Buddhism and Philosophy

Buddhism and Philosophy

VOLUME - II

C. D. Naik

KALPAZ

ISBN: 978-93-5324-241-1 (Set)
978-93-5324-224-4 (Vol. II)

First Published, 2020

Published by

Kalpaz Publications
C-30, Satyawati Nagar,
Delhi – 110052
Ph.: 011-47034999, 9811692060
www.kalpazpublications.com
E-mail: kalpaz@hotmail.com

Printed at: G. Print Process, Delhi

Contents

Chapter - 1

Buddhism in the Age of Crisis

B. A. Kausalyayan, C. D. Naik

Mr. President and Friends!

As it is not only my first visit to Canada, but even first gathering of Canadian friends, before whom I am expected to say something about Buddhism, particularly in the context of its meaning to Canadians in this age of crisis.

I wonder if you have read or heard of a novel written by Rumanian author- 25th Hour— Humanity is attacked by technological civilization.

I think this is a crisis- not for Canada alone, not for America alone, but for the whole world, as a whole.

To what is this crisis due to? And what is the way out of it? This crisis is due to the world's ignoring what the Buddha taught 2500 years ago. What did he teach? Before we say anything as regards his teaching, I feel like referring to the historicity of Buddha, for his historicity is not as controversial, as the historicity of a few well-known founders of some religions. Buddha's birth, enlightenment, his first sermon, his ministry of 45 years, his Parinirvana at the age of eighty. What did he teach in his first sermon? One of the epitherts of the Buddha was – vijja carana sampanno- he knew what one ought to know- the supreme knowledge. He lived as one ought to live- sublimity personified. What he knew to be true, he taught with utmost clarity.

1. This world is accidental. 2. This world is the creation of a God- always with capital 'G'. Why he did not believe in either of the two views? Instead he taught Law of Dependent Origination. Evam sati evam hoti: This being so, this comes into existence. The whole of this mind-matter world has also come into existence because of this Law of Dependent origination.

The philosophers of the world are divided on the question, whether mind is the real base of the matter, or matter is the real base for the mind. Those who believed and preached that, mind is the real base for the matter are known as 'idealists'. Those who believed that matter is the real base for mind are known as materialists. The Buddha was neither idealist, nor materialist. Just as Einstein says that matter and energy go together and even one is convertible to another. Similarly the Buddha said that mind-matter always stay together and mind is not something as 'mental' as it is presumed to be and similarly matter is also not as 'material' as it is presumed to be. A hungry man gets angry easily and an angry man's digestion is also disturbed with equal ease.

In a nutshell he taught-ye dhamma hetuppabhava hetu tesam tathagato aha tesan ca yo nirodho evam vadi mahasamano- preconditions of all such conditions which have a pre-condition are taught by the Buddha and the non-coming into existence of such conditions also have been taught by the Buddha. As every thing is conditioned, so suffering is also conditioned. Is suffering accidental? Is suffering somebody's creation?. Neither accidental, nor somebody's creation, but an outcome of the Law of Dependent Origination. Existing pre-conditions cause suffering. Non-existence of these pre-conditions does not cause suffering. Hence the best way to realize the elimination of all suffering is not to let such preconditions arise, as result in the coming into existence of suffering.

Suffering and pessimism, suffering past, present and future. This cessation of suffering does not take place by itself. One has to humbly exert for it. The way, the path that leads to the cessation of suffering is known as Noble Eightfold Path. It consists of an eightfold programme of not only individual emancipation, but also of social emancipation. 1. Samma Ditthi- Right Views. 2. Samma Sankappo, 3. Samma Vaca, 4. Samma Kammanto, 5. Samma Ajivo, 6. Samma Vayamo, 7. Samma Sati and 8. Samma Samadhi. Rhys Davids and Eightfold path. What is the central idea, the spirit or the essence of this eightfold path? At first five disciples— when their number arose to 61— Buddha said: Abstain O' Bhikkhus from the path of sensual enjoyment and abstain O' Bhikkhus from the equally fruitless task of self-mortification.

It appears that the whole world has ignored this teaching of the Buddha. European countries, America and Canada and Russia and to some extent even Japan have taken to the path of more and more sensual enjoyment and the eastern countries such as India to the path of self-mortification.

This globe of ours known as eastern hemisphere and western hemisphere is ist divided into five continents and those continents are again sub-divided into different countries or different states. Each country is occupied with her own problems. Nobody cares for the world as a whole. On one side – over population such as in India, China and Japan. On the other side- not enough people, such as in Canada and Australia etc.

If we think of the world as one whole, we can solve the problems of all countries. At present one religion is fighting with another religion, one state is fighting with another state and we are all clamoring for universal peace. We are all preparing for war. We are all preparing for peace. A real paradox, such as humanity has never known.

Buddhism-the Teaching of the Buddhism, Buddhism- the life recommended by the both can come to our assistance, provided we should seek guidance from it.

Reference

1. Talk of Dr. B. A. Kausalyayan, Toronto University, Canada.

Chapter - 2

Buddhism as Indigenous Movement

B. A. Kausalyayan, C. D. Naik

Venerable Sir, Brothers and Sisters in the Dhamma,

It was no less than two thousand and three hundred years ago, when the great Mahinda, perhaps the first Indian missionary to any foreign land proceeded from the birth place of Buddhism itself to Sri Lanka (known as Ceylon also). While introducing himself to king Devanamapiyatissa of Sri Lanka he said: samana mayam maharaja Dhammarajassa Savaka Tameva Anukampaya Jambudipadha Agata. "O! great king, we are the disciple of the king of righteousness and have come here from Jambudveepa to this land of yours to extend our compassion towards yourself."

Not only the great Mahinda, but later his sister, who was also a Buddhist nun named Sanghamitra had reached Ceylon. She had carried a sapling of the sacred Bodhi tree from Buddhagaya, which was transplanted at Anuradhapura, the capital of Sri Lanka in those olden days. Since then the Jay Sri Mahabodhi as it is always referred to in Sri Lanka, has blossomed forth into the most respectable oldest historical tree in the world.

Needless to state that the great Mahinda had not sojourned to Sri lanka all alone. While pointing towards mahinda's companions who were also dressed in yellow robes like himself, the king of Sri Lanka asked him if there were others like these who dressed similarly. Mahinda's answer was: kasaya pajjoto jambudipo, i.e. India was shining with the brilliance of yellow robes.

Mahamahinda had preached, according to the chronicles of Ceylon, in the language of the Island itself, which could not have been very different from his own language in those early days, because even now Ceylonese language is nothing else but an ancient dialect of northern India.

Here the most important point that is not only to be noted but stressed immensely is that even when the king, his queen and other so many courtiers got themselves converted to Buddhism, king Devanamapiyatissa of Sri Lanka enquired of the wise missionary of Buddhism in pre-Christian era, whether Buddhism had become an established religion in Ceylon or not. Mahamahinda's reply was a definite no. The king became simply bewildered. He himself had embraced Buddhism. His queen had become a Buddhist queen. His courtiers got themselves converted to Buddhism and still one who was compassionate enough to come all the way from India to Sri Lanka was saying that Buddhism had not become an established religion even then in Ceylon. What more he needed was the king's query. Mahamahinda's answer was that he did not consider that Buddhism had become an established religion in Sri Lanka as till then the sons of Sri Lanka yet remained to be ordained and had not joined the Order of the yellow robes till then.

In the wise answer given to the king of Sri Lanka by great Mahinda who had reached Ceylon on the very sacred day which we have gathered together to celebrate, here even in a far off land such as Great Britain, three irrefutable historical truths become quite apparent: first, it is of little use even if the mother country is shining with the brilliance of yellow robes if the Dhamma or the Law of Righteousness is not preached and taught to others and is not practiced by those who profess it "for the good of many and for the welfare of many"; second, a religion or a new way of life has to be taught and preached in the language of the people, who are to be benefitted thereby; third, a religion or any new way of life can only prosper and flourish in any country when it no longer remains an outlandish movement but becomes an indigenous movement and is taken up by the sons of soil.

In late 19th century when Buddhism was introduced by such pioneer Buddhist missionaries as Anagarika Dharmapala of Ceylon, Chandramani Mahasthavira of Burma, Kripasharana mahasthavira of Chitgong in foreign countries it remained an outlandish movement for a long time. But by and by thanks to the tireless activities of Buddhist missionaries like Venerable Saddhatissa and others Buddhism has become an established organized indigenous movement not only in England, but I learnt, in some other countries over the continent also.

In India, inspite of the best efforts of a great many teachers and preachers of Buddhism, it remained more or less an outlandish movement. Non-Buddhist Indians did not even take serious notice of it. They then thought of Buddhism, not as a modern religion of a great mass of humanity prevalent all over the world, but merely a subject befitting to satisfy the curiosity of a few oriental scholars interested in Archaelogical studies. But fortunately as we have it the historical conversion ceremony of at least half a million people under the leadership of Dr. B.R. Ambedkar at Deeksha Bhoomi Nagpur followed by a link of such similar conversion ceremonies at various places in which even greater number got themselves converted to Buddhism, has brought a tremendous change in everybody's outlook. Buddhism and its propagation is no more just a subject of oriental archaeological studies. It has become a living proposition for everybody concerned all over India. Come what may, Buddhism has come to stay.

We admit that it is being discouraged by our present Indian Government, we admit that we are being mercilessly harassed by Hindu orthodoxy, we are also very concerned as our Parliament is thinking of discussing such bills as the so called bill of the freedom of religion, which is intended to curtail the freedom of all religions with the exception of Hinduism. Inspite of such numerous hurdls and obstacles, which we have to face daily, Buddhist thought and Buddhism as a new way of life is gaining ground in India day by day. There were days when there were a very few Buddhist monks, but no Buddhist Vihara for them, where they could stay. Now we have enough Buddhist Viharas but not enough capable Buddhist monks, who could use them as their centre of activities.

Such days, when the Pali Tripitaka, though it was available in Roman script, Sinhali script, Burmi script and Thai script, was not available in Devanagari script of India. Now we have not only the whole of Pali Tripitaka available in Devanagari script but even most of the Pali texts and even some of the commentaries have been translated into some of the Indian languages. I myself have been able to prepare a Hindi Pali dictionary and get it published by one of our publishers.

On the life and teachings of the Buddha, we have any number of books in almost all Indian languages. Edwin Arnold's famous poetry "Light of Asia" too has been translated at least according to my knowledge into two Indian languages-Punjabi and Hindi. An exceptionally good book, the history of Pali literature too is available in Hindi. Acharya Narendra Deo, Rahul Sankrityayan and Bharata Singh Upadhyaya have written various such voluminous books in Buddhist philosophy and literature in Hindi, which would do credit to any author anywhere in the world.

We are really glad, though not fully satisfied, that now we have amongst ourselves, not only Buddhist scholars but even Buddhist poets, Buddhist dramatists, and Buddhist architects too.

Whether it is philosophy, whether it is history, whether it is poetry, whether it is music, whether it is painting, whether it is sculpture the same message, the same age old message, the same age old teaching of the Buddha or Tathagata has found expression there in the message of suffering and putting an end to the suffering.

To the extent, philosophy helped anybody to purify his life and enlighten his mind, to that extent alone, the Buddha admitted the use of philosophy and gave it its due place in his Dhamma-Vinaya, in his doctrine of righteousness and Discipline. He could not withstand the misuse of philosophy as a distortion and detraction from the real purpose of life, total annihilation of all suffering.

It is certainly true that there are a few topics, a few unprofitable subjects on which the Buddha has refused to commit himself. But these topics are just ten, and they are fixed and enumerated, such as –

1. Is the universe permanent?
2. Is the universe not permanent?
3. Is the universe with an ending?
4. Is the universe without ending?
5. Is the soul and body one entity?
6. Are the soul and body two entities?
7. Do the Tathagatas live after their passing away?
8. Do the Tathagatas not live after their passing away?
9. Do the Tathagata both live and not live after their passing away?
10. Do the Tathagatas both not live and not not live after their passing away?

When Malunkyaputta asked the reason for not having answered the above questions or for having not committed himself on the above topics, the Master replied: "I have not committed myself on the above topics as their discussion is purposeless, is fruitless, does not help anybody to remain nonattached to this world, does not help one to attain enlightenment and it does not help one to realize Nibbana. It is for this specific reason that I have not committed on these topics".

It is not only to be noted, but emphasized and underlined that this list of non-stated topics- avyaktas, as they are called, does not include or even does not suggest the conceptions or misconceptions of the existence of Atma and Parmatma, the Sanskrit synonym for soul and God. Hence it is not only incorrect, but even ischievous, if intentionally done, to suggest that the Buddha remained absolutely mum when he was questioned about soul and God.

Sabbe sankhara anicca – All is transient.

Sabbe sankhara dukkha – All is dissatisfying.

Sabbe dhamma anatta – Nothing consists of any changeless permanent entity, not even Nibbana.

These three pertinent aphorisms, to my mind, in a nutshell formulate the metaphysics of Buddhism. In this strange world, we are all surrounded by so many, who profess to believe in a big or small soul and a big God, always with a capital letter. But when you talk to them, you invariably find that even to them their soul and God is similar to a sign x in algebra, which may mean anything and everything.

According to Abhidhamma (which is an all inclusive, comprehensive, presentation of not only Buddhist psychology, as it is often wrongly supposed to be, but also of Ethics, also of Physics and also of Metaphysics) a man is either five Khandas or twelve Ayatanas or eighteen Dhatus. It is not easy to translate any of these words into any non-Indian language. Hence we are using these terms as they are, of course with their explanations as best as we can give. Five Khandhas are five groups of existence: Rupa (form), Vedana (sensation), Sanna (perception), Sankhara (no less than fifty mental differentiation or classifications) and Vinnana (consciousness). Twelve Ayatanas are six sense organs (Mind is enumerated as the sixth one) together with their six sense objects. Eighteen Dhatus are six sense organs plus six sense objects plus six eye consciousness etc…

Anything and everything of this universe can be assigned to this or that category. Everything is bound to come under one head or the other. All that exists is transient. That which is not transient does not exist. It has been rather well said that the changeless change is the law of nature.

Buddhism wholly corroborates with this statement. In fact this statement in itself is but an echo of what the Buddha declared centuries ago. Under no conditions should this change be misunderstood.This change is not an outward change of any changeless entity. It is total extinction of one condition and total new arising of another condition. The Buddha has clearly instructed: "The one that goes out of existence is another and the one that comes into existence is quite another."

It is really astonishing that this change, this law of transiency should always be misunderstood, as if in all circumstances it was a law for the worst. When a man passes away, we always say anicca vata sankhara- all things are transient. Why we cannot and why we should not repeat the same anicca vata sankhara – all things are transient when a child is born is beyond my comprehension. Anicca or the law of transiency is not biased, is not partial. Anicca is perfectly neutral, perfectly impartial. It is neither pessimism nor optimism. It is just a truism.

But as the scales are overburdened on one side, it is high time that we inaugurate reading a message of hope and a redemption in this law of transiency and say to ourselves, how fortunate the world is changeable. We can always improve ourselves. We can always improve others. We can transform our subjective life, we can transform our objective life. What else do we want?

The world is not Dukkha, is not misery, as it is generally misunderstood to be. It is Dukkha, it is misery only for the misinformed, only for the Putthujjana. If it is suffering, it is nobody's fault, but our own. We ourselves manufacture our hells and we can convert them into heavens if we so desire and endevour. We can conveniently do away with these hells and heavens, we can realize Nibbana.

Transient this universe is, but if one accepts it is intransient in one's thought, in one's feeling, in one's attitude, in one's behavior, one is bound to suffer, nobody can help him. Bereft of any abiding changeless entity this universe is, but if one takes it, as if it were a composition of separate changeless entities, known as souls or Atmas, one is bound to get into endless trouble, whoever one might be.

Thus the world is Dukkha-all suffering-only to the ignorant, most certainly not to the wise. True the Buddha has declared that all Upadana Khandas are suffering, but it only means that all grasping groups of existence are suffering. The Buddha's doctrine aims at the uprooting of this suffering, this suffering of the unwise, this suffering of the ignorant, as it is only for such as do not know. The way to put an end to this suffering is generally known as the Noble Eightfold Path, such as – 1. Samma Ditthi- Right View, right perspective. In case one does not possess even the right view nothing commendable can be expected of him, self-deception once yielded, everything follows; 2. Samma Sankappo- Right Aspiration, one's life is not so much composed of one's resolution as of one's aspirations and one's imaginations, we resolve not to smoke, not to drink but go on making mental pictures of the very same habits, how can we get rid of the clutches of such addictions, it is simple enough that we cannot; 3. Samma Vaca- Right Speech, no falsehood, no harsh language, no backbiting, no frivolous talk, it is not a joke to practice such noble tongue; 4. Samma Kammanto- Right Activities, it is one thing to know that it is wrong to tell a lie, it is one thing to resolve not to tell a lie, yet it is quite another thing to actually abstain from telling a lie, practice alone counts, nothing else does; 5. Samma Ajivo- Right Means of Livelihood, such means of livelihood as cause suffering and pain to others are of no value, one's means of livelihood should be beyond any reproach either from one's self or from others, doing business in such trades as selling of slaves, selling of meat, selling of ammunition, and selling of alchoholic intoxicant drinks are tabooed for a Buddhist aspirant; 6. Samma Vayamo- Vayamo literally means exercise, exercise this is but not physical exercise, it is constant endevour to see that any ignoble practice which may have become our habit as a result of our negligence should leave us, any new ignoble practice may not become our habit, any noble practice which has become our habit may not leave us and similarly any noble practice which somebody else possesses may be imbibed by us; 7. Samma Sati- Right Mindfulness, sati is also translatable as memory, but in this context it means wakefulness, awareness of one's smallest activities even such as sitting, standing and walking and later on of one's incoming and outgoing breathing also; 8. Samma Samadhi- Right Concentration, it is not concentrating on any one particular point, it is one-pointedness in one definite direction, concentration in the performance of noble activities is rightly termed as Right Concentration.

Important surely is the doctrine of impermanence in Buddhism, but no less important is the non-soul doctrine, the teaching of Anattavada. The Budha has condemned the superstition of soul in no uncertain terms: "And with such unwise considerations, he adopts one or other of the six views, one of them being- this myself, which can think and feel, and which now here, now there, experiences the fruit of good and evil deeds; this myself is permanent, stable, eternal, not subject to change, and will thus eternally remain the same. If there really existed the self there would exist also something which belongs to the self. As, however, in truth and reality neither the self can be found, nor anything that belongs to it is found, it is therefore really an utter fool's doctrine to say, this is the world, this am I; after death I shall be permanent, persisting and eternal. Such views are mere views, a thicket of views, a puppet show of views, a coil of views, a snare of views, and ensnared in the fetter of views the ignorant worldling will not be freed from rebirth, from decay, and from death, from sorrow, pain, grief and despair, he will not be freed, I say from suffering."

To me Paticca Samuppada or the Law of Dependent Origination as it is often translated is nothing more or nothing less than a positive statement of the doctrine of impermanence and of the doctrine of non-soul. It is not just a simple statement of cause and effect as it is often misunderstood.

Buddhism makes a subtle but no less clear distinction between the law of cause and effect and the Law of Dependent Origination. According to Paticcca Samuppada the subsequent origination is neither the same as previous origination nor quite different. Another important point is that the previous origination is absolutely necessary for the coming into existence of the subsequent origination. The subsequent origination does not and cannot come into existence without its previous origination. So we have Avijja Paccaya Sankhara (On delusion depends the Karmic formations), Sankhara Paccaya Vinnanam (On Karmic formations depends consciousness).

Various questions suggest themselves as soon as we utter the word consciousness. One of the often asked questions is: Is consciousness a monistic conception or a pluralistic conception? According to Buddhism all existence is compound. It is not impossible that our analysis of this universe might lead us to a situation where further analysis might become impossible. Budhism declares the whole world is a composition of exactly such ultimate entities which though further unanalisable are yet compound. Nothing is absolute neither in the exterior world nor even in the interior one. Our consciousness in its ultimate analysis is but a single name given to no less than 89 different types of consciousness. Each of these in its own turn happens to be one of the permutations and combinations of as many as 52 factors of consciousness, known as Cetasikas. Not a single type of consciousness can be conceived without being based on the interplay of some or the other factors of consciousness. All consciousnesses form our subjective world. How it is related to the objective world? In simple Buddhist phraseology what is the relationship which Vinnana bears to Rupa? Modern people have got used to think in terms of mind and matter and their conceptions of mind and matter is of the two entities standing poles apart from one another. It is also true that this attitude is changing for the better. Buddhism teaches neither mind is totally independent of matter, nor matter of mind. Both are transient. Both continue to rise and fall and only seen running their courses as if in a parallel.

It has been argued that if both mind and matter are transient and neither is permanent, nor there exists any other agency such as a soul of permanent nature, then how can the very experience of impermanency be explained? The answer is that it is on the basis of total impermanency alone that the experience of transiency can be explained. Any soul, any entity supposed to be permanent and changeless can have no experience whatsoever, for, the very capacity to observe any facts or witness any occurrences, presupposes transiency on the part of one who is presumed to be an experiencer. Two parallel trains running exactly at the same speed will never be able to experience the movement of each other, for, not only all movements, but even taking notice of the movement of both the trains is also relative. Buddhist Psychology and Physics fit in very well here, because according to these, although mind (Nama), and matter (Rupa) are both transient, although both seem to be running parallel yet there is a difference in the speed of the transiency of mind and matter. Hence the possibility of observing the impermanence of all transient nature.

The whole of Dhamma-Vinaya, which has been termed as Buddhism is not merely a set of philosophical tenets, it is a path of course the right path, which is capable to lead one to the total annihilation of all suffering. What a great hope that this annihilation of all suffering, this Nibbana is attainable in this very body of six feet!

"Two things, O Monks, I teach, suffering and the total annihilation of suffering, has been summarily said by the Blessed One."

Suffering can be of three kinds- past, present and future. Can we put an end to the suffering, which is a begone fact, which we have already suffered? Of course not. Can we put an end to the suffering, which is a present fact, which we are already suffering from? Of course not. Can we put an end to the suffering, which we might otherwise suffer in future? Of course. Hence this putting an end to the suffering is not putting an end to anything that is already existing. It is simply obstructing the coming into existence of some unwholesome experience which might otherwise come into existence. Dukkham Heyyam Anagatam. Only future suffering can be terminated. Only future pain, future troubles, future misfortunes are to be stopped from arising, are to be annihilated.

We have intentionally touched upon the transient nature of the universe. We have explicitly spoken of the dissatisfactory nature of the universe. We have with purpose referred to the absolute non-permanent nature of the universe. We have also mentioned the Law of Dependent Origination, and last but not the least the summum bonum of Budhism i.e. Nibbana. It is absolutely essential that one is conversant with the chief characteristics of Buddhism so that one may be able to appreciate the subtle and fine distinctions even in one respect between the various differing schools of Buddhism.

A hundred years, after the passing away of our Lord Buddha, there took place in Vaishali a conference, which is generally termed as the second Sangiti or the second convocation of the Buddhist monks. The differences which were underlined in that Sangiti, all related to Vinaya or Discipline of the Brotherhood. It was only in the third Sangiti or the Council of the Buddhist monks, held at Pataliputra or modern Patna, that there arose differences as regards Abhidhamma, the deeper study of the Dhamma. Leaving aside such differences as existed or still exist in the very minor sects of Buddhism we propose to illustrate today and then finish the subtle distinctions, which were upheld by the followers of the four well known specific Buddhist schools of thought. These schools are fairly well known and are designated as Sarvastivadi (Vaibhasikas), Sautrantika, Vinnanavadi (Yogacara), and Madhyamika (Sunnavada). According to Indian logic there are threemain proofs, which have been submitted as valid- 1. The proof of direct perception, 2. The proof of inference and 3. The proof of the spoken or written word, as found in the so called revealed books.

We see fire, with our own eyes and we say there is fire. This is direct perception. We do not see fire with our own eyes, but we see only smoke. We infer that there is fire because we see smoke. This is inference. We do not see, feel or cognize the existence of any soul or God; yet we proclaim that they do exist. Why? Because the books, which from our childhood we have been taught to regard as revealed books state so. This is the proof of the spoken or revealed word as found in the revealed books.

It is the special characteristic or singularity of Buddhist logic that it admitted the validity of only two proofs 1. The proof of direct perception and 2. The proof of inference. According to Sarvastivada (Vaibhasika) the objective world exists because its existence can be ascertained and maintained as a result of direct perception. Their contention is this that the consciousness or the subjective world exists independently. And it is the consciousness which experiences the existence of the objective world. What is the position of Sautrantikas? They also like Vaibhasikas accept the existence of the objective world, but they say there is no direct perception of the existence of the objective world. We have to infer to the existence of the objective world. According to Vinnanavada or Yogacara vinnana or consciousness alone exists. All that is assumed to be the experience of our senses – the sum total of the objective world- is nothing else but the mental creation of our consciousness. It does not recognize the independent existence of the objective world. To Vinnanavadi, a believer in the monism of consciousness the whole of the objective world is Asata, it does not exist at all.

It can be easily seen that how Buddhist Yogacara is the forerunner of Shankaracharya's Vedanta. Much advertised Shankaracharya and even his teacher's teacher Gaudapadacharya are greatly indebted to Yogachara form of Buddhism.

The fourth Buddhist school is that of Madhyamika. Their philosophical tenet is known as Shunyavada. They neither accept the independent existence of consciousness nor of the objective world.They deem that neither consciousness exists, nor all that which is supposed to be the object of cognizance by all the senses. Both are merely truths of every day life-voharasacca, none has got an absolute existence. Nagarjuna was the forerunner of Einstein and his comprehension of the Law of Dependent Origination or the relativity of the great scientist. Obeisance to the originator of the Law of Dependent Origination, the Blessed One, the Buddha, the Tathagata.

Reference

1. Reference: Talk delivered by Bhadant Anand Kausalyayan in USA and Canada.

Chapter - 3

Historical Sites in India and Nepal

Intelligence, Compassion and Courage are the three universally recognized virtues. – CONFUCIUS

The Sun I am, the seeds of life I shall sow. Even as I set, will leave behind an afterglow.

Suraj Hun Zindagi ki Ramaq chod jawun ga, Main Dub Bhi Gaya to shafaq chod jawun Ga. – SYED MUHAMMAD KHAN

Abstract

While Siddhartha Gautam was born in Lumbini and brought up in Kapilavastu in Nepal he became Buddha or Enlightened One at Bodh-Gaya and Buddhism was born at Sarnath in India.

Going back to the Indus Civilization of Mahenjo-Daro and Harappa we find archaeological remains of the Shraman Culture and same is to be continued by Shraman Gautama Buddha but it is considered as proto-historical civilization, although its matriarchal societal form corroborated with Buddhist social pattern as Sariputta-like names indicated the matriarchal remains of the period. Vedic civilization left nothing of the archaeological finds and facts on which post-Buddhist Hindu civilization is based and the latter has historical and archaeological sites but they are post-pala period in East India and Post-Kushan period in north-west India and are thus post-Buddhistic. So were the civilizations of Moghul and British empires, which were equally larger and vaster in archaeological and historical sites, though not equal to that of earlier Asokan India. So the only historical Indian civilization remains to be Buddhist to reckon with and to be proud of.

The National emblem of India is the Dhamma-Cakka (Buddhism) embossed on its tri-colour flag, and lion capital of Asokan Pillar found in Sarnath (Buddhism) as its official seal and punched on national currency also. Its Parliament Hall of Lok Sabha, where the Speaker occupies the appointed seat, bears the most signifying motto of Buddhism- Dhamma Chakra Pravartanaya (Foundation of the Empire of World Righteousness or Wheel of Buddhism) and architecture of the Courts and Supreme Court and that of the Rashtrapati Bhavan is of Buddhist dome orientation. Thus the living deity of Indian nation is naturally and factually Buddhism.

The popularity of Buddha and Buddhism in India in earliest historical period is recorded thus: Rulers of the time loved to claim the share of the Buddha's mortal remains to construct his monuments in their respective kingdoms and republics. So it happened that Ajatasatru, the king of Magadha; Licchavis of Vaishali; Sakyas of Kapilavastu, Bulis of Allakappa; Koliyas of Ramagrama; Mallas of Pava and Resident of Vethadipa (Drona) shared the same for the purpose in peaceful manner.

Such a great force in human form is the rarest phenomenon to take birth, for such an one is not born to a common place. But wherever such an one is born the name, fame, clan and nation of his birth is dignified with matchless glory as signified by the Dhammapada stanza: *dullabho purisajanno na so sabattha jayati ettha so jayati dhiro tam kulam patisevati*.

India of ancient Buddhist period was divided into six provinces namely (1) Middle country (Madhyam Desh), including Oligarchies and Republics such as i. Kashi, ii. Koshal, iii. Anga, iv. Magadh, v. Vajji, vi. Malla, vii. Chedi, viii. Vatsa, ix. Kuru, x. Panchal, xi. Matsya, xii. Shursen, xiii. Ashvak, and xiv. Avanti, (2) Northern Part including Kingdoms like (i). Gandhar, and (ii). Kamboj; (3) Western Part comprised the present (i) Sindh, (ii) Western Rajaputana, (iii) Gujrat and (iv) some parts of the Narmada basin., and (4) Southern Part included all extensive province spread from the Ganga to south and from Godavari to north called Dakshinapatha, (5) Eastern Part or Prachya country was located at the east of Madhya Desh. Its Western border touched Kajangala Nigama, Anga and Magadh Janpadas. The famous Tamra (copper) lipti port situated in it alone and was used for voyages to Suvarna-Bhoomi, Java, Lanka etc. by traders, and the sixth (6th) province was the Himavanta Pradesh.

India today has 28 states of which Sikkim is a Buddhist Kingdom. Andhra Pradesh, Arunachal Pradesh, Assam, Bihar, Jharkhand, Goa, Gujrat, Haryana, Himachal Pradesh, Jammu and Kashmir, Kerala, Madhya Pradesh, Chhattisgarh, Maharashtra, Manipur, Meghalaya, Mizoram, Mysore, Nagaland, Orissa, Punjab, Tamil Nadu, Tripura, Uttar Pradesh, Uttaranchal, West Bengal are states, and out of seven Union territories one is the National capital territory Delhi, and other UTs are such as Andaman and Nicobar

Islands, Chandigarh, Dadra and Nagar Haveli, Daman and Diu, Lakshadweep, and Puducherry having each UT and state the presence of Buddhist members in a small or large number.

So it is now high time that every Indian ought to be enlightened like the Buddha in sixth century B.C. himself and be the uniting force not only for territorial Bharata land but for extraterritorial gods and men as well (*satta deva manussanam*). Buddha attained the highest and absolute Mahaparinirvana at Kusinara in 483 B.C. and his last message was, "*Atta Dipo Bhav, Be Light unto thyself*" and in the *Mahâparinibbâna Sutta*, there is a passage that states that the Buddha, in his last moments in this world, spoke to his followers: "After I'm no more, O Ânanda, men of belief will visit these four places (Lumbini, Bodh Gayâ, Sârnâth, and Kusinagar) with faith, curiosity and devotion."

The author of these lines attempts to focus on how during the period of decline of Buddhism (1250 A.D.) it had lost and how during its revival phase it has regained and preserved its strength of material and mental forces and man power, the last one mainly through the single struggle and efforts by Dr. Babasaheb Ambedkar as almost 73 percent of Buddhist population in India owe their existence in Maharashtra to him alone.

Vote of Thanks

Let me first of all wish you all the very very much happy new year 2013 and heartily thank the Indian Council for Cultural Relations (ICCR) for organizing a Buddhist Conference at Lumbini, Nepal in collaboration with Embassy of India, Kathmandu and Lumbini Development Trust on *Buddhist and Historical Buddhist Sites in India and Nepal* during these two days. I thank them for invitation extended by the Director General of ICCR, Academic Coordinator Dr. Pannalankar Bhikkhu and Programme Coordinator Shri Vibha Mehdiretta, on behalf of Dr. Suresh K. Goel, Special Secretary, Ministry of External Affairs, to me as one of the six eminent scholars from India to participate in this event and for allowing me to make this presentation on the theme and I thank them again, not the least, for providing necessary requisites for travel and hospitality during this conference.

Introduction

Buddhism is a spirit of the Enlightened Being and universal uniting force. Lakkhana Suttanta of the Buddhist texts reads: "Whereas, in whatsoever former birth…Brethren, the Tathagata, then being human, put away abusive speech, revolted against abusive speech, what he heard here not repeating elsewhere, to raise a quarrel, against people here; and what he heard elsewhere not repeating here, to raise a quarrel against people there:- thus becoming a binder together of those who are divided, or fostering those who are friends, a peacemaker, a lover of concord, impassioned for peace, a speaker of words that make for peace, he by the doing and by the accumulating of that Karma, by the mass and the abundance of it, was when the body perished reborn after death in a bright and pleasant world. …(Lakkhana Suttanta).

However the historicity of Buddha and His Word is as certain as the two unequivocal and identical schools of philosophy waging war against exploitation and against evil of greed respectively.

Historical Background

The kingdom of Magadha, with its capital at Rajagaha (afterwards at Pataliputta) reigned over at first by King Bimbisara and afterwards by his son Ajatasattu, both were contemporary of Buddha. The daughter of one of the chiefs of Licchavis of Vesali, was married to Bimbisara. Moreover Pasendi's sister, the Kosala Devi, was the wife of Bimbisara, king of Magadha. Furthermore Ajatasattu was son of Bimbisara by his another wife, the Videha lady from Mithila. Kosala Devi died of grief of death of Bimbisara killed by Ajatasattu. The revenues of township of Kasi had been granted to the Kosala Devi as pin money (dowery) but after her death Pasendi confiscated that township. Angered at this, Ajatasattu declared war against his aged uncle (brother of his step mother). He was taken prisoner in the fourth campaign, and not released until he had relinquished his claim. There upon Pasenadi gave him his daughter Vajira in marriage with township of Kasi as her wedding gift.

It is stated that it was from the desire to associate himself by marriage with the Buddha's family that Pasenadi asked for one of the daughters of the Sakiya chiefs as his wife. The Sakiyas discussed the proposition in their Mote Hall, and held it beneath the dignity of their clan. But they sent him a girl named Vasabha Khattiya, the daughter, by a slave girl, of one of their leading chiefs. By her Pasenadi had the son, Vidudabha.

Three years after the marriage of Vajira with Ajatasattu Pasenadi's son Vidudabha revolted against his father, who was then at Ulumba in the Sakiya country. The latter fled to Rajagaha to ask Ajatasattu for aid; but was taken ill and died outside the city gates. Later Vidudabha and his brother-in-law Ajatasattu were in conflict with Sakiyans and Vajjians of Vesali respectively.

According to Rhys Davids, "The real reasons which induced Vidudabha to attack and conquer his relatives, the Sakiyas, were, most likely, the same sort of political motives which later on induced his cousin, Ajatasattu of Magadha, to attack and conquer his relatives, the Licchavis of Vesali. (p. 12)"

It was in consequence of the anger kindled in Vidudabha's heart at the discovery of the fraud that, having determined to wreak his vengeance on the Sakiyas, he, on coming to the throne, invaded their country, took their city, and put to death a great number of the members of the clan, without distinction of age or sex, when Buddha was 78 or 79 years old.

When Ajatasattu intended to attack his Licchavi relatives he sent his messenger Vassakara to hear the Buddha's forecast that eventually when the Licchavis had been weakened then he would be able to carry out this intention. Vassakara sowed seeds of dissension among the leading families of Vesali and the King swooped down the place with an overwhelming force, and completely destroyed it.

Ajatasattu fortified his capital Rajagraha, in expectation of an attack about to be made by King Pajjota of Ujjeni. In the 4th century B.C., Ujjeni had become subject to Magadha, and Asoka, when a young man, was appointed governor of Ujjeni.

Devadatta, about nine or ten years before the Buddha's death, created a schism in the community. Ajatasattu as the then Crown Prince, supported Devadatta, the Judas Iscariot of the Buddhist story. Ajatasattu carried out his deed of slaying the King Bimbisara at the instigation of Devadatta in the eighth year before the Buddha's death. Ajatasattu repented later at his deed and an illustration saluting Buddha on this occasion is depicted on the bas-relief of the Bharhut Tope. He built stupa on the relics of Buddha and supported the first Buddhist Council at Rajagaha.

To the north-west there was the kingdom of Kosala – the Northern Kosala – with its capital at Savatthi, ruled over at first by King Pasenadi and afterwards by his son Vidudabha, contemporary of Buddha. Educated at the celebrated seat of learning, Takkasila, in the extreme north-west, he was placed, on his return, by his father, Maha Kosala, upon the throne. Asked how the Buddha being so young, as compared with other already well-known teachers, could claim an insight beyond theirs the latter replied, "Who would show disrespect to a prince, or to a venomous serpant, or to a fire, merely because it was young?" Pasenadi's aunt Sumana became the Arhat after she entered Buddha's nun's order. The King's grandmother, father and aunt were alive during the life of Buddha. Pasenadi was an official epithet or a designation used for several kings and the personal name of Pasenadi was Agnidatta. On the bas-relief of Bharhut tope Pasenadi is represented as issuing forth on his chariot to meet Buddha and hear his teaching represented by the figure of the Wheel of the Law.

Southwards from Kosala was the kingdom of the Vamsas or Vatsas, with their capital at Kosambi on the Jumna, reigned over by King Udena, the son of Parantapa, contemporary of Buddha. And still farther south lay the kingdom of Avanti, with its capital Ujjeni, reigned over by King Pajjota, contemporary of Buddha.

The royal families of Kosambi and Avanti were also united by marriage. Vasula-datta, the daughter of King Pajjota of Avanti, became the wife, or rather one of the three wives, of King Udena of Kosambi. Samavati was his another wife. His father's name was Parantapa. He had a son named Bodhi. He survived the Buddha.

Avanti-putta, King of Surasena and the Eleyya were supporters of Uddaka Ramaputta, the teacher of Gotama.

New Kapilavastu was built after the old one was destroyed by Vidudabha. Sakya country was 60 yojanas (450 miles) from Rajagaha, 50 yojanas (375 miles) from Vesali, 6 or 7 yojanas (50 or 60 miles) from Savatthi, it is just on the border of Nepalese territory. Sakyas put up burial-mound over the portion they retained of the relics from the Buddha's funeral pyre and Asoka visited the Lumbini garden in which Buddha was born. Some names of Sakiyan townships included Catuma, Samagama, Khomadussa, Silavati, Metalupa Ulumpa, Sakkara, and Devedaha. Mother of Buddha, Mayadevi was born at Devadaha named after Prince Devadaha, a Koliyan chief. She was the daughter of Anjana Sakiyan. Koliyans were a subdivision of the Sakiya clan. Sakiyans were an Agricultural community. According to Buddhaghosa the Buddha had eighty thousand families of relatives on the father's side and the same on the mother's side. Sakya territory comprised of about a million persons by allowing six to seven to a family.

Young and old were alike present in the Sakiyan common Mote Hall (santhagara) at Kapilavastu. The political divisions of India then were tribal and not geographical.

Buddha

Birth and Childhood (Lumbini, Kapilavastu in Nepal)

Lumbini lies 19 Kilometres west of Siddharthanagar (Bairahawa) in Rupandehi district of the Lumbini zone of the Kingdom of Nepal. Emperor

Ashoka visited this sacred place in 249 B.C. He erected a stone monolith with an inscription that: "When King Devanampriya Priyadarshi had been anointed twenty years he himself came and worshipped this spot because Buddha Sakyamuni was born here- Hida Budhe Jate Sakyamuni ti." This was followed by the visit of Chinese monk scholar Fa-Hien in 406 A.D., who noted that for centuries the sacred place remained neglected. As late as in 1956 late King Mahendra visited this sacred place and celebrated the Democracy day here, and forbade slaughter of animals in the whole Kingdom of Nepal on every Vaisakh Poornima day, and consequently Lumbini Garden development commenced there since then. U. Thant, then Secretary General of the United Nations suggested His Majesty's Government of Nepal to develop LUMBINI as an international Pilgrimage and himself donated fund out of which a rest house was erected near the temple (Mayadevi) in 1967. The year 1986 as the International Year of peace hoped that not only the government and people of Nepal but also the governments and peoples of all nations of the world would co-operate in rehabilitating Lumbini, the luminary of Peace, as rapidly as possible.

It is interesting to note that Emperor Ashoka visited the stupa of Buddha Kanakamuni also at the Nigalive site, 13 miles north-west of Lumbini in 249 B.C., and left his pillar inscription there, which was discovered in 1895.

As soon as we utter the name of Kapilavastu what come to our mind are some sites and episodes like the three seasonal palaces created for Prince Siddhartha by the King Shuddhodana, Nyagrodharama created by the King for the Buddha (his son), Krakuchhanda Buddha, Kanakamuni Buddha, massacre of Sakyas in ancient Sakya kingdom by Vidudabha and so on. Lord Buddha first visited his home town seven years after his enlightenment and for that visit he had taken the rout from Venuvana via Rajgrih to Tilaurakot (ancient Sakyan capital), 27.5 Km southwest of Lumbini and after his arrival there he stayed for a couple of weeks at Nyagrodharama (currently known as Kudan), which is about 1.5 Km. south of Taulihawa, headquarter of Kapilavastu district in western Nepal.

In 1962 Tilaurakot and Kudan were excavated for secular and religious finds. Ten years later Dr. Fuhrer explored the sites of Krakuchhanda's birth and Nirvana. His monograph read, "The ruins of this large ancient city still exist between the modern villages of Lori-ki-Kudan and Gotiva, about 2 miles south-west of Taulihawa, and about 8.5 miles south-west of the Srinagar of Sirinagar Sagar, near which stood the southern gate of Kapilavastu. The three stupas and monasteries mentioned by Fa-Hien and Hiuen Tsiang are still visible except Kakusandha's nirvana stupa.

Nepal has an area of about 55,000 sq. miles with a population of approximately 9.5 millions. The Terai of Nepal formed part of India at the time of the birth of the Buddha. Since the Blessed One was born in Nepal, the earliest religion of Nepalese was Buddhism. Besides Gautama the Buddha, the names of Buddha Kasyapa and Buddha Kanakamuni were known to the people of Nepal even before Asoka visited Nepal in 250 B.C. and built a new city identified with the city of Patan near Kathmandu. The important shrines of Nepal include Bodh Nath (or Bodha Chaitya), Swayambhu Nath, Manjushree Chaitya and Charumati Vihara, Kirnyavarna Maha Vihara (Kwa Bahal), Maha Buddha Vihara and Bhatgaon Vihara. Besides there are two modern Theravada Viharas called Ananda Kuti Vihara and Sringha Vihara founded by Ven. Amritananda and Ven. Dharmaloka respectively. Nepali people follow shades of Theravada, Mahayan and Tantrayana Buddhism and Buddhist communities include Newars, Tamangs, Sherpas and Bhotiyas living amidst multitudes of Kirantis and Pravatis.

Fahiyan and Huen-Tsang recorded that Gautam was born in Lumbini near Kapilavastu, the capital of Shakyas in 563 B.C in the month of Ashadha. Lumbini Grove is 8 miles away in south of Kapilavastu. Mayadevi delivered the child while holding the branch of the Ashok tree. She passed away after seven days of Siddhartha's birth and left him in the custody of Mahaprajapati Gautami, her sister. Siddhartha was married to Yasodhara at the age of 16 and had son named Rahul. Siddhartha was sent to the nearest Vihara from the palace for his schooling befitting a prince. Siddhartha left his princely palace at the age of 29 after seeing all the three worlds at fire and the frequent quarrel between the Shakyas and Koliyas over the water of Rohini river flowing between them. He went to Vikatavana near Ramagrama (Shakya region), shaved his head and robed himself as a renunciate.

Search and Enlightenment (Bodh Gaya, Bihar)

At Uruvela Senani Nigam in Magadh he practiced severe penances and his five companions served him during this austerity. But seeing the futility of penances Gautam took to eating and his five companion ascetics mistook it for fall of saintliness and left his company for Sarnath. After taking rice-pudding at the hands of Sujata, the shephard's daughter Buddha left Uruvela for Pragbodhi hills in the north-east and thence to Peepal tree with vajrasana 3 miles away in south-west. He sat under the Peepal tree for seven days and was enlightened to the Middle Way, and spent another seven days while taking rounds of the tree. He attained to three knowledges- memory of former lives, divine eye and dependent origination at three phases of the night. After his enlightenment he doubted as to "*This that so many toils I have won, why should I then make it known, to folks with hate and lust consumed this truth will not be understood*". Having dispelled this doubt while sitting under the Bodhi tree after bath from Nerajana river Buddha remembered his former five companions, who were residing at Rishipatana deer park then, and went there, traced them and delivered his First Middle Path Sermon to them. Like his first five disciples he had his first two lay devotees, Tapassu and Bhallik from Utkal, whom he earlier administered the five precepts and ten norms of knowledge.

Dissemination of His Mission (Sarnath, U. P.)

Buddha spent his first rains-retreat at Sarnath. He ordained the Varanasi resident Yash as a monk. He had now 60 Arhat monks and laity during his first Varanasi round. From there he sent his disciples for propagation of his Dhamma in all directions and he himself went to Uruvela near Bodhgaya and initiated Kashyap brothers and their 1000 followers to his fold (Adityapariyaya sutta, Mahavagga, 1.20.20, 1.21). From Uruvela he went to Gayashirsh mountain, where Bimbisara himself with his numerous retinue approached Buddha and prayed him to visit Magadhan capital. Accordingly Buddha went to Rajgrih and rested there at Latthivana, where he addressed the king and his lakhs of following. Next day after giving meals to the Sangha headed by Buddha the King donated them the pleasance of Venuvana. Sanjay's disciples Sariputra and Maudgalyayan were also initiated to the Buddhist fold at Rajgrih, where Buddha spent his 2nd, 3rd and 4th lent before his next retreats at Vaishali, Mankulgiri, Tavantisaloka, Sunsumaragiri, Vaishali, Parileyyakavana, Nala Brahman gram, Veranja, Chaliyaparvata, Shravasti, Kapilavastu, Alavi, and Rajgrih. Again his 18th and 19th lents were spent at Chaliya Parvata before his next rains-residence took place at Rajgrih. His 21st to 45th, in all 24 rains-retreats were at Jetavanarama and Purvarama of Shravasti and his last lent was at Veluvagrama near Vaishali.

Regionwise Buddha was busy in his mission for the weal and welfare of mankind at Kitagiri Nigam (as per Kitagiri Sutta) in Kashi. His Sangha was economically prosperous in Kosal and spiritually and demographically strong in Magadh. Further demographic increase was added by adherence of Shakya-sons in Shakya Janapada to Buddhism. Vajji region contributed to the emergence of women wing to the Sangha and devotion of women towards the Buddha's norm. All this was additionally consolidated by the support of Udayan and Shyamavati in Vatsa region, and by his visit to Mathura, Thaneshwar, Sankissa, Kanyakubja and Champa, the capital of Anga Region.

The Buddha walked the land along the Himalayan Foothills and the Gangetic Plains during his 45-year long missionary life to preach his teachings for the well-being and happiness of all.

After his demise (mahaparinibbana) at Kusinagar at the age of 80 years the holy relics of his earthly body were, as found in Buddhist literature, divided into eight portions, and eight stupas (shrines) were built in various parts of the Jambudvïpa to enshrine these relics for public worshipping.

Death (Mahaparinirvana) at Kusinara, U.P.

Vaishali, Gridhrakuta, Ambalatthika, Nalanda, Patliputra, Kotigram, Nadita, Vaishali (Veluvagrama), Bhandagram, Ambagram, Jambugram, Bhoganagar, Pava, Kushinagar was the route of Buddha's last journey. Mallas took his body to cemetery crossing the river Hiranyavati.

Sukiti bhatinam sa-puta-dalanam iyam salila-nidhane Budhasa bhagavate sakiydnam. This text inscribed on the urn confirms the enshrinement of the relics of the Buddha by the Sakyas or in other words it confirms the statement of the Buddhist text Mahaparinibbanasutta that the Sakyas of Kapilavastu were one amongst the eight claimants to a portion of the relics of the Buddha after he was cremated at Kushinagar, and that they ceremoniously constructed a stupa over the relics. Since the texts mentioned that the Sakya's had built this stupa on the outskirts of Kapilvastu and latest excavations explored the sites associated with Buddha's life we can believe that Gautama Buddha's home town Kapilavastu has been finally found.

Buddhism and Archaeology

As we discussed in the above pages that after his demise (mahaparinibbana) at Kusinagar and building of shrines over his relics in various parts of the Jambudvïpa for public worshipping, a new genus of (1) images and icons, (2) temples, (3) monuments, (4) stupas, (5) cave-temples, (6) inscriptions, (7) literature, (8) arts (visual and performing) and (9) architectures flourished in India and Nepal on the basis of the life and teachings of the Buddha. All these are now a part of the cultural treasures of mankind. One of such treasures is historical/archaeological sites directly linked to the life and works of the Buddha. The impact of Buddhism and historical Buddhist sites has been phenomenal in shaping the Asian thought and culture. There are also many more historical Buddhist places in India and Nepal rediscovered in the 18th and 19th century. And there is a general consensus on their identity. It is high time that we now relook the Buddha and his heritage to promote mutual understanding and cooperation for sustainable and effective development and preservation of Buddhist historical sites across the border.

The teachings of the Buddha spread beyond India and Nepal and brought many Asian nations closer to each other in the spirit of brotherhood and friendship and tied them with a common cultural bond.

Monument illuminating important events in the life of Buddha and different phases of Buddhism: Sanchi

Based on the confluence of two rivers, the Betwa and the Bes, Sanchi Stupa is unique not only in its having the most perfect and well-preserved stupas but also in its offering a wide and educative field for the study of the genesis, efflorescence and decay of Buddhist art and architecture for a period of about thirteen hundred years, from the third century B.C. to the twelfth century A.D., almost covering the whole range of Indian Buddhism. According to the Chronicles (The Mahavamsa) of Sri Lanka, Mahendra, son of Asoka and his queen Devi, daughter of a merchant of Vidisha (modern Besnagar near Bhilsa or Vidisha), whom Asoka had married during his halt there on his way to Ujjayani as a viceroy, is said to have visited his mother at Vidisha, and the latter took him up to the beautiful monastery of Vedisagiri (Chetiyagiri) built by herself, Mahendra had stayed there for a month before he set out for Sri Lanka. The foundation of Sanchi establishment was laid by Asoka (circa 273-236 B.C.), when he built a stupa and erected a monolithic pillar here. He is said to have opened up seven out of the eight original stupas erected over the body-relics of Buddha and to have distributed the relics among innumerable stupas built by himself all over his empire.

About the middle of the second century B.C. the Sungas were ruling and they stone-encased and enlarged the stupa of Asoka, erected balustrades round its ground, berm, stairway and harmika, reconstructed Temple 40 and stupas 2 and 3 (about the same time circa 150 B.C. a large brick stupa, with a high stone railing and four gateways around it was Bharhut, about 15 kilometres to the south of Satna in Madhya Pradesh, was discovered).

In the next century the Satavahanas added to stupas 1 and 3 elaborately-carved gateways. When Scytho-Parthians and Kushanas (pre and post Christian Era) and their Kshatrapas invaded and annexed a large part of the land Sanchi was dormant in development till the Guptas (circa A D 400) conquered them and provided peace and prosperity for artistic pursuits. The local art of Sanchi once more came to the fore, and to this period belong the four images of Buddha seated under canopies against the berm of stupa 1 facing the four entrances. The female lay-worshipper Harisvamini made endowment in favour of the Buddhist community residing in the monastery of Kakanadabota, for maintaining lamps in the jewel-house and at places of the four Buddhas in A D 450-51.

In the first half of the sixth century Huna chief Mihirkula's invasion on western and central India was shattered by Yasodharman and till A D 606-647 Harshavardhana achieved political unity of northern India. After the death of Harsha the Pratiharas established themselves in Malwa region by the eighth century. Sanchi was swept then with images like Vajrasattva and Marichi under the impact of Vajayana. No Buddhist monument can be assigned to the thirteenth century A D., which was rife with plaques such as Vishnu, Ganesh and mahishasuramardini etc. From the fourteenth century onwards, Sanchi was left deserted and unnoticed till the year 1818, 1822, 1851, 1881, 1912-1919 and 1936 when General Taylor, Captain Johnson, Alexander Cunningham, Captain F.C. Maisey excavated and brought it to public attention. Otherwise the pillar of Asoka was broken into pieces by a local Zemindar, to be utilized as a sugar-cane press like the pillar of Sarnath was dismantled and used for Jagat Singh Market in Varanasi. Major Cole cleared off vegetation and restored the gateway, Sir John Marshall conserved edifices and Mohammad Hamid brought to light a monastery respectively.

The subject-matter of the carvings on the gateways are classified as A,B,C,D and E. Under A scenes from Jatakas such as Chhaddanta, Mahakapi, Vessantara, Alambasa, and Sama jatakas are covered. Under B scenes from the life of Gautama Buddha are depicted and they include his birth, enlightenment, first sermon, parinirvana, Maya's dream and conception, four drives, mahaabhinishkramana, Sujata's offering, grass offering by Svastika, temptation and assault by Mara, Buddha's chankaman, thinking out abhidharma in jewel-house, Naga king Muchilinda, Tapassu and Bhallika passing through Uruvela, presentation of bowls, Adhyeshana (whether to preach or not), miracle of the serpent in the fire-temple at Uruvela, miracle of wood and fire by ascetics foiled, Buddha walking on the river at Uruvela, visit to Kapilavastu, Buddha preaching to the Sakyas in the Nyagrodharama, Buddha's residence at Jetavana, miracle of Sravasti, Buddha preaching under the mango-tree at Sravasti, miracle of Sankasya descending, offering of honey by a monkey at Vaisali, Sakra's visit at Indrasaila near Rajgrih, Royal processions of Prasenjit. Under C are identified events in the subsequent history of Buddhism and they include 1. Siege of Kusinagara by Ajatasatru of Rajgrih, Sakyas of Kapilavastu, Bulis of Allakappa, Koliyas of Ramagrama, Mallas of Pava, Licchavis of Vaishali and Brahman of Vethadvipa after Mallas of Kusinagara took possession of the bone-relics left after cremation of deceased Buddha, 2. Stupa of Ramagrama guarded and worshipped by the Nagas and Asoka failed to secure the relics from here as he did from other seven original stupas, 3. Asoka's visit to the Bodhi-tree, construction of temple over vajrasana by him, destruction of Bodhi-tree by Tishyarakshita. Under D are scenes relating to Vipassi (Patali tree), Sikhi (pundarika tree), Vessabhu (sala tree), Kakusandha (Sirish tree), Kanakamuni (Udumbara tree) and Kassapa (Nyagrodha tree), Maitreya (Nagapushpa) and Gautama Buddha (Peepal tree). Under E are miscellaneous scenes and decorations such as worship of Buddha as symbolized by empty throne or stupa by human and celestial beings and animals and birds and motif of kalpa-valli (wish-fulfilling creeper).

Material Evidence for Words

Buddhism and Buddha were very earthly icons. They both do not look for above to help them but point to earth to reaffirm their truth and existence. Bhoomi Sparsha Mudra or Earth touching posture of Buddha, indicating the achievement of enlightenment at Bodh Gaya is an example of invoking the earthly witness for his Buddhahood, instead of any revelation made from above. Similarly Buddhism as an earthly philosophy accepts only two kinds of proof namely direct perception (Pratyaksha) and Inference (Anuman) in contrast to other proofs accepted by other systems of thought. Buddhist Middle path on human level avoids two extremes of self-indulgence and self-mortification on the one hand, and on philosophical level, Ashasvatam (neither eternal) and anucchedam (non-annihilation) on the other are materially and intellectually verified and verifiable by every reasoning person (paccatam veditabbo vinnuhi).

Revival of Buddhism in India and Nepal

The researches of all the explorers, archaeologists and scholars were helpful in creating a new awakening amongst the people. The systematic revival of Buddhism in India began in 1891 with the arrival of Anagarika Dharmapala, a young Sinhala Buddhist, who turned out to be the first great missionary of modern times. Ven. Kripasarana, a Bengali Buddhist monk founded Bengali Buddhist Association (Dharmankur Sabha). Mr. Rea discovered a casket containing bones of the Buddha at Bhattiprolu in Andhra Pradesh. Bhimrao Ramji Ambedkar was born in Maharashtra. Ven. Mahavir made Kushinagara an accessible shrine.

In 1896 Fuhrer discovered Asokan pillar at Rummindei (Lumbini). In 1998 a relic casket was discovered in the Lumbini garden by the owner of the estate, the casket was inscribed with words "This relic casket of the Divine Buddha is that of the Sakyas."

In 1909 Dr. D.B. Spooner discovered at Shahji-ki-dheri at Peshawar the Kanishka Stupa containing relics of Buddha enshrined by Kanishka. These relics were eventually replaced in a beautiful gold casket and presented by the Government of India to the Buddhists of Burma. In 1914 Sir John Marshal discovered relics of Buddha at Dharmarajika Vihara of Taxila with inscription "These relics of the Holy One (Buddha) were enshrined by Uraska, scion of Imtavhria, a Bactrian, resident of the town of Noacha, in the year 136 of Azes, on the 15th day of the month of Asadha. Two more caskets of the relics of the Buddha discovered from two minor Viharas near Dharmarajika Stupa, were presented by the Government of India in 1917 to the Buddhists of Ceylon and were enshrined in the temple of the Tooth (Dalada Maligawa) at Kandy. Yet another relic casket pertaining to the Buddha with inscription in pre-Asokan characters was discovered at Piprahwa in Basti District of Uttar Pradesh.

The Dharmarajika Vihara in Calcutta, opened in 1920 contained the sacred relics of Lord Buddha, so it became a symbol of Buddhist revival movement in India. Dr. Anandrao L. Nair founded the Buddha Society, Bombay in 1922 and Anand Vihara in 1931 with its publication of Buddha Purnima and Dharma-Chakra periodicals. Dharmananda Kosambi popularized Pali literature, wrote himself books in Marathi and Gujrati. He also built Bahujana Vihara in 1937 to satisfy the spiritual needs of the workers and labourers in Bombay, assisted by his disciple Professor N.K. Bhagwat. In Kerala C. Krishnan, Editor of the Mitavadi journal, converted himself to Buddhist fold with his headquarter at Calicut in 1925. He was assisted in taking Dhamma to the masses by Bhikshu Dharmakkhanda, a Malyali monk trained in Ceylon. In 1928, the great wheel-form Stupa, enshrined with a bone of the Buddha himself, built in 3rd century A.D., at Nagarjunakonda was excavated. In 1929, two Asokan Rock Edicts were discovered at Erragudi in Kurnool District and in 1931 in Raichur District of A.P. In the same year Mulagandhakuti Vihara built at Sarnath was opened. Anagarika Dharmapala entered the Sangha as Sri Devemitta Dhammapala and passed away in 1933. Hindi journal Dharmaduta spread Buddhism in North India since 1935. In 1939 Mahabodhi Society under Devapriya Valisinha, Ven. Sagharatana and Ven. Jinaratana opened Buddha Viharas in New Delhi and Assam, Karnataka (1940), Agartala (1946) and Madras (1947) respectively.

Buddhist revivalists like Rahula Sankrityayan, Anand Kausalyayan, Jagdish Kashyap brought Buddhism in Hindi and served the masses. Kalon

Tsewang Rigzin and Munshi Sonam Tsewang established Ladakh Buddhist Association in 1937. Nandabongsha and Jinaratan Mahatheras established All Assam Buddhist Association in 1939 and Kushak Bakula established Himalayan Buddhist Society, Kulu/Manali in 1942.

Buddhism as Mass Movement

Buddhist symbol of Foundation of World of Righteousness (Dhammacakka) and Lion-Capital of Asoka were adopted as national symbols of free India at the inspiration of Dr. B.R. Ambedkar in 1949. In the same year the sacred relics of Sariputta and Mahamoggalana taken in UK in 1851 were returned to India and enshrined at Sanchi. At the celebration of home-coming of the relics at Sanchi in 1952, Prime Minister of India, Jawahar Lal Nehru said that he saw in the teachings of the Buddha a path leading to progress and prosperity. Thus the Sanchi celebration opened a new vista for the revival of Buddhism in India. Further appreciating efforts of Anagarika Dharmapala towards Buddhist revival Rabindranath Tagore said that a Buddhist University should be established in India to honour such Buddhist revivalist and in 2012 the laying of foundation stone for the Sanchi Buddhist University in Madhya Pradesh took place. Buddha Gaya Temple Management Act was enacted by the Government of Bihara and now (2012) its management is wholly in the hands of the Buddhists as per the verdict of the Supreme Court unlike earlier. In 1950 Dr. B.R. Ambedkar asked his followers to celebrate the Buddha Jayanti in future every year. He also contributed an article to the Vaisakha Number under the title 'The Buddha and the Future of His Religion' stating that Buddhism was the only religion which the world could have because of its emphasis on reason, morality, liberty, equality and fraternity.

In 1956 the Buddhist Era, which commenced on the day of Mahaparinirvana of the Buddha, completed 2500 years. As was natural, on the occasion of the 2500th Celebrations the Buddhist shrines in India got a face-lift. Another event of home-coming of the sacred Relics of Moggaliputta Tissa, Kosikputta and Gotiputta, Mahavanaya, Apagira and Kodiniputta, and Vachiya Savijayata and others, contemporary of Asoka, which were in the possession of the British Museum, London were brought back by Shrimati Vijaya Lakshmi Pandit, Indian High Commissioner in UK. The Government of India presented the relics of Moggaliputta, Kosikputta and Gotiputta to the Government of Ceylon and those of Mahavanaya, Apagira and Kodiniputta and Vachiya Savijayata to Maha Bodhi Society of India, who enshrined them in the Sanchi Vihara.

Dr. B.R. Ambedkar arranged the production of two Gramophone records, through the H.M.V. Company in Pali relating to Trisarana, Panchsheel etc. Setting the foundation of world righteousness on 14th October 1956 Ambedkar Era of Indian Buddhism commenced. From 1956 to 1961 the Buddhist population registered a spectacular increase of 1670.71 percent as it rose from 1,80,823 to 32,50,227. In 1964-65 as a part of the Dharmapala Centenary celebrations in the capital of India, a Bo-sapling was planted on the 25th October 1964 in the Buddha Jayanti Park by Lal Bahadur Shastri, Prime Minister of India. The sapling, which was brought by Mrs. Sirimavo Bandaranaike, Prime Minister of Ceylon, from the Bodhi Tree at Anuradhapura, was taken there from the original Bo-Tree at Bodh Gaya by Princess Sanghamitra (Asoka's daughter) about 2300 years ago. In the same year the seventh but first conference of the WFB to be held in India took place at Sarnath, where the delegation was drawn from 23 countries. In 1966 the Magnificent Thai Monastery was constructed at Buddha Gaya. In 1967 the sacred Buddhist Suttas were for the first time recited in the courtyard of Parliament House by the Venerable monks led by Bhadant Anand Kausalyayan at the occasion of unveiling ceremony of the life-size statue of Dr. Ambedkar at the hands of Dr. S. Radhakrishnan, President of India. In 1968 Bharatiya Bauddha Maha Sangha convened a national conference in Bombay, which was inaugurated by Shrimati Indira Gandhi, Prime Minister of India and presided over by Prof. R.D. Bhandare. Another conference was held in Bombay under the aegis of the Buddhist Society of India in which His Holiness, the Dalai Lama was the inaugurator and Bhayyasaheb Y.B. Ambedkar was in the Chair and Dr. Ambedkar's Memorial at the Chaitya Bhoomi was unveiled by the Chief Minister of Maharashtra, Shri V.P. Naik with unveiling ceremony on the concluding day of the conference. World Peace Pagodas at Rajgir and Dhauli (where Asoka converted himself to Buddhism) marked the year 1969.

During post independent period some notable discoveries marked identification of Ghoshitarama, where the Buddha had stayed during his visit there at the invitation of king Udayana with his capital city Kausambi. At Vaishali, the remains of the stupa built by the Licchavis over their share of the holy relics of the Buddha has been discovered. At Devnmori in Western India remains of monastic establishment and relic casket in the stupa have come to light. At Pauni in Vidarbha, inscriptions and sculptures of the Sunga-Satavahana period (2nd century B.C.) have been found. At Sannotha, on the left bank of the Bhima river in Gulbarga District, nearly 2000 year old brick-built stupas and relics have been discovered. At Chaneti, near Jagadhri in Haryana, the remains of a Mauryan stupa have been found.

At Rajula- Mandagiri in Andhra Pradesh, at Gujarra in Madhya Pradesh, at Ahraura in Uttar Pradesh and at Bahapur, New Delhi four more Asokan Rock Edicts have been discovered. Ven. Dharmarakshita of Sarnath identified in 1969 the village Kadwar, on the river Gomati, about 10 miles to the north of Sultanpur in Uttar Pradesh, as the well-known Kesaputta of the Kalamas. India's Deputy Director of Epigraphy, Dr. N. Venkataramayya discovered in 1970, a vast complex of votive stupas neatly carved on the surface of the living rocks in the Akhanna and Madanna Hills at Vijayawada in Andhra Pradesh. The Patna University team, excavating the Mahbodhi temple in the centre of the University exposed and identified in 1971 the site of famous Vikramasila University in Bihara during the reign of the Palas (750-1162 A.D.). In the same year Dr. S.N. Deo, Head of the Department of Ancient Indian History, Culture and Archaeology of Nagpur University and his team discovered in the Chandla forest, 64 kms. from Nagpur an ancient Buddhist cave with inscription in Brahmi script and Prakrit language.

As against a meager figure of about 50,000 in 1891, India now has more than 3.2 million Buddhists (1971) and 1% of total population of India (2012). And to cater to the spiritual and religious needs of the ever-increasing Buddhist population, a large number of Viharas have come up; the number of Bhikkhus has increased; and a good number of Buddhist Societies are now engaged in the propagation and preservation of the Dhamma. This is true for India as it is for Nepal. Buddhism and historical Buddhist sites in India and Nepal go together to unite the territorial, geographical and demographic humankind. Let us promote, preserve and pass on this heritage and culture to the coming generations for their better and greater future.

Conclusion

During 483 B.C. and 275 B.C. full text of the Scriptures was settled at Rajgrih Council under the Presidentship of Ven. Maha Kassapa. Differences of opinion arose between Vajji monks and those led by Yasa and the Council held at Vaisali under the Chairmanship of Ven. Sabbakami gave verdict against the Vajji monks. This was the consolidation phase of Buddhism. During its systematic propagation phase (275 B.C.- 200 B.C.) Asoka (273 B.C. – 232 B.C.) made the Buddha-Dhamma the basis of all his actions in the spiritual as well as temporal fields. He launched a vigorous campaign after Pataliputra (modern Patna) Council under the Presidentship of Ven. Moggaliputta Tissa and sent missionaries to various parts of India and the neighbouring countries, issuing a number of Rock and Pillar Edicts and made Buddhism a national religion. However after about 45 years of his death Pushyamitra, Brahmin commander-in-chief of Brihadaratha, the last Mauryan King, treacherously assassinated the king and usurped the throne. During the phase of Buddhism as Popular Religion (200 B.C. – 500 A.C.) the Buddhist masses, despite persecution by Pushyamitra stuck to their faith, and gave unreserved support to the Sangha. Most of the stupas and railings at Sanchi and Bharhut were the creation of the pious lay devotees of the Buddha, who came about 50-100 years after Asoka. They formed the village committees to help building the railings at these places. Buddhism's popularity further increased when the Greek King, Menander (at the hands of Ven. Nagasena) and the Kushana ruler, Kanishka (78 A.C.- 101 A.C.) ruling North-West India (200 B.C.- 100 A.D.) embraced Buddhism and did their utmost to further popularize it.

Ashvaghosha, contemporary of Kanishka, took Buddhism to every hearth and home. Nagarjuna, contemporary of Satavahana King, Yajnasri Gautami Putra (166-196 A.D.) of Andhra gave a new and definite turn to Buddhist philosophy (Sunyavada). Asanga and Vasubandhu flourished in Punjab in the 4th century A.C. Asanga developed the Yogachara or Vijnanavada school of his guru, Maitreyanatha and Vasubandhu wrote Abhidharmakosa as an encyclopaedia of Buddhism. Buddhaghosha (5th century A.C.) as great Pali scholar, wrote commentaries and Visuddhimagga as key to Tripitaka and as post-Tripitaka literature. Buddhapalita and Bhavaviveka expounded Sunyavada doctrine of Nagarjuna in the 5th century. Dinnaga was the father of the Medieval nyaya as a whole.

During the phase of struggle for Survival (C. 500 A.C. -700 A.C.) while the Huna Chief Mihirkula mercilessly persecuted Buddhists in north-west india the Samanta rulers of Valabhi (Gujrat), the Maukharis of Kanauj (U.P.) and the Vardhana dynasty of Thanesar (Punjab) as Buddhist local chieftains ruling their independent states, endeavoured to rehabilitate their sacred religion. On Mihirkula's death Meghavahana in Kashmir undertook propagation and preservation of Buddhism with great zeal. When Rajyavardhana, elder brother of Harsha (606-647 A.D.) and Grahvarmana (his brother-in-law) were assassinated and Rajyashri (his sister) imprisoned by the king of Malva, Harsha later on, succeeded to annex Punjab, Haryana, part of Rajasthan, U.P., Bihar, Bengal and Orissa to his capital Kanauj. He foiled the twin conspiracies of the Brahmins against his own life and treated Hiuen Tsang (629-644 A.D.) with utmost reverence and hospitality. The latter reported that there were about 1000 monasteries and about 50,000 monks in India during the reign of Harsha. After the death of Harsha in 647 A.D. Buddhism began declining rapidly.

During the Decline phase of Buddhism (C. 700 A.C.- 1150 A.C.) we hear very little of Buddhism outside Kashmir, Bengal and Bihar, reports I-Tsing, who was in India from 673 to 685 A.D. (30 years after departure of Hiuen Tsing) and stayed at Nalanda for 10 years. Khadgas as first Buddhist dynasty ruled Bengal from 625 to 725 A.D. Pala rulers, another Buddhist family, ruled from 750 to 1162 A.D. and patronized Nalanda Maha Vihara and established famous monasteries of Vikramasila, Odantapuri and Somapuri etc. After the downfall of the Palas, Buddhism passed into oblivion in the North-Eastern region.

The phase of Dark Age (C. 1150 A.C.-1800 A.C.) began as the Muslim army advanced towards Bihar; sacked the Buddhist establishment at Nalanda, Vikramasila and Odantapuri; massacred most of the monks residing in them. The Buddhist laity were left without any guide; and in due course they went back to the fold of Hinduism. Asokan Stupa at Sarnath was dismantled in 1794 by Jagat Singh, the Diwan of Raja Chait Singh of Banaras, merely for the bricks required for the construction of a market in Varanasi (now called Jagat Ganj). A good number of Buddhist temples such as Mahabodhi Temple at Bodh Gaya, were converted into Hindu or Muslim places of worship. Every trace of Buddhism was effaced from the land of its birth.

During the Renaissance phase of Buddhism (1750-1890) Asokan inscription was discovered on Delhi-Mirath Pillar by Padre Tieffenthaler, Allahabad-Kosam (Kausambi) pillar was discovered followed by the discovery of Lauriya-Araraj (Radhia) Pillar in 1784 and Barabar Hill Cave inscriptions in 1785, Delhi-Topra Pillar at Ferozshah Kotla. As Captain James Hoare published in 1801 in the Asiatic Researches, Journal of the Asiatic Society of Bengal, facsimiles of the Delhi-Topra inscriptions attempts to decipher the Asokan lipi began in right earnest. In 1819 the Ajanta Caves, unique combination of architecture, sculpture and painting was discovered followed by discovery of Ellora, Nasik, Karle, Bhaja and Junnar etc. In 1822 first Rock Edict at Girnar, sacred mountain near Junagadh in Gujrat was discovered. In 1834 Allahabad Pillar inscription was published and in 1836 Shahbazgarhi Rock Edict in Peshawar District, Pakistan was discovered. The deciphering of the Asokan lipi and the identification of Asoka in 1837 enriched the history of India and of Buddhism. In 1840 Bhabru Edict on the rock at Bairat near Jaipur, in 1850 the Jaugada Rock inscription in Ganjam Distt., Orissa and in 1860 Asokan Rock inscription at Kalsi near Dehra Dun were discovered. In 1851 the Great Stupa of Sanchi rescued in 1818, was opened by Cunningham. He recapitulated the glorious history of the Buddhist remains and monuments scattered all over the country. He excavated Maha Bodhi as the Great Buddhist Temple at Buddha Gaya in 1870 and Mahastupa of Bharhut as finest Buddhist art in 1873-74. He researched on Bhilsa Stupa also. By this time, the Bairat Minor Rock Edict, the Rupnath Minor Rock Edict and the Rampurva Pillar Edict had been discovered. In 1882 Asokan Rock Edict at Sopara, Mansehra Rock Edict in Hazara District, Pakistan (1889) and Mysore Minor Rock Edicts (1890) were also discovered.

The discovery of Buddhist literature commenced with Winternitz with a history of Buddhist literature in French, Volume II. Burnouf published the first history of Buddhism in 1844 and French translation of Saddharma-pundarika in 1852 based on Sanskrit Buddhism. Fausboil studied Pali texts and published a Latin translation of the Dhammapada, his English translation of Sutta-nipata was published in 1881, his monumental work was the translation of Jatakas in English in six volumes published between 1877 and 1897. Hermann Oldenberg translated Vinaya Pitaka into English from 1879 to 1883, Patimokkha, Mahavagga, Cullavagga, in collaboration with Rhys Davids, appeared in Volumes XIII, XVII and XX of the Sacred Books of the East (1881-85). Rhys Davids learnt Pali in Ceylon and in 1879 published a translation in English of the Nidanakatha (Buddhist Birth Stories), in 1881 he founded the Pali Text Society in London. Mrs Rhys Davids also did a yeoman's service to the study of Pali and Buddhism. Rhys Davids edited texts of Dighanikaya (1889), the Abhidhammat-thasangaha (1884), Dathavamsa (1884) and a Manual of Yogavacara (1896). He translated Milinda-panho and Digha-nikaya also. In 1885, Sir Edwin Arnold, author of Light of Asia visited Bodh Gaya and was shocked to see the deplorable condition of the most sacred shrine of the Buddhists. He wrote a number of articles in the Telegraph, of which he was the editor, and drew attention of the Buddhists to the pitiable condition of the Maha Bodhi Temple and urged them to save it from further desecration.

We have already discussed systematic revival phase and Mass Movement phase of Buddhism above. From these we can make a practical suggestion as follows.

Suggestions

1. Buddhist historical sites such as Sankissa near Eta District in U. P., Satdhara and nearby sites near Sanchi and Bagh Caves in Madhya Pradesh and Sirpur in Chhattisgarh should be developed and preserved for our national interest and international peace.
2. Over and above the Atthamahathanani viz. Lumbini, Bodh Gaya, Sarnath, Kusinagara, Sravasti, Sankasya, Vaishali and Rajgir

visited by Asoka the following important centres of Buddhism should also be kept in mind for development: Amravati, Nagarjunakonda, Bhattiprolu, Jaggayyapeta, Ghantasala, Goli, Gudivada, Guntupalli, Adurru, Sankaram, Ramatirtham and Salihundrain in Andhra Pradesh; Salkusa in Assam, Nalanda, Pataliputra, Odantapuri and Vikramasila in Bihar; Junagadh, Dhank, Siddhasar, Talaja, Sanah, Valabhi and Kampilya in Gujrat; Thanesar and Sugh in Haryana; Mandi, Kulu and Nurpur in Himachal Pradesh; Srinagar and its outskirts like Saurasa, Simpor etc. in Kashmir; Srimulavasam and Cranganore in Kerala; Sanchi, Bharhut and Bagh Caves in Madhya Pradesh; Sirpur in Chhattisgarh; Buddhavedu and Nagapattam in Tamil Nadu; Bhaja, Kondone, Kondivite, Pitalkhora, Ajanta, Ellora, Bedsa, Pandu lena, Junnar, Karle, Kanheri, Mahad, Karhad and Nala Sopara in Maharashtra; Dhauligiri, Jaugarh, Baudh, Choudwara near Cuttack, Udayagiri and Ratnagiri in Orissa; Patti, Jullunder and Sirhind in Punjab; Nagar near Udaipur, Bairat near Jaipur, Dhamnar, Kholvi, Vinayaka and Hathigor in Rajasthan; Kanauj, Kausambi, Mathura, Prayag in Uttar Pradesh; and Jugaddala, Somapuri etc. in West Bengal.

3. They should be developed as they are immensely conducive to revival of Buddhism and enlightening on be-gone glory of Buddhist art and architecture.
4. The Asokan Edicts have been since 1750, discovered at 32 places within states of Andhra Pradesh, Bihar, Delhi, Gujrat, Madhya Pradesh, Maharashtra, Mysore, Rajasthan and Uttar Pradesh and since they are catalyst to Buddhist revival movement, they should be protected and well maintained by the Government of India.

References

1. Fuhrer, A. Dr. Antiquities of Buddha Sakyamuni's Birthplace in the Nepalese Tarai, Indological Book House, Varanasi, India 1972:19.
2. Dharmananda Kosambi, Vishva Vani Ka Bauddha Sanskriti Visheshank, May 1942, p. 504 and Dr. B.R. Ambedkar the Buddha and His Dhamma, Siddhartha Prakashan, Bombay 1957.
3. Bapat P.V., 2500 years of Buddhism, Govt. of India, New Delhi 1956, foreword by Dr. Radhakrishnan.
4. Dr. B.R. Ambedkar, The Buddha and His Dhamma, printed in Taiwan 2007.
5. Internet Surfing dated 21 Dec. 2012.
6. Dr. Avdhesh Singh, Chini Yatriyon Ke Yatra Vivran Mein Pratibimbit Bauddha Dharm Ka Ek Adhyayan, Ramanand Vidya Bhavan, New Delhi 1987.

7. Ahir D.C. Buddhism in Modern India, Nagpur 1972.
8. Carus Paul The Gospel of Buddha, Nagpur 1997.
9. Kuldharma Ratna Tuladhar, Buddhism and Nepal, Kathmandu 1986.
10. Sanchi, Archaeological Survey of India New Delhi 2001.
11. Tiwari Vinay Kumar, Sanchi, Bhopal Year of publication not mentioned.
12. Kausalyayan Ananda, Buddhism and Dialectical Materialism (Article) published in The Maha Bodhi, September 1952, pp. 327-332.
13. Kuladharma Ratna Tuladhar, Buddhism and Nepal, Dharmodaya Sabha, Buddha Vihara, Kathmandu, Nepal 1986.
14. The Kapilavastu Controversy: Part 1 posted on December 12, 2012 by buddhistartnews surfed on the same date on internet.
15. T.W. Rhys Davids, Buddhist India, Motilal Banarasidass, Delhi, 1st ed. 1971, rep. 1981 pp. 3ff.

Chapter - 4

Yoga

Introduction

Life is not a planned enterprise but a fraction of the vast existence and often considered in terms of life of mankind on the earth. Even human life is infinite though it is regarded as confined to living beings alone in intercourse with their other counterparts in various geographical societies and communities. Since life is wrongly understood as a finite and spatio-temporal affair commonly fraught with psycho-physical and social complexities and their attendant ills yoga as a remedy is quite often exhorted and adapted as if it was an additional component and extra burden for resolving the problems of life. Some yoga teachers and masters even go to the extent of imposing yogic technique to the great peril of both the taught and technique itself, resulting in further deterioration of health and attitude towards such remedy and its provider as well.

The point of view about yoga for consciousness and total life management as propounded by the author of these lines is to hold both life and yoga as natural as possible and as effortless as any human being can succeed in practicing the same. Of course, in the beginning some kind of effort cannot be avoided but it is only to the extent as we endeavour while taking any turns during walking along the road or driving. Thus said it is proposed and strongly recommended that some misconceptions about the life and Yoga called for revisiting and revaluation of Yoga for consciousness and total life management as suggested in the abstract and the detailed paper that follows is as a sequel to this theme.

Some authorities on Yoga are referred to in support of and to substantiate the above perspective:

Yoga

Gheranda Samhita (1:4) described 'Yoga' as power and *yogam Samasadya* as the technique of yoga. Chapter 2:6 of the same source reads that out of eighty four lacs of asanas eighty four of them are important and out of the latter only 32 of them are sufficient in this world of mortal beings. Gheranda Sanhita chapter (5:8/15) itself restraints the beginning of the exercise of yoga in the season of Hemant, Sishir, Grishma and Varsha as causing sickness, if it is practiced. Instead it recommends that starting it in Vasanta or Sharada makes it easily successful. Further 5:78 exhorts that *sukhena kumbhakam krtva manascha bhruvorantaram, santyajya vishyan sarvan mano murcha sukhprada* i.e. by performing kumbhaka comfortably, fixing the mind between the eye-brows inside and detaching oneself from all objects there arises enjoyable tranquility of the mind. While 6:19 observes that *chanchalatvanna drshyte* subtle yoga awakening kundalini is not perceived because of high frequency of vibration. 6:20 describes subtle yoga as meaning dhyanayoga along with Sambhavi mudra, which is not easily attainable even by the gods (devanamapi durlabham), where Dhyana is defined in Brihadyogiyajnavalkya Smrti as the control of buddhi, ahamkara, manas and indriyas with their objects in one place, 7:1 equated the supreme yoga with Samadhi (samadhishcha paro yogo).

In ShivasamhitaYogi is attributed as always engaged in gyan marg (1:31), perceiving self by self in self (1:63) and dissolving the world (laya kurvanti). In 2:5 it says that yogi knows this body as universe (Brahmanda sanjnake dehe).

Swami Jnaneshvara Bharati (Swami J. com) of Traditional Yoga And Meditation of the Himalayan Masters (Self-Realization through the Yoga Sutras, Vedanta, Samaya Sri Vidya Tantra, surfed on 14.9.12) "Yoga is to do with mind and transcendence, not the physical body, as is the modern misperception".

Religious leaders say that Yoga is spiritual. Paramahansa Yogananda, the well-known author of Autobiography of a Yogi is one of them. George Feurstein, another well recognized scholar and teacher, in response to the question "How would you describe Yoga today" wrote in the online LA Yoga Magazine that "It is a mess". David Frawley, an internationally recognized scholar and teacher is reported to have said in the issue of Yoga Journal that "Yoga in the West has only scratched the surface of the greater Yoga tradition. Yoga community in the West is currently at a crossroads. Its recent commercialization should be used to build the foundation for a more profound teaching, aimed at consciousness of humanity. In his interview in CBS television in 2005 Bikram Choudhary said, "Yoga is a perfect marriage between body and mind. Then, you can reach and knock the door to the spirit". Pandit Rajmani Tigunait, Head of the Himalayan Institute of the

USA wrote, "To hold Yoga primarily as a set of practices for increasing strength and flexibility while calming the physical system is to mistake the husk for the kernel". Swami Chidananda Saraswati, head of the internationally known Sivananda Ashram Yoga Life Society in Rishikesh, India explained that Yoga is not mere acrobatics. Physical practices are at best as an auxiliary or a minor form of Yoga.

According to Hatha Yoga Pradipika, a 13th century text outlining the practice of Hatha Yoga has its last chapter on Samadhi (the Higher Consciousness) noted that the focus of Yoga is Samadhi. All of the practices of Hatha Yoga and Laya Yoga are means to Samadhi (4:103). Swami Satyananda Saraswati, founder of Bihar School of Yoga, explained that the main objective of hatha Yoga was to create an absolute balance of the activities and processes of the physical body, mind and energy. B.K.S. Iyengar, a well known teacher and author wrote, "Yoga is the means and the goal. Yoga is Samadhi and Samadhi is Yoga. Swami Rama in his Path of Fire and Light declared that the word 'Yoga' has been vulgarized and does not mean anything now".

The Columbia Encyclopaedia, sixth edition, 2001-07 interpreted Yoga as a general term for spiritual disciplines propounded by Buddhism, and throughout S. Asia directed toward attainment of higher consciousness and liberation from ignorance and suffering. Funk & Wagnalls New Encyclopaedia enlightened on the word Yoga as affirming the doctrine that through certain disciplines one may achieve liberation from the limitations, delusions of senses, and the pitfalls of thought and thus attain union with true knowledge or seek perfect self-knowledge.

Swami Jnaneshvara warned that if you are a sincere seeker of the higher authentic goals of Yoga, you are sometimes exasperating journey that is filled with joy. It is infinitely fraught with challenges along the way. Mark Singleton in his Yoga Body: The Origin of Modern Postures, Oxford University: 2010 rightly pointed out that "Yoga as popularly practiced today owes a great debt to modern Indian Pundits, even more surprisingly, to the spiritual aspirations of European body-builders and 20th-century women's gymnastic movement of Europe and America, than it does to the ancient Indian Yoga. Not Yoga Facebook Group playfully devoted to the ways in which yoga is misrepresented, uttered that "Much, if not most of today's Yoga can be called *gymnastic yoga* as it has emerged from the gymnastic practices of the late 1800 and early 1900s, not from the ancient traditions of yoga. Other "styles" of modern yoga are simply gross distortions.

Consciousness while life

While an individual is leading his or her life normally and naturally as per Shakespearian expression, "There is a tide in the affairs of men. Which, taken at the flood, leads on to fortune; Omitted, all the voyage of their life Is bound in shallows and in miseries. On such a full sea are we now afloat...", then the consciousness one possessed at the moment of birth is as impermanent a force as waves rising and falling on the surface of ocean if one pursues the deliberately thoughtful way of discarding the unwholesome and following the wholesome thoughts in the human state and develop psychological vectors till the attainment of path and fruit of deathlessness or nirvana and assures liberation from total suffering then one's life's deed worth doing is accomplished as the goal of life is found within, not in institutions.

This expression is corroborated by the references, one of which for example is as follows:

From the Majjhima Nikiiya, in the Vatthupama Sutta we read:

Alattha kho Sundarika Bharadvajo brahmano Bhagavato santike pabbajjam, alattha upasampadam. Acirupasampanno kho pan' ayasma Bharadvajo eko vupa kattho appamatto atapi pahitatto viharanto nacirass' eva yass' atthaya kulaputta samma-d-eva agarasma anagariyam pabbajanti tad anuttaram brahrnacariyam pariyosanam ditthe va dhamme sayam abhinnaya sacchikatva upasampajja vihasi: khina jati, vusitam brahmacariyam, katam karaniyam naparam itthattayati abbhannasi, annataro kho pan' ayasma Bharadvajo arahatam ahositi.

Then the brahmin Sundarika-Bnaradvaja received the going forth [pabbajjam]in the Lord's presence, he received ordination. Soon after he had been ordained, the venerable Bharadvaja, abiding alone, aloof, diligent, self-resolute, not long after• wards, by his own super-knowledge [abhinna], having precisely here-and-now realized the matchless culmination of the Brahma-faring [brahmacariyam] for the sake of which young men of family rightly go forth from home into homelessness, abided in it. He comprehended : Destroyed is birth, brought to a close the Brahma-faring, done is what was to be done, there is no more of being such and such. So the venerable Bharadvaja became one of the perfected ones [arahatam]. This formula is actually a formula about how one goes about

Management

Abraham Maslow introduced a model of developmental psychology that has become extremely well known not only in the field of psychology, but also in management and other human science. Maslow said that to develop a next higher level requires a reasonable level of completion at the previous level. *Physiological needs* such as needs for food, water, air, and sleep are to be satisfied first, then the *safety needs* for safe lifestyle and safe environment, safe housing, financial security, job security, as well as physical, mental, and emotional safety and freedom from threats are met. Beyond that are *social needs* for belongingness, having family, friends, and community, giving and receiving of love and nurturing that arise for our attending to. Thereupon the *esteem needs* for self-respect, achievement and recognition by others, for aesthetics and knowledge come and they are followed by *self-actualization* by attaining one's full potential as a human being living in the world, involving the seeking and expression of justice, wisdom, benevolence and creativity. This brought forth the force of the humanistic psychology preceded by depth psychology of the ego structure and behavioral psychology. There was further breakthrough in psychology by introducing the needs for *transpersonal level* beyond self actualization.

Yoga psychology is about self realization in that it goes beyond, transcend even transpersonal level or all six needs hierarchy of Maslow and relates to subtle, causal and absolute reality. Collectively all needs operate in the gross level but Yoga contains a total of four broad levels or stages, though there may not be much recognition of the higher levels when one is still working on a lower level. The deeper levels are functioning substratum, which is generally quite out of view by most people. While gross level is called vaishvanara the subtle level is known as taijas or astral, occult, psychic plane in Indian culture. Transpersonal communities never talk or write about the xcausal or prajna plane of development though it is the substratum out of which the subtle and gross spring. It is the fountain of intuitive and formless knowing, deeper than subtle experiences, visions, sounds, visitations or vices. Parallel to the forth force of humanistic psychology is the Yogic state of Absolute or Turiya in which pure consciousness permeates and transcends both the subtle and causal planes.

These four stages of developmental Yoga Psychology are symbolically represented in the four parts of the OM Mantra analysed into three sounds A, U and M along with the *silence* that follows. This four part framework of OM Mantra is one of the finest simple roadmaps of the four broad stages of Yoga Psychology.

Reality expresses or manifests itself in four levels of consciousness and three domains of consciousness as shown in the following table.

Table - 1

S.N.	*Levels of consciousness*	*Domains*	*Of*	*consciousness*
1	Waking/conscious/gross level	Waking state of consciousness	Conscious mind	Gross realm of manifestation
2	Dreaming/unconscious/subtle level	Dreaming state of consciousness	Unconscious level of mind	Subtle realm of manifestation
3	Deep Sleep/subconscious/causal level	Deep Sleep state of consciousness	Subconscious level of mind	Causal realm of manifestation
4	Absolute/consciousness/self-realization/brahmam/god as immanent compared to god as transcendent	Experience of movements within these three levels of consciousness	Mental functioning is happening at one of three levels interacting each other without one's awareness	Gross universe, subtle world and causal plane coexist in mutual interaction

The 3 states of consciousness, waking, dreaming and deep sleep are like surface, undercurrent and bed of a river. In the waking state of consciousness conscious mind experiences gross realm of existence while unconscious and subconscious minds are out of conscious view as are subtle and causal realms. In the dreaming state conscious mind recedes back into the subtler levels and it loses awareness of gross world. Latent impressions from subconscious mind arise into the dreaming state. In Yoga meditation access to subtle realm is let go as it is a diversion from the true self realization. In the deep sleep state awareness of both the activity of gross realm and subtle realm is lost. Conscious mind and unconscious processing part of mind recede back into the latent bed of subconscious from which they emerge. Through Yoga Nidra deep sleep state is experienced while fully conscious. In this state all visible subtle and gross objects, pictures and impressions remain in their latent, dormant potential formless form.

Yoga meditation is performed in waking state of consciousness and allows unconscious impressions and subconscious to come forward, which gradually expands its conscious state to unconscious and subconscious, so that it is all conscious and comes in direct experience of Turiya. Yoga Nidra, though an extremely relaxing, insightful state of being is still short of Samadhi and Turiya.

Similarly three states of mind, conscious, unconscious and subconscious are active life, microchip in a computer and hard disk drive of a computer respectively. Impressions arising from the bed of subconscious cause a stirring of unconscious and conscious emotions, thoughts, actions, speech, objects and people, whose memory or images the mind draws from subconscious in the dreaming state. In Yogic meditation as the conscious mind becomes quiet, the veil between conscious and unconscious is gradually opened, allowing more thoughts, feelings, sensations, images or impressions to come forward from the unconscious to the conscious, and as they are allowed to drift away, in a spirit of non-attachment the conscious mind is expanded in such a way that it goes beyond all aspects of the mind.

In the same way the three states of manifestation, namely gross, subtle and causal are to be explained as consciousness expresses itself in the domain of five elements of earth, water, fire, air and space as Bhutas, the same in etheric aspect as tattvas and in lightness (sattvas), heaviness (tamas) and activity (rajas), respectively, which is derived from pure consciousness itself.

Total

Total means a common ground for all. When consciousness is not individuated then it is total. At this level the pure consciousness flows equally throughout all. It is silence. This is the source of all states of consciousness, all states of mind and all states of manifestation. It is not subject to death, decay or decomposition. It was never born and it never dies. It is absolute and indescribable. This is indivisible. This is the depth of the ocean of consciousness. Those rare few who seek to know the source out of which both gross and subtle planes emerge, seek to know Prajna (pra= supreme, jna= knowing), the formless causal plane of pure potential. This causal plane is the place from which the creativity of the subtle and the gross emerges. One who becomes aware of this deepest state of mind through the process of Yoga Nidra begins to have access to thought patterns in their latent form and weaken these latent habit patterns called samskaras, and can effectively reduce the effect on karma or actions that would play out as a result of the sanskaras. In the deepest deep sleep state of consciousness subconscious mind is encountered, and in which awareness has no gross or subtle objects on which to focus, but instead can focus on the formless forms of the potential, latent, inactive thought patterns, as they rest in the bed of the mind-field. Thus deep sleep state of consciousness, the subconscious state of mind and the causal realm all operate at the Same level of reality or existence.

Conclusions

Thinking there is only one way comes from ignorance.

Chapter - 5

Osho, Kashyap and Kausalyayan

After finishing his MA, Jagdish Kondur, desiring to doctoral work in Buddhist philosophy, was advised to study Pâli, and so resolved to go to Sri Lanka, to his parents' dismay. They relented in 1933 and he joined the Vidyalankara Pirivena (now the University of Kelaniya). He was ordained by Venerable L. Dhammananda Nayaka Mahathero. During his time at the Vidyalankara Pirivena he translated the Digha Nikâya into Hindi.

On a trip to Japan he was stopped by the police in Malaysia due to his involvement in Gandhi's non-cooperation movement. He spent a year living in Penong, learned some Chinese, lived in a Chinese vihara, and published a collection of lectures.

In 1936 he returned to Sri Lanka to spend time in a forest hermitage to practice meditation, which was quite unusual for a bhikkhu in his day, so much so that his teachers tried to dissuade him. Bhikkhu Kashyap continued to practice meditation throughout his life. Towards the end of 1936 he returned to India and in 1937 settled at Sarnath where he was involved in scholarly and translating work, principally of the Pâli Canon into Hindi. In Sarnath he became associated with the Mahabodhi Society and was soon helping with the institutional organisation and social services. He became the headmaster of a new high school founded by the Mahabodhi Society General Secretary, Devapriya Valisinha. While in Sarnath he also persuaded officials of Banares Hindu University to offer courses in Pâli which he taught for free - even occasionally walking the 22 mile journey into Varanasi.

During this time Bhikkhu Kashyap took on a young English monk as a live-in student for about nine months. Sangharakshita went on to found the Western Buddhist Order in 1968, and considers Bhikkhu Kashyap to have been an important teacher in both the spiritual and secular senses.

In 1947 India became independent and there was a new sense of identity for Indians. In 1949 he toured his ancestral homeland, the ancient province of Magadha, which was also the centre of ancient Buddhism. For the first time in many centuries the villages in Magadha saw a yellow robed bhikkhu, and were pleasantly surprised to find that he spoke their local dialect Magadhi. The locals had long forgotten their own history and Bhikkhu Kashyap was able to furnish many details. The very name of the state of Bihar comes from presence of so many Buddhist viharas in the past. He was able to point out the true identity of the images of Buddhas and Bodhisattvas which were being worshipped as Hindu gods or local deities. Villages such as Sari-chak, near Nalanda, had previously had an association with the Buddha's chief disciple Sariputta. Finally he was able, by quoting passages from the Pâli texts, to demonstrate that Magadhi is still closely related to the Magadhi dialect.

After this visit Bhikkhu Kashyap offered to teach Pâli at Gaya College and at Nalanda College in Bihar-Sharif. Later, when the Bihar state government decided to start an institute for Pâli studies at Nalanda, he was the obvious choice to head the project. In 1951 the institute became the Nava Nalanda Mahavihara.

1956 was the 2500th anniversary of the parinibbana of the Buddha, celebrated by the Indian government as the Buddha Jayanti. As part of the celebrations, Bhikkhu Kashyap's work of bringing out a Devanagari edition of the Pâli Canon was accepted as an official project, and was jointly sponsored by the governments of Bihar and India. The first volume appeared in 1956 on the occasion of the Buddha Jayanti, and the rest followed over five years - guided to completion with enormous effort and marathon labour by Bhikkhu Kashyap. At one point he sold his house to pay the salaries of workers when payments had been delayed.

During the Buddha Jayanti project Bhikkhu Kashyap returned to Varanasi and in 1959 was asked to become the first Professor of Pâli and Buddhism at the Sanskrit University of Varanasi. He remained there until 1965 when he returned to Nalanda for a second term as Director of the Nava Nalanda Mahavihara. He retired in 1973. Having earlier developed diabetes, he became seriously ill in 1974 and spent his last two years bedridden in the Japanese temple in Rajgir, from where he could see the Vulture Peak and the newly constructed Peace Pagoda. He died in 1976.

About him Ven. Sangharakshit gave his own account of intimacy and discipleship in the following pages:

"Tonight I'm just going to reminisce about my eight most important Buddhist teachers, I'm going to start off with Bhikkhu Jagdish Kasyap.

I don't know how many of you have heard his name before, so I'll just repeat it: Bhikkhu Jagdish Kasyap. Kasyap-ji as he was usually called ('ji' being an honorific suffix), was Indian, he was in fact a Bihari; Bihar being that province or that state in India in which Bodhgaya, where the Buddha was enlightened, is situated. He used to talk to me a bit about his earlier life, his ancestry. He came of respectable, peasant or small landholding stock and seems to have been a rather religious-minded youth. Of course, he was born as a Hindu. And while he was still in his teens, he joined a Hindu organization, a sort of Hindu reform organization, called the Aryasamaj, founded by Swami Dayananda Sarasvati in the last century. This particular Samaj, this organization, was opposed to image worship, not very much in favour of the caste system, and strongly emphasized Vedic Hinduism. Kasyap joined the Aryasamaj, became a Hindu Sannyasin, and embarked upon the study of the Vedas, the most sacred scriptures of the Hindus. He embarked on their study because these were the texts which the Aryasamaj so strongly emphasized, and all Hindus believed that the Vedas were the foundation of their faith, of their practice, contained all possible mysteries — and often Hindus believe that the formula for the manufacture of the atom bomb is to be found in the Vedas — so Kasyap was very excited and very thrilled to be able to embark on the study of the Vedas. And of course he had to learn Sanskrit, including Vedic Sanskrit which is rather different to classical Sanskrit. But he was very disillusioned. He didn't find any wisdom, he told me, he didn't find any philosophy. He found hymns to this god, that god, especially hymns to Indra, a sort of thunder god, rather quarrelsome, rather fond of fighting, often getting drunk — a rather edifying sort of god; he found all sorts of rituals described, all sorts of chants, he found all sorts of magic spells to destroy your enemies and attract love — and he felt, Well, where is the sublime philosophy that I was promised? He used to say to me subsequently that the best way of weaning a Hindu away from Hinduism is to get them to study the Vedas. Because normally they're not studied, you very, very rarely find even a Brahmin who possesses a copy of the Vedas, they're very rare indeed. You used to find the Vedas in the libraries of the scholars in the West; you don't find them in India".

"Any way, to cut a rather long story short, he did become very disillusioned with the Vedas, with the Aryasamaj, with Hindusim — so he started exploring other faiths: for example, Sikkhism and Buddhism. And when he came upon Buddhism, which don't forget had been actually dead in India for hundreds upon hundreds of years, he decided that this was the faith, this was the religion for him. He went to Sri Lanka, he became a bhikku there, he studied Pali, and became in fact a Tipitaka-Acarya, that is to say he studied the whole of the Pali canon in the original Pali language — in the royal Thai edition this is some 45 volumes. Kasyap had studied them all, and was therefore eventually granted this title. But though he had studied the Tipitaka in Pali in Sri Lanka, though he'd become a bhikkhu there, he did not in fact have a very high opinion of the Sri Lankan Bhikkhu Sangha. He used to tell me some rather amusing stories which rather illustrated their approach to the Dharma, even their formalism. I remember him telling me once that — well, I should explain that in Sri Lanka, among the bhikkhus, there are various sects. There are three main sects, so how do you tell them apart? They dress a little differently. Monks belonging to two of them, when they go out, out of the monastery, they cover both shoulders with their robes. Monks belonging to the other one do not: they leave the right shoulder bare. And there's a difference of umbrellas, I might add while I'm on the subject. One sect carry a black umbrella, one carry a Burmese-style, parasol-type umbrella because they originate from Burma, the other are very strict, they make do with a big plantain leaf. In this way you can tell them apart. So it's very important, apparently, in Sri Lanka, to know which Nikaya, or sect of the sangha, a bikkhu belongs to; and bikkhus I suppose like to know which Nikaya another bikkhu who they happen to meet belongs to. Kasyap was always being asked this question when he travelled around in Sri Lanka — which Nikaya do you belong to? So Kasyap, who had after all come into Buddhism from the outside, was not a Sri Lankan, used to say Nikaya? I belong to Buddhanikaya. So that didn't satisfy them at all, so they used to probe a little, and they used to ask him, he told me, Well, when you go out, when you leave the monastery, do you cover one shoulder, or do you cover two? Kashyap used to say, Well, when it's hot I cover two shoulders, when it's very hot, I cover only one, when it's very,very hot I don't cover either. So he could not be caught; and he used to tell me other stories too. He told me that one day he was giving a lecture, and he was invited to give a lecture on the *anatta* doctrine, the doctrine of no-self as it's usually translated; and he started off by saying that you couldn't understand what was meant by *anatta*, or non-self or no-self, unless you first of all understood what was meant by *atta*, or self. So at that moment, as soon as he'd said that, various Sri Lankan bikkhus got to their feet and shouted We don't want any of that Hindu philosphy here. Kasyap tried to explain that he wasn't preaching Hindu philosophy, he was only trying to clarify the concept of *anatta*. But they would not accept it, they actually shouted him down, they forced him to resume his seat. So he used to tell me stories like this; and at the end, as I believe I've related in *The Rainbow Road*, he said to me — because as you know the Pali Tipitaka, the Pali scriptures, were admittedly preserved in Sri lanka by the Sri Lankan bikkhus — but he said, Sangharakshita — this is how he used to talk — Sangharakshita, those Sinhalese bikkhus, they are a set of monkeys, sitting on a treasure, the value of which they do not understand. This is what he said.

He also told me one or two little stories about the laity to illustrate their attitude, and he said one day that he was going for alms, he was begging with his begging bowl, and he was quite a new monk, a new bikkhu, and couldn't keep his robe up; it kept slipping down. But in some sort of miraculous way, when you've been in the robes for five or six years, the robe just stays up. And believe it or not, this is my own experience: if you are a monk of some experience, of some standing, you can actually do a prostration and your robe won't fall off. But anyway, Kasyap found his robes slipping down. So what did he do? He had his begging bowl in his hand, so he just put it to one side on the ground while he adjusted his robe. An old woman saw him doing this, and at once started screaming what sort of a bikkhu is this here, who doesn't even know how to respect his bowl, he's ignorant of the Vinaya — because there is an obscure Vinaya rule which says bikkhus mustn't put their begging bowl on the ground. So the old woman knew that somehow, and she was screaming at him and abusing him for being a bad bikkhu. Anyway, this was Kasyap's experience, or some of his experience, of Sri Lanka. Anyway he left Sri Lanka and for a while he was in Penang, with Chinese bikkhus, staying in a Chinese Buddhist temple; and he was of course a Theravadin, not a narrow-minded one, quite a liberal-minded one, but nonetheless at this time — which was about 15 years before I met him — he wasn't quite so liberal-minded as he afterwards became. And what happened with this? And this is a story he related to me personally. He used to visit Chinese Buddhist temples, that is to say, Mahayana Buddhist temples with his Chinese friends, and they used to bow down to the Buddha image, bow down to Kuan Yin that is to say Avalokitesvara, bow down to all the other Bodhisattvas. Kashyap however, being a good Theravadin, he only bowed down to the Buddha, and not the Bodhisattvas. So his friend, who accompanied him to the temples, didn't say anything. But that day, when they got back to the house, and lunch was served, Kashyap found he'd only been given rice. So he didn't really like to say anything, but nonetheless he looked to his friend and after a while he said &Where is the curry? so the friend said Well, the rice is the main course. He said it's just like that with the Buddhas and Bodhisattvas. Admittedly, yes the Buddha is the main thing, but the Bodhisattvas are also necessary. So, yes rice is the main thing, but curries are also necessary. So Kashyap said he learnt his lesson because he was someone who could take a point. Whenever he went to the Mahayana temples thereafter he bowed down to the Bodhisattvas too.

Thereafter he came back to India, and when I came to know him, which was in 1949, he was professor of Pali and Buddhist philosophy at the Benares Hindu University — I've written about this in *The Rainbow Road.* He'd been professor of Pali and Buddhist philosophy for 12 years, but he was feeling very frustrated because he had very few students, I think only four or five. And why was this? Benares Hindu University had been founded mainly by orthodox Hindus, and they were very keen on Sanskrit, they weren't very keen on Pali. The only reason why they had the department of Pali was that one of their very great benefactors, whom they didn't wish to offend, had insisted on there being a department of Pali and had offered to pay all the expenses of that department. He happened to be a patron of Kashyap's. But what they did was this — I don't know how many of you are familiar with academic goings on — but they made, the university made a rule that yes, you could study Pali if you wanted to, but you couldn't take Pali unless you also took Sanskrit. So very few people were so eager to learn Pali that they were willing to learn Sanskrit, which is much more difficult, at the same time. So in this way, Kashyap came to have very few students; and when I met him, and started staying with him and studying with him, he was always very frustrated for that reason. I personally found him to be an excellent teacher — again I've written about this in *The Rainbow Road.* He was not only extremely well-versed in the subjects that I studied with him, that is to say logic, both Buddhist and western, Abhidhamma, and Pali; he often knew the texts by heart. And I stayed with him probably nearly a year. After that he wanted a bit of change, he took me on pilgrimage in Bihar to places like Nalanda and Rajgir and he took me up to Kalimpong which I'd never heard of before; and to cut a long story short he left me there with the parting injunction Stay here and work for the good of Buddhism — which I tried to do. I was then 24. Subsequently Kashyap left the Benares Hindu University, and he founded the Nalanda Pali Institute in the vincinity of the ancient Nalanda Mahavihara or monastic university. And the NPI I believe has been raised to university status by the government of Bihar. He also edited in Devanagari characters the entire Tipitaka, writing prefaces in English to every volume and summaries of all the suttas.

I remember that while I was with him in Benares at the university, he told me he'd gone through the entire Tipitika so many times in Pali that he felt that he had it right here in the palm of his hands. And it was then his intention to write a book in Pali — because he spoke as well as wrote Pali and sanskrit and I heard him give Sanskrit lectures — a work in Pali of the essence of the Tipitaka, which would just give you the essence of the Buddha's teaching as recorded in the Pali scriptures. I'm afraid he never actually got around to it, but that was his original intention. Thereafter I did see him from time to time. The last time I saw him was in 1966 at Nalanda, at the Nalanda Pali Institute which was then flourishing, and I took some pictures of him — I had a picture of him feeding his peacocks; he was very fond of these peacocks. He used to come out of his residence every morning with some grain, and these peacocks would come flying through the air and he'd feed them. So that's my last memory of Kashyap. He died some years ago. But his work, I'm delighted to say, his work for the Pali language and literature is being continued by his nephew, who is also a scholar in Pali and Buddhism. And I was very interested to learn that Saramati had been one of his students. The nephew is now retired, living in India in Sarnath: he was formerly teaching in the States and has founded an institute of Pali and Buddhist studies in memory of his uncle Jagdish Kasyap, and has invited the cooperation of the FWBO, which obviously we will be very glad to give. Perhaps I should just give a few personal details: Kashyap was of medium height, very dark in complexion and very, very fat. He told me shortly after I'd met him that had I come a year earlier he would have been unable to go out with me, go for a walk, because he was unable to walk he was so fat. He used to go everywhere by cycle rickshaw, he used to give the rickshaw wallah double the fare. He was very humble, very unassuming: despite his vast learning he never arrogated anything to himself. He was in some ways quite a childlike sort of person, very simple, very simple in his way of life with regards to dress, to accommodation. I also remember that he was a terrific worker: he could work day and night without food, without sleep. But if he had no work, he'd simply lie on his string bed and sleep hour after hour. If there's no work to do, why not just sleep? I used to be studying in the next room and if I had a problem, if I'd come to some knotty point of grammar or logic or Abhidhamma, I'd just go into his room — the door was always open — he'd just open one eye so, and when I put my question, he'd yawn and then answer. And he knew exactly where that verse or that passage came in a text, he wouldn't need to look; and he could explain it without opening more than one eye. So clear, so much to the point. I'd say, Thank you Bhante, he'd close his eye... so that was what he was like. That was Jagdish Kasyap, and obviously I have very fond memories of him indeed. Perhaps I should also add that I very much regarded him as my teacher — well, he was — though he always used to say that I was his friend. And he said he learnt a lot from me, which I very much appreciated (though I didn't really agree about that).

About Kausalyayan the following lines would introduce the reader this great Hindi scholarly monk, who was my teacher, who told me about Jagdish Kashyapa that there is no teacher as great as to put complicated matter into simplified way and no child as simple as this Bhante Kashyap.

Born on 5th January 1905 Vishwanatha was a Punjabi Arya Samaji as Jagdish Kashyapa and he graduated from Lahore as the class mate of Bhagat Singh, the martyre of Independence of India. He came into contact with Swami Ramodar Das, later known as Rahul Sankrityayan and went to Sri lanka and was ordained by his preceptor, Lunupokane Dhammananda. He was deputed to work in UK in 1933-34 under the Mahabodhi Society. he was a professor of Hindi in Vidyalankara Pirivena in Sri Lanka till 1969. then he came to India and made Deeksha Bhoomi his main abode, from where he educated and brought many Maharashtrian youths as Buddhist monks, who later became well-known as scholars and high officials whether as laymen or monks. He wrote about seventy books on Buddhism and was the General Secretary Hindi Prachar Samiti, Wardha and establed Hindi nagar there. He championed the cause of the downtrodden and the Ambedkar Mission and founded Buddha Bhoomi on Nagpur-Kamptee Road. He visited England several times particularly in 1979 and 1982 during this author's residence in UK. He passed away on 22nd June 1988 at Buddha Bhoomi, Nagpur.

It will not be out of place if Osho's view on some Buddhist monks are cited herewith. He said in his lecture entitled Osho's interaction with Buddhists that "I love the Gautam Buddha as I have loved nobody else. I have been speaking on him throughout my whole life. Even speaking on others I have been speaking on him. Take note of it, it is a confession. I cannot speak on Jesus without bringing Buddha in; I cannot speak on Mohammed without bringing Buddha in. Whether I mention him directly or not that's another matter. It is really impossible for me to speak without bringing Buddha in. He is my very blood, my bones, my very marrow. He is my silence, also my song.

Ordinarily religions like Christianity or Mohammedanism are afraid that if they allow somebody to come too close, they may lose their own identity. Buddhism was never afraid, and it never lost its identity.

I have been to Buddhist conferences where people from Tibet and Japan and Sri Lanka and China and Burma and other countries were present, and that has been my one experience-that they all differed with each other, but they were still connected with a single devotion towards Gautam Buddha. About that there was no problem, no conflict.

And this was the only conference-I have attended many conferences of other different religions, but this had something unique about it, because I was using my own experience in interpreting the teachings of Buddha. They were all different, and I was bringing still another different interpretation.

But they listened silently, lovingly, patiently, and thanked me, "We have not been aware that this interpretation is also possible. You have made us aware of a certain aspect of Buddha, and for twenty-five centuries thousands of people have interpreted it, but have never pointed this out."

One of the Buddhist leaders, Bhadant Anand Kausalyayan, told me, "Whatever you say sounds right. The stories that you tell about Gautam Buddha look absolutely true, but I have been searching into scriptures-my whole life I have devoted to the scriptures-and a few of your stories are not described anywhere."

I asked him, "For example?" And he said, "One story I have loved. I looked again and again in every possible source-for three years I have been looking into it. It is not described anywhere; you must have invented it." The story I have told many times. Gautam Buddha is walking on the road. A fly sits on his head, and he goes on talking with Ananda, his disciple, and mechanically moves his hand and the fly goes away. Then he stops, suddenly-because he has done that movement of the hand without awareness. And to him that is the only wrong thing in life-to do anything without awareness, even moving your hand, although you have not harmed anybody. So he stands and again takes his hand through the same posture of waving away the fly-although there is no fly any more. Ananda is just surprised at what he is doing, and he says, "The fly you have brushed away from your face long before. What are you doing now? There is no fly."

Buddha said, "What I am doing now is…that time I moved my hand mechanically, like a robot. It was a mistake. Now I am doing it as I should have done, just to teach me a lesson so that never again anything like this happens. Now I am moving my hand with full awareness. The fly is not the point. The point is, whether in my hand there is awareness and grace and love and compassion, or not. Now it is right. It should have been this way."

I had told that story in Nagpur at a Buddhist conference. Anand Kausalyayan heard it there, and three years later in Bodhgaya-where there was an international conference of the Buddhists-he said, "The story was so beautiful, so essentially Buddhist, that I wanted to believe that it was true. But in the scriptures it is not there." I said, "Forget the scriptures. The question is whether the story is essentially characteristic of Gautam Buddha or not, whether it carries some message of Gautam Buddha or not." He said, "It does, certainly. This is his essential teaching: awareness in every action. But it is not historical." I said, "Who cares about history?"

And in that conference I told them, "You should remember it, that history is a Western concept. In the East we have never cared about history because history only collects facts. In the East there is no word equivalent to history, and in the East there was no tradition of writing history. In the East, instead of history we have been writing mythology. "Mythology may not be factual, but it has the truth in it. A myth may have never happened. It is not a photograph of a fact; it is a painting. And there is a difference between a photograph and a painting. A painting brings out something of you which no photograph can bring out. The photograph can only bring out your outlines.

"A great painter can bring you out in it-your sadness, your blissfulness, your silence. The photograph cannot catch hold of it because they are not physical things. But a great painter or a great sculptor can manage to catch hold of them. He's not much concerned about the outlines, he is much more concerned about the inner reality."

And I told the conference, "I would like this story to be added to the scriptures because all the scriptures were written after Gautam Buddha's death-three hundred years afterwards. So what difference does it make if I add few more stories after twenty-five centuries, not three centuries. The whole question is that it should represent the essential reality, the basic taste."

And you will be surprised that people agreed with me; even Bhadant Anand Kausalyayan agreed with me. This kind of understanding and agreement is a Buddhist phenomenon, it is a speciality which has happened in different branches of Buddhism.

And I am not even a Buddhist. And they went on inviting me to their conferences. And I told them, "I am not a Buddhist." They said, "That does not matter. What you say is closer to Gautam Buddha than what we say-although we are Buddhists." You cannot expect that from Christians or Mohammedans or Hindus. They are fanatics. Buddhism is a non-fanatic religion.

There exists now in Sarnath a great institution teaching the philosophy of Buddha and his language, Pali. The director of the institute, Bhikkshu Jagdish Kashyap, invited me to his institute to speak on Gautam the Buddha, but I had to leave after one day. He had come to take me to the station. He said, "This is strange; why are you leaving after one day?" said, "For the same reason that Gautam Buddha left this place after one day."

He said, "It is strange, but we have been discussing…" and he was a Buddhist, "We have been discussing for all these centuries why he did not stay."

I said, "You are all idiots! Just see! I have moved around the whole country but I have never seen such big mosquitoes." And Buddha was not using mosquito nets. It would have been difficult carrying a mosquito net, he was traveling and traveling.

But I told Jagdish Kashyap, "You should at least give mosquito nets to every student and scholar and researcher in your institute, not only for the night but for the day too." I stayed there for twenty-four hours inside a mosquito net!

I have experienced many times-because I have lived with many so-called saints-that saints are the worst company in the world. You cannot imagine: to live with a saint for twenty-four hours is enough to make you decide never to be a saint. From the morning till the night they are moving like robots, everything according to principle.

The Buddhist monk has thirty-three thousand principles. I told one Buddhist monk…he is an Englishman, converted at an early age-now he is very old. Bhikkhu Sangha Rakshita is his name, and he has lived in Kalimpong between Tibet and India, almost his whole life. He has written beautiful books on Tibetanism, and is certainly one of its authorities as far as scholarship is concerned.

Just by chance I was holding a camp in Bodh Gaya where Buddha became enlightened, and he had come to pay homage to the temple and to the tree where Buddha became enlightened. Just by coincidence I was also there sitting under the tree when he came. We became friends.

I told Sangha Rakshita, "I cannot visualize myself ever becoming a Buddhist monk because my memory is not good. Thirty-three thousand principles! Following all those principles is out of the question; I cannot even remember them. And if you are following thirty-three thousand principles in such a small life, where will you find time to live or to breathe? Those thirty-three thousand principles will kill you from all sides."

I had a case sent to me from Ceylon, which is a Buddhist country, with so many Buddhist priests preaching Vipassana meditation.... The technique is so simple, but they have never done it themselves. To teach anything to anybody which you have not done-and experienced all its possibilities, consequences, difficulties, problems that it can lead you into-then you are a criminal. This man who was sent to me was a Buddhist monk. He had lost his sleep for three years, and every treatment was done but no treatment was successful; no medicine would work. He had been told by his teacher-I cannot call him a master-to do Vipassana in the night. Even if you do Vipassana in the day, its effects will carry into the night; that's why I am suggesting the most distant point, before sunrise. Just two hours are enough; more than that...even nectar can become poison in a certain quantity. Vipassana for ten hours a day can drive anybody mad....Vipassana is one of the greatest meditations, but only in the hands of a master. In the hands of a technician it is the greatest danger. Either the man can become enlightened or the man can become mad; both possibilities are there, it all depends under whose guidance it is being done.When the Ceylonese monk was sent to me I said, "I am not a Buddhist, and you have been under the guidance of Buddhist monks. What was the need for you to come to me?" He said, "They have all failed. They have taught me, but they cannot cure me. And I am going crazy. I cannot sleep a single wink."

When he told me this...Buddhist monks are not supposed to laugh, but I told him a joke. For a moment he was shocked, because he had come very seriously. I told him that a man in England, no ordinary man but a very rich lord, was asking another lord-with the English attitude, mannerism: "Is it right that you slept with my wife last night?" And the other lord said, "My friend, not a wink."

Even the Buddhist monk laughed. He said, "You are a strange person. I have come from Ceylon and you tell me a joke! And I am a religious man."

I said, "That's why I am telling you a religious joke. If you stay with me I will tell you irreligious jokes too." I said, "Your problem is not curable by any medicine. Your problem is created by your Vipassana."He said, "Vipassana? But Vipassana was the meditation of Gautam Buddha; through it he became enlightened." I said, "You are not a Gautam Buddha, and you don't understand that Vipassana done after sunset is very dangerous. If you do Vipassana for just two hours in the night, then you cannot sleep. It creates such awareness in you that that awareness continues the whole night."

I have been searching for jokes which have their origin in India. I have not found a single one. Serious people...always talking about God and heaven and hell and reincarnation and the philosophy of karma. The joke does not fit in anywhere.

When I started talking-and I was talking about meditation-I might tell a joke. Once in a while some Jaina monk or a Buddhist monk or a Hindu preacher would come to me and say, "You were talking so beautifully about meditation, but why did you bring in that joke? It destroyed everything. People started laughing. They were getting serious. You destroyed all your effort. You did something for half an hour to make them serious, and then you told a joke and you destroyed the whole thing. Why in the world should you tell a joke? Buddha never told a joke. Krishna never told a joke." I would say, "I am neither Buddha nor Krishna, and I am not interested in seriousness." In fact, because they were becoming serious, I had to bring in that joke. I don't want anybody to become serious. I want everybody to be playful. And life has to become, more and more, closer to laughter than seriousness.

Bibliography

1. D.C. Ahir. The Pioneers of the Buddhist Revival in India. (Delhi, Sri Satguru Pub. : 1989).
2. Reminiscences of C.D. Naik about Bhante Kasusalyayan.
3. Osho, no mind 03.
4. Osho, book 06.
5. Osho, dark 30.
6. Osho, Mystic 40.

Chapter - 6

Japanese before American Aviators

C. D. Naik

Introduction

Discussion on Vipassana led to creativity of Vipassana mind and in that context the speaker happened to mention the inventors of first aeroplane design were Japanese called Chuhaci Ninomiya and Tsuneo Noguchi, who have lost public demonstration of their skill just by a day of that of Wright Brothers in America. The details are as under:

Models of Chuhachi Ninomiya's (1866) Tamamushi (Jewel Bug above by Tsuneo Noguchi and flew it 50 m in April 1991) and karasu or Crow (below) (Wednesday, 30 April 2003)

Models of Chuhachi Ninomiya's (1866) Tamamushi (Jewel Bug above by Tsuneo Noguchi and flew it 50 m in April 1991) and karasu or Crow (below) (Wednesday, 30 April 2003)

If not for lack of money, a Japanese aviation pioneer could have beaten the American Wright Brothers to achieving the world's first powered and fully controlled manned flight - a Japanese aviation expert claims.

Almost the Father of Flight

Chuhachi Ninomiya

Chuhachi Ninomiya was a young man with a dream. He wanted to invent a flying machine. He watched birds fly for hours and hours. He also studied insects and flying fish to get ideas. Did Ninomiya's dream come true? The story of his life will give you the answer.

Ninomiya was born in Japan in 1866. As a boy, he loved flying kites. People called him "Kite-flying Chuhachi." Ninomiya also loved to design kites. His kites were unique because they had pockets. Some businesses used Ninomiya's kites for advertising. They put advertisements into the pocket of a kite. The pocket opened and let the ads fall to the ground. Then the pocket closed again.

Ninomiya built his first model of a flying machine in 1891. He was just 24 years old. He called his model "The Crow," which is the name of a kind of bird. It had a propeller and landing gear, but its wings did not move. Ninomiya's model actually flew!

In 1894, Ninomiya became a soldier in the army. He thought flying machines could be very useful in a war. He gave his engineering plans to the army. The plans had drawings and specific directions for building a flying machine. However, the army didn't pay attention to Ninomiya. They said: "Humans are not supposed to fly." They thought he was crazy.

Ninomiya left the army in 1898. He continued to design airplanes. He started to build a plane that was more like a

According to Agençe France-Presse, former aerodynamics professor Tsuneo Noguchi is convinced Chuhachi Ninomiya - the fourth son of a samurai born in 1866 - would have beaten the Wright brothers by about a decade if he could have raised the money to buy an engine for the aircraft he designed.

While this year will mark the centenary of the achievements of Orville and Wilbur Wright, it also marks the 112th anniversary of the unmanned, powered flight by Ninomiya's revolutionary Karasu, or Crow, model monoplane which had fixed wings, a rubber band-powered propeller and tricycle landing gear - an innovation that only became the norm on aircraft from about 1930 onwards. Ninomiya's pioneering work was celebrated in Japan earlier this week.

According to Noguchi, Ninomiya's design principles - especially fixed wings when most European pioneers were experimenting with flapping wings - were on the right track to achieve manned, powered flight.

It is no idle, nationalistic boast: Noguchi built an aircraft based on another of Ninomiya's designs - the Tamamushi (Jewel Bug) - and flew it 50 m in April 1991. "The original Tamamushi design is not capable of flight because of the stability problem. Chuhachi might have failed at the first flight, but it wouldn't have taken him long to figure it out and fly," said the aerodynamics expert, who only had to add a horizontal stabiliser and tailfin to the craft he flew.

"If he had got a 12 horsepower engine, he could have flown before the Wright brothers' success, because the difference [between his design and their flight] is 12 years," said Noguchi, now the head of an aviation consulting company.

Perhaps the most impressive part of Ninomiya's story is the fact that he arrived at an understanding of the key principles of aeronautical engineering - the relationship between lift force, speed and wing area - through observation, independently of aviation pioneers elsewhere.

"Many papers were published in Europe, and aviation pioneers shared information, but Chuhachi Ninomiya didn't have any relationship with Europe," Noguchi said. He developed his own ideas independently, and didn't have any education in science. But he was interested in flying since childhood and just observed nature - birds and insects - and made measurements such as their wing area."

Ignored by the army

Ninomiya's success was set back by his need to acquire an engine which was prohibitively expensive. After his requests to the army for financial backing were repeatedly rejected started a chemical business in Osaka to raise the money. But, said Noguchi "it took a long time to be successful, and he was too late."

The successful flight by the Wright brothers' left Ninomiya disheartened. "After he heard the news of the Wright brothers' successful flight, he stopped the development [of his designs] and burned most of his documents and designs." But the designs sent by Ninomiya to the military survived, allowing the contsruction of the Tamamushi.

Ninomiya, who died in 1936 at the age of 70, did not end his days in embittered obscurity. In 1921, the officer who had rejected Ninomiya's ideas wrote a belated apology to him, awarding him a commendation, and he became known as the 'father of Japanese aircraft' to the Japanese aviation community of the day. And every April in Japan, the pioneering work of Ninomiya - almost unknown outside aviation circles - are quietly celebrated in his home country.

modern airplane. Ninomiya's plane wasn't a model this time. It was a real, full-size plane.

The plane was almost finished. All Ninomiya needed was an engine, and he ordered one. Then one day, he read in the newspaper about the Wright Brothers. These two men from the United States flew their first plane in December of 1903. Ninomiya read about the brothers' success just one day before he received his engine. This was bad news for Ninomiya. He stopped building his plane, and he never built another one. After that, he became a Shinto priest.[1]

"The Crow"

Most people think the Wright Brothers designed the first airplane. But this isn't true. Ninomiya designed and flew model planes many years before the Wright Brothers did. However, the Wright Brothers flew their first plane before Ninomiya finished his full-size plane. Unlike Ninomiya's plane, the Wright Brothers' plane did not have landing gear. It also had a kind of wing that wasn't as modern as the wing on Ninomiya's plane. In 1991, an expert in aviation used Ninomiya's engineering plans to build an airplane. He said that Ninomiya's plane was better than the Wright Brothers' plane.

Ninomiya never lost his interest in airplanes and flight. He even built a shrine[2] for people who died in airplane accidents. Before he died in 1936, he received an apology[3] and an award[4] from the army. Today, he has the greatest honor of all: The Japanese call him "the father of Japanese aircraft."

Wright Brothers

Original 1903 Wright Flyer in the National Air and Space Museum in WashingtonThe Wright brothers, Orville (August 19, 1871 – January 30, 1948) and Wilbur (April 16, 1867 – May 30, 1912), were two American brothers, inventors, and aviation pioneers who are generally credited[1][2][3] with inventing, building, and flying the world's first successful airplane. They made the first controlled, sustained flight of a powered, heavier-than-air aircraft on December 17, 1903, four miles south of Kitty Hawk, North Carolina. In 1904–05 the brothers developed their flying machine into the first practical fixed-wing aircraft. Although not the first to build and fly experimental aircraft, the Wright brothers were the first to invent aircraft controls that made fixed-wing powered flight possible., D.C.

Wilbur and Orville Wright were American inventors and pioneers of aviation. In 1903 the Wright brothers achieved the first powered, sustained and controlled airplane flight; they surpassed their own milestone two years later when they built and flew the first fully practical airplane.

Jump to First powered flight - (Because December 13, 1903, was a Sunday, the brothers did ... The following is Orville Wright's account of the final flight of ... Education: Orville 3 years high school; Wilbur 4 ...Nationality: American

The Wright Flyer was the first successful heavier-than-air powered ... The brothers tossed a coin to decide who would get the first chance at piloting, and Wilbur won. Buoyant over the success of their 1902 glider, the Wright brothers were no longer content to merely add to the growing body of aeronautical knowledge; This object is on display in the The Wright Brothers & The Invention of the Aerial ... 1903, making a 12-second flight, traveling 36 m (120 ft), with Orville piloting.

The Wright brothers, Orville (August 19, 1871 – January 30, 1948) and Wilbur (April 16, 1867 – May 30, 1912), were two American brothers, inventors, and aviation pioneers who are generally credited[1][2][3] with inventing, building, and flying the world's first successful airplane. They made the first controlled, sustained flight of a powered, heavier-than-air aircraft on December 17, 1903, four miles south of Kitty Hawk, North Carolina. In 1904–05 the brothers developed their flying machine into the first practical fixed-wing aircraft. Although not the first to build and fly experimental aircraft, the Wright brothers were the first to invent aircraft controls that made fixed-wing powered flight possible.

Orville demonstrating the flyer to the U.S. Army, Fort Myer, Virginia September 1908. Photo: by C.H. Claudy.

Sources

1. Wikipedia extract taken on 11th May 2017
2. Curiosity of the author on the theme

Chapter - 7

Fire Thy Name is Peace

Introduction

Peace is a fire and silence speaks to inmost spirit with a voice of thunder as views freed by wisdom leads to speechlessness. In a sleep you meditate while maintaining creativity of dream state into waking life and blending richness of dream state with clarity of the waking state.

Buddhist peace is distinct and universal. Peace is realization of at least hundredth part of what we understand and becoming Buddha on the spot. An intellectual has a strong creative element in his thought. Physical as well as psychological and spiritual babies grow in the same way.

Peace Dharma is not to be falsified by objectification of Buddha's Peace. Buddhist spiritual life is not to talk in terms of monks, monasteries etc. Even intellectuals' understanding of running down intellect or transcending it remains purely intellectual.

Majority of books on peace are the product of ill-digested information, muddled thinking, unconscious realization, downright delusion and confusion and reading them is to distract one's mind. There is a need of thorough knowledge of a small number of works, rather than a superficial knowledge of many. Buddha's teaching has bearing on spiritual life.

Which is greater oceanic water or human tears, oceanic water or human blood, oceanic water or human restlessness (SN 15.3, PTS: S ii 179, CDB i 652, Assu Sutta: Tears, translated from the Pali by Thanissaro Bhikkhu © 1997)?

At Savatthi. There the Blessed One said: "From an inconstruable beginning comes transmigration. A beginning point is not evident, though beings hindered by ignorance and fettered by craving are transmigrating & wandering on. What do you think, monks: Which is greater, the tears you have shed while transmigrating & wandering this long, long time — crying & weeping from being joined with what is displeasing, being separated from what is pleasing — or the water in the four great oceans?"

"As we understand the Dhamma taught to us by the Blessed One, this is the greater: the tears we have shed while transmigrating & wandering this long, long time — crying & weeping from being joined with what is displeasing, being separated from what is pleasing — not the water in the four great oceans."

"Excellent, monks. Excellent. It is excellent that you thus understand the Dhamma taught by me.

"This is the greater: the tears you have shed while transmigrating & wandering this long, long time — crying & weeping from being joined with what is displeasing, being separated from what is pleasing — not the water in the four great oceans.

"Long have you (repeatedly) experienced the death of a mother. The tears you have shed over the death of a mother while transmigrating & wandering this long, long time — crying & weeping from being joined with what is displeasing, being separated from what is pleasing — are greater than the water in the four great oceans.

"Long have you (repeatedly) experienced the death of a father...the death of a brother...the death of a sister...the death of a son...the death of a daughter... loss with regard to relatives...loss with regard to wealth... loss with regard to disease. The tears you have shed over loss with regard to disease while transmigrating & wandering this long, long time — crying & weeping from being joined with what is displeasing, being separated from what is pleasing — are greater than the water in the four great oceans.

"Why is that? From an inconstruable beginning comes transmigration. A beginning point is not evident, though beings hindered by ignorance and fettered by craving are transmigrating & wandering on. Long have you thus experienced stress, experienced pain, experienced loss, swelling the cemeteries — enough to become disenchanted with all fabricated things, enough to become dispassionate, enough to be released." (See also: SN 15.13. ©1997 Thanissaro Bhikkhu. PTS: S ii 187 CDB i 658 Timsa Sutta: Thirty translated from the Pali by Thanissaro Bhikkhu © 2009).

Now on that occasion the Blessed One was dwelling in Rajagaha, in the Bamboo Grove. Then thirty monks from Pava — all wilderness dwellers, all alms-goers, all triple-robe wearers, all still with fetters — went to the Blessed One and, on arrival, having bowed down to him, sat to one side.

Then the thought occurred to the Blessed One, "These thirty monks from Pava...are all still with fetters. What if I were to teach them the Dhamma in such a way that in this very sitting their minds, through lack of clinging, would be released from fermentations?"

So he addressed the monks: "Monks."

"Yes, lord," the monks responded.

The Blessed One said, "From an inconceivable beginning comes transmigration. A beginning point is not evident, though beings hindered by ignorance and fettered by craving are transmigrating & wandering on. What do you think, monks? Which is greater, the blood you have shed from having your heads cut off while transmigrating & wandering this long, long time, or the water in the four great oceans?"

"As we understand the Dhamma taught to us by the Blessed One, this is the greater: the blood we have shed from having our heads cut off while transmigrating & wandering this long, long time, not the water in the four great oceans."

"Excellent, monks. Excellent. It is excellent that you thus understand the Dhamma taught by me.

"This is the greater: the blood you have shed from having your heads cut off while transmigrating & wandering this long, long time, not the water in the four great oceans.

"The blood you have shed when, being cows, you had your cow-heads cut off: Long has this been greater than the water in the four great oceans.

"The blood you have shed when, being water buffaloes, you had your water buffalo-heads cut off...when, being rams, you had your ram-heads cut off... when, being goats, you had your goat-heads cut off...when, being deer, you had your deer-heads cut off...when, being chickens, you had your chicken-heads cut off...when, being pigs, you had your pig-heads cut off: Long has this been greater than the water in the four great oceans.

"The blood you have shed when, arrested as thieves plundering villages, you had your heads cut off... when, arrested as highway thieves, you had your heads cut off... when, arrested as adulterers, you had your heads cut off: Long has this been greater than the water in the four great oceans.

"Why is that? From an inconceivable beginning comes transmigration. A beginning point is not evident, though beings hindered by ignorance and fettered by craving are transmigrating & wandering on. Long have you thus experienced stress, experienced pain, experienced loss, swelling the cemeteries — enough to become disenchanted with all fabrications, enough to become dispassionate, enough to be released."

That is what the Blessed One said. Gratified, the monks delighted in the Blessed One's words. And while this explanation was being given, the minds of the thirty monks from Pava — through lack of clinging — were released from fermentations.

Pacific Relations Conference

Paper entitled "Mr. Gandhi and the Emancipation of the Untouchables" was written by Dr. B. R. Ambedkar for the session of the Pacific Relations Conference at Mont' Tramblant in Quebec in Canada in 1942 addressed that Imperialism, Racialism, anti-semitism and free traffic have been the plague glands in which nation's cruelty to nation and man's inhumanity to man have their origin. These problems must be tackled if a new and a better world is to emerge from the ashes of this terrible and devastating war.

Mute Peace

Mute peace belongs to the beast. Human peace is turbulent. What is the use of such peace which belongs to the beast and which leaves the humanity pauper? In his "Evolution of Provincial Finance in British India" Dr. Ambedkar wrote, "English man can look back on theirn work in India, if not with unalloyed satisfaction, at least with some legitimate pride. They have conferred on the people of India what is the greatest human blessing-peace. ....But whether mere animal peace is to be preferred to economic destitution, let every one decide for himself."

Untouchables as Peace Lovers

One of the roots of untouchability lies in the hatred and contempt which the Brahmins created against those who were Buddhist, said Dr. Ambedkar. Buddhists were and are peace lovers. The broken men as followers of Buddhism regarded Brahmins as impure. Abbe Dubois in his "Hindu Manners and Customs, 3rd ed., p. 61 f.n." reported that the Pariahs, under no circumstances, allowed a Brahmin to pass through their huts as they firmly believed it would lead to their ruin." Mr. Hemingsway, the Editor of the Gazetteer of the Tanjore District (1906, p. 80), said that Parayan and Pallan or Chakkiliyan castes of that District strongly objected to the entrance of a Brahmin into their quarters believing that harm would result to them therefrom".

Consequently Manusmriti treated the Untouchables as impure and prescribed means of purification also. Nilkant in his Prayschit Mayukha (ed. Gharpure, p. 95) referred to the matter as follows:

"If a person touches a Buddhist or a flower of Pachupat, Lokayat, Nastik and Mahapataki, he shall prify himself by a bath." Since the Brahmin changed his behavior from peace to violence and found that the Untouchable is adherent to peaceful Buddhism despite being threatened to be made most degraded in society, he was made untouchable for his love of Buddhism even at this cost.

Spark of Peace

Spark of peace can be derived from the following quotes:

1. *"Helping others is a question of being genuine and projecting that genuineness to others. This way of being doesn't have to have a title or a name particularly. It is just being ultimately decent." ~ Chogyam Trungpa.*
2. *"You cannot really eliminate pain through aggression. The more you kill, the more you strengthen the killer who will create new things to be killed. ~ Chogyam Trungpa.*
3. *"We can change the world, definitely. The problem is that we don't smile when chaos occurs to us. When chaos occurs, even within that chaos, we can smile which cures confusion and resentment." ~ Chogyam Trungpa.*
4. *"A true warrior is never at war with the world."~Chogyam Trungpa*
5. *"What are you rushing toward? Your death?" ~ Chogyam Trungpa*
6. *"If we learn to open our hearts, anyone, including the people who drive us crazy, can be our teacher." ~ Pema Chodron*
7. *"The most fundamental aggression to ourselves, the most fundamental harm we can do to ourselves, is to remain ignorant by not having the courage and the respect to look at ourselves honestly and gently." ~ Pema Chodron*
8. *"We don't set out to save the world; we set out to wonder how other people are doing and to reflect on how our actions affect other people's hearts." ~ Pema Chodron*
9. *"At the root of all the harm we cause is ignorance." ~ Pema Chodron*
10. *"If someone comes along and shoots an arrow into your heart, it's fruitless to stand there and yell at the person. It would be much*

better to turn your attention to the fact that there's an arrow in your heart..." ~ Pema Chodron

11. *"Freedom is not given to us by anyone; we have to cultivate it ourselves. It is a daily practice...No one can prevent you from being aware of each step you take or each breath in and breath out." ~ Thich Nhat Hanh*
12. *"People have a hard time letting go of their suffering. Out of a fear of the unknown, they prefer suffering that is familiar." ~ Thich Nhat Hanh*
13. *"Walk as if you are kissing the Earth with your feet." ~ Thich Nhat Hanh*
14. *"When another person makes you suffer, it is because he suffers deeply within himself, and his suffering is spilling over. He does not need punishment; he needs help. That's the message he is sending." ~ Thich Nhat Hanh*
15. *"We have to continue to learn. We have to be open. And we have to be ready to release our knowledge in order to come to a higher understanding of reality." ~ Thich Nhat Hanh*
16. *"We can never obtain peace in the outer world until we make peace with ourselves." ~ Dalai Lama*
17. *"If a problem is fixable, if a situation is such that you can do something about it, then there is no need to worry. If it's not fixable, then there is no help in worrying. There is no benefit in worrying whatsoever." ~ Dalai Lama*
18. *"Our prime purpose in this life is to help others. And if you can't help them, at least don't hurt them." ~ Dalai Lama*
19. *"If you can cultivate the right attitude, your enemies are your best spiritual teachers because their presence provides you with the opportunity to enhance and develop tolerance, patience, and understanding." ~ Dalai Lama*
20. *"The true hero is one who conquers his own anger and hatred." ~ Dalai Lama*

Buddha's Fire Sermon

Thus I heard. On one occasion the Blessed One was living at Gaya, at Gayasisa, together with a thousand bhikkhus. There he addressed the bhikkhus.

"Bhikkhus, all is burning. And what is the all that is burning?

"The eye is burning, forms are burning, eye-consciousness is burning, eye-contact is burning, also whatever is felt as pleasant or painful or neither-painful-nor-pleasant that arises with eye-contact for its indispensable condition, that too is burning. Burning with what? Burning with the fire of lust, with the fire of hate, with the fire of delusion. I say it is burning with birth, aging and death, with sorrows, with lamentations, with pains, with griefs, with despairs.

"The ear is burning, sounds are burning...

"The nose is burning, odors are burning...

"The tongue is burning, flavors are burning...

"The body is burning, tangibles are burning...

"The mind is burning, ideas are burning, mind-consciousness is burning, mind-contact is burning, also whatever is felt as pleasant or painful or neither-painful-nor-pleasant that arises with mind-contact for its indispensable condition, that too is burning. Burning with what? Burning with the fire of lust, with the fire of hate, with the fire of delusion. I say it is burning with birth, aging and death, with sorrows, with lamentations, with pains, with griefs, with despairs.

"Bhikkhus, when a noble follower who has heard (the truth) sees thus, he finds estrangement in the eye, finds estrangement in forms, finds estrangement in eye-consciousness, finds estrangement in eye-contact, and whatever is felt as pleasant or painful or neither-painful- nor-pleasant that arises with eye-contact for its indispensable condition, in that too he finds estrangement.

"He finds estrangement in the ear... in sounds...

"He finds estrangement in the nose... in odors...

"He finds estrangement in the tongue... in flavors...

"He finds estrangement in the body... in tangibles...

"He finds estrangement in the mind, finds estrangement in ideas, finds estrangement in mind-consciousness, finds estrangement in mind-contact, and whatever is felt as pleasant or painful or neither-painful-nor-pleasant that arises with mind-contact for its indispensable condition, in that too he finds estrangement.

"When he finds estrangement, passion fades out. With the fading of passion, he is liberated. When liberated, there is knowledge that he is liberated. He understands: 'Birth is exhausted, the holy life has been lived out, what can be done is done, of this there is no more beyond.'"

That is what the Blessed One said. The bhikkhus were glad, and they approved his words.

Now during his utterance, the hearts of those thousand bhikkhus were liberated from taints through clinging no more.

Ambedkar's Peace Talk

Dr. Ambedkar reviewing the Russell's book on "the principles of reconstruction of society" in 1918 showed that the book in question was against war but it is not for quietitutde or peace as Russell minded use of force as energy, thus putting premium on impulse as spring of action.

Ambedkar suggested directional use of force to effect man's well-being. This was correctly perceived by Albert Einstein also who on his notes on pacifism said, "peace cannot be kept by force, it can only be achieved by understanding."

Dr. Ambedkar criticized the discipline of comparative religion for holding the illusion that all religions are equal and good and held that religion is both normative and descriptive logic in that it is a prescription for moral life and it is subject to the test of wrong or right or true and false and further said that no one could uphold Buddhism truly without studying the other religions also scientifically.

While delivering the talk on BBC London on May 1956 Dr. Ambedkar said, "I prefer Buddhism, because it gives three principles in combination which no other religion gives. Buddhism teaches Prajna (Understanding as against superstition and supernaturalism), karuna (love) and samata (equality). This is what man wants for good and happy life. Neither god nor soul can save him from the hell of his own doing.

Conclusion

That Buddhism is a synonym for peace and its summom bonum nirvana also means the same. Its eightfold path is nothing but living in nirvana here and now within this five and half feet body of ours in day to day routine.

Bibliography

1. Ambedkar B R, The Buddha and His Dhamma, Peoples' Education Society, Mumbai 1957.
2. Christopher Queen, The Fourth turning, USA 1998.
3. Naik C D, Dr. B. R. Ambedkar : Contributions in nation building, Songir 10th March 2018.

Chapter - 8

Human Rights

> We must get people to realize this (caste) is an international struggle for human rights on the same level as the battle against apartheid in the last century, and against slavery the centuries before.
>
> – Revd David Haslam[1].

> Jat Jat mein Jat Hai Tin Kelan Ke Pat Ravidas Na Mans Na Ban Sake Jab Tak Jat na Jat – Shri Guru Ravidas Ji argued that there are castes with castes just like there are banana leaves within leaves. Until caste is annihilated human beings will not be liberated.
>
> – Ravi Das

Present Status

In the year 2000 there were 126434 court cases out of which 11605 were acquitted because victims depended on their oppressors for their livelihood, they do not have financial resources to pursue their oppressors, the oppressors used their influence, money to bribe, and political muscle to intimidate the officers to rule in their favour and thousands of cases do not get reported because fear of humiliation by police and by village elders.

Total no. of atrocities committed against untouchables in the year 2002 were 16494 including 486 murders, 3298 grievous bodily harms and 1034 rapes. These atrocities pertained to SCs alone. About STs their atrocities will again multiply this figure.

Commitment of United Kingdom

The Hindu Council UK has raised question about how widespread is Caste Discrimination in UK and whether it is necessary to prevent this form of discrimination in law. These concerns were never raised by Hindu Council UK when Race Relation Act was going through Parliament to protect black and ethnic minorities from racial discrimination. HCUK said that the caste system should and will undergo reforms in the social arena, through education and CastWatchUk is in full agreement with this part of HCUK's statement.

However the Federation of Ambedkarite and Buddhist Organisations UK appealed that instead of denying the existence of caste prejudices, the Hindu Council UK must join them and our Prime Minister Dr. Manmohan Singh who considers that caste discrimination and untouchability are a blot on humanity in assisting the UK Government to remove this blot which has threatened, destroyed and dehumanized millions of Indians in the past and now threatens to spread its tentacles to other progressive world societies.

All those from Indian sub-continent settled in United Kingdom who are concerned about this problem, have suffered from caste prejudice or have witnessed others being victimized due to their caste should urge their MPs to support the inclusion of the outlawing of caste discrimination in the forthcoming "Single Equality Bill".

It became self evident that caste prejudices are passionately believed in and practiced amngst the people of the Indian subcontinent residing in Britain. It is beginning to penetrate into education, Industrial relations, media and the political life of Britain. It requires the foremost attention of the law makers and parliamentarians to secure safeguards against it. There is now a great opportunity for caste discrimination to be included in the proposed 'Single Equality Bill'. A suitable punishment should be prescribed by law for anyone responsible for caste-based discrimination no matter which religion they practice.

The minority fundamentalists must not be allowed allowed to undermine this process of integration or bring the evil of caste from the Indian subcontinent to law-abiding Britain.

Meena Varma, DSN Director said, "DSN has just become engaged in supporting the campaign by 1.3 million manual scavengers, cleaning the dry toilets of the upper castes in India, for the eradication of this worst job in the world by 2010. Jeremy Corbyn MP, Chair of the Dalit Solidarity network (UK) assured that 'In the light of what has been said today we have a real responsibility to continue the struggle, inside the UK Parliament and outside, to raise the consciousness of people in the UK'. Gurpal Gill of Shri Guru Valmik Sabha International warned the Hindu Council UK by stating that "We object to your plans to stall our lobbying work with the UK Parliament for an amendment in legislation to include Caste

Discrimination in the Single Equality Bill, so that the victims of caste discrimination may seek legal remedy and the perpetrators are brought to books."

Councillor Khan commented "the Biradari system is disgusting. We live in the Western society, I was born and red in Birmingham, yet certain people criticize me for my caste. It has all come down to a gutter level of politics. The people were saying 'Tariq is from the clan or this part of Pakistan' nut I am British through and through. I represent every part of the community, English, Afro-Caribbean, Irish, every Religion and every Race; my politics are to work with people, all people. This is gangster politics in Birmingham and I won't tolerate it. We are in 2008 but we cannot progress until we eradicate the Biradri System."

The former Mayor of Coventry, Ram Lakha, a labour Councillor who is a Dalit contested in elections in a ward which was largely populated by Indians. During campaigning he was often told that he would not get people's votes as he was a "Chamar". So he filed his nomination in a non-Asian constituency and was able to win. This case is supported by the experience of Lord Nazier Ahmed, member of House of Lords, who stated on record that in Peterborough, Bradford and Birmingham, candidates from jat caste or Rajput, regardless of their politics, when it comes to voting people will vote for their own.

Councillor Mr. Joshi, chair of the Social Equality Department of Coventry Council wrote in the booklet of 1995/6, entitled A Guide to ethnic minorities:- their beliefs and culture that 'the caste is inherited by birth and one cannot change or leave one's caste. Hindus in Britain may wish to observe the caste system and wish to avoid dining and inter-marriage with members of other castes.' In Bedford there is a Public house'Gardner's Arms' owned by a English person, it is called by the Indians "Chamar pub'.

Future

The Government of Australia has apologized to their victim Aborigines for taking their land and destroying their cultural way of life. Mr. Blair as Prime Minister of Great Britain apologized for the Slave trade. The Americans have apologized to native Americans for taking their land and the massacre of over fifty million of them. The German Government have also apologized to the Jews for their massacre during the Second World War. Other societies are expected to do the same. The Indians must be aware that due to Caste prejudices, the Caste Issue has been debated in

British Parliament. The European Parliament has passed a resolution condemning Caste prejudices. The United Nation's Human rights Commission brought out a report highlighting the plight of the Untouchables in India and the suffering they endure every day. The Hindus must acknowledge, accept responsibility and apologige for past executions of the untouchables, and undertake to act decisively to prevent further injustices from happening in the future- said the Resident FABOUK, Mr. Chanan Chahal.

Neither the hindus remained the same as before nor the Untouchables. The commitment of world society to eradicate human rights abuse and oppressive features from any society or culture made the United Nations to pur the strategy to realize this objective and the international media exposes hidden characteristics of oppression from all cultures. Globalisation will also expose all discriminatory elements of the society. The South Asian Human Rights Documentation Centre expressed that "It is shameful tragedy and irony of the fate for the hapless Indians belonging to the Scheduled Castes and Scheduled Tribes that inhuman and barbaric treatment is meted out to them by their own countrymen."

Review

Under 'What is "Human Rights" in The Modern World' Darmitha-Kotte wrote that Much is being reported in the newspapers about human rights these days because the 2nd Session of the Human Rights Council Geneva has just been concluded on 18th September,2006. The Daily Mirror carried two articles on 19th and 22nd September, 2006 on this subject. One article titled "Human Rights Situation Remains Alarming" was a very lengthy speech made by Ms. Louise Arbour, United Nations High Commissioner for Human Rights and the other titled "UNHCR Accuses Govt. and LTTE of Human Rights Violations."

The Universal Declaration of Human Rights proclaimed by The United Nations on 10th December 1948 states "*The General Assembly proclaims This Universal Declaration of Human Rights as a common standard of achievement for all peoples and all nations, to the end that every individual and every organ or society, keeping this Declaration constantly in mind, shall strive by teaching and education to promote respect for these rights and freedoms and by progressive measures, national and international, to secure their universal and effective recognition and observance, both among the peoples of the Member States and among the peoples of territories under their jurisdiction.* "This Declaration carries 30 Articles of which

Article 30 states" *Nothing in this Declaration may be interpreted as implying for any State, group or person any right to engage in any activity or to perform any act aimed at the destruction of any of the rights and freedoms set forth herein.* " Articles 1-29 talk of specific areas on rights and in Article 30 it sums up the entire Declaration through the above quote.

(1) "Developed" and "Developing" Countries in The World:

When we look at the world picture we can see two main sections to which the world can be divided (1) The "developed world" under which the USA, UK, Europe, Nordic Countries, Australia, South Korea, Singapore and Japan can be categorized, and (2) the "developing world" in which Africa, Middle-East, Latin American countries, Russia (former Soviet Union) and Asian countries (including North Korea and China) are categorized. Based on the Universal Declaration of Human Rights, each of the countries in the world are free and independent.

May we ask the pertinent question "is this really so?" or "how free are the developing countries?" This is where the great misconceptions of "Human Rights" and injustices lie. Reason being, that the developed world has taken it on themselves as the superiors, to dictate terms to every aspect of the lives of the developing countries without giving due respect to the history, culture, ethnicities, religious affiliations and social fabric of these countries. The developed countries (based on their values and standards) consider it their right, to bulldoze over the developing countries dictating what should or should not be done. If we are honest and objective, we will realize that this is the blatant truth!

(2) Who Commenced Violation of Human Rights:

History has it on record, that when Africa, Persia, Messapotamia, Babylonia, Indus Valley, India and China (even tiny Ceylon) already had rich and prosperous civilizations/ cultures of their own many thousands of years ago, the now "developed countries" were living in the jungles! The purpose of stating this is not to insult any country but to show how "human rights" were violated for the *"now developed countries"* to become "developed." Colonial powers plundered every grain of minerals, metals, gems, ivory, spices etc from those countries and left these countries bankrupt, to suffer the ignominy of starvation. Once rich, the developed countries returned to these countries to dictate how countries now categorized as "developing countries" should govern their countries in the form of IMF, World Bank, Asian Development Bank, United Nations, G7, NORAD, JICA, USAID, CIDA, etc. 5-6 countries in the Security Council decide on the very existence and future of all nations of the world. Is this done with the interests of the developing countries in mind, or with the interests of the developed countries in mind? Whose rights are being violated and by whom, is a matter that needs to be microscopically analyzed before making scathing attacks against the developing countries on matters related to the violation of human rights.

(3) How are Human Rights of Nations Violated & By Whom?

Article 30 of The Universal Declaration of Human Rights states: "*Nothing in this Declaration may be interpreted as implying for any State, group or person any right to engage in any activity or to perform any act aimed at the destruction of any of the rights and freedoms set forth herein.*"

If all countries have been following this declaration to the very letter, there would be no problem in this world and we would be living in a very peaceful and harmonious environment. However, we all know that this is not the case and it never will be, as long as the developed countries disregard and insult "the rights " of other countries to determine their own future. No matter how well the Universal Declaration is formulated, equality can never be achieved as long as the developed countries deem it "their right" to undermine the sovereignty and independence of countries that are considered to be "developing countries."

(a) Manufacture and Sale of Weapons: Why would arms manufacture be necessary if countries were following Article 30 of the Universal Declaration of Human Rights? Can we in our wildest dreams, imagine that large-scale manufacture of weapons by the developed countries, is to spread "love" in the world? Once they are produced, can they sell their arms to countries without violating as stated in the Universal Declaration of Human Rights "*.......... implying for any State, group or person any right to engage in any activity or to perform any act aimed at the destruction of any of the rights and freedoms set forth herein.*" Does this seem logical or honest by any standards?

To find markets to sell the weapons, these countries need to utilize their intelligence services to create an environment in which these arms/ weapons can be used-to do that, they have to create an environment in developing countries where the human rights of those countries are violated, the peace of those countries are destroyed. Is that not the case?

If it is good for USA, UK, France, Japan and Norway to produce nuclear weapons, weapons of mass destruction, or chemical weapons- then it should also be permitted for Iran, Iraq, Russia, India, Pakistan, China and North Korea to produce the same weapons and sell them to markets that are willing to buy them for their own self-protection. Is this not the logical argument?

Why should the USA think that it is "their right" to impose sanctions on developing countries with capabilities of producing weapons thereby violating "the rights" of these countries? Where is the "equality" that the Universal Declaration talks about?

Where does the Universal Declaration of Human Rights stand in their Article 30 when terrorism is encouraged by developed countries, for them to make profits through the sale of arms to both the terrorists and the respective governments involved in such conflicts? Whose rights are being violated? Is it not the "rights" of citizens who wish to live in peace and harmony? Who is instigating and conspiring the destruction of human rights in the developing countries- is it very difficult for us to see the utter hypocrisy and blatant violations? The USA has been terrorizing the entire world with their arrogance, invasions and intimidations but the Universal Declaration of Human Rights has not been used by The UN to stop their atrocities-why? Because they consider themselves "The Super Power" with authority to rule over others while destroying the human rights of other nations!

What action has been taken against Norway by The UN for their active involvement in encouraging terrorism, aiding and abetting with the LTTE terrorists in Sri Lanka? Is this not considered to be a violation of the Universal Declaration of Human Rights? As per the Declaration"………. *implying for any State, group or person any right to engage in any activity or to perform any act aimed at the destruction of any of the rights and freedoms set forth herein."* Does the Democratically elected sovereign Government of Sri Lanka have the "right" to decide on how to protect her citizens from terrorists? Are we to protect the "rights" of minority terrorists against the majority citizens of this country? Why should Norway, which has blatantly violated the Universal Declaration be permitted to remain in the SLMM when it has been proven that they are part of the LTTE terrorist outfit? Why the double standards? Is this how the USA is treating Iran, Iraq and Muslims as a whole after they dared to challenge the USA?

(b) "Religious Rights" of Developing Countries: Every country in the world has a "right" to determine how to govern their own countries based on the historical, socio-economic and religious heritage of their particular countries. The developed countries must respect "that right" and avoid as per the Universal Declaration of Human Rights "………. *implying for any State, group or person any right to engage in any activity or to perform any act aimed at the destruction of any of the rights and freedoms set forth herein."*

How can the developed world justify their acts of blatant disrespect for "rights" of developing countries to safeguard their own socio-economic and religious identities? Where is the impartiality of the United Nations Universal Declaration of Human Rights when it comes to acts of unethical conversions being conducted by Christian religious groups with vested interests invading developing countries and destroying the inherent rights of that country? Do countries with majority Islamic, Hindu or Buddhist cultures have a "right" of their own?

What "right" does the USA, UK, Europe or South Korea have, to conduct "religious invasions" of non-Christian countries to force Christianity on countries, which have a history of religious harmony within their own countries. That harmony has been destroyed by these insensitive and selfish Evangelical Christian groups who even have the audacity to write reports criticizing independent countries which want to protect their countries of contamination.

True to US arrogance, they have recently put out a report "International Freedom of Religion Report-2006" in which Sri Lanka is stated as one of the countries which discriminates against minority religions. This is absolutely incorrect given the history of religious tolerance that Sri Lanka has maintained even at the risk of American Evangelists using even the Tsunami of December 2004 to carry on their unethical conversion activities. Their aggressive and arrogant methods are disgusting, to say the least. In the true sense of the term "service to humanity" evangelists must not use 'conversion' as a bait for material benefits! Let us kindly request the USA to permit Muslims to spread Islam freely within the territory of the USA because that would be their "right" to spread their religion just like the American Evangelists are doing in developing countries! The Universal Declaration means nothing to American Evangelists and they are by no means respecters of countries, persons or cultures as we have witnessed in Sri Lanka and we have no doubt that they use the same arrogance in all other developing countries.

If Sri Lanka wishes to bring in an Anti-Conversion Bill to safeguard our citizens, what right does countries like USA and UK have to dictate terms and threaten sanctions against Sri Lanka if the Bill was implemented? Will the USA or UK permit Muslims to invade their countries and spread the Islamic faith within their countries? In France, the government even brought legislation to prevent Muslim women from wearing the Hijab in public because it breaks down the social fabric of French society and culture- isn't that so? Why cannot the same rules be applied to developing countries?

In an article which appeared in the Daily Mirror of 20th September 2006 reported by AP titled "Bush Promoting His Middle East Strategy Before a Skeptical UN" it states; " *George W.Bush is trying to persuade skeptical world leaders to embrace his vision for the Middle East in a speech before the United Nations today where he is calling on the world to "stand up for peace" in the face of violent extremism"* Who is George W. Bush and is he a Muslim for him to have a vision for the Middle-East? What right does he have to decide on the past, present or future of another country or countries which are independent? Is he respecting "the rights of Middle Easterners" by thinking that he has the authority and right to decide for them? No one in his decent right mind, will justify what Bush has done in Iraq let alone the Middle East-except for Tony Blair who prefers to nod his head to everything the US says.

Why doesn't the UN penalize the violators of the Universal Declaration of Human Rights when they blatantly disrespect "the rights" of other countries. Is it because the perpetrators these countries which are also members of the Security Council think that they can violate any regulation human rights or otherwise, and expect developing countries to tolerate their audacity and arrogance?

Conclusion

Ms. Louise Arbour, the UN High Commissioner for Human Rights in her address has touched on the situation in Darfur, Iraq, Sri Lanka and Nepal and the issue of International Migration and Development. In her reference to Iraq states "My colleagues in Iraq continue to report on the breakdown in law and order as well as on daily attacks, extra-judicial killings, kidnappings, arbitrary detentions, disappearances and torture. Cases of violence are inadequately investigated and remain unpunished..............."

Who initially started the violation of "human rights" in Iraq and with what authority? The USA which is thousands of miles away from Iraq decided that it had to punish Iraq, brought out some lame excuses about chemical weapons(even if they had, it is not for the USA to decide how to punish Iraq), brought in their army and began to attack Iraq with venom! Iraq is an independent country with a culture of their own & it is for the people of Iraq to decide without foreign interference. The USA is not the United Nations for them to take unilateral decisions against any country in the world! The UK true to its colonial heritage backed USA not with the best interests of Iraq in mind but their own vested interests-why this hypocrisy? Ms. Arbour has not made even one reference to the abhorring violation of "human rights" inflicted by the US forces against the Iraqi detainees and citizens whose "human rights" have been desperately violated as per the Universal Declaration "……….. *implying for any State, group or person any right to engage in any activity or to perform any act aimed at the destruction of any of the rights and freedoms set forth herein."*

Her reference to Sri Lanka and the LTTE terrorists is equally hollow in the fact that it is obvious she does not understand who is violating "whose rights"? Does she expect the Sri Lankan Government to sit back and watch all the atrocities committed by the terrorists and do nothing to protect the citizens of this country. Let Ms. Arbour not think that the terrorists are representing the Tamil community. The terrorists are a law unto themselves and are even against the majority Tamil community let alone the Sinhalese or the Muslims living in this country.

We are quite familiar with the Sri Lankan issue and it is obvious that the likes of Ms. Arbour do not understand the core problem of the issue related to the LTTE terrorists. First and foremost, it would be prudent to investigate extensively and find out as per the Universal Declaration "……….. *implying for any State, group or person any right to engage in any activity or to perform any act aimed at the destruction of any of the rights and freedoms set forth herein."*

Sri Lanka is a sovereign country with a democratically elected government. Any terrorist activities against the state or her civilians have to be stopped by the government and the Armed Forces which are there to protect and defend our nation. A mythical assumption of the LTTE terrorists have been pampered by countries like Norway and other western countries until recently when they began to blacklist them as "terrorists" and curtail their activities within their countries. Who has been selling arms to the terrorists? Why have they not been charged according to the rules of the Universal Declaration for violating the "rights" of a peace-loving nation? For nearly 30 years, the terrorists have been conducting their killings, abductions and atrocities but western countries chose to ignore these activities because their INGOs could prosper and thrive in Sri Lanka so long as they could talk about "conflict resolution" and "peace and harmony" and "ethnic conflict."

Westerners should accept the fact that Sri Lanka does not have "an ethnic conflict" and there never was such a problem. How come Muslims, Tamils and Sinhalese all live together in other parts of Sri Lanka except in the North and East of the country?

Western countries and world bodies need to be honest with what they are doing. Show the world that they really and truly respect equality, human rights and fundamental rights of the developing countries. All these terminology is not there only to serve the vested interests of the western powers. Understand the core issues before passing rash judgements and sanctions against governments. Most conflicts in developing countries have been created with the instigations of developed countries, to achieve their agendas.

Just as much as western powers want to protect "their rights," developing countries also would like to protect "our rights." If developing countries blindly listen to the dictates of western powers or western aggressors as we may call them, then we will continue to be "developing countries" until the next millennium! We need to stand up and speak up for what is "our right" and work towards building solidarity amongst developing countries, we must not fall prey to the "divide and rule policy" of western powers who continue to create rifts between nations[2].

References

1. Chair of the Dalit Solidarity Network Trustees-March 23rd 2007:54.
2. Darmitha-Kotte, What is "Human Rights" in The Modern World' Surfed Dated 17. 04. 2009.

Chapter - 9

Empowerment

Introduction

Despite the fact that there were 26 lakh Dalits in Government establishments' employment in India in 2001, lakhs of them are still unemployed due to the sixty years of backlog in the service sector left unattended by the well-intentioned official machinery and in elementary, secondary and higher level education of the reservation-facilitated increasing number of Dalit youths. Two hundred years of Dalit struggle under the leadership of Kratiba Jyotirao Phule (1827-1890), Maharshi Shahu Maharaj of Kolhapur(1865-1920) and Dr. B.R. Ambedkar (1891-1956) respectively in facilitating knowledge, in providing fifty two percent reservation and constitutionalizing the political, economic and social equality rights for the Dalits cannot be wiped off within six generations as Muller pointed out about the 13-15th century Spanish, Morrocan, and South African communities, who vanished in history owing to forgetting their history.

Yet the burning question of the contemporary social-economic-educational-politico-scenario in respect of Dalits in India is "why" less share of Dalits in politics, why less number of Dalits are educated in all levels, particularly in technical, scientific, professional studies and private enterprises and why they lag behind in life's dignified standard compared to the prosperous generality?

Answer to this "why" may be sought on two fronts, (1) within Dalits themselves and (2) within their surrounding including 75 percent population amidst whom the scheduled castes and the scheduled tribes survive with their common lot of deprivation against their every odd. A list of numerous causes can be produced. Political, economic and social historical causes can be traced. But pointing to one major cause out of them for the backwardness of Dalits in higher education is a strenuous and rewarding exercise of research for the practical solution of the "why" of the Dalit plight.

Empowerment on social level is seen by the famous sociologist Prof. Nandu Ram in terms of (1) social awareness and consciousness, (2) resistance to injustice and exploitation, (3) employment in white collar jobs, (4) access to power and authority, (5) improved life-style and changed world-view and on personal level it is reflected in (1) individual personality traits or psychology, (2) his/her attitude and behavior and (3) mind set (see seminar brochure). Despite Governmental measures towards facilitating avenues of higher education for the SC-ST students the latter lacked social mooring and family tradition that put them at stake of availing such measures and finding employment in higher posts in an adequate number if not in large scale, if any succeeded to have it at all.

In this paper the author attempts to discuss various facets of the issue and throw some light on it in details through the pages of the main text.

Foreword

It is quite possible that all the Dalits are not qualified to enter the stream of higher education. This loophole is always a hurdle for Dalits themselves and their well-intentioned Government as well to mark the point that their representation is therefore minimal in the scientific and technical as well as professional education in spite of measures adopted by the government. But given the fact that the Dalits have increased in their qualification as graduate and post-graduate in a large number the government in cahoot with court also finds it inexcusable as to their recruitment in suitable jobs in public undertakings and institutions. In fact the reflection of political superstructure visible overtly has the unjust social foundation underground that being covert is hard to hit at squarely.

Brahamization

In the prescribed curriculum of Indian schools, colleges and universities, Dalit characters are not only far and few but even those which find space in the pages of the text-books, feature as poor, uncultured and ignorant people.

An ICSSR study (1970) conducted that "Schools and colleges have not functioned effectively as melting pots for caste boundaries in the matter of friendships." The adverse learning environment experienced by the Scheduled-Caste pupils impacted their educational aspirations, achievements and their alarming the drop-out rate and this problem is live both in rural areas in metropolitan cities, where the children are abused on caste angles publicly.

In Oriya literature, one studies Gopinath Mahanty or Fakir Mohan Senapati but not Bhim Bhoi or Sameer Ranjan or Basudev Sunani and Om Prakash Balmiki or Bama in other regions. This is so because they are the voices of the dissent, they are the voices of the marginalized.

Dalit literature as a subject has already been introduced in many foreign universities. But in India even a full-fledged University of Delhi and Jawaharlal Nehru University have not felt it necessary to introduce it as a subject. Dalits have been compulsorily studying and reading the literature which is not their own. No text books ever present Dalit culture as an integral part of Indian culture. Most of the time they are bundle of lies about them, yet they have to study. Dalit autobiographies, novels, poetry and short stories exist in many regional languages and many of them have already been translated into English. These writings represent the true culture and identity of the Dalit communities. Dalits also have a story about themselves and a history. The aim of introducing Dalit literature in higher education is to realize that caste system is an evil which must be eradicated from the society. Teaching Dalit literature in higher education aims at debrahmanization and de-hinduization of knowledge. Paulo Freire (1993) once wrote,...sooner or later being less human leads the oppressed to struggle against those who made them so.

Discrimination

Ninety-nine percent of dalit students are enrolled in government schools that lack basic infrastructure, classrooms, teachers and teaching aids. They are made to sit in the back of the classroom and endure verbal and physical harassment by teachers and students both. According to the UN special rapporteur teachers held that dalit pupils "cannot learn unless they are beaten". This is another cause of the low literacy and high dropout rates for dalits. Upper-caste hostility toward dalits' education is linked to the perception that dalits, if educated, will pose a threat to village hierarchies and power relations.

The European Parliament also in 2007 found India's efforts to enforce laws protecting dalits to be "grossly inadequate," and "atrocities, untouchability, illiteracy, and inequality of opportunity continue to blight the lives of India's dalits". They suggested that Indian social reform would be a salutary move, in an era when the need for 'reforms' is being trumpeted from every television station and political party.

Chandrabhan Prasad said that "Khairlanji conformed to a familiar pattern of Dalits' systematic exclusion, which extends all the way from the remotest villages to elite institutions such as the All India Institute of Medical Sciences. AIIMS' Dalit students cannot live in *savarna* (upper-caste)-dominated hostels or eat at the same table. The administration also refused to cooperate with an official committee appointed to look into allegations of caste discrimination.

According to the media the suicide of a Dalit research scholar, Senthil Kumar in University of Hyderabad and the recent clash between different caste based groups in Dr. Ambedkar Law College in Chennai had at the root the caste based discrimination against the Dalits in higher education.

When Two Circles. net talked to some of the Dalit students of history in Patna and Magadh Universities, they found that upper caste people have devised plans to stop SC-ST students from entering the educated, cultural and powerful class." Even after clearing their Pre Research Tests (PRT) 2-4 years back they haven't yet been able to enroll because of the alleged lack of vacancy under any of the faculty who could take a Dalit as his or her research scholar.' But whenever students of their own caste come to them they easily take them under their supervision. They revealed that when their supervisors agree to guide the SC and ST students they ask from the candidate half of his or her stipends which the SC and ST students are entitled to get from Rajiv Gandhi Foundation. Not only the SC and ST students but even the teachers belonging to these communities are at the receiving end.

Dr. Phulo Paswan, a dalit scholar and also the Chairperson of Department of Maithili, Patna College, Patna University while he was attending a meeting on September 1, 2004 was verbally abused and assaulted by DN Jha, the contemporary Controller of Examination of Patna University, asking him how dared he a Dalit sit in a meeting with people of upper caste. Although Mr. Paswan filed an FIR but there hasn't been any action against him yet.

Patna and Magadh universities in Bihar haven't yet constituted the SC-ST cell to look into the grievances of SC-ST students and to supervise the proper implementation of schemes meant for them as directed by UGC.

PG ST student Arihant in the School of Languages (SL) from Jawaharlal Nehru University (JNU), pointed out that "The caste based discrimination is more subtle here. It is particularly prevalent in the departments on which saffron inclined faculties have penetrated."

The vice chancellor of Patna University, Shyam Lal said that even after sixty years of independence the caste based discrimination in India is still prevalent. The caste based discrimination in the higher education is mere an extension of the discrimination which is being practiced in the society and it gets its legitimacy in the society first. The root cause of the discrimination is the attitude and the feudal mindset of the upper caste people which their modern education couldn't dispel. The other reason for the discrimination is the provision of reservation itself. To root out the caste based discrimination any one step won't suffice. It needs a multi-pronged strategy which includes the government, the political class and the civil society to come together and think about it.

In West Bengal all the Bengali medium schools where the Dalit and Adibasi children normally take their education stopped teaching English language with a view to increase the percentage of literacy in the state and seriously damaged the future career of the Dalit children.

The Ministry of Higher Education laid the condition that SC-ST category students should get admission to the UG-Honours or PG-courses if they secured minimum 90 percent marks. As a result not a single student of reserve category could have their admission in a number of reputed colleges in Kolkata.

B.G. Verghese in 'Deccan Herald' dated 2009 pointed out that Mayawati as Dalit-ki-beti (daughter of a dalit) blunted her original appeal as a Dalit leader intent on forging a wider social alliance."

Ravinder Goel on 30 December 2008 submitted that in the Department of Political Science of the Delhi University, (headed by one renowned leftist) qualified SC and OBC candidates were denied admissions to Ph.D. on reserved seats in September 2008. They were the products of the same Department of the University with a high second class at MA level, and awarded M. Phil degrees. Moreover, the victimised OBC candidate Vibha Maurya has qualified NET twice and is eligible to teach at UG and PG levels as per the UGC guidelines. In their place one general category candidate without M Phil degree was admitted to Ph D. Thus teachers and the officials of DU helped the 'efforts of Supreme Court' to fill the vacant seats with the general category students.

Lag

The following table shows the percentage of Dalits in education compared to that of the general category in 2005 and the hurdles the Dalits have been facing in getting scholarship in Government schemes in Indian society.

(In Percentage)

Category S.N.	*SC*	*ST*	*All*	*Age-group*	*Stage*
I	2.1	1.1	12.1	06-11	Primary (I-V)
II	1.2	0.6	7.4	11-14	Up-Primary (V-VIII)
I+II	3.3	1.7	19.5	06-14	Elementary (I-VIII)
III	1.5	0.8	9.4	14-18	Sec/Senior Secondary (VIII-XII)
IV	1.9	0.9	10.1	18-24	Higher Education (XII-B.A., M.A., M.Phil.)
I+II+III+IV	6.7	3.4	39.0	06-24	All Education

Source: www.Scrid.com/doc/11569307/education-statistics-2005-06.

Only about 3 SC students and hardly two ST students can reach standard I to VIII for every twenty students of other categories in elementary education while only one SC student and not even one ST student can make to the secondary education against the nine students of general category in the secondary stage of education. Hardly two SC students and one ST student can reach the higher education from stnd. XII through B. A., M. A. to M.Phil. against the ten general students. In all education SC-ST students together cannot reach the point on par with other category students who are four times ahead of their counterparts. The above table shows that the number of SC-ST students enrolled in all stages of education from 1st standard to M.Phil. degree is respectively about seven and thirteen times lagging behind that of the other students in all stages of education said above.

In the present existing (2008) more than three hundred universities, over twenty thousand colleges and 121 institutes recognized as Deemed Universities one finds only the general category students dominating the scene. There is a reciprosity between the increase in private institutions and decrease in government schools for the advanced stages of education. The fees of the private institutions and the cost of the Science and professional courses are so exorbitant that the weaker sections could hardly afford them.

Dr. Ambedkar in 1924 while writing testimony on the Bombay University Reform, questioned the quality maintained by the private educational establishments while imparting higher education. He said, "At present the teachers are attached to the colleges and their pay and status are regulated by the authorities governing them. But the colleges did not seem to be making the appointments solely from the view of obtaining the most qualified persons nor from the sense of regulating their grades, tenure, pay and promotion in such manner as to open a career to the best and most qualified members of the staff. In private educational Institutes self-interest was more important than quality and equity in education".

As education is privatized, less privileged youths were denied access to professional and technical education. It was this denial and exclusion from education and jobs that made them prey to the fundamental right wing forces.

Role of Society

Society is a larger field for the Dalits to lean upon. Indian society is consisted of Dalit poor and Dalit literate along with general poor and general literate, which are considered worthy of Governmental measures to alleviate their poverty and provide them education. Indian diaspora settled in foreign countries also do their best to voice the grievances of the weaker sections of India and put pressure on Indian government and international forum for doing needful in that respect. There is an international society also which has been aware of the problems of the Indian Dalits and it tries to assist financially Government of India and NGOS working for the amelioration of the deprived people due to caste and politico-economic backwardness. International organizations, IMF, Asian Bank, United Nations are such bodies which are effective in pressing matter to take positive form in development, empowerment and education in India as well as in other developing countries' weaker classes. The other intellectual society consisting of the academicians and professional classes are at least theoretically wedded to resolve the issues of social nature like untouchability, caste, education and empowerment of Dalits in India and abroad, who by their writings, speeches and literary contributions assess the situation and advise the national and international agencies working for this end to incorporate their views in right earnest and direction and help to reduce the suffering of the unfortunate humanity.

The above role of society is well expressed by Society for Dalit Empowerment (Reg. No. 389/2007) in south India which aimed at putting before one the ideals of the great leaders like Buddha, Karl Marx, Jyotiba Phule, Shahu Maharaj, Dr. Ambedkar, Bhagat Singh, Mother Teresa and others. It held that the architects of the society will be the students, scholars, academicians, Poets, Artists, Social Activists and Philanthropists committed to the amelioration of Downtrodden India (dalits, tribals, minorities, backward classes & economically poor upper class), through non violence and democratic means. Under its goals the prominent one is to espouse pride in Dalit identity and Culture. Similarly Dr. Ambedkar Mission INC, Canada, Dalit organizations in America and Federation of Ambedkartie and Buddhist organizations in UK help raise voice, grievances and issues of Dalits on international forum.

Leo Bashyam, in his paper on *International Development Aid: Addressing Dalit Issues*, said that Dalits are seen as a combination of all the Scheduled Castes and Tribes. Within their categorisation of Scheduled Castes and Tribes the Indian Government refuse to recognise Dalits who have converted to other religions, such as, Christian and Muslim Dalits. This is wrong and it is important that International organisations work with all Dalits irrespective of their religious beliefs.

There are approximately 300 million Dalits living in India. A total of 270 million people live below the poverty line. In India as a whole 345 million people live below the poverty line, therefore Dalits make up approximately 78% of all Indians living below the poverty line. Dalit women are discriminated against twice, firstly for being a Dalit and secondly for being a woman, as a result there is the need for a specific focus to be put on addressing gender imbalances, especially in relation to the position of women. A majority of bonded and child labour are also Dalits.

In 1999 Charity Aid Foundation and Voluntary Action Network India estimated 18,000 NGOs in India. Similarly another 4,000 NGOs were granted temporary permission during the period.

Subsequent to the opening of India's economy to Multi National Corporations (MNCs) as a part of India's Structural Adjustment Programme (SAP) there has been an increased flow of funds into the country. However, the impact of foreign aid on India's development policies is highly controversial. While most aid is"tied" and in many instances given according to the political and commercial interests of donor countries, in some cases foreign aid has served to challenge some of the Indian government's policies on poverty alleviation.

It is estimated that under 25% of official aid is spent on poverty alleviation, and most official aid is channelled through the central government which sometimes uses it for political ends that are not strictly development-related. The growing tendency of bilateral and multilateral agencies to fund local NGOs directly is a cause for some concern. There is a danger that direct funding could effectively transform local NGOs into contractors, reducing their independence and undermining the empowerment process.

Till 1997, the volume of foreign contribution to NGO sector was nearly \$568 million (Rs. 26, 000 million). The official development assistance (ODA) in 1998 was \$1,594.6 millions.

Bilateral assistance from Organisation for Economic Co-operation Development (OECD) countries goes to India's central government. Multilateral aid goes for government-sponsored development programmes in the form of grants and loans and is channelled through agencies like UN organisations (UNICEF, UNESCO, FAO), the IMF, the World Bank and regional development Banks (the Asian Development Bank) and other institutions such as the European Commission. International solidarity groups, international trade unions and other international organisations are funding their Indian counter-parts and, international non-governmental development aid agencies and private trusts have funded mostly the NGO sector in India. USA, GERMANY and the UK, contributed more than half of the foreign contribution.

Sri Satya Sai Centran Trust and Maharishi Vedvigyan Viswavidyapeetham alone received 25% of the contributions. "Development NGOs" received only 20% of foreign aid. However, they have also come under criticism for promoting donor driven policies, pushing western ideas on gender, and causing a mushrooming in the number and size of NGOs in certain regions. The impact of NGOs work at the micro level is being questioned in 21st century. People are asking whether the present structures, policies and strategies of many NGOs are still relevant, and whether the capacity of NGOs to bring about change is keeping up with the changing environment.

A third of India's population continues to live below the poverty line. At least 50% of aid to poverty alleviation programme should be allocated to programmes that focus on Dalits. In India adequate representation should be given to dalits at senior levels. Aid agencies and international bodies should allocate money for development education programmes that help strengthen civil society.

Findings

So we can conclude from the above that social consciousness is not cultivated even up to the half mark. Resistance to injustice and exploitation has been going on from the sufferers, who represent in education and jobs far below their other counterparts of society; Dalits share power and authority only to axe their roots and any change in their outlook and standard of life is confined to a few and far between. As far as the attitude, mindset and psychology of the higher caste learned supervisors is concerned they have been exercising their roles as the new millennium Dronacharyas against contemporary Eklavyas. On national and international level Indian diaspora, NGOS and Academicians have been doing their best to grapple with the problem of less education, less employment and less participation of Dalits in Socio-Politico-Economic affairs of the country.

Suggestions

1. There should be a fair representation of the oppressed castes and their life experiences in educational texts and in the selection committees, academic councils and executive bodies of the educational establishments.
2. The number of boys' and girls' hostels should be increased. The Pre-Matric and Post-Matric scholarships for the students of SC/ ST/OBC communities should be given on the monthly basis, the amount of the scholarship should be increased to cover the maintenance cost and the number of scholarships should be heightened to reduce deprivation of students from this scheme.
3. That NCERT, SCERT, NCTE, AIU, UGC, AICTE, Bar Council of India, Medical Council of India, Council of Architect, Central Council of India, Pharmacy Council of India, Indian Nursing Council, the Council of Higher Education and Distance Education Council should make their educational policies and curriculum in such a way as to enable the weaker section students to compete with others in this global economy because without their education and empowerment our country's welfare can never be materialized.
4. Fortunately in Maharashtra in all private unaided professional colleges the students of SC, ST, NT, VJA are getting the full reimbursement and OBC students got 50 percent fees concession. So the Government at the centre should apply this policy in all states of India and enable them to pursue professional courses and higher studies in Medical, Engineering, Agricultural, Pharmacy and Nursing disciplines.
5. That backlog in SC-ST reservation and implementation of 17+8+27 percent reservation for the SC-ST-OBC in IIT, IIM and Central Universities should be strictly implemented so that their progress in education in the present scenario after independence can be assured.
6. "That education should be related to life and the need of a person, the process of modernization should speed up development and

inculcate social values and there should be an equalization recommended equalization of educational opportunities". This was the recommendation of Kothari Commission in the sixties. Elementary education should be free and compulsory according to Article 21C under the Fundamental Rights after the 93rd constitution amendment carried in 2001.

7. That SC-ST students cannot be expected to forego their right and opportunity to reap the benefits of the highest education to the fullest extent as Dr. Ambedkar said.
8. The Government should reduce delay in disbursing the scholarship amount and enable the scholars to pursue higher education with increase of slots under Rajiv Gandhi National Fellowship Scheme started in 2005 and secure jobs of higher caliber to the qualified weaker section people.
9. The Government should help students of weaker sections in taking up entrance examination of foreign universities and adopt criteria of intellectuality rather than that of seniority in resolving the tie between two students and their final selection under National Overseas Scholarships for SC students.

References and Bibliography

1. Vandana Shiva, India Divided Diversity and Democracy under Attack: Bangalore, Seven Stories Press, 2005: 77.
2. Vasant Moon ed. Dr. Babasaheb Ambedkar Writings and Speeches, 2nd Vol: Bombay: Education Department, Government of Maharashtra, 1982: 303.
3. Katkar, Education Policy in India from C.D. Naik ed. Buddhism and Dalits: Social Traditions and Philosophy, Kalpaz Publication, New Delhi, 2009.
4. Internet surfing dated 23 November 2009.
5. Ilaiah, Kancha. 1996. Why I am not Hindu. Calcutta: Samya Publications.
6. Zelliot, Eleanor. 1996. From Untouchable to Dalit. New Delhi: Manohar.
7. Dangle, Arjun. (ed.) 1992. Poisoned Bread: Translation from Modern Marathi Dalit Literature, Bombay: Orient Longman.
8. Quoted in the article, "Alternative education", http://www.avehi.org/.
9. Gail Omvedt, Dalit Visions, op. cit., p. 18.
10. Joshi, Barbara R. 1986. Untouchable: Voice of the Dalit Liberation Movement. New Delhi: Select Book. Fucoult, Michael. 1984. Power/Knowledge, ed. by Paul Rabinow, New York: Peregrine.
11. Frontline, Volume 23 - Issue 25:: Dec. 16-29, 2006, India's National Magazine from the publishers of THE HINDU reported.0
12. Submitted by admin on 26 December 2008 - 9:34 am. by Md. Ali, Two Circles.net
13. N.N. Oza ed. Chronicle year Book, Noida< Chronicle Pub. Pvt. Ltd, 2009: 155.

14. In Dalit Diary:1999-2003–Reflections on Apartheid in India *by Chandra Bhan Prasad; Navayana Publishing, Chennai, 2004;pp 264 (paperback), Rs 225.*
15. Leo Bashyam, Head of Asia Team, Christian Aid, 35,Lower Marsh, Waterloo, London SE1 7RT, Tel: 44-020-75232337, Fax: 44-020-7620, E-mail: *lbashyam@christian-aid.org* (internet surfing dated 1st December 2009).

Chapter - 10

Gender Study

It is an established fact that the Dalit women and their empowerment were a seriously pondered and successfully institutionalised issue under the dispensation of the Truth-Finder Thathagata Buddha in ancient Indian society. In contemporary India, Dalits were made aware of their Buddhist legacy by Babasaheb Ambedkar, who broke their age-old shackles and set them free so as to enable them to be their own sentinels. One look into the vision of Dr. Ambedkar, which essentially calls for the establishment of the casteless society, one is more than convinced how the modern social scientists arrived, after their long and strenuous researche, at the same findings and suggestions as presaged and predicted by one of the greatest thinkers of the last millennium.

How foresighted and prophetic were the findings and suggestions of Dr. Ambedkar made in 1944 in comparison with those of recent investigators can be illustrated by citing a couple of examples. Firstly, Meena Ramkrishna, the contemporary sociologist suggested that Dalit women should not rely on Dalit men, or on the mainstream women's movement but actively support and work with women from other vulnerable sections for leading Dalit women's movement. This observation can be contrasted with Dr. Ambedkar's advice to the Scheduled Castes six decades ago that they must organize themselves under one leader, one party and one programme of the Federation to remove caste distinctions. Secondly while Prof. Subhabrata Dutta of the Department of Social Welfare Administration in the Tata Institute of Social Sciences, Mumbai investigated that the Dalit women were denied both minimum and equal wages, Dr. Ambedkar foresaw as early as in 1944 that the day will come when it would be possible to guarantee a minimum wage, provide housing for labour and pensions as an insurance against old age to the poor.

While the plight of womenfolk as shown in the above table no. 4 is being intensified with their insecurity in respect of their being members of the so called criminal tribes, in respect of their endangered persona as victims of rape, incest, sattee, police and judicial biases, illiteracy, enforced widowhood, Devadasee system, gangrapism, public riot, less Governmental budgetary concern, economic dependence, abject poverty, social taboos, prostitution, parading naked and killing as witches etc. the talk of their empowerment amidst such odds with far more serious and intricate issue of Dalit women will only be a farce if not ferocious unless their insecurity is lifted and their material empowerment is impelled.

Dalit women and their empowerment was a seriously pondered and successfully institutionalised issue under the dispensation of the Truth-Finder Thathagata Buddha in ancient Indian society. Contemporary Dalits were made aware of their Buddhist legacy by the modern Buddhist revivalist Bharatratna Boddhisattva Babasaheb Ambedkar, who broke their age-old enslaving shackles and made them free so as to enable them to be their own sentinels. The following essay, based on the secondary data, attempts to highlight how the modern social scientists arrived, after their long researches and strenuous investigations, at the same findings and suggestions as presaged and predicted by the great thinker of the millennium Dr. Ambedkar sixty years ago.

Introduction

All Scheduled Castes and Scheduled Tribes men and women are Dalit but the latter are more Dalit than the former in respect of gender inequality, wage inequality, legal treatment, occupational inferiority, educational backwardness, social prejudice, economic dependence, intellectual discrimination, and prevailing inequality in all walks of life in international community in general and Indian society in particular.

A scavenger woman is more degraded because of her unclean occupational routine and of her Dalit status in society. All women are equally placed as biological realities but there are unequal gradations among them according to their occupational, economic position and within themselves social gradations vary from section to section such as Dom, Dumna, Walmiki, Bhangi and Mehtar women etc.

Dalit woman is the weakest person even amongst general womenfolk. She can be identified as a person as manual labourer in agricultural occupation in villages or as a slum dweller in a town or city.

Dalit Women

The population of Dalits in the country is 22 crores[1] and about half of this number accounts for Dalit women populace.

In Haryana Bhiwani District at Jatuluhari village Dalit groom taking barat on mare was prohibited even in this current twenty - first century[2].

In 2001 the then President of India Sri K.R. Narayanan, while addressing the nation on the Republic Day, said, "That untouchability was abolished by law but its shadow was inherent in the outlook sustained by caste system. He further deplored that Dalit women were being subjected to most despised insults by the high caste males' passion[3]."

A sociologist by name Meena Ramkrishna, writing on National conference of Dalit Organisations in Rampur, Uttar Pradesh (150 Dalit Organisations in 15 states) reiterated the Dalit issues as under:

1. There is devastating impact of privatisation, liberalization and globalisation on the Dalit community and the Government is adopting economic policies, which will lead to a shrinking of employment opportunities for Dalits in all sectors.
2. Eighty percent of the Dalit population is connected with land, and so the agricultural policy of the Government is critical as agricultural reforms in consolidating small pots of land (which Dalits own) into larger ones allowing private entrepreneurs to enter agriculture, and mechanization of all agricultural operations meaning a large scale loss of work to Dalits currently employed as agricultural workers.
3. Disinvestment policies of the Government will result in loss of reservation quotas in the public sector and taking away existing jobs, closing an important avenue of employment for Dalits in the future.
4. The ever-expanding private sector is exploitative and existing labour laws are unproductive to Dalits working in them.
5. Large-scale displacement of Dalits is taking place, without their consent, and without any plans for their rehabilitation in the name of development.
6. Dalits are unable to pay the high fees at school and higher-level education and are being further excluded during privatisation of educational institutions.
7. So job reservations in the private sector, distribution of ceiling land to the landless Dalits, quotas for technical education are being demanded by Dalits.

   She further exposed the current socio-economic plans and policies and accountability of Government by referring to the Ninth Five year Plan which spent less than two percent of its budget on SCs/ STs, whereas they formed more than 22 percent of the total population. The gap between the literacy of Dalit and non-Dalits, which was 16.89 percent in 1961, had increased to 20.28 percent in 1991[4]. She had suggested to the Dalit women that they should not rely on Dalit men, or on the mainstream women's movement but actively support and work with women from other vulnerable sections like nomadic and de-notified tribes for leading Dalit Women's movement. She also recommended that there be critique of the educational system, including the curriculum, to make the pedagogic and delivery mechanism unbiased and Dalit friendly.

There is also another aspect to Dalit women issue. In India unlike in any other country communities of populace take birth as criminal tribes and untouchables. The stigma of being criminal from one's acts hurled on an individual is understandable but the hereditary stigma of criminality attached to a whole community is beyond one's comprehension. Created (Born) in 1871 such criminals are still being stigmatized and brutalized with prejudice in fiercer measures. Our Home Minister (Lal Krishna Advani) too endorsed such view about criminality, which is even more stunning.

In 2001 on July 19 one police Inspector K.L. Jadhav of Malabar Hill, Mumbai issued the circular to alert the residents of Malabar against Bihari and Nepali servants as innate criminals.

Moreover there are criminal tribes such as Bhils, Pardhis, Kanjar, Lolyar, Sansi, Bedias, Mushwer, Chhasa, Janjam, Bedkut, Saismal, Nut etc. at Khandesh and Coastal Narmada regions in Maharashtra, Dhikaros tribe of Santhal Paragana in Veerbhum and Zarkhand; Kheria Sabar of Bengal and scores of such tribes in Madras, Hyderabad, Mysore presidencies altogether ranging upto 180 tribes (8 % of total population) till 1924.

According to the recommendations of the Advisory Body constituted under the National Human Rights Commission chaired by Hon. Justice Venkatchalaiah (1998 May 4), " This is beyond imagination that a class of people of society, who were the aboriginal inhabitants of this subcontinent and who formed the six percent of the population, were neglected and are being deprived of respectable life even after half a century of independence."

One woman named Jalan of Paradhi criminal tribe of Maharashtra was on her way to Vadodara to participate in Seminar on Denotified (anadhisuchit/vimukta) and Nomadic Tribes . She was wearing a new saree. Police arrested her and stripped her naked amidst the crowd of people because she did not produce a cash memo of her saree and Police hypothesized that it must be stolen by her, who belonged to the so called criminal tribe[5]."

Empowerment of Dalit Women

Empowerment connotes both material and mental power to be endowed within one's person. In respect of woman it means that they are given opportunities and occasions to gain these powers within themselves and strive in life as any other person in society.

As for empowerment of Dalit women in respect of their status and dignity Amit Sengupta has rightly pointed out that " They just can't accept the changed reality that Dalits can actually demand social and economic dignity. They refuse to accept the constitution of India. They don't believe in a multi-cultural, multi-religious, multi-lingual egalitarian India. They don't want the Untouchables to be touched by the freedom of secular democracy", and he further warned the so called "They" by the phrase " But if they still choose to be blind, then not even the holy cow can save them" despite Acharya Giriraj Kishore's prophetic claim that "a cow is more valuable than five Dalits lynched to death[6]."

According to Subhabrata Dutta, a faculty member in the Department of Social Welfare Administration in the Tata Institute of Social Sciences, Mumbai, " ST women are denied both minimum and equal wages[7]."

There is a sensational report published in Jansatta on Sunday Nov. 17, 2002 by Anurag, who described how an Orissa woman by name Manjulata Sahoo, desperate in hunger, sold her seven days twins for only Rs. 250 /-.

As for the economic conditions of Dalit women, the point can be made as under. One of the drawbacks in transforming Dalits into a businessman/ woman class was the inability of Dalit bureaucratic class and the political leadership to turn administrative and managerial skills among the Dalits and Tribals into a social capital of the community as the upper castes had done[8].

United Nations' Development Programme (UNDP) reported that despite infinite resources the Arab countries are wanting three important principles – Independence, Knowledge and Women Empowerment and 50 % Arab women cannot even write and read today[9].

According to the National Crime Record Bureau between 1990 and 1996 within a span of 7 years as many as 86,291 rapes have been committed on women[10] and "In many respects women are main victims of Gujrat genocide and their bodies are battlefields[11]."

There is no difference between Dalit and woman's status as Laxmisingh pointed out in her essay on 'Dalit Enquiry', a research paper published in *kathan* of Oct.-Dec. 2002 issue[12].

Societal domination of male and female also makes difference in woman's treatment. Children born in matriarchal society in Kerala and some South Indian communities were found to be better in skill and more intelligent than those in the Hindi belt, observed Dr. Ram Manohar Lohia[13].

The Book of Levictus of Old Testament and Hindu Scriptures prohibit menstruation of women, not to liberate them spiritually[14].

In Madhya Pradesh District of Ratlam there is a Bancchhara community among whom the custom of transforming minor girls into goddess prevails and under this custom the divine girls are being sexually exploited[15].

Even in Vedic time there was no equality given to the women. Yajnavalkya threatened Gargi with cutting her throat and silenced her in the course of debate when he was being defeated. According to the Brihdarnyaka upanishada (6.4.7) a husband could forcibly cohabit with his wife against her will. Atharvaveda (3.3.7.10) mentioned that husband could beat his wife with a slit bamboo in case she left outside for entertainment against her husband's wishes. In Rigveda the women were listed among the articles of gift such as animals, cart etc[16].

In Thailand as many as 8 lakh young women are engaged in prostituion and among them 2 lakh 80 thousand are girls of minor age. They are being assisted in the occupation by 60, 000 agencies. United Nations estimated in 1990 that Thailand earned in that year an income of 400 Dollars a month[17]. Against Thai prostituion there are as many as about 10 lakh prostitutes in India and 30 percent or 3 lakh of them are child prostitutes (against 35 % in India)[18].

There have been four incidents of parading Dalit and Tribal women naked in U.P. and M. P.[19].

A few years ago Dr. Kanta wrote a terrorizing Hindi novel called *the Fish of the Sand,* which was ranked by Yashpal as high as the English book *Freedom at Midnight*. In her novel Kanta roared on man: dehus] rsjh Hkk'k.kckth gks x;h\ py cSB xkMh esa A Debased, have you finished with your lecturing? Off and get in the car[20].

The former Chief Minister of Orissa Srimati Nandini Satpathi even endorsed her support and praise to the burning of woman on dead husband's pyre (Roopkumvar 18 Devrala town, Rajasthan, 1987 Sept. 18; Charan

Shah 55, Bundelkhand, U.P. 1999; Kattubai aged, Panna district, M.P. 2002) [21] and custom of devadasi or child prostitute earlier and off late she said that women themselves were accountable for inviting rapes on them[22].

Relief to and empowerment of woman and riot-hit victims is being given on the basis of their religious status. For a death of the Hindu the compensation amounts to Rs. 2 lakh and of the Muslim only Rs. 1 lakh. Even today women as victims of domestic violence are also victims of terrorism and social violence[23].

Lata Sharma referred to an idiom popular in her cowbelt that " A mother of one son is blind and of two a deaf[24]."

Manisha wrote in the column of Truth-False under Rashtriya Sahara and posed the question: " Can those who ridicule women's rights answer "Why women in Bihar and Madhya Pradesh are killed in the guise of being 'devil'; why not a man is killed in the guise of a 'demon'"[25].

Prem Bhardwaj, writing on the pain of widows, said "There are over four thousand widows in Vrindavana, out of which ninety percent belonged to Bengal. The same is true of Benares. Forced to leave for Vrindavana by their relatives, evicted from their own property, in toto they are numbering their days in the wait of death the widows of Vrindavana and Benares are living example of pain and neglect, who appear to be moving but are in fact living dead bodies[26]. According to 1991 census India has about 3.3 crore of widows, the largest number in the world.[27]

In India out of total working force 28.66 percent are women[28].

For the last 30 years compared to the number of males, the women's population has continuously been declining. A married woman is still a slave under her husband lord. For a woman it is a crime to be childless and it is punishment to be a mother of girl child[29].

While on the one hand the medal of Miss World 2000 organised in Millennium Dome in London, won by Priyanka Chopra of India exhilarated all the beauty competion lovers of the world the then Chief Minister of Uttar Pradesh Shri Rajnath Singh underwent pain of Indian mind and tradition,[30] on the other hand in Nigeria, where on 7th December 2002 110 beauty contestants were to exhibit themselves, a woman named Ameena aged 31 was sentenced to death by stonning by Islamic Court after being found guilty of illicit sexual relations and of giving birth to a child. To protest against this cruelty 19 beauty contestants boycotted the beauty competition. The other countries which supported this boycott include France, Belgium, Denmark, Norway, Iceland and Switzerland etc. Shame to India for keeping mum on the issue. A funny thing about Indians is highlighted in this humour. A foreigner was referring to his country's development and told about the women of his land that they were so industrious that they could claim equal pay (salary) for equal work as men. At this point an Indian proudly said that in our country the pace of development is on such progressive hight that our women do nothing but appropriate the whole salary package of their men[31].

Woman is a biological reality not a historical one, said Simon De Bouor in her novel, "The Second Sex"[32].

Brinda Karat, speaking on women and food insecurity, wrote, " Sarkari prescriptions for women's empowerment miss one of its main prerequisites, namely, to be able to live a hunger free life[33].

In view of the Judicial bias justice to women folk seems to be distant. Caste and gender discrimination in the courts may be assessed from the following courts' verdicts. Rajasthan Government's Women's Development Programme (WDP) called Sathin and its member Bhamvari Devi, a Dalit woman was gangraped in full sight of her husband for she exerted to stop child marriage. The District and Sessions Court on November 1995 decided that delinquents be acquitted on the grounds that (1) the middle aged people indulging in rape is unthinkable, (2) they were respectable citizens incapable of committing such a crime and (3) the high caste men could not have committed rape with a low caste woman. A July 1996 case of the rape of a three year old girl by her father in which Supreme Court concluded that the wife's " attitude to the petitioner, even de hors the allegation involving the child, was vengeful" and like in Bhamvari Devi case the Court disbelieved that a father could molest his infant child in Satish Mehra V. Delhi Administration and another; and in Suman Rani custodial rape case, (Prem Chand and another V. State of Haryana) the Supreme Court refused to apply the minimum ten-year sentence under 376(2) to the police officers charged because of the victim's questionable character on the opinion of medical officer (1989 Supp(1) SCC, P. 287) and in a rape case in the State of Karnataka, the Supreme Court in October 1983 reduced the sentence to less than ten years provided by section 376(2) of the Indian Penal Code[34].

Finally a word or two may be stated about annihilation of caste by means of conversion to other religion than non-proselytizing religion. In India there are two types of societies and religions, one is that society and religion which believe and practice in changing society and religion by conversion and the other is a static society and religion which believe and practice no change whatsoever in any matter of conversion. Between the two types, the first one inducts recruits from the other and the proselytized have to change not only their religion but culture also. Buddhism belonging to the first type have more advantages in respect of its being the indigenous religion the adoption of which warrants no change in culture and it renders a proselytized person casteless status. Suneet, the sixth century prototype of the present scavengers, was promoted to the noble Buddhist status by Buddha because of this advantageous position of Buddha's Dhamma. Prakriti, an outcaste woman was equal to any noble member of Bhikkhuni Order. Both men and women of socially downtrodden class became equal with other higher caste members during Buddhist period and they declined in status during the Hindu rule till they were led to reserved category and equal status on par with any other member of Indian society under the leadership of Dr. Ambedkar from the first quarter of the twentieth century, through sixties to the present millennium of empowerment of women in global scenario[35].

Political Participation of Dalits with Perspective of Dr. Ambedkar

When one thinks of this age long problem of caste and gender discrimination prevailing in Indian society one cannot help but postulate by way of remedy two measures. One, humanization of Dalit and women in Hindu society and two, capitalization of Dalit dormant abilities as Justice Garg of Patna High Court suggested and Kanta Tyagi has done during her 47 years service among the tribal women in Madhya Pradesh and won 2002 Award for the same[36]. Shri Chandrabhan Prasad also dealt with participation of Dalits in Indian politics and made a point when he said that what Dr. Ambedkar repeatedly maintained by the representation of Dalits in bureaucracy, Executive, Legislature and Judiciary was nothing but his concern about participation of Dalits in Indian governance, not by pseudo representation but by real, loyal and actual Dalit representation in the key positions of State affairs of Indian society[37]. These suggestions and Dr. Ambedkar's statements of the matter may be juxtaposed and evaluated as under.

Dr. Ambedkar's addresses (1) on "The Awakening of Women" delivered on July 20, 1942 (P.118), (2) "The Problem of the Scheduled Castes" dated 29th January 1944 (P. 119), (3) "The communal Problem of India and Drafting a Constitution (Bombay 6.5.1945 P. 224), (4) "Cultivate More Strength and Power" (25.5.1947, P. 262), (5) "What Constitutes Good Government (25.9. 1947, P. 271), and (6) "Advice to the Prostitutes of Bombay" (16.6.1936 P. 668) indicate how the powerless ones be empowered. For instance in the first address mentioned above he dealt with the problem of awakening of Dalit women and said, "I measure the progress of a community by the degree of progress which women have achieved. There cannot be an occasion of greater happiness to any one interested in the advancement of the Depressed Classes than to witness this gathering of woman. Women should give education to their children, learn to be clean, keep away from all vices, instill ambition in children that they are destined to be great, remove from their minds all inferiority complex, not to be in a hurry to marry in respect of themselves and their children unless they both are financially able to meet the liabilities arising from marriage, bear in mind that to have too many children is a crime, that the parental duty lies in giving each child a better start than its parents had and above all let each girl who marries stand up to her husband, claim to be his friend and equal and refuse to be his slave. This is the way to bring honour and glory to women and Depressed Classes as Dr. Ambedkar as a labor Member in Governor General's Executive Council exhorted to Dalit women at the All India Depressed Classes Women's Conference held at Nagpur on the 20th July 1942[38].

In the same address Babasaheb Ambedkar further reiterated that meekness self-imposed is not a virtue of Ahimsa, for the latter consisted two parts namely (i) love and kindness towards all creatures and (ii) destruction of all evil doers as the great saint Tukaram in his abhanga expressed भले तर देऊ काठीची लंगोटी नाठाडाचे माथी देऊ काठी । The second part of this principle of non-violence is missed and Dalit women are subjected to dishonour, inglorious name, loss of chastity and judicial infamy as a lamb of Upanishadic story, which went to God and lodged a complaint saying that he was the father of all the creatures and all creatures were, therefore brethren but that notwithstanding this, every creature, said the lamb, was threatening its life forgetting all brotherly affection. To her complaint the God is alleged to have said, "You look so meek that even I am tempted to devour you"[39].

Dr. Ambedkar suggested to the Scheduled Castes classes as a whole to inculcate in their minds the ideal of becoming a ruling race in the free India. As early as in 1944 he said, "We must resolve that in the Free India of the future, we will be a ruling race. We refuse to continue to play a role of subservience or accept position in which we should be treated as servants, not masters. If and when a Swaraj Government was established in India, Hindus, Muslims and the Scheduled Castes, three parties in the country would share the political power. The days of domination of one community over another were certainty over and I want to make it known that the scheduled castes are determined to fight for their rights and claim due share in the administration of the country. Unless they had the political power in their hands they would not hope to bring about the desired improvement in the condition of the poverty stricken people. I visualize the day when it would be possible to guarantee a minimum wage of Rs. 30 a month, provide housing for labour and pensions as an insurance against old age to the poor. I regard as more important the freedom of the scheduled castes in India, the community which has been the victim of domination and oppression for over two thousand years. I refuse to recognize as a leader any one who recognizes caste distinction or religious differences. I ask you to ponder over the causes of your sufferings extending over a long period of thousands of years. The Hindu Dharma, is the main cause of your suffering. Of all religions in the world it is Hinduism that recognizes caste distinctions and untouchability. This was the cover, the cloak for all injustices perpetrated on the scheduled castes by the castes Hindus. The position even today, I regard to say, is that in villages they can not live with self-respect. We must discard Hinduism and refuse to submit to indignities any longer. What struck me most was that my community still continues to accept a position of humiliation only[40].

According to Dr. Ambedkar the communal problem can be solved on the basis of principles and their applications to all parties concerned without a fear or favour. Accordingly the following tables show impartial representation of Indian communities in their empowerment in legislature, executive and services.

Table 1: Showing share of power in Central Assembly (1945)

S.No.	*Name of Community*	*% of population*	*% of representation*
1.	Hindus	54.68	40
2.	Muslims	28.5	32
3.	Scheduled Caste	14.3	20
4.	Indian Christians	1.16	3
5.	Sikhs	1.49	4
6.	Anglo Indians	0.5	-

Table 2: Showing share of power in Bombay Assembly (1945)

S.NO.	*Name of Community*	*% of population*	*% of representation*
1.	Hindus	76.42	40
2.	Muslims	9.98	28
3.	Scheduled Caste	9.64	28
4.	Indian Christians	1.75	2
5.	Anglo Indians	0.07	1
6.	Parsees	0.44	1

Table 3: Showing share of power in Punjab Assembly (1945)

S.No.	*Name of Community*	*% of population*	*% of representation*
1.	Muslims	57.06	40
2.	Hindus	22.17	28
3.	Sikhs	13.22	21
4.	Scheduled Caste	4.39	9
5.	Indian Christians	1.71	1

The preceding tables shown are based on the following principles of distribution of representation.

1. Majority rule is untenable in theory and unjustifiable in practice. A majority community may be conceded a relative majority of representation but it can never claim an absolute majority.
2. The relative majority of representation given to a majority community in the legislature should not be so large as to enable the majority to establish its rule with the help of the smallest of the minorities.
3. The distribution of seats should be so made that a combination of the major minorities should not give the combine such a majority as to make them impervious (inadmissible) to the interests of the minorities.
4. The distribution should be so made that if all the minorities combine they could without depending on the majority form the Government of their own.
5. The weightage taken from the majority should be distributed among the minorities in inverse proportion to their social standing, economic position and educational conditions, so that a minority which is large which has better social, educational and economic standing gets a lesser amount of weightage than a minority whose members are less and whose educational, economic and social position is inferior to that of the others.

This was a proposal of balanced representation for a united India put forth by Dr. Ambedkar in 1945 in which the majority was warned against situation that took place in Ireland where the leader of the Irish Nationalists once told Carson, the leader of Ulster, "Consent to United Ireland. Ask for any safeguards and they will be granted to you." To this offer Carson said, "Damn your safeguards. We don't want to be ruled by you." The minorities of India have not said this; they are ready to be satisfied with safeguards[41].

Dr. Ambedkar's Advice to the Prostitutes:

Unlike the scavenging women the women trading in their own flesh are more degraded and despised by the nature of their occupation. They are generally known as 'prostitutes' to whom Dr. Ambedkar had given the advice in the following terms:

"Whether you change your religion along with us or not, it does not matter much to me. But I insist that if you want to be with the rest of us, you must give up your disgraceful life. The Mahar women of Kamptipura are a shame to the community. Unless you are prepared to change your ways, we shall have nothing to do with you and we shall have no use for you."

"There are only two ways open to you, either you remain where you are and continue to be despised and shunned or you give up your disgraceful profession and come with us."

"You will ask me how you will earn your livelihood. I am not going to tell you that. There are hundreds of ways of doing that. But I insist that you must give up this degraded life as women of other classes do and not continue to live under conditions, which inevitably drag you into prostitution[42].

While delivering his address at Lucknow on 25th April 1948 Dr. Ambedkar advised the Scheduled Castes that they must organize themselves under one leader, one party and one programme. They remove all castes distinctions and organize themselves under the aegis of the Federation[43].

With regard to the empowerment of Dalits Dr. Ambedkar was of the opinion that Dalits are concerned with double loyalty. They have loyalty to their people inhabiting this country and all difficulties faced by them should be met by them. They have also loyalty to this country. They should not be disheartened because their people in some villages have suffered and are undergoing great sufferings. They shall have to pursue their task with determination and decide to be organized. There need not be any fear of suffering in this country – cultivate more strength and power for more suffering and sacrifice[44].

How foresighted and prophetic were the findings and suggestions of Dr. Ambedkar made in 1944 in comparison with those of recent investigators can be illustrated by citing a couple of examples. Firstly, Meena Ramkrishna, the contemporary sociologist suggested that Dalit women should not rely on Dalit men, or on the mainstream women's movement but actively support and work with women from other vulnerable sections for leading Dalit women's movement. This observation can be contrasted with Dr. Ambedkar's advice to the Scheduled Castes six decades ago that they must organize themselves under one leader, one party and one programme of the Federation to remove caste distinctions. Secondly while Prof. Subhabrata Dutta of the Department of Social Welfare Administration in the Tata Institute of Social Sciences, Mumbai investigated that the Dalit women were denied both minimum and equal wages, Dr. Ambedkar foresaw as early as in 1944 that the day will come when it would be possible to guarantee a minimum wage, provide housing for labour and pensions as an insurance against old age to the poor.

Table 4: Showing year, place and event

Year	*Place*	*Event*
1924	India	180 tribes or 8 % of total population of India are still criminal tribes.
1983	Karnataka	Rape case punishment of 10 years for police officer, u/s 376 (2) of IPC was reduced
1987	Rajasthan	Satee Roopkumvar
1989	Haryana	Suman Rani custodial rape and Judicial bias
1991	India	Gap between literacies of Dalit and Non-Dalit classes increased from 16.89 % in 1961 to 20.28 % in 1991
1991	India	3.3 crore widows in India, largest in the world
1995	Rajasthan	Bhamridevi gangraped and Judicial bias
1996	Delhi	Infant girl's rape by her father and Judicial bias
1998	India	6 % criminals of total population according to Justice Venkatchalaiah of National Human Rights Commissions
1999	U.P.	Satee Charan Shah
9th Five Year Plan Period	India	Only 2 % of budget lay out was spent on SCs/STs
2001	Mumbai, Malabar	Bihari and Nepali servants were declared to be criminal
2001	Maharashtra	Jalan, Paradhi woman stripped naked as criminal
2002	Orissa	Manjulata Sahoo in hunger sold her 7 days old twins for Rs. 250 /-
2002	Hariyana, Jatuluhari village	Dalit groom's barat on a mare was prohibited.
2002	Gujrat	Women were victims of public riots
2002	M.P.	Bancchhara Devdasis' exploitation
2002	M.P.	Satee Kattubai
2002	U.P. and M.P.	Parading Dalit women naked
2002	Bihar and M.P.	Women killed as witches
2002	India	10 lakh prostitutes in India

While the plight of womenfolk as shown in the above table no. 4 is being intensified with their insecurity in respect of their being members of the so called criminal tribes, in respect of their endangered persona as victims of rape, incest, sattee, police and judicial biases, illiteracy, enforced widowhood, Devadasee system, gangrapism, public riot, less Governmental budgetary concern, economic dependence, abject poverty, social taboos, prostitution, parading naked and killing as witches etc. the talk of their empowerment amidst such odds with far more serious and intricate issue of Dalit women will only be a farce if not ferocious unless their insecurity is lifted and their material empowerment is impelled.

Findings

1. There are 11 crore Dalit women in India.
2. Dalit groom taking barat on a mare is not tolerated even today.
3. Woman is a villager, manual labourer or slum dweller.
4. For Dalits employment opportunities in all sectors are shrinking. There is a large scale loss to 80 percent Dalit agricultural workers due to wrong land reform and agricultural policies. Disinvestment is taking away existing jobs and future job reservations of Dalits.
5. Exploitative private sector and unprotective labour laws are against Dalit interests.
6. Development is working in displacement of Dalits on a large scale.
7. The gap between the literacy of Dalits and Non-Dalits increased from 17 n percent in 1961 to 20 percent in 1991.
8. Cow is more valuable than a man called Dallit.
9. ST women are denied even minimum wages.
10. 86,271 rapes have been committed during a span of 7 years from 1990 to 1996 and women are even victims of public riots in India.
11. Woman is treated biasedly under male dominated society.
12. Religious books decree against women's interests.
13. Devadasi religious prostituion prevails in certain parts of India.
14. There are 10 lakh women prostitutes and 3 lakh child prostitutes in India.
15. Relief to Dalit victims is given by step motherly treatment as relief of Rs. More than 1 lakh is given to a Hindu dead and less than that amount is to non-Hindu dead person.
16. Women are treated as witches and killed as such.
17. Women formed 29 percent of the India's total work force.
18. Women population has been declining census by census and childless woman is a crime and mother of a girl child is punishment.

19. Beauty competition is despised in India and capital punishment to woman in Islamic countries is not denounced by Indian leaders.
20. Judicial bias is working against women's interests in India.
21. Religious conversion from Hinduism to Buddhism is desirable for establishment of caste-gender-race-place- of- birth- free secular egalitarian society.

Suggestions

1. Education system should be unbiased and Dalit friendly.
2. Administrative and managerial skills among the Dalits and Tribals may be transformed into a social capital of Dalit community.
3. All round development of women and Dalit must be the aim of Developmental Agencies.
4. Women's empowerment should mean women to have her say and decision on every issue related to her own.
5. Married woman should not be a bonded woman but free person.
6. Real representatives of Dalits be elected by constituting suitable constituencies and giving weightage of minorities whose economic, social and educational standing is comparatively weaker.

Notes and References

1. Sanjaykumar Rokde, Savarna mediamen are not interested in raising issues related to Dalits, media did no justice to the Dalits, 2002 Nov. 30, Dainik Bhaskar, p. 8.
2. Rashtriya Sahara, 2002 Nov. 26, p. 8.
3. Shamsul Islam on Rising Inhumanity of Dalit Atrocities, Rashtriya Sahara, Sunday, Umang.
4. Meena Radhakrishna, A Statement of Self-confidence, The Hindu, 2002 Nov. 3, p. 3.
5. Anil Kumar Pandey, Who are the Criminal Tribes, Jansatta, 2001 August 23, Delhi.
6. Amit Sengupta, Buddha's Smile, Hindustan Times2002 Nov. 8, p. 8.
7. Subhabrata Dutta, Tribal Welfare, Social and Government support is vital, editorial, Statesman, 2002 Nov. 24/25.
8. Kancha Ilaiah, The Bhopal Dalit Declaration, Cow and Culture, The Hindu dated 25.10.02, p. 10.
9. Shweta Mishra, Arab, Rashtriya Sahara 2002 Sept. 21, p. 8.
10. Viddhullata, Social concern programme is meaningless without awarding respect to women, when will women be liberated from insecurity, Dainik Bhaskar, 2002 Oct. 9, p. 13 (In 1998 NCR Bureau showed 15,033 rape victims, Hindustan, Nov. 22, 2002, p. 10).

11. Gopa Joshi on Woman in the Hindutva Laboratory, Woman Panel Fact Finding Report, Jansatta, 2002 Oct. 18, p. 6.
12. Rajkishor on Swakiya in Rashtriya Sahara Nov. 3, 2002, p. 9.
13. K. Vikram, Memory, Rashtriya Sahara 2002 Oct. 12.
14. Janet Chawla, Programme of Divine women theory, Hindustan 2002 Oct. 25, p. 6.
15. Sarojini Bisht, Daughters on Stake, Jansatta, 2002 Oct. 27, p. 3.
16. Suhas Kumar on Status of Women during Vedic Period, Hindustan 2002 August 23.
17. Sudhir Kumar Singh on Child Prostitution in South East Asia, Hindustan 2000 March 3.
18. Sarojini Visht on Series of Neglect and Insults, Rashtriya Sahara Sept. 10, 2002 p. 8.
19. Manimala on Body of Dalit Woman, Adhi Duniya, New Delhi 2002 Sept. 28, p. 9.
20. Mudrarakshas on Cost of Woman's autonomy, Rashtriya Sahara Sept. 15 2002, p. 8.
21. Mrinal Pande on Satee, Loktantra aur Hum, Hindustan, New Delhi 2002 Aug. 18
22. Point on How Accountable is woman, Rashtriya Sahara August 8, 2002, p. 8.
23. Mrinal Pande on Women and Blind tunnel of Violence, Hindustan, New Delhi 2002 March 8.
24. This is not a female child but a male, Rashtriya Sahara 2002 Nov. 9 p. 9.
25. Rashtriya Sahara, New Delhi, 2002 Nov. 9, p. 9.
26. Rashtriya Sahara, New Delhi Sept. 10, 2002, p. 8.
27. Megha on Excluded from Society in Madhurini, Dainik Bhaskar 1999 Jan 13.
28. Manoj Verma on Code on Prevention of Sexual Abuse (Atrocities), Kusum Nautiyal, Hindustan, New Delhi.
29. Arvind Jain on Womb, Law and Cruelty, Hindustan, New Delhi 2000 March 3, p. 29.
30. Bhanupratap Shukla on "Shamelessness in the name of women's liberation", Dainik Jagran 2002 Oct. 25.
31. Manisha, Truth-False, Have shame, Rashtriya Sahara 2002 Nov. 16, p. 9.
32. Prabhat Ranjan, on About the women, Rashtriya Sahara 2002 Nov. 25, p. 9.
33. The Hindu 2002 Oct. 23, p. 10.
34. Human Rights Watch, Broken People: Caste Violence against India's Untouchables, USA 1999 March, pp. 177-178.
35. Dr. B.R. Ambedkar, The Buddha and His Dhamma, Siddhartha Publication, Mumbai 1957.
36. Dainik Bhaskar dated 12.12.2002, pp. 8 and 12.
37. Dainik Bhaskar, ibid.
38. Dr. Babasaheb Ambedkar: Writings and Speeches, Vol. 17 of Miscellaneous Writings, Edu. Deptt., Govt. of Mah. 2002, Speech of 1942, p. 118.

39. Dr. Ambedkar's Address 1942, ibid., p. 117.
40. Address of Dr. Ambedkar on the Problem of the Scheduled Castes, 1944, p. 119.
41. Dr. Ambedkar's Speech delivered in the meeting of the Scheduled Castes Federation, Bombay on the 6th May 1945 incorporated in the Volume No. 17, pp. 224-229.
42. In 1936 the prostitutes of Bombay held a meeting in Devdas Thackersay Hall on the 16th June in support of conversion movement of Dr. Babasaheb Ambedkar. This meeting was largely attended by men and women belonging to the Devadasi, Patraje, Bhute, Aradhi and Jogiti sects; p. 668, ibid.
43. Dr. Ambedkar's speech on what constitutes Good Government delivered at Lucknow on 25th April 1948, pp. 271-285, ibid.
44. The 55th birthday message of Dr. Ambedkar to the Scheduled Castes, Delhi on 14th April 1946, pp. 262-265, Vol. 17, ibid.
45. Punjab Census Report 1881. para 214.

Chapter - 11

Social Work

Social Science and social work are complementary disciplines. A great man is endowed with sincerity, courage and intellect as Phule and Ranade were in their time and we are inspired to follow in their footprints today. Social scientists lay essential principles from the empirical components and facilitate social work to redress social wrongs of members, groups and communities at large.

It is alarming though that adhering to one single identity has its dangers and religion is no excuse for divorcing reason. Therefore what an organ is for the whole living organism a part is vital for the functioning of the whole society in general.

Becoming proud of our generational dancing for outward civilization of our time is very superficial aspect of the reality and it warrants questioning our existence as adequate manly power and cultured psyche.

Only variegated interests of the diverse social classes and communities can tell the story of a whole truth and thus they have right to be voiced and protected by special and pragmatic concern and safeguards. Especially the weaker and marginalized community deserves more attention and care of the social workers for their amelioration unconditionally.

Thus social reform has precedence over political reform and no law and army can secure social safety unless the public conscience and social psyche is ready to do that job and help auxiliary weapons to get strength to combat social ills.

It is not true that adaptability of religion or of a child for that matter is always wholesome. Sometimes it is a sign of weakness and a cause for shame as when someone adapts himself to eat and digest dung.

Morality of a nation can be seen from the domestic lenses of its inhabitants in day to day routine. Small reforms are harmful for big reforms and small immoralities can bring great calamity of national demoralization from which a great being can save.

Globalization and education in elementary base and technical level have removed local context and brought individual occupational mobility but utterly failed in adjusting present generation with social heritage creating culture-lag in terms of Ogburn and invited suicidal effects on them without contributing to collective social advancement in any aspect.

Gujarat had provided furnace for Ambedkar to go through his life's ordeal and sacrifice for the collective social survival and progress with educational vision and economic prosperity to cheer the nation in caring order of world.

There is further hope for the sons of the soil that Buddha developed compassion after uprooting self-interest and ran for the needy to lighten his burden and get enlightenment for his happy life career and this legacy can light the path of the true soldiers of social aims and ideals.

Do not get disintegrated despite challenging odds surrounding you and have an openness of sky and depth of ocean as your remaining life's flying wing.

Attempt has been made to discuss these points in more details in the following pages of this address.

Introduction

Social Science is a knowledge of social life as a whole and social work is a treatment of social ills and diseases. Under these categories both theoretical and practical issues of society will be discussed.

Society today is infested with some serious old problems like caste, language, religion, tradition, culture and new problems such as violence, terrorism and social change across the communities in the world. This is a great scope for social work and its application for these evils.

Dr. Ambedkar's views are reflected on the concepts pertaining to the part and whole, castes' merit and demerit, independence, principle and rule in this paper.

Dr. Ambedkar equipped himself with academic excellence in Economics, Sociology, History, Public Finance and Administration, Comparative Religion, Comparative Constitutions, Ethics, Education, Philosophy and other branches of social sciences and social work from America, England, and Germany, and put his input in practice of social reconstruction, Labour welfare, Nation-building, social change, state-socialism, removal of caste-class- gender discrimination, exploitation and inequalities by means of social, economic and political democracy based on the eternal principles of equality, liberty and fraternity to establish justice and ethical Dhamma in Indian life realities.

During his lifetime and post-Ambedkar age many a school, college, hostel, library, periodical, satyagraha, struggle and endevour was made and today we see the neglected masses gradually coming up in the forefront in all spheres of life and asking for human rights and fighting to materialize the same within their limited means deriving infinite inspiration from this store of energy, intelligence and light, the Babasaheb Ambedkar as was well known amongst his lovers across the world.

Treatment of society as the heart of Social Work

Social Work Education was founded in western countries. Through Social Work activities in various forms have been a part & parcel of our religious, political, social & cultural life in India, systematic instructions in Social Work education in Indian set up commenced with the establishment of Tata Institure of Social Sciences in Mumbai in 1936. However till 1980 the concept of Social work Education was unknown to Marathwada Region, where first & single college of Social Work Education came in 1992 & only one college of Social Work called Dr.Babasaheb Ambedkar Marathwada University's College of Social Work[1] was established in Aurangabad District in 2007.

Social work is a discipline involving the application of social theory and research methods to study and improve the lives of people, groups, and societies. It used other social sciences as a means. It is a profession committed to the pursuit of social justice, to the enhancement of the quality of life, and to the development of the full potential of each individual, group and community in the society, simultaneously addressing and resolving social issues and economic status at every level of society including the poor and sick. Naturally social workers are concerned with social problems, their causes, their solutions and their human impacts.

The Centre for Ambedkar Studies established at Rani Durgavati Vishwavidyalaya, Jabalpur in July 2006 studies and re-examines the life, works and thought of Babasaheb Ambedkar, an Epoch-Making Thinker of India and helps to ameliorate the condition of the deprived and depressed sections of Indian society.

Theoretically Lena Dominelli's *Social Work: Theory and Practice for a Changing Profession*, may be helpful to help the reader understand the changing context of social work practice as she recognizes social work as a force for change at an individual and structural level.

Mel Gray of the University of Newcastle, Australia calls 'Social work as a *a Dying Profession* and questions its future in 'the rule of white middle-class elites' through 'gendered, classist, homophobic, disablist and racist orientations'? However he resolves the challenge before a social worker by his adage that 'when the going gets tough, the tough gets going'!

Out Institute namely Baniss meant for research and orientation to the weaker sections development with the perspective of Dr. Ambedkar. I remember one student of our Institute belonged to Gujarat while she was pursuing her M.Phil. studies and she selected her dissertation study area her home town and was shocked and alarmed to see that what she never believed was a reality in the study area i.e. domestic violence.

And now you have this new centre called Dr. Ambedkar Thought centre in Vadodara, Gujarat to study and treat social issues and bring about social transformation. So in all one can see a flurry and fervour in taking up social work and apply Ambedkar's thought to uplift the marginalized masses to bring them on par with the generality and this is but a most welcome trend.

Great man

According to Ambedkar Mazzini was wrong to say that 'you may kill men, you cannot kill a great idea' for, 'men are mortal and so are ideas' which do not take roots propriovigore. He further observed that small reforms are the worst enemies of great reforms and we are surviving because our too many enemies in the form of besetting problems have not devoured us yet. You cannot be political Radicals and social Tories and be sincere.

Lecky the great historian said, "The foundation of a Nation's strength and prosperity laid in pure domestic life, in commercial integrity, in a high standard of moral worth, and of public spirit, in simple habits, in courage, uprightness, and a certain soundness and moderation of judgment which springs quite as much from character as from intellect. If you would form a wise judgment of the future of a nation, observe carefully whether these qualities are increasing or decaying, observe carefully what qualities count most in public life. Is character becoming of greater or less importance? Are the men who obtain the highest posts in the nation, men of whom, in private life, irrespective of party, competent judges speak with genuine respect? Are they of sincere convictions, consistent lives and indisputable integrity? It is by observing this current that you can best cast the horoscope of a nation."

Rights since their inception in America and France have been protected not by law but by the social and moral conscience of society. Law can punish a single solitary recalcitrant criminal (Burke) but social conscience-to use the language of Coleridge-is that calm incorruptible legislator of the soul, without whom all other powers would "meet in mere oppugnancy- is the only safeguard of all rights fundamental or non-fundamental."

Intelligentsia divided in schools of orthodox belief with unpolitical outlook on the one hand and modern belief with political view on the other hand must ponder on the right understanding of a social reformer endowed with sincerity, courage and intellect.

Dr. Ambedkar said, "A man is great because he finds a way to save society in its hour of crisis. A great man must be motivated by the dynamics of a social purpose and must act as the scourge and the scavenger of society." Environmental forces whether impersonal or social if they are the first are not the last things. Time may suggest possible new ways. But to step on the right one is not the work of time. It is the work of man.

We are now aware that President of America Barak Obama inherited from his predecessors economic slump from the start and at such economic and social crisis Paul Croogman, a renowned nobel prize winner economist ran to direct him across world depression through his advice of creating employment for at least ten lakh citizens and investment of about of 800 million (arab) dollars in the national social and public work projects while maintaining real estate industry at low interest rate, which is difficult as Government interest rate is at its lowest i.e. (.5) percent.

Social work as profession depends on the spirit of a social worker to whom the systemic conditions may be threatening and only his personal greatness can overcome his and his surrounding mass crisis given the right understanding of the situation and application of three pronged (sincerity, courage and intellect) strategy at right time. For this Dr. Ambedkar's life and struggle is a strong force to get going with it.

Nature of society according to Sociologists

Thomas Ward studied all the text books of sociology published between 1950 and 1967 and came to the conclusion that sociological theories had 27 definitions of its discipline, which are mostly nothing but logical deductions and understood as laws, generalizations, postulates and common idioms. They have originated from the source of their propounders as Comte in France, Herbert Spencer in England and Lester Frank in America, who stressed biological approach for understanding social problems.

Social fact, social development, contract and organism are related to social life. Durkheim held 'every fact regulating man's conduct is a social fact. Social fact is not produced by an individual. Every society has facts already prevailing.' MacIver and Page called 'increase in specialization of units or organs social development'. It has various stages but today because of progress in communication a primitive society can arrive at a developed state without being entered into the mediating stages of social development. Man and society do not originate in the same way. Man has created society for his facility and this approach leans on social contract theory of understanding society while considering society as an organism and an individual as just an organ in the body of that society views organic theory of society as suitable approach.

Unlike Dr. Ambedkar Herbert Spencer believed that today the ancient societies have ended and new societies are being formed. But in India this is not the case as Dr. Ambedkar observed in his book on nation-building, 'What Congress and Gandhi Have done to the Untouchables?' This is not the book alarming critique on Congress and Mahatma but it is a new vision into reconstruction of Bharat.

How mutual relationship of society and individual impacts each other is described in the views of Charles Cooley, Parsons and Merton when they said that 'individuals by their mutual relationship form society, whereas society endevours to make an individual a social being'. There is a functional relationship among the units of structure as a systematized form of mutually related institutions, agencies and social norms, as well as statuses and roles assumed by every member of a group in society. System goes on while an individual dies and after his death social system survives and runs. Persons alone make culture. But Merton observed that cultural factor is not always functional to all societies. Religion functions to relieve a group of its prevailing tension. However industrialization and urbanization as civilization called globalization, modernization, post-modernization etc., set in dis-organizational changes in society during the end of 18th and beginning of 19th centuries that brought in structural-functional approach of society to question.

Despite the fact that the above structural-functional approach had been used by Einstein in Physics, C. Bernard in Physiology, Carrel in Biology, White Head in Philosophy, Cobler in Psychology, T. Litt. in Law it neglected historical factor. For MacIver and Page "Society" meant cooperation crossed by conflict, for Ambedkar it meant participation and circulation. George Simmel defined conflict positively and stated that conflict as feeling never upsets equilibrium of society in contrast to thinkers during the period between 1907 and 1930. Similarly Dr. Ambedkar said "Hate and love are forces for a social worker to employ in his profession, greater their intensity stronger will be their results, I dislike Jinnah and Gandhi because I love nation more.

Like participation and circulation concepts of Ambedkar Homans' and Peter Blau's Social Exchange is indicative of social cooperation and precedes monetary system in the form of exchange of objects. Exchange of economic goods is possible only after individual's intellectual and psychological decision in social field. Exchange occurring between two persons at least is indicative of its social aspect and feeling of need by man is expressive of his intellectual and psychological side. Exchange does not give rise to social relations, but social relations induce possibilities of exchange. In 1970s Homans remained adhered to social behaviorism and distinguished animal and human conduct in degrees, not in quality. Peter Blau also told that social exchange is different from economic exchange in that exchange takes place when goods, services and other benefits are exchanged in anticipation of their return in equal proportion. To secure future services or surrender from others is to gain power, in which exchange takes place but not in physical restraint or 'boycott' as Ambedkar denounced. This exchange power is a result of some conditions of exchange or lack of those conditions. By giving economic or social assistance to a person and putting him under pressure are beneficial, for we desire that maximum people in society should owe to us, through whom we can derive maximum power and be successful. Thus exchange of gratitude benefits personal interest and requires social relationship.

Social traditions in all differentiations as accumulated legacy of any society influence all levels of an organization, such as value system, social structure and individual structure said Professor Yogendra Singh in his *Tradition and Modernity in India.* We are invaded by the issues of culturalization, westernization, ruralization (downward devolution), universalization and violence and terrorism. The last has been spreading in the unequivocal or equivocal forms as in Khalistan demand of Khalsa faction in Punjab, Hizbul aggression supported by Pakistan in Kashmir, Naxalite terrorism in Bengal and Bihar, Bodo and Ulma movements in Assam etc. as the principal examples of the same. Amartya Sen pointed out that this terrorism as a form of violence rests on singular unique identity.

It is possible to understand the nature of social life through any social approach, whether structure, exchange, contract, organism, identity and so on but the issue is how to deal with problems faced by victims of such social conditions immediately and at its critical juncture unaided by any social assistance. That is why social conscience and public opinion in democratic set up are assets of saving men from peril and developing the same for future contingencies.

How unique Identity leads to Violence

As referred to above Amartya Sen said, "In our normal lives, we see ourselves as members of a variety of groups we belong to all of them. Central to leading a human life, therefore, are the responsibilities of choice and reasoning. The imposition of an allegedly unique identity is often a crucial component of the "martial art" of fomenting sectarian confrontation. The uniquely partitioned world is much more divisive than the universe of plural and diverse categories that shape the world in which we live."

People can not be uniquely categorized based on religion or culture. When interpersonal relations are seen in singular intergroup terms, paying no attention to other groups (involving economic, social, political, or other cultural connections), then much of importance in human life is altogether lost, and individuals are put into little boxes.

The world of practice is systematically fed by the confusion between having a religion and ignoring the need for reasoning-and for freedom of thought- in deciding on matters that need not be "locked up" by religious faith. Amartya Sen emphasized intellect, courage and moral aspects when he referred to visionary leaders of civil society such as Asma Jahangir and I.A. Rehman in Pakistan, fighting for the freedoms of women, minorities, and other threatened people, Pakistani economist and former finance minister, Mahbub ul Haq, who pioneered in the world the Human development approach to understanding economic and social progress by judging progress not merely by the growth of gross national product but by the enhancement of people's living conditions, The foreign minister of Singapore, who, at the World Conference on Human Rights in Vienna in 1993 warned the "universal recognition of the ideal of human rights can be harmful if universalism is used to deny or mar the reality of diversity, The Chinese delegation and Chinese foreign Minister who put on record "regional diversity" in the prescriptive framework adopted in the declarations and the proposition that the Asian priorities demand that "Individuals must put the states' rights before their own respectively.

As for the global challenge of terrorism, he expected from the world leaders working against it, rather greater clarity of thought and recognition of multiple identities. In the downplaying of political and social identities as opposed to religious identity, it is civil society that has been the loser, precisely at a time when there is a great need to strengthen it. (p. 83).

Mr. Sen held democracy as primarily about public reasoning, and debates, "global doubts", discontent are a major global phenomenon, and signs of its concern for implicitly humanitarian ethics and politics across the world.There is a compelling need in the contemporary world to ask questions not only about the economics and politics of globalization, but also about the values, ethics, and sense of belonging that shape our conception of the global world. Dr. Ambedkar defined democracy not only as a form of government but also as a form of society also.

Is a part insignificant in the Whole?

Realizing that a vital part of any national life cannot be ignored the H.M.G.made constitutional changes in 1920 and called RTC to be represented by Untouchables separately and independently of Congress or any other political party. The govt. of India Act 1935 also recognized the Untouchables a minority. According to Mr. Gandhi's own admission in his weekly called the Harijan of 21st October 1939 the Untouchables were the only real minority in India. British Government overruled Mr. Gandhi and recognized Untouchables as separate and distinct element in national life of India by their Award entitled to same safeguards as other minorities of India such as Muslim, Indian Christians etc., Cripps proposal of 1942 also marked separate representation of Untouchables in Constituent Assembly. Simla Conference of June, 1945 also agreed that untouchables were a separate and distinct element in the national life of India. Lord Linlithgow at Orient club, Bombay on January 10, 1940 and in the statement dated 8th August 1940 spoke that the established policy of H.M.G. was to guarantee safeguard to Muslim minority and Scheduled castes and not to transfer their responsibility for peace and welfare of India to any other government whose authority was directly denied by large and powerful elements in India's national life. Rt. Hon'ble Mr. L.S. Amery, Secretary of State for India, in House of Commons on 14.8.1940 declared Untouchables a community outside the main body of Hindu community which is represented by Congress, and the extract from letter by Lord Wavell to Mr. Gandhi dated 15.8.1944, p. 541 revealed that their offer was made conditional upon framing of a constitution agreed by main elements of India's national life and safeguard interest of racial and religious minorities of Depressed classes and Indian states.

But contrary to this the Cabinet Mission's first statements of May 16, 1946 and the supplementary statement of May 25, 1946 recognized only three communities (1) Hindus, (2) Muslims and (3) Sikhs for political purpose at the cost of the Depressed classes, power of legislature of a free India altering constitution and abrogating clause dealing with protection of minorities and, took no note of admission by Sir Stafford Cripps that the system of election of the untouchables as determined by the Poona Pact was iniquitous and, justified its decision on results of elections to Provincial legislature Assembly of February 1948 in which causes of failure of DCs in that election were (1) Hindu electorate were anti-British and did not cooperate willingly in war effect and (2) Scheduled castes were pro-British and cooperated in war effort.

Ambedkar suggested that the constitution framed by constituent assembly contained clauses putting limitations on constituent powers of Indian legislature and prescribing conditions precedent to be fulfilled before alterations in minority safeguards are made as provided in the constitution of USA and Australia. (Vol. 10, p. 549 Cabinet Mission and Untouchables).

Thus all the forces including the British, Congress and Gandhi ignored a part and leaned on the classist prejudice ignoring the other vital parts of the whole and missed the opportunity of rectifying the structure of Indian society for weal, welfare and happiness of "sarvajana", to use the phrase of UP Government CM Mayavati.

Whether India is an ancient society or modern society

What is the mark of an anciency and modernity? Dr. Ambedkar attached great importance to the passage in the Bible which read conversation between Mother-in-law Naomi and daughter-in-law Ruth thus, "(11) And Naomi said, Turn again, my daughters; why will ye go with me? (12) — go your way – (14) And they lifted up their voice, and (15) And she said, Behold thy sister-in-law is gone back unto her people, and unto her gods; return thou after thy sister-in-law. (16) And Ruth said, Intreat me not to leave them; or to return from following after thee; for wither thou goest, I will go; and where thou lodgest, I will lodge; *thy people shall be my people, and thy God my God.* (17) Where thou diest, will I die, and there will be buried; the LORD do so to me, and more also, if ought but death part thee and me". Here in this passage the reference to God as associated part of the human group signified its earlier phase of social life and this has a sociological value and Prof. Smith, also agred that it helped to distinguish modern society from ancient society. Ruth's statement "Thy people shall be my people and thy God my God" defined ancient society by its most dominant characteristic namely that it was a society of man plus God while modern society is a society of men only. Dr Ambedkar included women also in men and said "Pray remember that in men I include women also.

About this passage Ambedkar said to the addressee "As an oriental I belong to a society which is still ancient and in which God is a much more important member than man is." Even man is classified into two as governing and as servile, with sympathy for some and antipathy for others, the best man and the worst man belonging to governing class and servile class respectively and in attitude towards each other as much fratricidal as two opposing nationalities can be.

In India ancient tradition and modern civilization are coexisting. Even to this day in villages and towns or inland and abroad Indians travel with a kit of their deities securely fastened to their baggage. Dr. Ambedkar advised that "Nothing should be done whereby the best shall be superseded by one who is only better and the better by one who is merely good and the good by one who is bad…"

How to bring different big and small communities together

Community of purposes and unity of thought can help bring different communities together.The Mutiny of 1857 changed British attitude towards Indians. The days of Lawrence to hold victory by sword' are gone. Argument of British Government against India's freedom that Indians had incapacity for parliamentary institutions and Lord Rippon's attempt to give political training to Indians in Local self-government and Montagu-Chelmsford's reform in the field of provincial government changed to give way to the India's right to freedom and independence, frame constitution as suggested by Cripps proposal. But this change was not so much as to lift a condition before Indians for independence that their constitution had concurrence of the important elements in the national life of the country.

Indians also changed their inferiority complex and upto 1886, they learnt who ruled them and how they were ruled. The Congress upto 1910 agitated for good Government. It demanded self-government first. During 1919 Montagu-Chelmsford reform they demanded for self-government. Their 1917 Memorandum of the Nineteen Indians were content with diarchy in the Provinces. They superseded Sir Dinshaw Watcha and Mr. Samartha's 'we are not fit for responsible Government' as Mr. Montagu noted in His

Indian Diary, p. 147. In 1930 Congress resolution insisted on Independence, and went ahead of Mr. Gandhi's contentment with Provincial autonomy as he revealed at RTC. The representatives of the Non-Congress parties at the RTC are credited with the 1935 Government of India Act containing elements of responsibility at the centre. As to the unity of thought Indians' non-accord on the sort of constitution they wanted for their country there was halt in this direction from 1939.

Between 1920 and 1942, demonstrations staged by Congressmen of one form or the other by weapons of-non-co-operation, Boycott, Civil Disobedience and Fast could not bring unity of mind among communities in India. The reckless use of sanctions had made partition of India starker, surer and nearer. It was only during the shortlived Khilafat agitation that Muslims once took part in it, the untouchables never took part in it. They feared that freedom of India would establish Hindu domination which was sure to close to them and for ever all prospect of life, liberty and pursuit of happiness and that they would be made the hewers of wood and drawers of water. They did not wish to be placed under Hindu Raj in which the governing class would be the Bania and the Brahmin with low class Hindus as their policemen, all of whom have been the hereditary enemies of the Untouchables. Free India should be made safe for democracy. The Congress regarded the freedom of India from British Imperialism to be the be-all and end-all of Indian nationalism. This was the contention of the matter of oneness in intention.

The Untouchables were anxious to make India safe for democracy, while the Congress, if it was not opposed to democracy, was certainly opposed to creating conditions which would make democracy real. Congress opposed safeguards or checks or balances granted by every constitution to keep the political field a free pasture for the Hindu Majority by using nationalism as a cloak for a free field for rank communalism. So right to speak in the name of the country formed a vital issue and those who did not accept this had no alternative but to challenge it.

The untouchables could not forget the fate of the Negroes. It was to prevent such treachery that they had taken the attitude with regard to Fight for Freedom. In doing this they only followed Burke's advice, who had said, "It is better to be accused of timidity than to be ruined by over confident security."

But the Congress opposed the British proposal on the grounds that the condition prescribed by the British Government put a veto on freedom of

India in the hands of the Untouchables and that British Government was not honest.

The Untouchables however did not make unreasonable demands as Carson's demand to Redmond that "Damn your safeguards. We don't wish to be ruled by you". notwithstanding the unsocial and undemocratic character of its ethics, provided the constitution gave them reasonable safeguards. But what the Congress wished was a free India with full, unrestricted freedom to the Hindus in a free India to dispose of the Untouchables in any way they liked. So Untouchables refused to take part in such a dishonest agitation, elevated though it may be by such high sounding name as "Fight for Freedom"!

Safeguards for fearing community

The evolution of the Indian Constitution appeared to Ambedkar to have established a sort of a logical syllogism. In dealing with it one must deal as one is required to do with a syllogism, in which both conclusion as well as the premise are fundamental. And to close the argument it is not enough to deal with the conclusion and omit to examine the premise.

You cannot have feeling of union and separation at the same time. A common religion means a common cycle of participation. Cults have such common cycle of participation. Social sense is indicative of connubium and commensalism. When there is no touch, no association, only savarnas and avarnas, chaturvarnikas and panchamas how can there be any mode of intermingling and loving. If the untouchables and the Hindus were parts of one single community by religion because both worshipped same gods, go to same pilgrimages, hold same supernatural beliefs and regard stones, trees, mountains sacred then the Belgians, Dutch, Norwegians, Swedes, Germans, French, Italians, Slaves, etc. are all Christians by religion and so should be parts of one single community as they worship the same god and accept Jesus as their saviour, have same religious beliefs, and a complete religious unity between all of them in thought, worship and beliefs. Yet the French, Germans and Italians and the rest are not a single community. The Whites and the Negroes in the USA too have a common religion as both of them are Christians, yet the two on that account cannot form a single community. Indian Christians, Europeans and Anglo Indians also profess and follow the same religion yet they do not form one single community. There are Sikhs, Mazbi Sikhs and Ramdasia Sikhs, all professing Sikkhism but not forming one community. The fallacy of common religion is to presume social union and of separate religion social disunity. There is no concomitance between the two and that the Sikhs and the Hindus differ in religion but they are not socially separate. They dine together; they marry together; they live together. In a Hindu family one son may be a Sikh, another a Hindu. Religious difference does not break the social nexus. The Musalmans and the Indian Christians have been given separate political recognition not because they were Muslims or Christians but fundamentally because they formed in fact separate elements from the Hindus.

Religion is a binding force among the Europeans but it is not powerful enough to withstand other forces such as the sentiment of race tending to divide society. Between Hindus and Sikhs religions are separate but there is no social separation. The worst case is this that there is religion and separation exists because religion prescribed it. Caste is another name for separation and untouchability typifies the extremist form of separation of community from community. They are among the foremost observances prescribed by Hinduism in the conduct of one's daily life.

The dogma and conduct of caste and untouchability is not mere imaginary as between the Portuguese and their rivals for colonial possessions. It is not like the colour line which has length but no breadth and which one may observe or one may not observe, it is not like the race line, which involves distinction but no discrimination. Factually the Hindus and the Untouchables are divided by a fence made of barbed wire. Notionally it is *cordon sanitaire* which the Untouchables have never been allowed to cross and can never hope to cross.

Hinduism and social union are incompatible. By its very genius Hinduism believes in social separation which is another name for social disunity and even creates social separation. If Hindus wish to be one they will have to discard Hinduism.

Social Reform as action project against social ills

The sickness of Indian society in the form of the Untouchables remained under the Hindu God and the Hindu State until the advent of the British. Sick in vision but sound in body they helped the East India Company conquer India and the latter under their system of compulsory education for Indian soldiers and their children both male and female gave them a new vision and new value.

Social reform began with Raja Ram Mohan Roy in Bengal and from there had spread all over India and ultimately culminated in the formation of the Indian Social Reform Conference, with its slogan of Social Reform before political reform by Ranade (1846-1901). Social reform conference was killed and the problem of untouchability was declared social by the killers. But unlike the problems of dowry, widow remarriage, age of consent, etc., the untouchability problem is a problem of securing to a minority liberty and equality of opportunity at the hands of a hostile majority which believed in the denial of liberty and equal opportunity to the minority and conspired to enforce its policy on the minority. Viewed in this light, the problem of the Untouchables is fundamentally a political problem.

Even if it were a social problem political recognition of and political safeguards for the security of the untouchables should not retard their social unification with the Hindus if there is a genuine desire to set in motion processes which will bring about such a result. How can social solidarity between the Hindus and the Untouchables be advanced by one day devoted to joint voting if for the rest of the five years they are leading severely separate lives and how can one day devoted to separate voting in the course of five years make greater separation than what already exists or contrarywise how can one day in five years devoted to separate voting prevent those who wish to work for union from carrying out their purposes.

Every society consists of groups associated together in various ways and for various purposes. Some are like kindred closely bound together by blood or language, some are of the nature of social classes differentiated on the basis of rank and status. Others are religious associations upholding particular dogmas, including political parties and industrial corporations, criminal gangs and so on in an endless variety with differing aims and bound together some loosely some closely by differing degrees of affinity. But stating that Castes in India are not different from group and classes in Europe and America is an arrant nonsense. They may be same to look at. But isolation and exclusiveness are the hall-marks of the castes in India, which are maintained as matter not of routine but of faith none of which characteristics is to be found in the group or class system of Europe or America. When group interest mischief is counteracted by non-political means then constitutional means is not a necessity. Endosmosis or a broadening and socialization of its aims and purposes between groups in Europe affects dispositions and produces a society which can be depended upon for *community of thought, harmony of purposes and unity of action*. In India exclusiveness and isolation of castes have no interaction and no modification of aims and objects. What a caste or a combination of castes regard "as their own interest" as against other castes remains as sacred and inviolate as ever. The fact that they mingle and cooperate does not alter their character. These acts of cooperation are mechanical and not social. Individuals use one another so as to get desired results, without reference to the emotional and intellectual disposition. The fact that they give and take orders modify actions and results. But it does not affect their dispositions. That being the case; the Indian constitution must provide safeguards to prevent castes with "their own interests" from doing mischief to other helpless castes.

Mutual relations of the groups are not the same everywhere. In one society groups may be only non-social in their attitude towards one another. But in another they may be antisocial. And the class which has been the victim of antisocial spirit must be given protection by proper safeguards. In India the castes are not merely nonsocial. Often they are anti-social to allow water from well, entry in schools, travel in buses and the same railway compartment, wear clean clothes, jewellery, put tiles on the roofs of the houses, to own land, keep cattle, sit when superior is standing, which are emanations of the permanent anti-social attitude against the victims.

Untouchability is vanishing. Is it? Untouchability as touch-me-not-ism and as a mental attitude manifesting itself in social discrimination are two different things. The former may be vanishing gradually in towns in some degrees. You cannot untwist a two-thousand-year-twist of the human mind and turn it in the opposite direction.

Is Adaptability of a Religion a virtue?

Capacity of adaptability is not always a virtue. It is a great vice also. Many people would not regard such a capacity in a religion as a virtue to be proud of just as no one would think highly of a child because it has developed the capacity to eat dung and digest it. The best adaptability of Hinduism is its adjustability of Allahupanishad which the Brahmins of the time of Akbar produced to give a place to his Dine-Ilahi within Hinduism and to recognize it as the seventh system of Hindu philosophy. The beef-eating Hinduism absorbed the non-violence theory of Buddhism and became a religion of vegetarianism. But it has never been able to absorb the untouchables or to remove the bar of untouchability.

Loss of untouchability means much more loss to the interest group of 75 crores of Hindus served by 25 crores of Untouchables to maintain their pomp and show, pride and dignity befitting a master class which cannot be fostered and sustained unless there is beneath it a servile class to look down upon, to be used as forced labour, to work on mere pittance, as scavengers and sweepers, as lower job holders and as shock absorbers in slumps and deadweights in booms to be fired first and employed last respectively.

Untouchability is more than a religious system. It is also an economic system which is worse than slavery in which the master takes no responsibility for the maintenance of the enslaved untouchable, exploits without obligation, takes liberty to exploit not unmitigatedly but uncontrolledly under absence of independent public opinion and impartial machinery of administration, police and judiciary. For untouchability to vanish it is the Hindu who must change.

How to combat Moral Wrong?

One must have righteous indignation against a moral wrong. Righteous indignation against a moral wrong requires awakening to the sense of putting oneself with God and man and give up the economic and social advantages which untouchability gives. History shows that where ethics and economics come in conflict victory is always with economics. It would be most stupid-if not criminal-to take vanishing of untouchability into account in considering the demands of the untouchables for constitutional safeguards and ignore the hard facts of the present and their certainty to continue in the immediate future.

The reason for cessation of the 1930 movement was the deficiency on the part of some leaders to give up their vested interest, the public had the only blame that they could not drive out such leaders on one side and produce other dauntless heroes. (p. 56).It is well known that the Russian nation builder Lenin would give the pieces of dried bread kept on his desk for others to be fed while starving himself. Karl Max spent his whole life in misery in anticipation of seeing the proletariats of the world out of suffering. More than two and half millennium ago Siddhartha Gautam Buddha had abandoned his royal homely life in order that the humanity struggling in the midst of self-interest could lead life ever so happily.

Social Science and Social Work in Contemporary situation

Buddha said "We shall be loving men amidst hating people". There is need of loving culture in the spirit of the Moghul prince, Dara Shikoh, who had translated the Upanishads, of Muslim Pathan rulers of Bengal, who arranged translations of the Sanskrit Mahabharata and Ramayana, and Buddhist scholars, who revived literary tastes of our traditions. There is need of being critic in the spirit of Pundit Javali, who not only not treated Rama as God, but called his actions 'foolish'. There is need of reviving cultural heritage of India after a Buddhist emperor of India, Ashoka in the third century BCE, who laid down the oldest rules for conducting debates and disputations with the opponents being 'duly honoured in every way on all occasions', continued by Mughal emperor Akbar in 1590 when the Inquisition was in full swing in Europe.

Amartya Sen believed that "The argumentative tradition, if used with deliberation and commitment, can also be extremely important in resisting social inequalities and in removing poverty and deprivation. Voice is a crucial component of the pursuit of social justice. The critical voice was the traditional ally of the aggrieved, and participation in argument is a general opportunity, involving members of disadvantaged groups. Let no one entertain that India is the land of religions, the country of uncritical faiths and unquestioned practices and analytical reasoning and critique are only western or European traditions?

The Indian scenario seems bleak as women and downtrodden men became the victims of dominant interest. During the year 2006-2007 Bindu Devi, Ramffajju Manjhi, Bhola Chowdhary, and Sanoj Paswanin in Bihar; Rakesh in Haryana; Asha, Vidhya, Hakim Jatav, and Urmila in Madhya Pradesh; Asha, Bhaiyalal, and Madhukar in Maharashtra; Bant Singh in Punjab; a 14 year old mentally challenged girl in Rajasthan; Anju, Mukesh, and Puja in Uttar Pradesh have been victims of such heinous atrocities. Notwithstanding this ogre under anti-social conditions and political safeguards Dalits have long way to go in literacy and education in comparison to the general literacy in terms of percentage as shown in the following table:

Decade	*Literacy percentage gap between Dalit SC/ST Males and General Males*	*Literacy percentage gap between Dalit Females and General Females*	*Literacy percentage gap between SC-STs & Non-SC-STs*
1951-61	12.66	9.66	16.48
1961-71	14.78	12.28	17.09
1971-81	18.24	16.85	12.83
1981-91	18.78	15.53	02.25
1991-01	18.53	NA	NA

This is to be observed that on gender line literacy gap is more than on caste line.

A century earlier the report of the Board of Education of the Bombay Presidency for the year 1850-51 quoted the most liberal and large-hearted administrator, Mr. Elphinstone's observation, that "The missionaries find the lowest classes as the best pupils…they are not only the most despised, but among the least numerous of the great division of society and if your system of education first took root among them, we might find ourselves at the head of a new class superior to the rest in useful knowledge, but hated and despised by the castes to whom their new attainments would always induce to prefer them."

Social atrocities caused economic degradations also. One of the most serious causes of chronic poverty in India is social discrimination between genders, ages, ethnicity, castes and races, and impairments. The composition of chronic poor in India consisted SCs and STs in agricultural and casual labour, unskilled sector, food insecurity and access to assets. Even in developed state such as Gujarat the very poor and poor in rural and urban areas were estimated at 7 and 22, and 12 and 28 percentages of its population in 1993-94. Fortunately the India's 69 most backward districts (2003) did not include those in Gujarat state. India's global position on human development is 0.619, not better than 0.743 (of Sri Lanka in 2005) and gender development index is 0.600, worse than 0.525 (of Pakistan in 2005). However poverty ratio in Gujarat in 2006-07 was 4, which is below advanced state's percentage of poverty i.e. 9 (2004-05). During the year 2006-07 the percentage of people living below poverty line in India is 30 approximately. Poverty ratio in rural-urban combined during rediscovery of poverty regime in 2007 was 19.3 per cent. Out of 14 million Dalits only 1.1 million (8%) made use of reservation in 1991. Under globalization privatization hit reservation policy, the sole contributor to advancement of the Dalits.

Gujarat in relation to Ambedkar's Life Events

Gujarat is related to the life events of Dr. Ambedkar also. He wrote penta-linguistic dictionary of Pali in Gujrati also alongside Marathi, Hindi, and English. Pali words are similar to Gujrati as these examples show:

Pali	*Gujarati*
akallo	Ashakya
akalo	Akalik
akusalo	Akushal
Akkodho, akkodhano	Akrodh
akhando	Akhand
akhilo	Akhu(all)
akha	Ankh
Akkharam, akkharo, akkharso	Akshar
akkharam	Akshay
akkhata	Jo kathan kareche te
akkhayika	Akhyan
agacchati	Avavum (come)
agato	Nahi gayelo
agadho	Agadh

(*Contd...*)

aganno	Agewan (chief)
aggato	Agal अगळ
aggalo	अडगरो
aggi	Agni
ankuro	Ankur
anganam	Angan
ankhattho	Angutha
ankhali	Angali
acchariyo	Ashcharyajanak
ajjatagge	Aaj pachi (from this day)

A 87 year old Gujrati from Visnagari town in Gujrat namely Babaldas B. Chavda (94389 60548) narrated his life story in the national seminar at our Institue in Mhow on last October 2008 that his surname was Chava but he changed it to Chavda to hide his identity of caste and confuse Indians to wonder whether he belonged to higher Rajput caste or SC to escape contempt of casteist people in India today.

But even 97 years ago the event in Dr. Ambedkar's life was a testimony to such occurrence in Indian society. When the graduate Ambedkar was appointed as a Deputy collector at Visnagar on 17th January 1913 by the Maharaja of Baroda State Sayajirao Gaikawad the local orthodox Hindu of Visnagar boycotted him, knowing that Dr. Ambedkar belonged to the Untouchable or downtrodden caste. He immediately left for Baroda on the same day. He discussed the matter with Maharaja, the latter then appointed him as an Lieutenant of Baroda State. No sooner the fifteen days elapsed than he was compelled to resign his such high official post. The incident is well known. He was looking for rented accommodation and no one let him in in the entire city because of his untouchability. So he too showed him off as Parasi to accommodate him in Parsi dharmashala in Vadodara but notwithstanding his disguise he was detected who he was and maltreated by the so called advanced Parsi community members of the time so much so that seated under the shade of a Banyan tree tears rolled on his cheeks as he was not spared a single day to look for another shelter. This took place in about 1917. How to expect change in society when social consciousness is not prepared to change and religion and philosophy preached vasudaiva kutumbakam on paper and acted contrary in practice. All is Brahma in speech but no one at par with Brahman in reality. There was cruel perversion in ethics and philosophy that denied manhood to Indian man and woman.

Buddhist culture as representative of Indian true spirit of Bharat

In the light of Buddha and Kabeer, Phule and Ranade, the whole India and world are bound to reconsider Ambedkar's slogan for Education, Agitation and Organization of new world order with great men as characters of sincerity, courage and intellect.

As a part of Indian culture Buddhist thinkers such as Nagarjuna, Vasubandhu, Dignag, Dharmakirti, Prajnakaragupta and Jnanashri developed Nyaya philosophy of the Brahmin Pundits Akshapada, Vatsyayan, Vachaspati, Udayanacharya, and Gangeshopadhyaya. Parallel to Panini was Chandragomin and to Katyayana and Patanjali were Jayaditya and Jinendrabuddhi and Purushottamadasa and alike hailing from Buddhist tradition during the Nalanda Age.

Lexicographer Amarsinha (Buddhist), Ayurvedic chemistry master Nagarjuna were wellknown. Buddhist Kalidas and Dandi were Ashvaghosha, and Chandragomin and Harsha. The pioneers in Apabhransha poetry impacting nirguna poetical trend were the 84 siddhas. Places of sculptures such as Sanchi, Bharhut, Gandhar, Mathura and Amravati (Dhanyakataka) are world known; of painting Ajanta, Bagh, Alchi and Sumra are unforgettable; and of architecture Ajanta,Ellora, Karla and Bhaja are on the tongues of indigenous and foreign admirers. Needless to stress that Ambedkar's philosophy had roots in Buddhism and mission to make the Indians realize that the social philosophy affirming a life of liberty, equality, and fraternity cannot be found elsewhere but in Buddha's Bharat alone.

Change through remaining life's flying wing

According to the Professor of Rajiv Gandhi Chair, Barkatullah University, Bhopal "Both the concepts of education and the concept of social justice are time specific and therefore dynamic. Both the Bhagavadgita and the Laws of Manu emphasized that it is better to perform one's own duties poorly, even to die doing so, than to perform another's well. And the proper discharge of the duties of one's station will be rewarded in the next life. This practice was accepted and encouraged by the existing value system and the dominant public opinion. It is said that village was a self sufficient republic and collectiveness was the main binding force which united and sustained self sufficiency of Indian society. Education was inequalizer and those who possessed it had higher social status and those who could not do so, had lower social status. Eklavya during the Mahabharat and Shambuk during Ramayana period were perceived as violators of normative structure of Vasudaiva kutumbakama. Education during those days was not only informal, privately managed but also directed to isolation and exclusion for vast majority of Indian population especially women, poor and all those who are today termed as marginalized population. During this modern period also education could not include the excluded population. British education created and contributed to the formation of India within Bharat. Education could not contribute to social justice. Seed of inequality was sown by Varna system and its doctrine became big tree".

Education and Perception of industry as the temples of modern India proved to be poles apart. If one organ of society will go downward and the other in the opposite direction the result will be chaos called "cultural lag" by Ogburn. Beteille (1965) presented case of Shripuram village in which the Brahmins (first recipient of modern education) did not even recognize those of other castes in their count of the village's population, and non-Brahmin caste Hindus likewise did not count untouchables (p. 25). This situation is a routined affair in Indian society.

Modern education eroded tribal culture who knew about Mahatma Gandhi but not about their own social reformers from their own locality. They know about modern cough syrup but they did not know about herbs and medicinal plants meant for removal of cough available in their own locality. Education made them unfit to compete for education-based-new occupation. Hence they are neither local nor global. Their bride-price system was replaced by dowry system for educated tribal youth. There is positive correlation between education and dowry.

The new education system eroded the feeling of collectivity. Their leadership is from upper castes and existence of poverty, illiteracy, hunger deaths, crime against women, poor quality education in rural schools, casteism, regionalism, and corruption are rife in their locality. New change agents are also suffering from the trauma of "deresponbilization" as their predecessors suffered.

Modernization in India contributed to economic development without social change. Y.B. Damle in one of his articles rightly said that modern education is an effective instrument of occupational and social mobility in individual's life. It is not an effective instrument of social change in Indian society. Technical education is global minus local. Its result in increase of middle class in size and national economy created bottlenecks between regions and communities. Students from marginalized group entering more technical education suffered from cultural conflict and unable to adjust they committed suicides as a Mumbai IIT Dalit student is an example.

Because of coming of globalization gap between state and society is further accelerated. In the past there was collective voice of protest against state led oppression but increasing individualism coupled with lust in favour of consumer culture and modern life style have damaged the voice of collective protest. Hence the situation compels us to debate the thought and philosophy of Ambedkar as an argumentative Indian to borrow the phraseology of Professor Amartya Sen and instill hope among the hopeless during this crisis.

To sum up there is no better piece than an excerpt from 2008 Nobel Prize winner French poet, Jean-Marie Gustav Le Clazio's poem on "Flood" as under:

A lot more takes place around me

I do not disintegrate

There is in my blood…

An openness of sky
And depth of an ocean-
Perhaps this is the remaining life's take flying wing…

Conclusion and recommendations

1. Infinite inspiration on weaker sections of Babasaheb Ambedkar cannot be exaggerated. More incentive and facility to the study of Ambedkar Thought is the need of the day.
2. Social work as profession depends on the spirit of a social worker to whom the systemic conditions may be threatening and only his personal greatness can overcome his and his surrounding mass crisis given the right understanding of the situation and application of three pronged (sincerity, courage and intellect) strategy at right time. For this Dr. Ambedkar's life and struggle is a strong force to get going with it.
3. Great man upholds social reform prior to political reform since all reforms depend for their success and safety on social foundations of greatness consisting morality, courage and understanding.
4. It is possible to understand the nature of social life through any social approach, whether structure, exchange, contract, organism, identity and so on but the issue is how to deal with problems faced by victims of such social conditions immediately and at its critical juncture unaided by any social assistance. That is why social conscience and public opinion in democratic set up are assets of

saving men from peril and developing the same for future contingencies.

5. Thus unique identity and unquestioned authority are the causes of terrorism and violence and extremism in the world and doors of one's head, heart and mind are to be slammed open for widening circle of human understanding and relationship of close affinity.
6. However numerically small any group might be its unique culture and identity cannot be destroyed by a majority iniquitous authority. That is why safeguard convention is in vogue in advanced countries like Australia and America. The same can be provided in respect of the Indian marginalized weaker sections also.
7. In India ancient tradition and modern civilization are coexisting. Even to this day in villages and towns or inland and abroad Indians travel with a kit of their deities securely fastened to their baggage. Dr. Ambedkar advised that "Nothing should be done whereby the best shall be superseded by one who is only better and the better by one who is merely good and the good by one who is bad......".
8. Thus when sympathy and concern divorce each other separation and partition entertain the interests. Feeling of our men and belongingness to one was missing then and it has not been cultivated appreciably even to this day. So Dr. Ambedkar's call for fraternity in polity and society can make the plan of unification of India more successful.
9. Thus putting a bar on any group or community by the power of majority strength is to put it under eternal fear and cordon sanitatire to use the technical term and to withstand this the big brother needs to take pain in broadening his view and wish to incorporate the neglected and despised one in his bosom.
10. For a social worker community of thought, harmony of purpose and unity of action is to be comprehended clearly and nature of mechanical unity and inner feeling and intention distinguished from group to group and society to society is to be detected to succeed in his mission of social transformation since groups and associations are not equally on particular stage of social process of endosmosis and need to be treated in a particular specialized skill or manner.
11. Adaptability is not always a virtue. Sometimes it turns out to be stupidity and hence social worker is advised to be alert on this by rigorous observation and experimental verification of the truth.

12. By shunning avarice in ugly means of profiteering from economic gain of untouchability one can avoid wrong in morality. Buddha advised to uphold right understanding, right morality and right clarity of mind to be morally disposed.
13. By knowing the facts of the situations in the matter of atrocity, poverty, ethics, religion, education, culture and politics one can express one's voice against the malpractices and uphold what is right despite numerous opposing frownings in accordance with the saying, "They are coward who dare not be in the right with two or three" - Cowell.
14. Gujara put Ambedkar in the furnace of severest ordeal and Dr. Ambedkar came out successfuly as tried and tested great man.
15. Akkodhena jine kodham is the legacy of Buddha and morally it is far superior to all varieties of morals and principles preached by every religion in the world. So it is a true spirit of ideal Bharat and every worker in social field cannot do without it as Yash in ancient Aparantaka showed.
16. The remainder of time from our life is not be wasted as insignificant moment and has to be used to give last blow to the mighty anti-social challenge. So do not surrender and fight unto the last for removal of disgrace of our society in the name of caste, untouchability, extremism or terrorism.

References

1. Principal Smt.Hemlata Kulkarni, Opp. Chemistry Deptt. University Campus, Aurangabad, **Telephone Nos:**- 0240-2403398,2403387, **Fax**:-240-03113, 2403335 **e-mail**:-Social work 03 @ readifitmail com. Last Updated On Sep 4 2008 12:34 PM.
2. Lena Dominelli, Social Work: Theory and Practice for a Changing Profession. Malden, MA: Polity Press, 2004. $69.95 hardcover. Mel Gray, The University of Newcastle, Australia.
3. Devi Ahilya Visvavidyalaya, Theoretical Perspective in sociology, Indore 2006.
4. Amartya Sen, Identity and Violence, The Illusion of Destiny, Allen Lane, Penguin Books Ltd., England 2006.
5. Vasant Moon ed., Dr. Babasaheb Ambedkar Writings and Speeches, Education Department, Government of Maharashtra, Mumbai 1991, Vol. 9, pp. 166-198.
6. Vasant Moon ed., Dr. Babasaheb Ambedkar Writings and Speeches, Education Department, Government of Maharashtra, Mumbai 1991, Vol. 10, pp. 529-549.
7. Vasant Moon ed., Dr. Babasaheb Ambedkar Writings and Speeches, Education Department, Government of Maharashtra, Mumbai 1998, Vol. 16, pp. 439-6299.
8. Bhadant Anand Kausalyayan, Jo Bhool Na Saka, Buddha Bhoomi Prakashan, Nagpur 1994, pp.

9. Amartya Sen, The Argumentative Indian, Penguin Group, England 2005, pp. ix-xix.
10. Government of India, Ministry of Social Justice & Empowerment, Shastri Bhawan, New Delhi D.O. No. 13-16/2008 PREM(SCD-Res) dated 31.7.2008.
11. Kumar Anand, Political Sociology of Poverty in India: Between Politics of Poverty and Poverty of Politics, CPRC-IIPA Working paper, Chronic Poverty Research Centre, New Delhi 2004.
12. Babaldas B. Chavda alias Kavi Buddhidhan Visnagari, 15,New Cottonnagar Society, Gomtipur, Ahmedabad-380021 (94389 60548) was a college student at Baroda in 1945 and met Dr. Ambedkar.
13. S.N. Chaudhary, Rajiv Gandhi Chair Professor, Barkatullah University, Bhopal delivered Dr. B.R. Ambedkar Memorial Lecture at Baniss, Ambedkar Nagar (Mhow) on 9th September 2008.
14. Dr.B.R. Ambedkar, My Philosophy of Life, All India Radio Broadcast of speech on October 3, 1954 incorporated on page 503 of Vol. 17, part III.
15. B.R. Ambedkar, Ranade Gandhi and Jinnah, Address in Poona in 1943.
16. Author's translation of Hindi version by Krishnakumar Rattu 'bahut kuch ghatata hai mere aas paas, main bikharta nahin hum, mere khoon mein hain…aakash ka khulapan aur samudra ki gahrai-shayad yahi hai shesh jindagi ki parvaaz ke pankh…' published in Dainik Bhashkar, Indore, 10th October 2008, p. 10.

Chapter - 12

Inclusive Governance

Introduction

Inclusive governance is going to be the governing agency caring and sharing all the available national resources for the elevation of the most backward communities of the country with free and fair rule of equality, liberty and fraternity and do justice to the all inclusive growth vis-a-vis international competitive development on par with the developing and getting closer to the developed nations in the globe. This will take care of both governance and justice in society like India.

As far as the concerns and strategies are concerned they revolve round identification of such communities and doing needful to them through planning, commissions and effective measures to alleviate the severity of their plight and bring them on par with the main stream.

There are various good-intentioned organizations, institutions whose services in the sphere of socio-educational and cultural activities may be harnessed and policies framed such that the targeted groups are benefitted by useful strategies and such process is set that leads to tangible transformation of their conditions and social status. Why deprive socially and economically and educationally also those who are already traditionally degraded for centuries? Governance and justice need to work together here and resolve the most imminent and persistent Indian social issues.

Inclusive Governance

Inclusive governance is a name of political, constitutional and parliamentary democratic system of enforcement of inclusive policies for eradication of poverty, human trafficking, bonded labour, social evil prostitution, child abuse, rape, corruption, exploitation, mental perversion, crooked thinking and maladjustment so that there is a perrinial resources for continually rising social evils. Such system is invariably and independently associated with the Justice System to set the aberrations of Government on right track if and when such check is needed to be pronounced by constitutional legal authority in the hands of the courts in the state and supreme court for the whole nation and citizens.

Some of the most backward communities in the state of Madhya Pradesh along with immediate action plan for their elevation are cited here with as under:

Issues

1. There is a Banchada community among the scheduled castes in western M. P. particularly in the districts i.e. Mandsaur, Neemuch, Ratlam, etc., practising traditional prostitution by engaging the eldest daughter of their family in the business. To eradicate this social evil of traditional prostitution, Govt of M.P. has created the Banchda Development Authority to rehabilitate this community with respectable professions.
2. The Institute has conducted an empirical study in 38 districts of M.P. which reveals that eradication of manual scavenging is not possible until and unless the social stigma attached to this community is removed. Therefore the manual scavengers among SCs needed to be declared as the most backward group so that special rehabilitation scheme be launched which will provide them dignified occupational opportunities for their livelihood.
3. It has been noticed that the undignified scavenging professions have mostly been practised in the cities and towns. Therefore they may be rehabilitated by earmarking percentage of shops for them in shopping complexes being constructed by Municipal Corporations, Nagar Nigam and development authorities and also by private builders who constructed shopping malls or shopping complexes.
4. There are some most backward communities among the SCs engaged in lifting dead animals and removing the skin from dead animals namely Mochis/Dhors in the country. This community should be rehabilitated by shifting them from the traditional occupation to a dignified jobs. Besides, they should be given interest-free loans to establish their dignified means of livelihood. They should also be alloted some shops in cities and local town markets.

5. Reservation in the service sector under govt has been shrunken to the level of zero percentage for the groups in employment. The most of the population of such communities are employed only in group D category. Due to the effect of LPG the most of the employment opportunities and resources had gone to private sectors and the same private sector is not following the reservation policy. As a result, marginalization of SCs from the main stream of society has increased.
6. Bonded labour is also the most backward group among the SCs across the country.

Measures

The following criteria should be adopted at the national level to identify and protect the most marginalised SCs communities.

Social: *All such SC communities who are still being* segregated, stigmatized and engaged in unclean occupation should benumerated among the most backward SC communities, in which tradition is the test.

Economic: Those getting less than 200 days wages or labour should be recognized as belonging to the most backward communities among the SC, in which amount of wage-day is the test.

Education: Those communities having female literacy rate less than 20% of the average literacy rate of the respective states should be considered as monst backward SC community in which female literacy below 20 percent is the test.

SC/ST Development Corporation in the analogy of the existing SC Financial Corporation, a separate specially Backward SC Financial Corporation should be set up.

Those people and institutions working for social integration of most backward SC communities should be appreciated and felicitated.

There is a need to provide the quality education and skill development in modern occupation as per the market demands. For their educational requirement there is a need to open Ashram schools with all modern facilities to bring them from the depleted situation to a progressive environment.

Being engaged in unclean occupation and to overcome their social stigma attached with it the people involved in these occupations are becoming addicted to alcohol and other intoxicants which adversely affect their health and development. Similarly in the case of female scavengers;

because of working in dust and dirty places they too became addicted to taking intoxicants which lead to deterioration of their health. Because of the undignified work, the community is not able to develop confidence in themselves. It has been also noticed that sweepers are educationally and economically not so backward because of their employment in the govt and private establishments. However, they have not been able to live a dignified life in the society because of their stigmatized profession.

To help them to live in a dignified manner the govt should give priority to create sanitation facilities in the cities and towns and also in the villages.

The profession of these communities should be improved and mechanised as well as should be given entrepreneurship training and govt should provide funds and support to establish their business. Most of these communities need economical and infrastructural support. They are purely depended on the services and nowadays, service sector has been almost privatized and outsourced. Due to lack of education and quality training they are lagging behind in the competition of the emerging sector of economy. Hence they should be imparted training for upgradation of skills and entrepreneurship. It has been also observed that because of the poverty and unfavorable social and family environment, children of these communities are engaged in their socially stigmatized profession. To overcome this problem most of the states have created residential schools (like Ashram schools in Madhya Pradesh) where alongwith accommodation, food and quality education are being provided by the govt. Such schools should be created to the level of graduation and post-graduation to educate them for personality development and for employment opportunities in govt and private sectors.

Empirical study reveals that most of the communities are landless agricultural labourers engaged in undignified occupation in cities and towns due to resourceless conditions. To overcome this problem in the rural areas they should be provided land; either Govt land or govt purchased land in residential complexes in cities, towns and villages.

As far as Bonded labour is concerned there should be stringent application of Minimum Wages Act in this respect. Besides this, there should be employment opportunity, protection against economic exploitation, housing and separate settlement provided by the government on a large scale for this group. There should be allocation of cultivated plots or appropriate compensation in terms of capital during the period of their labour, when they were exploited on the land or in the household. In addition to this there should be separate cell for the implementation of POA and

PCR Act. The representation of these groups in the main stream should be ensured on village, taluk and district level in every states. Social participation of these groups in the main stream in terms of status, education and livelihood and other spheres of life should be ensured.

Special Package

Special package may be continued to provide them education, economic empowerment, skill training, etc. Most of such communities are involved in superstitions, black magic, unhygienic conditions, undignified social and cultural practices, alcoholism, etc.

They are facing court litigation, criminal offences in petty matters in biased manner. To provide them protection against these social evils, legal awareness cell (Samajik Vigyan Kendra) in each district should be created by MOSJE on the analogy of Krishi Vigyan Kendra of Ministry of Agriculture. These Samajik Vigyan Kendras should provide legal aid for prevention of atrocities and social justice to the victims of atrocities, skill development to create entrepreneurship imparting education to create awareness against superstitions, social disabilities, relief and rehabilitation to the victims and their family, preventive measures against social evils, etc on regular basis.

To bring them into the main stream-:

(1) There should be reservation in posts created either by govt or private sector.

(2) There should be reservation in allotment of shops in shopping complex being constructed by private developers, development authorities in the town and cities in appropriate proportion to the population of the most backward communities. If precautions are not taken SC/ST/OBC groups automatically will be segregated from the main habitants and settlements of the cities and towns.

Justice

Justice is a name of free and fair treatment by the ruling majority towards ruled subject in social, political, economic, educational and all aspects and spheres of life. In no way there can be such condition where the wish of the mighty is tantamount to justice.

There are various shades of justice and its classification is made according to their applicability in the context of nature of issue in the backdrop of governance and the governed. The above empirical data and measures are underlined above keeping in mind the Social Justice specifically focusing on the rights of women, Dalits, tribals, minorities and other vulnerable groups including a pioneering role in demonstrating the successful operation of institutional intervention in the field of law.

Findings of researches conducted in Madhya Pradesh by the Institute

Similarly in 1998 survey conducted on Bedia women in Raisen district rvealed hat girls of 10-13 age group were all prepared to take up their position in the trade of prostitution. The Bedias themselves were not hesitant in accepting prostitutions as a profession in Sukha and Pathari study areas. Women were head of the family as matriarchal household. Men could be seen loitering around or sitting under the tree, playing cards and smoking. One of the recommendations put forth was this that "the children, both boys and girls, have to be reared away from their families of origin, to avoid the prevalent socialization pattern through foster parents, NGOs, Ashram schools and SOS villages.

Manual scavenging survey was conducted in the year 2010-11 in ten districts namely Dhar, Jhabua, Barwani, Khargone, Betul, Rajgarh, Indore, Bhopal, Vidisha and Raisen by the author of this line himself. External evaluation of Govt. of India's self-employment Scheme for Rehabilitation of Manual Scavengers (SRMS) was conducted in respect of ineligible scavengers under the scheme in other districts.

Excerpts of Research and Findings with practical recommendations

1. In 1992 the main causes of adjournment in the PCR Act cases was transit of presiding officer, non-availability of npresiding officer and absence of accused and witnesses. The local JMFC may be handed over the charge of the PCR Act cases.
2. In the same year Dryland Farming Technology for water conservation and income enhancement of the farmers of Malwa region suggested that the rationality of the usefulness of the techniques in rain-fed areas for enhancing productions would have to be judged in the framework of traditional wisdom and individual risk bearing capacity of the farmers.
3. In the same year a study on premenstrual symptoms among Bhilala and Banjara tribes showed that premenstrual synmptoms were reported to a greater extent in women of middle and higher socio-economic classes.

4. In the same year integrated rural development programme in Damoh District was evaluated and found that contrary to the guideline those whose income was above poverty line were assisted in the study area.
5. In the same year the New Tendu Patta Policy of Madhya Pradesh was evaluated and found that the new policy had been a failure in namesake cooperation and in bureaucratization of trade.
6. In 1993 reason for diarrhoeal diseases in tribal women in Dhar District was the problem of availability of safe drinking water for households in remote villages.
7. In the same year infant mortality rate in Jhabua district was the result of a toll taken by poor transport facility and poor hygienic surroundings of illiterate women.
8. In 1994 Tribal Migration and Man-Power Planning in Jhabua found that even after the planning for man-power utilization within the clusters, quite a large number of tribals still had to migrate out for work.
9. In the same year the adolescent girls development was adversely affected by a large scale migration of tribes on Bhabra Block.
10. In the same year the scheme of post-matric scholarship to SC and STs in Madhya Pradesh and Rajasthan evaluated and recommended that the existing income cealing of Rs. 2000 per month should be revised to Rs. 4000 with effect from July 1, 1994 for inclusion of restricted students of scholarship due to restriction of income ceailing.
11. In the same year comparative study of ICDS Project run by voluntary agencies and state government in Madhya Pradesh revealed that there was an urgent need to equip anganwadi workers with skills and need based training and orientation courses with doctors and para-medical staff for health services under ICDS project.
12. In 1995 a study of status of education and causes of drop-outs among Scavengers revealed that there was lack of interest and psychology to overcome their problems.
13. In the same year Impact of Shikshak Samakya Pariyojna I.e. increasing enrollment rates, retention rate, attendance of learners on primary education in Dhar and Panna districts was positive as 80 percent children of the class attended but in respect of enrollment in all the schools it had not reached 90 percent target set in the objective.

14. In 1996 Tribals and Panchayats in Madhya Pradesh revealed that there was a need of Panchayat Raj Institutions to delivery of social services like education, health, supply of drinking water on priority basis.
15. In 1997 in six districts of Madhya Pradesh the nature of atrocity varied from heinous crime like murder, grievous hurt, arson and rape to physical torture (i.e. beating and minor physical injury), sexzual assault and discrimination especially on the ground of untouchabilirty. In order to eliminate caste system, the root cause of atrocities, intercaste marriages should be promoted by giving incentives in the form of prizes, financial help, relaxation in age of government services, preference in allotment of shops, residential plots, housing and other loans etc. for the boys and girls marrying outside their caste.
16. In the same year Handicraft Artisans census conducted in 45 districts of M. P. including Chhattisgarh identified 52, 000 artisans engaged in various skills and products of handicrafts.
17. In the same year Effectiveness of Social Forestry Programme in Environmental Consercvation and increasing Availability to Weaker Sections in Indore Social Forestry Range revealed that the tree co-operative scheme was successful only at the level of selecting the beneficiaries for the scheme, but miserably failed in maintaining and conserving the plantation.
18. In 1998 in Bihar and Assam states illiteracy, lack of production assets like land and capital, inadequate wages and poor income level, lack of gainful employment opportunities, indebtedness etc. constituted social disabilities of the victims of atrocities. The Central and state governments should jointly plan with adequate budgetary allocations, on long term basis, for the overall development of the backward regions with major focus on the employment of the SCs and the STs.
19. In the same year Human resource development, utilization and change among scavengers was found discouraging.
20. In the same year Adoption of Control Strategy of Drought revealed that the basic planning philosophy missed governance of rebuilding up of natural resources base and providing options to the people of study area to strengthen the survival base by opting less risky step.
21. In the same year Bedia Women were surveyed found that the girls got into the traditional profession and boys just did nothing.

As for their rehabiliatation older women should be given financial security so that they should not motivate girls to accept their traditional prostitution because of financial insecurity and for boys and men Govt. employment generation schemes like TRYSEM be implemented.

22. In the same year thirty Muslim communities were recommended for inclusion in the OBC list as identified by the Baniss research project.
23. In the same year Impact of Special Component Plan on Socio-Economic Development of Schedule Castes in the context of Rural Development and Forestry Sector was studied in Madhya Pradesh and what the 200 beneficiaries of IRDP, Jivan dhara, Indira Awas (Rural development programmes) and 200 beneficiaries of forestry schemes operating under SCP programme recommended was to make the Department of Scheduled Castes Welf are as Nodal Department for planning, implementation and monitoring of the SCP.
24. In 1999 in Madhya Pradesh because of being untouchables the respondents were deprived of their rights to self respect, ownership, use of transport, cooperation, power, dignity, food, water, house, electricity, clothes, job, education, business, property and participation. Removal of untouchability be made the main plank of the GENDA OF THE Panchayati Raj System throughout Madhya Pradesh and whole India.
25. In the same year the Baiga scheduled tribes of Madhya Pradesh also revealed that the near total absence of skill, technology and higher education placed the Baigas in a position where they cannot come up for any better way of living.
26. In the same year Centrally sponsored Scheme of Post-Matric Scholarship to Students of SCs and STs in M.p. was studied and found that the two tier system tended to leave the scope for manipulation to manage and get income certificates below the maximum income cealing so as to become eligible for scholarship and it affected mainly the service sector, who need to produce income certificate from the employer while leaving the rest of the occupational categories free.
27. In the same year Pilot Study on Aspirations and Achievements of SCs in the last 50 years in Madhya Pradesh revealed that an All India study was necessary to take a proper stock of the position of

development and for understanding problems of SCs , who are of diverse nature.

28. In the same year In-Depth study of Pre-Examination Training Centres in M.P. and A. P. showed invariably that both had similar facilities as far as infrastructure was concerned but the latter had an upper edge by having higher stipends and book grants for its students.
29. In 2000 in Madhya Pradesh the housing patterns and settlements in the studied villages showed a distinct pattern caste concentration. It was recommended that the modules of rural settlements planning for social harmony be designed and developed for different regions a national level rural housing policy should be formulated, giving priority to removal of the stigmatized site and situation of the SCs basttees.
30. In the same year status of scavenging and scavengers in M. P. showed that there was deficient and careless urban planning.
31. In the same year Seasonal Rural out-migration of SCs and STs communities from Chhattisgarh correlated with effect of irrigation i.e. increasing irrigation effected lower out-migration in top land and unbunded areas where the second crop was grown in the rabi season.
32. In the same year Nutritional Deficiencies in Tribal areas showed that women and children of tribal population were deficient in vitamin A, iron, calories and intake etc. They should be advised to improve their nutritional status within the ambit of their own resources.
33. In the same year Register of Handicraft Artisans of M.P. was prepared by Baniss for the use of Ministry of Textiles, Govt. of India, New Delhi.
34. Criteria of backwardness among religious minorities should be worked out at individual or family level but not at community level as suggested by research project of Baniss, year not mentioned.
35. In 2001 Socio-Economic and Political Status of SC and ST women in M. P. showed that they were addicted to alcohol both in rural and urban areas.
36. In the same year Girl Infanticide in Chambal Division revealed that the first born girl child stands high percentage of chances of survival in comparison to the second and the third born girls.

37. In 2002 in M.P. SCs were restricted use of common crematorium, social endosmosis. Elite persons should take an initiative and participate in the cremation of SCs ion the crematorium of the high caste.
38. In the same year in Kalukheda the Zamindar unauthrizedly occupied the land of Scheduled Castes to whom the surplus agricultural land was allotted by the Government. The actual possession of surplus land be ensured at the time of distribution of patta (lease deed). Once the allotment of the surplus land was made the lease deed should be distributed without delay.
39. In the same year to check falling of trees in the tribal areas warned that in the period between February to May in the western belt of Madhya Pradesh and from December to April, excepting March food security must be provided by the Government on a sustainable basis.
40. In the same year Comparative study of SC Financial Development Corporation programmes for Socio-Economic Upliftment of SCs in A.P. and M.P. was conducted in which it was observed that although the A. P. SCFDC was certainly far ahead in its organization and functioning than M.P. SCFDC, the former was not able to eradicate fully the cumulative deprivation of the scheduled castes because of the challenges of the market forces and the hostile role of dominant castes who were neutralizing the fuller impact of its development efforts.
41. In 2003 graded inequality was clearly visible within Samaj of Parichay Sammelansa and Samuhik Vivah in Malwa region of M.P.
42. In the same year rehabilitation of scavengers under liberation of scavengers in Madhya Pradesh and Karnataka revealed that the conceptualizations of the scheme did not trickle down as expected and conceived.
43. In the same year UNDP Study on Training Needs Assessment of Elected Representatives in Schedule V Areas of A.P., Orissa, Gujrat and M. P. revealed that there are knowledge-gaps, skill-gaps and attitude-gaps and there was lack of awareness among the masses as well as their representatives about the role of Gram Sabha and provision of PESA.
44. In 2004 it was observed that the status of women was very low due to the caste factor, worsened by unemployment, illiteracy, ignorance and poverty.

45. In the same year Impact of formulation and implementation of Special Component Plan on SCs in M. P. was examined and the study clearly showed that implementation of the SCP schemes and other welfare measures in the region have generated positive socio-economic impact on target groups at limited level in spite of the various constraints in implementation of SCP schemes.
46. In 2004-5 the scheme of land allotment to SCs and STs in M.P. was evaluated and observed that in spite of lapses in the execution of the programme which resulted in its low affectivity it was in itself a bold step towards providing social justice to the under-privileged, building in them a feeling of self-esteem and initiating a process of social change by empowering them.
47. In 2005 in Manpur Tribal Cluster Area social change underlined was in naming the children. Bhils had started using popular names, borrowed from the celebrity, cinema stars, TV serials etc.
48. In the same year Bonded labour in Raisen district numbered 427 as researched by the project.
49. In the same year in Panna district there were 607 bonded labourers, in Vidisha 1405, Shivpuri was not exception, as detected by the research project team.
50. In the same year study was conducted in Gujrat to find impact of Post-Matric Scholarship scheme on SCs and it was observed that in order to improve functioning of post-matric scholarship scheme in the state, the guidelines of its implementation should be simplified and be followed by state with utmost sincerity and commitment with a view to provide maximum benefits of the scheme to the target groups.
51. In the same year in Tamil Nadu an evaluator study was conducted on utilization of SCP attached to special central assistance and it was observed that people and political leaders as the main sources of information, were not clear in case of special component plan and special central assistance had been more popular among smaller projects than in the bigger ones, which needed to be increased with potential entrepreneurs.
52. In 2005-6 Bonded Labour of Raisen District offered rehabilitation lacked provision of productive assets and skill to enable them to throw the yoke of this enslavement.
53. In 2006 the hurdles faced by the organizations attempting to apply Dr. Ambedkar Thoughts and philosophy in their sphere of activities

were mainly incorrect grasp of Ambedkar's thought and perpetuating in old traditional set up of life pattern.

54. In the same year Released and Rehabilitated Bonded Labour in Satna and Ratlam, Shivpuri, Guna, Sagar, Bhopal Harda, Khandwa, Dhar, Shahdol and Vidisha districts of Madhya Pradesh were just reflective of the system prevalent in the state, the 2890 suspected cases with still widespread cases need to be explored and examined further by the competent authority for further action.
55. In 2006-7 Land Alienation and Indebtedness among Tribals of M.P. underlined the importance of employment guarantee schemes being made more effective in the tribal areas.
56. In the same year Training needs of the elected representatives of Panchayati Raj Institutions in M. P. were identified and it revealed that the Panchayati Raj Institutions were one of the best sources for empowerment, upliftment and overall development of low socio-economic background people.
57. The role of anti-poverty programme in removal of poverty in rural areas of Bastar district, Chhattisgarh underlined the need of universalization of elementary education and promotion of higher and technical education among the tribals for their development, the research study recommended, year not mentioned.
58. Final evaluation of Bamboo Plantation project in Jabalpur district revealed that Bamboo Plantation was done following the traditional methods only, which must be replaced by modern methods of plantation and protection of the plants, so that survival rate could be enhanced, recommended the study, year not mentioned.
59. In the year 2008 the status and problems of Buddhist minority in Nagpur pointed out the error of Maharashtra Lok Sabha and Vidhan Sabha and Panchayats in proportion to their population (Mahar and Buddhists forming 6 per cent) while enumerating SC population (Mang, Chambhar, Dhor forming 10 per cent) of the total population of the state (9,68,78,727 as per 2001 census).
60. In 2008 Perpetuation of socio-economic backwardness among cotton cultivators in Vidarbha (Maharashtra and Nimar (Madhya Pradesh) regions was caused by suicides and agrarian distress.
61. In 2009 In the same year, mid-term evaluation was conducted on skill enhancement of rural youth with self-employment in Sousar-Chhindwara district and observed that intervention of Council for advancement of People's action and rural technology, Ministry of

rural development, Govt. of India, New Delhi (CAPART) has generated awareness about new areas of income generation in self-employment sector with the help of technical skill development.

62. In the year 2009-10 Malnutrition among Tribal Children (0-6) in Western Madhya Pradesh became deplorable due to poverty and lack of income.
63. In the same year Welfare Measures for Economically Backward Classes included coverage under a comprehensive National Health Insurance Scheme with a provision of cash-less treatment of all major diseases making required facilities and services available in the respective primary health centres as suggested by the investigator of the research project.
64. In 2010 self-employment and rehabilitation of Beneficiary Manual scavengers and identification of non-beneficary Manual scavengers found that the list provided by the main source was much to be desired in respect of correct addresses and specifications of the target.

Doctoral Researches and Findings with Recommendations

Since the inception of the Institute in 1988 there have been more than 87 doctoral researches awarded to the internee of the institute. Swome of the later researches have been mentioned here for presentation before in this international gathering:

1. In 2009, Comparative study of status, power and gender roles in Orissa and Delhi revealed that from sociological point of view the structural reforms (1991 onwards) during the era of LPG (liberalization, privatization and globalization) brought out opportunities for the women and their share increased significantly in the occupation of both government and private jobs.
2. In the same year, study was conducted on emotional maturity of divorced and deserted women and emotional stability of their children and found that divorced women fared better than deserted women in maturity of emotional control. Muslim divorced women fared better than Hindu divorced women in this respect while both Hindu and Muslim deserted women fared equally on emotional maturity. As for the children those who belong to the deserted mother were of better emotional stability than those who belonged to the divorced mother.

3. In 2010, the study of ICT (information and communication technology) and women's empowerment revealed that Hindu women dominated in modern ICT occupation because of thweir educated urban elite and English medium background.
4. In the same year, the research study on impact of water resource conservation and protection on farms and socio-economic development of scheduled tribes in western Madhya Pradesh was conducted and it was found that constructive change took place both in productivity of farms and development of scheduled tribe in study area.
5. In the same year, study was conducted on life and work conditions of migratory women labour in unorganized sector and it was found that migration flowed from villages to urban centres and it affected adversely on relational affection of their relatives during migration period.
6. In 2011, the geographical research study on changing role of forests and impact on regional development in Mandla district underlined the loss of forest impacting regional and tribal economy adversely on one hand, and Governmental projects contributed in changing nature, form of forests and to facilitating transportation in the region that impacted the tribal identity and culture and education, on the other hand.
7. In the same year the research study was conducted on changes in use of cultivable lands in Narmada basin and observed that the crops of kodo, kutki, jagni etc. disappeared and the crops of maze, jawar, cotton, groundnut etc. comparatively showed decline, and compared to the base year (1970) crops as mentioned above the production of dollar-earning soyabeen replaced them at present.
8. In the same year the research study was conducted on sociological study of Impact of modernization on scheduled tribe women and it was observed that as a result of modernization the dowry custom rose in place of their old tradition of bride price, which gave better position to a wedded woman in tribal society than those in other societies. So there is need of restoring the traditional values of tribal society based on equality, fraternal feeling and like.
9. In the same year, research study was conducted on emerging gender differences among the Gonds and Korkus in which it was revealed that in their tribal society the status of women is inferior to men, who are oriented to patriarchal household system and

there is a need of establishing parity between these tribal men and women.

10. In 2013, research was conducted on contribution of modern agricultural techniques in the development of the tribes in Khargone district revealed that although the tribal farmers used modern tool for farming with irrigation facility, insecticide etc. However they lack education for which workshops, seminars etc. should be organized in villages from time to time to boost the farmers' educational interest.

References

1. Constitution of India, Govt. Publication, Ministry of Law and Justice, New Delhi.
2. Dr. B.R. Ambedkar, States and Minorities, Vol.1 of Writings and Speeches of Dr. Babasaheb Ambedkar, Education Department, Government of Maharashtra, Mumbai 1979.
3. Constitutional Assembly Debates, Parliament, Govt. of India 1956.
4. C.D. Naik & Dr. R.S. Kureel, Dr. Ambedkar's Vision for Nation Building, Indore 2014.
5. C.D. Naik & Dr. R.S. Kureel, Thoughts and Philosophy of Dr. B. R. Ambedkar, Indore 2014.
6. C.D. Naik & Dr. R.S. Kureel, Bodhisattva, Indore 2014.
7. Dr. R. S. Kureel, Dr. P. C. Bansal, Social Evils: Challenges and Remedies, Baniss Silver Jubilee Publication of Empirical research, Mhow, 2014.

Chapter - 13

Social Change

Meaning and connotation

Education means to draw out from within an individual a spring of action. However modern formal education is a process of stuffing individual minds with thoughts and things from outside into inside. Though education as power cannot be disagreed it is also characterized as "force for social change, as a means to combat poverty, to empower women, to safeguard children from exploitation, to promote human right and democracy, to protect environment, to control population growth and to lead to peace and security. Education is one of the best investment a country can make in order to prosper and related to literacy, mortality rate, fertility rate, life expectancy, population growth, nutritional status and economic progress"[1].

According to the Behaviouratic psychology referred to by Bertrand Russell in his book on the Principle of Reconstruction of Society[2] the meaning of education is to activate within man a sping of action. Social Psychology put premium on the modification of inner tendencies as importing education in true sense.

Buddhist Educational Background

In the beginning education was in the form of intellectual religious debates carried out between groups of different sects in Indian cultural setting. Intellectual gathering was organized under the auspices of royal dynasties as exemplified in the cultural historical periods of Vedic Age, Asokan (300 B.C.) and Harsha Period (700 A.D.)[3]. The initial provision of Buddhist monk training stressed that a Bhikkhu should be sharply intellectual.

Education is expected to reduce socio-economic disparities and develop individual potentialities to solve challenges of life. To remove suffering from the life of humanity was the Buddha's goal and he propounded Buddhism as medicine to humanity's mental ailment. The Buddhist monasteries were transformed into the educational universities with the aim of sharpening intellect of Buddhist monks with the help of economic patronage of the royal families and intellectual freedom of monastic tradition. Fahian and Yuan Chwang gave testimony of Vihara Educational establishments since or prior to 100A.D.

These Vihara universities were preceded by the Vedic and Brahmanic education systems, which compared to the Buddhist system marked the following features:

Vedic System

It was a Gurugrih system in which disciples sat at the feet of a teacher and learnt. It was executed in domestic atmosphere. Its scope was not exceeding its domestic limits.

For under one class of orthodox teachers big educational organizations cannot be developed.[4] Under this system beliefs in the Vedas, God, superiority of birth and rituals and sacrificial rites are underlined and are validated by law. Books were written and recommended in Sanskrit language. Dr. Kane mentioned in this system of 14 lore, four Vedas and six branches such as rules of vowels, astronomy, astrology, grammar, derivatives, and religion. He further referred to such branches of learning as the 18 Puranas, Logic, Mimansa and scriptures in addition to the four auxiliary Vedas called Ayurveda, Dhanurveda, Gandharvaveda and Arthashastra.

Vedic system necessitated reference to gotra of a student at the time of admission to Vedic institution of education. Education was imparted only through the Brahmin teachers. Entrants to it without certainty of gotra or clan as the Shudras and the outcaste were prohibited from learning. Strict observance of rules of discipline was maintained in the institute and breach of rule was accompanied by penance. Upanayan sanskar was a part of observance and a student was called Brahmachari after undergoing this ceremony. He is to take ablution, chant , worship fire and observe taboos with regard to touching the Shudras and at their breach undergo disciplinary actions as many as three, six or twelve times a year according to the gravity of breach of conduct including taking bath three times a day and survive on gruel for two months, on milk and buttermilk for a month and a half respectively on ghee, alms, water and fasting during the period of 8, 6, and 3 days and one.

Brahmanic System

Under the Brahmanic education system a Brahmachari was partaking religious instructions and dependent on a teacher or upadhyaya, who would teach a small class of students seated on the ground under the sky with their teacher holding umbrella over his head as shown in the museum at Mathura. Teaching was imparted by words of mouth and based on memory since inscription of copper plate found have no mention of script or writing material in the list of students' requisites. Only a Brahmin could be a teacher, who would teach the twice-born disciples alone. The subjects taught comprised Vedic hymns, Brahman texts, religious rites, procedure of sacrifice, criminal procedure, official rules of financial matter besides auxiliary sciences related to phonetics, grammar, etymology, astronomy, sacrificial lore; the Upanishadas covering dialectics, mathematics, chronology, warfare, knowledge of elements, deities and ethics. Education was patronized by the regal decrees. Conditions for admission to the Brahmanic educational establishment included purity of gotra (clan) and sacrificial act.

A Brahmachari was prohibited from visiting cremation ground, Samya and Shudra as outcastes[5]. Bad odour, corpse, Chandal and Shudra were taboos[6]. According to Manusmrti Vedas shall not be chanted in the presence of a shudra. The goal of Brahmanic educational system was to increase knowledge, make students dutiful and build their characters. Violation of educational rules by an outcaste was punished by poring molten lac, tin or glass into the ear of such Shudra, who listens to chanting of Vedic hymns knowingly, by slitting his tongue for their chanting and by splitting his body into halves for his memorizing them[7]. Mayne, Ramakrishna, Mulla, Gupte and Kane laid stress on the Manusmrtis, the Vedas, traditions, customs and choice as springs of the Hindu laws while according to Raghavachariar, the sources of the Hindu laws were Sruti, smrti, commentaries and digests, verdicts of courts, constitutional legislations, and customs.

Even Lokmanya Tilak discouraged the weaker sections of society to aspire political empowerment when he expressed, "Are the Telis, Tambolis, Farmers to drag the plough or hold the scale by going into the Council?

Buddhist System

Buddhist education system was called Vihara system. Education was one of the features of Buddhist Vihara life. Vihara establishments sprang in Bihara and Bengal on a large scale. There were thousands of teachers and students in the Buddhist Vihara precincts. Students flocked there even from foreign lands. This development culminated through 1500 years of educational flurry of centers at Nalanda, Vallabhi, Vikramshila, Jagaddala, Odantapuri as representatives of Buddhist universal educational system till it was reduced to ashes by the fierce anger-fired Turushk or Turk Bakhtiyar Khilji in 1200 A.D[8]. Teachers discussed on routines of a monk and curriculum that included Discipline, Jataka Stories, Morals, Verses, fundamental doctrines, readings of scriptures, and recitation at special occasions(sangayana). Teaching methodology included thinking, arguments, decisions. There were set accepted valid procedure of submitting points of controversy before the Order. Voting was cast by ballots called sticks (shalakas). A learner Bhikkhu had unrestricted freedom to cross, debate and counter-argue. When the Bhikkhus spent night without sleep in study, debate and recital the subsequent instruction session was concluded in short while to make over rest missed in the preceding night.

The psycho-philosophical technique was used to grasp the special doctrinal meaning of the texts of metaphysics. Experts of discourses discussed the doctrinal principles. The essences of above discourses were summed up in the Abhidhamma. Teachers and students both would reflect on wrong views. "Learning and discussion would run down a day too short", said Yuan Chwang. Viharas were transformed into the Universities in about circa 100 A.D. due to its inherent qualities of betterment, ability and rational persuasion. Its syllabus comprised religion, philosophy, agriculture and architecture-sculpture. Different Buddhist traditions were represented in educational instructions received by the students called manava[9] charged nothing against their lodging and teaching costs. The Nalanda University founded near Rajagrih at Bargaon village in Bihar, had 1500 professors and 10,000 inmates of the campus as students. Bargaon museum contained official seal engraved on stone with emboss of wheel flanked by deers and lettered 'The Honourable Bhikkhu Sangha of the Nalanda Mahavihara'. Vikramshila University settled on the hills of the banks of the Ganges under Palas had six great gates each supervised by Gate-Scholar- called Dvar-Pandit, whose status was equivalent to a Master of Arts degree holder. Vallabhi University of Western India oriented to Theravadi Buddhist tradition was highlighted as the greatest orthodox school university of the time by Chinese travellors Yuan Chwang and I-Tsing[10] respectively of 7th century[11]. Students used to stay there for two to three years as a normal period of studies[12]. Memory and alphabetics were used in the instruction methods[13], time table was prepared, hours of instruction were regulated by clepsydra or contraption, in which small bowel dipped into the water of large bowl signifying a duration of 15 minutes each time it dipped.

The most famous libraries of the Naland University[14] were Sea of Jewels (Ratnadadhi), Ocean of Jewels (Ratnasagara) and Jewel-adorned (Ratnaranjaka), its building as high as nine stories. Overriding traditional, national and religious barriers Viharas became medieval European Stadium Generale after 5th-6th centuries onward and welcomed all kinds of seekers of knowledge into them[15]. Nalanda[16] University's Acharya Shilabhadra[17] was well-known, under whom Chinese scholar Yuan Chwang studied, who later established one of the 15 Chinese schools called Fa-Hsiang. His colleague Thomni Sambhot became a Minister of Tibetan King. About three centuries later Deepankar, completing his studies in the Odantapuri University became the Chief of Vikramshila University in 1034-1038 A.D. and introduced the Lama tradition in Tibetan Buddhist society. In Western Bengal near Darjeeling at Ghoom stood the Tibetan Vihara in which stone sculpture of Deepankar Atish has been enshrined amidst various deities. His Tibetan disciple was Nagtcho. Deepankar died in Nethan. Odantapuri University contained one thousand inmates and became prosperous during the Pala dynastic rule. Later the first Buddhist monastery built in Tibet was modeled after Odantapuri Vihara architecture. King Ramapala of Bengal had its capital at Karatoa called Ramavati, where the Jagaddal University was founded (1084-1130 A.D.). During its 150 years of mission many a noted scholars had been produced.

British Period

Prior to 1846 when Ray Hislop founded the first English school in Nagpur even Bhonsale rulers of Nagpur did not feel that the education was the duty of the ruler, king or government. After East India Company's education principle of Filtration Theory, Charles Wood in 1854 pleaded for education for all, and sympathized with women's education and education for the Muslims but there was dearth of an iota of thought for the education of the Untouchables. In Central Province and Berar Education Department was established in 1862 with opening of a High School in Sagar. In 1870 the principle of equal treatment was enforced but despite it the Depressed classes students were discriminated against. Students of all above schools belonged to the wealthy and superior classes of society with conspicuous absence of the Untouchable students. So the untouchable reformers turned their attention to open hostel arrangement for their children.

C. P. & Berar Census Report of 1911 recorded 13 untouchable castes amounting to 30,60,232 population, whose proportion in education was less than 100 in every thousand members of them. In the year 1920-21 some 42 schools were run for the untouchable students, of which 14 were unaidedly run by private agencies and remaining 28 run by the Government, the District Council, the Municipal Body and the Religious Missions had intake of 1235 boys and 34 girls from among the untouchable castes. The other general schools represented 27496 children at primary level, 2287 at Middle Schools and 20 at High School level with sitting arrangement on bare ground and segregated from other caste children.

Modern education is deemed to be the duty of the State. But during the period between 1915 and 1935 when the Central Province Depressed Classes Association and the Untouchable reformers established hostels named after Mahar Saint Chokhamela and Chamar Saint Ravidass at Amravati, Akola and Nagpur and demanded by their memorandum dated 24 February 1929 to Statutory Commission or Simon Commission on behalf of Mahar, Mang, Chambhar and Bhangee castes financial aid from the British government the Inspector M.S. Staley and Commissioner W.N. Maw of Nagpur Divison informed the Government that grant should not be given to any depressed class hostel as it would create the feeling of segregation and induce missionaries also to demand the same.

Ambedkar Age

Educational legacy of Phule (1827-1890) was carried forward by opening hostels and colleges in Maharashtra for the education of the downtrodden sections of society by Ambedkar during the period between 1924 and 1946. Establishing Society for the Welfare of the Excluded in 1924, Depressed Classes Education Society in 1928 and the Peoples' Education Society in 1945 Dr. Ambedkar started the High School Boys Hostels in Sholapur in 1925, five more Middle School Boys Hostels and four Degree Colleges namely (1) Siddharth Arts and Science College, Mumbai in 1946, (2) Siddarth Law College, Mumbai in the same year, (3) Milind Arts and Science College, Aurangabad in 1950 and (4) Siddharth Commerce and Economics College, Mumbai in 1953.

Despite all these efforts of Ambedkar literary rate of the Scheduled Castes and the Scheduled Tribes lagged behind the national literacy rate by 14 to 20 percentage respectively at the end of the three decades since the introduction of Government of India's New Education Policy after Parinirvana of Ambedkar.

Ambedkar used to be worried as to "When the six and a half crores of the Excluded Classes of society would be be filled with knowledge and when the tree of national unity would grow healthy and alive."[17] The young excluded India was being awakened by his inspirational words recalling their sacrifice in the battlefields of Egypt, Palestine, Mesopotamia and elsewhere for the establishement of British Empire that neglected them at their cost.[18] In 1893 the Society for the Removal of Anaryan Defects at Dapoli had protested against the ban on the recruitment of the Untouchables in the army.[19]

As one of the 321 selected intellectuals of the country Ambedkar advised the Mumbai University Reform Committee in 1924 to adopt the aims and functions of the University education as proposed by the educational inspectors Board of England and pointed out the want of education-orientation in the existing university system, and the lack of role of leading the society to the awareness of its history and culture necessary for mutual harmony and cooperation among its different sections.

While the University Act of 1857 was replaced by that of 1904 with explicit provision for undertaking educational duties on the part of University besides examination affairs there was need to revamp the legislative, executive and academic bodies to represent the various interests and views and establish coordination between the intellectual classes and social life.

In respect of Primary, Middle and Higher education the smallest class of Indian society occupied the highest rank and the largest classes of population were at the lowest scale of education from the beginning.[20]

Rising to support the proposal of the amendment put by Mr. Jadhav during the discussion of the third Mumbai University Act Amendment Bill in the Mumbai Legislative Council on 3rd August 1927 Ambedkar exhorted that the first duty of any modern university was to extend the facilities of the higher education to the backward classes of society.

On 29th October 1942 Ambedkar submitted his memorandum on the Grievances of the SCs and STs to H.E. the Governor-General in New Delhi stating that in order to bringing reformation and change in the status and conditions of the weaker sections their youths must get key posts or higher administrative offices.

To represent the educational interests of the scheduled castes boys and girls Dr. Ambedkar advocated that their members should be appointed at the Senate Body in University and at the Central Advisory Board for higher technical educational schools in the domain of Mining Engineering and Geology so that the picture of the Scheduled caste members at the bottom of social ladder and the policy of last to be hired at the time of economic prosperity and last to be fired at the time of economic depression in Indian economy could be rectified.

Formerly hardly any scheduled caste boy, let alone girl, could be seen in the echelons of higher education. Ambedkar was the first matriculate studying in the then Elphinstone High School and was the only and lonely graduate among the 16 lacs of Dalit population of Bombay Presidency with other six depressed classes members as matriculate boys in the year 1920. But since the establishment of PES and its colleges in Mumbai and Aurangabad thousands of the scheduled caste students became graduates and winners of medals in sport and debate competitions, awards and prizes in academic performance and as competitors in technical, industrial, research, oratory, literary and scientific circles as their colleges concerned the social useful and on UNESCO suggested topics concerning Food, Grains and the People and consequently rose in popularity among the masses and media.

Ambedkar was deploring the Indian Education System as factory of Beggars where ninety pecent of population was illiterate and apprecitated the Brahmadesh model in this respect where same number of people were equally literate. Now America, Germany and China are the three most highly educated countries in the world. In China alone as many as 30,000 Ph. D. Degrees were awarded in the year 2004[21]. This trend is telling about higher level of education on the one hand and lower quality and harder competition in intellectual and job opportunities.

It was not surprising in the least then that in rural Maharshtra people are used to chant the couplets, “May we be blessed with such son as would make his flag hoist in the three worlds”.

Education and Change

After governmental and non-governmental efforts put in changing the traditional structure of our society during the past five decades a tangible change can be perceived as taking place among the scheduled castes. The very people of the scheduled castes themselves have shown that they have changed in socio-economic-political-educational-religious-cultural and general spheres of life to a certain extent.

During the 60 years span of period from 1931 to 1991 the scheduled castes marked increase in rate of literacy from 1.9 to 37.4 respectively and males are becoming literate faster (49.9) than their female counterparts (23.8) as per the figures of 1991. Of course the general rate of literacy is higher than that of the above in all respects. Scheduled caste boys and girls enroll at primary level of education from class I to V at higher ratio than they do from class VI to VIII during the period from 1990-91 to 1998-99 with their drop-out rate declining from 67.8 in 1990-91 to 66.6 in 1997-98. The boys and girls belonging to scheduled castes are luckier who reach the level of education from VIIIth class to matriculation or Xth class and above. Such ones receive scholarsdhips which are held by SC students, particularly for their post-matric education in ascending number from about 14 lakh in 1999-00 to the 15 lakh and a quarter in 2000-01 approximately. Such educational progress among the SC students is due to the following facilities made available by the government under planning and constitutional provisions such as hostels, residential schools, scholarships at pre-matric and post-matric levels, book banks, upgradation of merit, special developmental educational programmes, national scholarships to meritorious students, relaxation of norms for opening of primary schools within one k.m. of walking distance, concession and free education, free books and uniforms, other scholarships and vocationalization of education in the main.

In this regard it may be mentioned that the educated boys and girls among the scheduled castes people are getting aware of life and works of Dr. Ambedkar also. So this trend is positive in the matter of understanding Dr. Ambedkar's life and ideals to the extent of the more the education the better the result in learning Dr. Ambedkar.

The second dimension of change is in the sphere of economical conditions. The above draft showed that Government's organizations like NSFDC, NSKFDC and SCDC are providing credit and market for their employment, income generating and economic independence which can be seen in the increasing number of SC beneficiaries under vcarious schemes of SSCDC from 28.69 lakh in 1980-85 to 29.22 lakh in 1985-90 though that number is declining from 5.42 lakh in 1990-91 to 3.71 lakh in 1997-98 respectively. However IRDP, Swarna Jayanti Seva Rojgar Yojna and Swarna Jayanti Sahakari Rojgar Yojana and sectoral departments of State governments helped over 10 lakh SC families and 400 Safai Karmacharis in income generating activities. During 1994-95 to 1997-98 monitoring under point 11-A of 20-point programme assisted 26,96,412 and 20,65,987 SC families economically to cross the poverty line and lessen their poverty rate which marked 57.60 in 1983-84 and declined to 48.37 in 1993-94 during which period the percentage of SC population below poverty line was 53.10 rural, 54.30 urban and 48.11 rural and 49.48 urban respectively.

The third dimension of change is social justice- which was instituted by doing structural changes in administrative level by Government of India and Government of Madhya Pradesh providing separate Ministry for SCs and STs so as to administer focused attention on development of them separately. Exclusive special courts have been set up to expedite disposal of cases pertaining to social discrimination, crimes and atrocities and untouchability practices. No. of cases registered under PCR Act 1955 shows downward trend from 1794 in 1994 to only provisional 537 in 1998 respectively. Along with administration and Act social justice is related to the statutory Bodies such as National Commission for SC/ST/Safai Karmacharies also, which have been set up to oversee the implementation of provisions under the constitution of India. It is also related to government policies one of which called reservation as positive discrimination enabled SCs claim for services from 13.7 % in 1974 to 16.9 % in 1994.

They also benefit from the strategy of special component plan funds for other general development sectors and SCA funds to States in income generation activities for SC families.

In short changes are marked in educational, economic, social, and judicial dimensions due to government efforts and further steps need to be taken to improve SCs conditions in coming years.

World Scenario

Higher education in France is organized nationally, with centralized control being almost marked as in primary and secondary education. All course structures have to be validated by a national regulatory body responsible to the Minister of Higher Education. National degrees are generally regarded as mere prestigious and valuable than those awarded by the individual university and by the state, since they are supposed to conform to guaranteed uniform standards. A certain range of occupations in government are only open to the holders of national degrees, which are also favoured by most industrial employers. All teachers in schools, colleges and universities in France are State employees. Rates of pay and the broad framework of teaching duties are fixed centrally.

While in the United States of America the high proportion of colleges and universities are in the private sector ranging to 54 percent including the most prestigious universities, such as Harvard, Princeton and Yale. But the distinction between Public and Private in American Higher education is not clear-cut as students at Private Universities are eligible for public grants and loans, and public research funding and public universities often possess substantial endowments and donations by private firms and research grants from private industrial sources.

The British system of higher education is more decentralized than that of France, but more unitary than that of the USA. Universities and colleges are government-financed and teachers at all levels of the educational system have their salaries determined according to national wage-scales despite diversity in organization of institutions and curricula.

In 1937, the total number of undergraduates in British Universities was approximately as much as the number of full time university academic staff in 1981[22] and 75 percent of all the graduate students in the country were registered at the University of London.

Between 1945 and 1970 the higher education system in Britain grew four times as large. Polytechnics comprise 400 colleges concentrate more on vocational courses than the universities. The Council for Natonal Academic Awards ensures uniform standard in degrees.

A degree from Leicester or Leeds is the same standard as one from Cambridge, Oxford or, from a Polytechnic or College of higher education. Yet Oxford and Cambridge are noted for a highly selective intake, about half of which comes from public schools (fee-paying schools). Their degree confers greater chances of reaching a high economic position than a qualification from most other universities.

In spite of post-war expansion, the proportion of the British population in universities, and in higher education is still well below that of other western countries. Only 6.6 percent of eighteen-year-olds entered university in Britain in 1986 compared to over 10 percent in most other European countries and about 30 percent in Italy in the same year. The then ruling government held view that universities should be places where ideas are freely explored and academic excellence is pursued for its own sake opposed to 1980 conservative government's view of a learner, cheaper, more utilitarian system of higher education.

According to Kogan and Kogan[23] between 1989 and 1985, 5,600 academic posts in universities disappeared and 18,000 undergraduate places were lost. Despite the Government's aim to reduce waste and academic drift, there is growing opposition to a set of policies which seem to jeaopardize the universities' distinctive contribution to national life: the commitment to rational, disinterested solutions to all kinds of problems.

The government's aim to cut down on expenditure on higher education has led to demoralization in some sectors of the university system, and to the feeling that the universities' ability to train and teach the students whose skills will be needed in the years to come is endangered.

Education and inequality

The expansion of education has always been closely linked to ideals of mass democracy. Reformers value education for its own sake – for the opportunity it provides for individuals to develop their abilities and aptitudes. Education has also consistently been seen as a means of equalization. Universal education will help reduce disparities of wealth and power by providing able young people with skills to enable them to find a valued place in society. Education tends to express and reaffirm existing inequalities far more than it acts to change disparities.

Social and family backgrounds are the major influence over school performance, and are thus reflected in subsequent levels of income.

In 1960 investigation on educational inequalities resulting from differences of ethnic background, religion or national origin carried out as per 1964 civil rights Act by James Coleman, a sociologist and Director of the research programme and result was published in 1966. Half a million pupils underwent a range of tests assessing verbal and non-verbal abilities, reading levels and mathematical skills and gave information, sixty thousand teachers provided data from four thousand schools. The report found that segregation of school children into black and white; 80 percent or less black students schools contained 10 percent or less black students; whites and Asian Americans scoring higher in achievement tests than blacks or other ethnic minorities; black schools with worse facilities, larger classes and inferior buildings made little difference to educational performance; the decisive influence was the children's backgrounds. Inequalities imposed on children by their home, neighbourhood, and peer environment are carried along to become the inequalities with which they confront adult life at the end of school[24]. Students from deprived backgrounds who had close friendships with others who were better off were likely to be more successful at school. Children from minority groups would do better in school if mixed with students from more affluent backgrounds. This influenced public debates about school integration in Britain as well as the USA.

Coleman's study could not analyse changes as it was confined to a single point in time. Michael Rutter carried out a study in London, looked at the educational development of groups of boys over several years – 1970 (When children were about to finish primary schooling, their social background and academic performance were observed to 1974 (when boys had been in secondary school for three years; within the group, a number of schools were selected for intensive study; pupils and teachers were interviewed and classroom activities observed).

The findings indicated that schools do in fact have an influence upon the academic development of children. The factors Rutter found to be important were (1) the quality of teacher-pupil interaction, (2) an atmosphere of cooperation and caring between teachers and students, and (3) a well-organized course preparation. Influences prior to, and outside, school are most decisive in perpetuating social inequalities. Rutter's results help us to understand just why schooling tends to maintain inequalities. Differences in school organization and atmosphere can counteract outside influences on academic attainment. Improvement in teaching quality, the social climate of the school, and patterns of school work can help deprived children improve academic performance. Coleman, Hoffer and Kilgire, 1981 reached similar conclusions in later research. Jenk Christopher (Inequality 1972, Oakes 1985) reaffirmed the findings that educational and occupational attainment are governed mainly by family background and non-school factors, and that educational reforms on their own can have only minor effects on existing inequalities.

A.H. Halsey reported (1980) in UK a boy from the service class (people of professional and managerial background) during the post-war period was ten times as likely as one from the working class to be in school at the age of eighteen, and was eleven times as likely to go to university.

Craft and Craft (1985) studied ethnicity and educational achievement and reported that in 1985 only 5 percent of West Indian school-leavers obtained one or more passes at 'A' level in 1981-2, compared to 13 percent of the white population.

Theories

Basil Bernstein argued that children from varying backgrounds develop different codes or forms of speech, during their early lives, which affect subsequent school experience (1975). There are systematic differences in ways of using language, particularly contrasting poorer and wealthier children. The speech of lower-class children represents a restricted code – a way of using language containing many unstated assumptions which speakers expect others to know. A type of speech tied to the cultural setting of a lower-class community or a district. Many lower-class people live in a strong familial or neighbourhood culture, in which values and norms are taken for granted, and not expressed in language. Lower class parents tend to socialize their children directly by the use of rewards or reprimands to correct behaviour. Language in a restricted code is more suitable for communication about practical experience than for discussion of more abstract ideas, processes or relationships. It is characteristic of children growing up in lower class families, and of the peer-groups in which they spend their time. Speech is oriented to the norms of the group.

The language developed of middle class children involves the acquisition of an elaborated code – a style of speaking in which the meanings of words can be individualized to suit the demands of particular situations. The ways in which children from middle-class backgrounds learn to use language are less bound to particular contexts; the child is able more easily to generalize and express abstract ideas. Middle class mothers, when controlling their children, frequently explain the reasons and principles which underlie their reactions to the child's behaviour. While a lower-class mother might tell a child off for wanting to eat to many sweets by simple saying, "No more sweets for you!" a middle class mother is more likely to explain that eating too many sweets is bad for one's health and the state of one's teeth. Children who have aquired elaborated codes of speech are more able to deal with the demands of formal academic education than those confined to restricted codes.

Joan Tough backed the thesis that lower-class children generally have less experience of having their questions answered, or of being offered explationations about the reasoning of others[25].

Labov 1978 opined that lower-class language is as selective as elaborate, and abstract, as middle-class speech, although its grammatical character is different.

Samuel Bowels and Herbert Gintis observe that education has not been a powerful influence towards economic equality. Modern education should be understood as a response to the economic needs of industrial capitalism. Schools help to provide the technical and social skills required by industrial enterprise; and they instill respect for authority and discipline into the labour-force. Relations of authority and control in school, which are hierarchical and include an emphasis upon obedience, directly parallel those dominating the workplace. The rewards and punishments held out in school also replicate those in the world of work. Schools help to motivate some individuals towards 'achievement' and 'success', while discouraging others, who find their way into low-paid jobs.

They accept that the development of mass education has had many beneficial effects. Illiteracy has been virtually eliminated, and schooling provides access to learning experiences, which are intrinsically self fulfilling. Because education has expanded mainly as a response to economic needs, the school system falls far short of what enlightened reformers hoped from it.

Modern schools reproduce the feelings of powerlessness. The ideas of personal development can only be achieved if people can control the conditions of their own lives, and develop their talents and abilities of self-expression. Under the current system, schools are destined to legitimate inequality, limit personal development to forms compatible with submission to arbitrary authority, and aid in the process whereby youth are resigned to their faith (p. 266). Bowles and Gintis argue, if there were greater democracy at large, a system of education could be developed providing for greater individual fulfillment.

Ivan Illich described modern economic development as a process whereby previously self-sufficient peoples are disposed of their traditional skills, and made to rely on doctors for their health, teachers for their schooling, television for their entertainment and employers for their subsistence. Everett Reimer and Illich argue that the very notion of compulsory schooling – now accepted throughout the world – should be questioned[26]. Bowles and Gintis and Illich stress the connection between the development of education and economic requirements for discipline and hierarchy. Schools cope with the provision of custodial care, the distribution of people among occupational roles, the learning of dominant values and the acquisition of socially approved skills and knowledge. The school has become a custodial organization because attendance is obligatory, and children are kept off the street between early childhood and their entry into work.

Schools tend to inculcate passive consumption – an uncritical acceptance of the existing social order – by the nature of the discipline and regimentation they involve. The hidden curriculum teaches children that their role in life is to know their place and to sit still in it[27].

Since schools do not promote equality or the development of individual creative abilities, why not do away with them in their current form?

In place of schools there should be several types of educational framework – material resources for formal learning stored in libraries, rental agencies, laboratories, information storage banks, communications networks, vouchers to use educational services as and when any student wishes. Education would not just be a form of early training, confined to special institutions but would become available to whoever wished to take advantage of it.

Cultural reproduction[28] refers to the ways in which schools, in conjunction with other social institutions, help perpetuate social and economic inequalities across the generations[29].

Ethnic and gender differences are marked in education. Newspaper, radio, TV, and Computers have been globalizing social life. World society has become increasingly[30] interdependent – a process known as globalization. The development of world social relations involves large-scale inequalities between the industrialized and third world societies. The largest disparities of wealth and living standards are those separating the rich industrialized countries from the poorer third world states.

Most third world societies are in areas of the world, which underwent western colonial rule. Many have only become independent states in the period since the second world war. Although most third world societies are impoverished compared to the industriakised nations a minority (NICs, or newly industrializing countries) have recently experienced rapid economic development.

Milllions of people in the world each year die of hunger or diseases associated with multinutition, yet, even with rapid population growth sufficient food is produced to feed everyone in the world. Large amounts of food are destroyed or stored indefinitely by the western countries, even though people in other parts of the world are starving. The level of regular food aid provided by the rich to the poor countries is low.

The distribution of the world's food supplies is strongly influenced by the impact of agribusiness – the industrial production, processing and storage of food. Agribusiness firms operating in third world countries are geared to export for western markets rather than stimulating local agriculture.

Theories of imperialism and non-imperialism, dependence theories and world system theories emphasized external economic pressure, dominating relationship of industrial nations and centralized world economy respectively, as factors leading to global inequalities. The process of world development is a result of interdependence of countries in the world economy and activities of transnational companies across national boundaries.

Telecommunication technologies, advanced transportation system and non-state agencies to deal with international collaboration or communication facilitated a frequent and rapid exchange of goods from country to country. Despite the fear of rise of media imperialism an international order of production, distribution and consumption of informational goods came into being that makes one feel as inhabiting one world today[31].

Remedial Measures for Higher Education of Weaker Sections

Why higher education is important for the backward classes, what constitutes its backwardness? Given the Indian social structure of hierarchy of highest, middle and lower statuses depending on economically happier, less happier and miserable positions education bridges such gaps and it evokes the principle that the richer the education the higher the socio-economic upliftment as an operative rule.

Dr. Ambedkar was not for the rule that individual everybody must be highly elevated in order to elevate any community's status. He was a practicably wise reformer in believing that the contempt valley of ascending hatred and descending humiliation for a particular community of Indian society can be overcome by producing something like 30 engineers, 20 doctors, 10 barristers and same number of professors within that community to be highly looked at as respectable class of members[32].

Hill Theory: How the rural people will get economic help? For this the governing agencies should raise their status – a status of rural backward class et al, not individually. Their doctors, lawyers, professionals among them will draw respect for them all. No primary, secondary schools for this community are needed to raise their status, for, out of 100 school-going children among them only 20 remain and 80 are drop-outs. If there be such schools then they should be opened in their locality and admit their boys and girls in them. Then collect best boys from primary schools, give them food, shelter and education in the schools themselves away from their parents upto their matriculation examinations. After that send them to college and give them tution fee. Then select a number of students from amongst them and send them for higher education to Europe, Germany, France, America and similar foreign countries, where they can get the best of education as there is no social atmosphere in our country to give their children equality of opportunity and such social setting mars their academic progress and upliftment. After that give them service in the government departments. Spend at least one crore of rupees for the scheduled castes and scheduled tribes. As a result they will become vocal and thus you will create a few people with high qualification and place them in higher posts and it will be 2000 times better than the 2000 boys educated in Marathi or Gujarati schools.

Community education will take a shape of hill but education to a few at top will take a shape of tower. Tower will fall and hill will remain.

Burmese education system can be cited as best example. On par with the Banares Hindu University and Aligarh Muslim University there ought to have been Indian SC or Buddhist University to be financed by Government of India by required amount of rupees for educating their students.

As the Member of the Viceroy's Executive Council, besides opening the girls' schools, and distribution of prizes apart, one day Dr. Ambedkar went to the Viceroy and asked him – "Would you not mind if I ask you some question?" "No", said the Viceroy. Ambedkar asked, "My first question is whether you would reckon me as an individual to surpass 50 to 500 university graduates or not?' "I admit it," replied the Viceroy and when Ambedkar queried further "why" the Viceroy replied, "I just don't know but the fact is there." Ambedkar explained, "I am one of those highly qualified and educated persons who are on a marke ki jagah or key offices. I can check any wrong being done and there are only a few persons who can occupy such positions." After being convinced by Ambedkar's explanation the Viceroy consented to invest Rs. 3 lacs in the foreign education of the scheduled castes and 26 candidates were dispatched to foreign countries on his behest then despite Rajgopalachari's muddling in the matter.

How to speedily remove the educational backwardness of the community? Produce big people among them as above and then their inferiority complex – a sort of backwardness would go[32].

Education system meant for the removal of untouchability and gender discrimination presuppose (1) change of attitude, (2) reform of family system, (3) nationalization of land, (4) awareness of the oppressed, (4) social welfare schemes, (5) upliftment of women, (6) Education of secular pattern, prescribing (i) lessons on job-orientation but not on Chaturvarna, caste and untouchability, (ii) taking up Booker T. Washington model, (iii) training untouchables in the discipline of engineering, medicine, ship-building and mechanical work, and (iv) giving increasing maintenance and scholarship sufficient to carry out education in Arts and Commerce, training in industrial and vocational on the part of the SC and ST students.

It is also suggested that education imparted on the basis of ancient tradition and customs be dropped and such education should be given as would create among them a sense of social endosmosis.

No schooling be conducted inside a temple precinct but in separate buildings constructed for that purpose.

Private institutions running primary and secondary schools should not mention caste and sub-caste of students in their school registers. However reforms are to be made in management of temple affairs so that its proceeds could be utilized for the welfare of the backward communities and instead it be made a house of education by doing away with privileges of priests or pujaris by legislation as was done in respect of the Princes and ICS Officers and sanad or licence be given to a proficient religious candidate as it is given to an advocate.

Summary

1. Meaning and connotation: *Though education as power cannot be disagreed it is also characterized as "force for social change.*
2. Buddhist Educational Background: *The initial provision of Buddhist monk training stressed that a Bhikkhu should be sharply intellectual.*
3. Vedic System: *Vedic system necessitated reference to gotra of a student at the time of admission to Vedic institution of education.*
4. Brahmanic System: *According to Manusmrti Vedas shall not be chanted in the presence of a shudra.*
5. Buddhist System: *There were thousands of teachers and students in the Buddhist Vihara precincts. Students flocked there even from foreign lands. This development culminated through 1500 years of educational flurry of centers at Nalanda, Vallabhi, Vikramshila, Jagaddala, Odantapuri as representatives of Buddhist universal educational system till it was reduced to ashes by the fierce anger-fired Turushk or Turk Bakhtiyar Khilji in 1200 A.D*[8].
6. British Period: *the Inspector M.S. Staley and Commissioner W.N. Maw of Nagpur Divison informed the Government that grant should not be given to any depressed class hostel as it would create the feeling of segregation and induce missionaries also to demand the same.*
7. Ambedkar Age: *On 29th October 1942 Ambedkar submitted his memorandum on the Grievances of the SCs and STs to H.E. the Governor-General in New Delhi stating that in order to brining reformation and change in the status and conditions of the weaker sections their youths must get key posts or higher administrative offices. Ambedkar was deploring the Indian Education System as factory of Beggars where ninety pecent of population was illiterate and appreciated the Brahmadesh model in this respect where same number of people were equally literate.*
8. Education and Change: *In short changes are marked in educational, economic, social, and judicial dimensions due to government efforts and further steps need to be taken to improve SCs conditions in coming years.*

9. *World Scenario: All teachers in schools, colleges and universities in France are State employees. Rates of pay and the broad framework of teaching duties are fixed centrally. But the distinction between Public and Private in American Higher education is not clear-cut. The British system of higher education is more decentralized than that of France, but more unitary than that of the USA. The Council for Natonal Academic Awards ensures uniform standard in degrees. Only 6.6 percent of eighteen-year-olds entered university in Britain in 1986 compared to over 10 percent in most other European countries and about 30 percent in Italy in the same year. According to Kogan and Kogan*[23] *between 1989 and 1985, 5,600 academic posts in universities disappeared and 18,000 undergraduate places were lost.*
10. Education and inequality: *Education tends to express and reaffirm existing inequalities far more than it acts to change disparities. Rutter's results help us to understand just why schooling tends to maintain inequalities.*
11. Theories: *Basil Bernstein argued that children from varying backgrounds develop different codes or forms of speech, during their early lives, which affect subsequent school experience (1975). Modern education should be understood as a response to the economic needs of industrial capitalism. Modern schools reproduce the feelings of powerlessness. Ivan Illich described modern economic development as a process whereby previously self-sufficient peoples are disposed of their traditional skills, and made to rely on doctors for their health, teachers for their schooling, television for their entertainment and employers for their subsistence.Cultural reproduction perpetuates social and economic inequalities across the generations. Ethnic and gender differences are marked in education. Despite the fear of rise of media imperialism an international order of production, distribution and consumption of informational goods came into being that makes one feel as inhabiting one world today.*
12. Remedial Measures for Higher Education of Weaker Sections: *Hill Theory. Burmese education system can be cited as best example. I am one of those highly qualified and educated persons who are on a marke ki jagah or key offices. I can check any wrong being done and there are only a few persons who can occupy such positions. Education system meant for the removal of untouchability and gender discrimination presuppose (1) change of attitude,*

(2) reform of family system, (3) nationalization of land, (4) awareness of the oppressed, (4) social welfare schemes, (5) upliftment of women, (6) Education of secular pattern.

Notes and References

1. Carol Bellamy, Executive Director, Education, Unicef, The State of the World's Children, 1999, Report of 2001, pp. 96-1142.
2. Ambedkar's review: 1917.
3. Bouddha Sanskrit Grantha (400 A.D.) referred to principles and rules of debate; Maitreya's Saptadasabhoomishastra (Nanjio 1170) incorporated seven chapters on an art of debate; the Buddhist monks represented medieval school in the history of Indian logic, their writings disappeared in India but the founder of Medieval school of Indian Logic, Pandit S.C. Vidyabhushan discovered their works in Tibet and published them in 1907.
4. Prof. Mukerjee, Ancient Indian Era.
5. Apastambhasmrti, N.6,9, P.1, Patala 3 and Part 9.
6. Gautamasmrti, Niyam No. 19.
7. Gautama, adhyaya xii, Shlokas 4, 5 and 6.
8. Buddhist Chinese, Tibetan Edicts and manuscripts.
9. Sharat Chandra Das, Indian Pandits in the Land of Snow, 1893.
10. Captain Wadell, Lhasa and Its Mysteries, 1905.

9. Admission was open for all Bhikkhus and Non-Bhikkhus, Buddhist and Non-Buddhist students free of charge. The latter category of students were distinguished by designation of Manava (commoner) and Brahmachari living and learning there free of cost. Bhikkhus offered mainly various other cultural subjects such as teachings of other religions, philosophical systems and socially useful subjects including agriculture, architecture, which foreran since the beginning of writing skill in the first century A.D. and a store of the manuscripts of Nalanda, Vikramashila and other Vihara University libraries.

10. I-tsing in his edict No. 35 described Indian educational method of imparting education that taught compulsory subjects including Sanskrit Grammar, even Panini's Grammar as mentioned in the commentaries of Yasomitra, Panini sutra, Dhatupatha, Ashtadhatu, Unadi-Sutra, Kashikavrtti, Churni (like Patanjali's great commentarial treatise), Treatises of Bhrtrihari, Vakyapadiya and Peina or Bedavrtti as youth scholars took interest in them as well as in logic, metaphysics, inferences grasped rightly through the study of Nyaya dvaratarkashastra. Jatakamala developed their grasping power. Even Buddhist monks would study besides Vinaya Texts the Sutras and the Shastras and dismiss heretic views as the hunters would drive the deer through plains and refute them as the vapour melts the fogs.

11. Taranatha, History of Indian Buddhism, Early 18th Century, Colophones.

12. P. V. Bapat ed. 2500 Years of Buddhism, Government of India, New Delhi 1956, p. 168.

13. Bouddha Dharma Ke Abhilekh, pp. 182-83: Intellect is developed by repeated memorizing and idreas are stabilized by letters.

14. See King Yasovarman's Edicts on stories of Nalanda University, Hui-Lee on lodging and Yuan Chwang (629-646 A.D.) on magnificence of the building of the Nalanda Centre of Learning. This development took place during the 200 years gap between Fa-Hian (405-411 A.D.) and Yuan-Chwang. The former visited in Patliputra two viharas belonging to Theravada and Mahayana traditions that were large and beautiful in respect of disciplinary and intellectual atmosphere attracting merited characters and truth-seekers from all quarters. He told that kings and wealthy merchant chiefs built the Viharas for the monks furnished with farms, houses, groves, gardens and animals with the assistance of local folks. Royal gift was inscribed on metal plaques and this tradition was continued unbroken from one dynasty to another. When a king offered alms to the Order he would take his crown down and feed them in company of his relatives and ministers at his own hands. Lay families would supply the monks requisites in plenty lest there should be no shortage of anything. At the end of the 7th century the Viharas became abundantly rich and the contempory travellor I-Tsing teasingly expressed, " Such an abundance of wealth in the Viharas, the granaries overfilled with the grain at the brink of going waste, many a men and women servants and wasteful collection of properties and assets in a treasury are not good." Such was the maintenance and endowments under the jurisdiction of the central Maha Vihara.
15. For lectures and discussion hundred platforms per day were arranged. Both Brahman and Recluse cultures were represented in syllabus on spiritual and secular subjects. Choice of subjects from among the available lot was of learners. The topics studied in Nalanda can be estimated from the Hwui-Lee's biography of Yuwan-Chwang, a Mahayan Buddhist scholar. Accordingly there were constant number of 10,000 inmates, be they visiting or residential and all would study the Mahayan Buddhism and treatises of the eighteen different Buddhist sects, besides general study of heretical and secular books such as Vedas and other scriptures, Hetu-vidya, Shabda-vidya, Chikitsavidya, Jaduvidya (Atharvaveda) and Sankhya philosophy and miscellaneous books. During the period of I-Tsing (671-695 A.D.) this number reduced to little more than 3000 of learners. Compared to Vallabhi in the western part of India, Nalanda in the eastern India was well-equipped with study-rooms, lecture-halls, libraries, rules of attendance of lecture and admission, character and discipline and awards of punishment for breach of rules, and institutional administration as a whole.
16. One Shilabhadra alone studied and digested the aggregate of fifty baskets of aphorisms and treatises, otherwise dealt with by ten Masters of Law (Dharmavida), an aggregate of thirty baskets of Sutras and Shastras to be dealt with by five hundred scholars and twenty baskets of aphorisms and treatises that required one thousand scholars to deal with respectively. Under him Yuan Chwang, his biographer Hwui-Lee reports, studied Yogachara system of philosophy for the period of more than five years.
17. Mooknayaka, Marathi fortnightly dated 9th October 1920.
18. Mooknayaka, 23.10.1920.
19. Amnbedkar's address at the Depressed Classes Conference, Kolaba in 1927.
20. The Report of the Director of the Government Public Instruction Department of the Year 1923-1924.

21. Dainik City Bhaskar, Indore, 8th March 2005, p. 20.
22. Carswell, 1985, p. 1.
23. Cogan and Cogan, 1988, p. 11.
24. Coleman et al., 1966, p. 325.
25. Tough 1976; Barbara Tizard and Martin Hughes 1984.
26. Illich 1973.
27. *Ibid.*
28. Bourdieu 1986, 1988; Boudieu and Passeron, 1977.
29. Anthony Giddens, Sociology, Polity Press, UK 1989, pp. 421-423, 437, 519-549, 530-533 and 729.
30. *Ibid.,* p. 547.
31. Report of the Backward Classes Commission, Volume III, Delhi 1956, pp. 73-75.
32. Nirmal Kumar Bose, Anthropology and Some Indian Problems, Calcutta, 1988, p. 275.

Chapter - 14

Social philosophy

We are to discuss in this paper society, its meaning, fundamental principal of foundation of society, principle of change and reconstruction of society, religion, ideal society and new order based on the principles of liberty, equality and fraternity as naturally justified principles of Ambedkar's conception of new age society.

Unfortunately there is no independent school of sociology that represents social and religious values besides the five major schools namely (1) Mechanistic, (2) Geographical, (3) Biological, (4) Bio-Social, and (5) Sociological school. Malthus in his book entitled *An essay on Principles of Population* (1768) echoed the Buddha's dictum, which in Pali reads *sabbe satta aharatthitika*, i.e. all beings depend on food for their existence. But the former added to the law of subsistence by telling that the means of food and edible stuff are subjected to diminishing return in mathematical progression (1,2,3,4..), and the law of human births multiplies by geometrical progression (1,2,4,8...). However Sadler viewed that although the sex instinct is universal fecundity diminishes as the population increases. Thus bio-social or demographic school studies social events through such speck of biological and livelihood rules.

August Comte (1798-1857) was the first thinker to believe that social science could be studied scientifically and his successor Emile Durkheim (1858-1917) reinforced that belief by actual application of scientific method in social sciences. Karl Marx (1818-1883) presented the historical evolution as product of social economic forces. However Von Wiese distinguished between sociology as a discipline and sociology as a science of social reality and concentrated more on social processes like sociation, association and dissociation.

Pitirim A. Sorokin in his book *System of Sociology* (1920: 769) said that *sociology has been, and either will be a science of the general characteristics of all classes of social phenomena, with the relationships and correlations between them, or there will be no sociology.*

Thus sociology is a study of intra-mental and impersonal and interpersonal relations of society. But are social form, quality and subject matter (man) different from social thought? According to Rollin Chambliss *social thought is concerned with human beings in their relationship with their fellows*[1].

But R. N. Mukherjee called it *a branch of thought which primarily concerned with men's general social life and its problems as created, expressed and endured by human interrelations and interactions*[2].

E.S. Bogardus simplified the definition of social thought as he expressed that it is thinking about society problems by one or a few persons here and there in human history or at the present[3].

As Babylonian and Egyptian social thoughts expressed in *The Epic of Gilgamesh* and *Code of Hammurabi* went against modern principle of equality so were the thoughts of Plato (427-347) about social stratification and of Aristotle (384-322) about impossibility of social change contrary to later thinkers like Lucretius (96-55 B.C.), Cicero (106-43 B.C.), Marcus Aurelius (121-180 A.D.), St. Augustine (354-430), Thomas Hobbes (1588-1679), John Locke (1632-1704), Rousseau (1712-1778), Montesquieu (1689-1755), August Comte (1798-1857), etc. before Dr. Ambedkar (1891-1956) and his contemporary social thinker Radhakamal Mukerjee (1889-1968).

So R. N. Mukherjee is right when he said that "social thought is that branch of human thought which is primarily concerned with human interrelations and interactions in their socio-historical settings[4]". According to Rollin Chambliss Comte's mode of thought was universally acceptable. "Comte denied that positivism is atheistic, since it is in no way concerned with the supernatural. He also claimed that it is not fatalistic, since it asserts that the external order is modifiable; or optimistic, since it lacks the theological roots of optimism; or materialistic, since it subordinates material to intellectual forces. Positivism is concerned with the *real* rather than the fanciful; with useful knowledge rather than all knowledge, with facts that are certain to the degree that the prevision is possible. It is concerned with precise knowledge rather than value impressions, with ever changing organic truth rather than the eternal verities, with the relative rather than the absolute. Finally, positivism is *sympathetic*, in that it binds in one fellowship all those who share its spirit and method. In short, positivism (science) is a mode of thought which can be universally accepted."[5]

Religion as one of the means of social regulation is recognized by H. Spencer and Emile Durkheim opined that every religion has society as its real basis. Therefore according to him "The Kingdom of Heaven is a glorified society". While Comte laid the foundation of sociology in France, Durkheim cemented the structure of this science....One of the Durkheim's aims was to establish sociology as independent science and to divorce it, in particular, from philosophy.

Karl Marx in his Capital (Vol. I, p. 776) rightly pointed out that "Force is the midwife of every old society pregnant with a new one". According to T. Veblen "Social structure changes, develops, adapts itself to an altered situation, only through a change in the habits of thought of the several classes of the community; or in the last analysis, through a change in the habits of thought of the individuals which make up the community. The volution of society is substantially a process of mental adaptation on the part of individual under the stress of circumstances which will no longer tolerate habits of thought formed under and conforming to a different set of circumstances in the past". To the Marxists Protestantism is a by-product of the rise of capitalism. But Weber came to the opposite conclusion in his analysis of the development of modern industrial capitalism and of Protestantism and his study of their relationships.

To C. H. Cooley (Social Organisation, p. 23) Family, play group and neighbourhood as primary groups are characterized by intimate face-to-face association and co-operation. They are primary in several senses, but chiefly in that they are fundamental in forming the social nature and ideals of the individuals.

About social mobility Sorokin expressed that "There has never existed a society in which vertical social mobility has been absolutely free and the transition from one social stratum to another has had no resistance. Social institutions including religion, according to Talcott Parsons are on a certain level, the most fundamental mechanisms of all, and only when they break down does it become necessary for more elaborate and specialized mechanism to come into play.

The social function of an organization helps to determine the structure...just as the structure helps to determine the effectiveness with which the functions are fulfilled, said Robert K. Merton. According to R.K. Mukherjee society is an organization and accumulation of values.

In the above statements we have seen that religion, spirituality and values formed the important part of social organization and Dr. Ambedkar observed that social life required discipline of either Dhamma or Law. Let us discuss his social philosophy here.

Who were the Shudras (1946) and *the Untouchables* (1948) by Ambedkar point to the salient feature of political history of India that in former time reference to ruling classes was a general way of recording political events of the time. Mention of leading social classes was also made in the writings of religion or scriptures. In any national life the leading social class also held power at the helm of affairs of the state.

According to Jyotiba Phooley such was the Brahman domination in India that "From many customs (Let the kingdom of Bali come and all troubles and misery go Vs. Let the kingdom of Bali go respectively wished by a Shudra and a Brahmin on Dussehara occasion and like customs) traditionally handed down to us, as well as from the mythological legends contained in the sacred books of the Brahmins, it is evident that there had been a hard struggle for ascendancy between the two races. The wars of Dev and Daitya, or the Rakshas, about which so many fictions are found scattered over the sacred books of the Brahmins, have certainly a reference to this primeval struggle. The original inhabitants with whom these earth-born Gods, the Brahmans, fought, were not inappropriately termed Rakshasas, that is the protectors of the land. The incredible and foolish legends regarding their form and shape are no doubt mere chimeras, the fact being that these people were of superior stature and hardy make. Under such leaders as Brahma, Purshuram and others, the Brahmins waged very protracted wars against the original inhabitants. They eventually succeeded in establishing their supremacy and subjugating the aborigines to their entire control. Accounts of these conquests, enveloped with a mass of incredible fiction, are found in the books of the Brahmins. In some instances they were compelled to emigrate, and in others wholesale extermination was resorted to. The cruelties which the European settlers practiced on the American Indians on their first settlement in the new world, had certainly their parallel in India on the advent of the Aryans and their subjugation of the aborigines. The cruelties and inhuman atrocities which Parshuram committed on the Kshatriyas, the people of this land, if we are to believe even one tenth of what the legends say regarding him, surpass our belief and show that he was more a fiend than a God. Perhaps in the whole range of history it is scarcely possible to meet with such another character as that of Parshuram, so selfish, infamous, cruel and inhuman. The deeds of Nero, Alaric or Machiavelli sink into insignificance before the ferocity of Purshram. The myriads of men and defenceless children whom he butchered, simply with a view to the establishment of his coreligionists on a secure and permanent basis in this land is a fact for which generations ought to execrate his name, rather than deify it[6]".

Perhaps the Best Bakery case in which the burning train took toll of many men, woman and children in Godhra, Gujrat and an Apex Court Bench describing the government officials as Neros looking elsewhere while human beings were burning to death at Godhra spot may even be insignificant before the incident cited above[7]. If this is offendable to refer to Parshuram in such manner on his jayanti, which falls on 22nd April every year another example of latest political events that occurred in the capital of the country's biggest state in terms of largest number of Lok Sabha seats, Uttar Pradesh may be mentioned, which fell on the birth day of BJP leader Lalji Tandon when sarees were distributed to the Dalit women, who gave their lives, along with their children in the stampede that ensued and made the face of India crestfallen despite the Governmental pill of Feel Good philosophy freely propagandized at such juncture of General Election.

Thus social affairs are supreme and they form the goal of political activities. This has been deftly put in the words of Ambedkar thus:

> "As a student of history I have been profoundly impressed by the view that however important political forces may be in the regeneration of a community, social, economic and moral forces are only a means to the social, economic and moral regeneration of a people. I have from the very beginning laid greater stress on social movement than on political movement. A very large part of 25 years of my public life has been mainly devoted to the cause of social uplift of the untouchables. I mention this only to correct the impression that I am only a politician. For it is a wrong impression. I want the public to realize that I have played no insignificant part in giving momentum to the new moment and fostering its growth[8]"

Furthermore dwelling on the relationship between society and religion Dr. Ambedkar said, "Religion in the sense of morality must therefore, remain the governing principle in every society" and replying to the Radhakrishnan's statement regarding greatness of the Hindus because they survived so long against odds he said, "For an individual as well as for a society there is a gulf between merely living and living worthily."

Even the Buddha founded his Order on the principle of *everything is perishable* and realization of that principle is sought by the methodology of observation, remembrance, comparison and conclusion or the dictum of meditation on thought. In the modern era Ambedkar revived not only the body Buddhica of India but resuscitated the Principia Buddhica both in letter and spirit. This is the reason why he underlined the social warfare between the leading classes and projected the struggle for ethical supremacy going on between the religious orders and political systems of the time.

Society is a conglomeration of people living in a fixed territory under certain political rule bound by socio-economic-cultural ties. Society is variously observed by different social scientists with their emphasis on various salient features of social life. The important thing about society is its unit, whether it is caste(s) or an individual, the former being a sign of primitive society and the latter of civilized one. Thus society is of two types according to the reference of point of time and its evolution during the process of its course in the history. By characteristics society may be classified as free or bound societies also. By advancement of science and technology the development of society is identified as industrialized developed society or urbanizing developing society or underdeveloped societies. All societies have one common mark as its basic nature or function.

Meaning of Society is to identify that common thread running through all kinds of societies as described above for instance. Fraternal relationship among people of world is an ideal social and moral condition. It is an organization of human relations running undisturbed by any social eruptions. However this definition is ethical value loaded and therefore it is ideal kind of social relationship. This is corroborated by the definition of society given by Dr. Radhakamal Mukerjee. According to him, "Society is the sum of social structures and functions that establishes, safeguards and transmits an ordered and systematized pattern of ethos, beliefs, relations and behaviours[9]".

Fundamental principles of foundation of society include man's egregious nature and sociability for leading associated life together and fulfill the needs of self and others to one's own maximum satisfaction through such collective mode of living. Thus there is society for a man to develop his self and there are various groups of people bound by the relationship of common needs and common ends promoting their association to conduct one another in material respect and mutual exchange of goods and ideas for their material and mental sustenance.

This idea may be compared with Talcott Parsons' Theory of Action, which is approved by the largest majority of sociologists. He defined the society as the total complex of human relationships in so far as they grow out of action in terms of the means-end relationship, intrinsic or symbolic (Society, New York, 1953, p.231). Talcott said that "Reduced to the simple possible terms, then, a social system consists in a plurality of individual actors interacting with each other in a situation which has at least a physical or environmental aspect, actors who are motivated in terms of a tendency to the 'optimization of gratification' and whose relation to their situation, including each other, is defined and mediated in terms of a system of culturally structured and shared symbols." Further, the social system is essentially a net-work of interactive relationships.There are in tern two aspects of this reciprocal inter-relation with each of the others. First, a social system cannot be so structured as to be radically incompatible with the conditions of functioning of its component individual actors as biological organisms and as personalities of relatively stable integration of a cultural system; secondly, in turn the social system, on both fronts, depends on the requisite minimum of support from each of the other system. It is indeed a very general phenomenon that social forces are directly responsible for injury to or destruction of some individuals and some of the wants or needs of all individuals, and though this may be reduced, it is highly probable that it cannot be eliminated under realistic conditions. To cite a very simple case, a war cannot be won without casualties and acceptance of war is sometimes a condition of survival of a social system as a distinctive system.

This is corroborated with principle of reconstruction of society as mentioned in Russell's writing of the book of institution of war, where violence is referred to be one of the impulses as spring of action as psycho-social school also might approve of it.

According to Parsons "The elements for this new generalized system of action are four in number: (1) heredity and environment, as the ultimate conditions of action; (2) means and ends; (3) ultimate values; and (4) zeal or effort – the name for relating factor between normative and the conditional elements of action[10]".

In any concrete system of action a process of change so far as it is at all explicable in terms of those elements of action formulated in terms of the intrinsic means-ends relationship can proceed only in the direction of approach towards the realization of the rational norms conceived as binding on the actors in the system. That is, more briefly, such a process of action can proceed only in the direction of an increase in the value of the property rationality (ibid., p. 751). Since action is a process in the actor-situation system which has motivational significance to the individual actor, or, in the case of a collectivity, its component individuals. A social system consists of a plurality of individual actors, interacting with each other in a situation, and whose relations are defined and modified in terms of a system of culturally defined structure and shared symbols.

About regulating society T. Parsons gave the mechanism of means of social control on gross scale which are on a certain level the most fundamental mechanism of all, and only when they break down does it become necessary for more elaborate and specialized mechanism to come into play.

Principle of change and reconstruction of society revolves round the natural law of flux and identity. This phenomenon has been expressed in the phrase 'na ca so na ca anno' in Buddhist terminology meaning thereby "neither the same nor the totally different one", since sameness precludes new formation and absolute difference cuts off itself from causal connection with total destruction of precedent and complete new arising of subsequent entity appearing as identical process like a series of lighting going off and on continuously and looking rotating due to that effect as the process of continuity links two consecutive moments at the two ends of the present state.

Religion as said above remains the governing principle of every society although by religion is meant not ritual but only morality from Ambedkar's standpoint.

Ideal society is an association of human beings for satisfactory performance of social, economic, political and above all fraternal or moral activities resulting in peace, harmony and happiness of all members.

New Order means free, frank and fair society without castes, without classes, without constraints of any kind be they of culture or of system not leaving its individuals to degenerate but providing environment for them to fare better and bring revolutionary and radical change in their present status quo through the lower stratum to the higher plane.

Thus it is a matter of great significance for both the individual and the society that one should not mind the distance traversed by one in the course of time but one must mind the direction in which that distance has been traversed by one during that process or time.

According to Wittgenstein, "Philosophy is a therapeutic activity". Social thinkers such as MacIver and Page defined society as a net of human relationships". So social philosophy is a therapy of social ills. Ambedkar's social philosophy is a combination of philosophy and sociology respectively of Wittgenstein and Durkheim both.

There are numerous social evils of Indian society be they religious, economic or political. Above all the ills the social exclusiveness is of prime importance. Varna, caste, religion, language, politics, economy, philosophy have each contributed to disintegrate Indians into separate warring camps between the warriors and the priests on the one hand and between the Buddhists and the Brahmins on the other hand. The warriors and the Buddhists formed the present Shudra castes and minorities respectively in Indian social hierarchy with priests and the Brahmin class usurping the topmost position in education, wealth, power and other matters of life.

Historically speaking the nobles were revolutionary people, warrior race and of Buddhist culture while the Vedic tribes were counter revolutionary, caste bound and of no-change establishment.

There is a philosophy of Burke, Carlyle, Marx that recognizes non-human material and divine forces as creative powers of life and does not recognize man as creator of his own destiny. Only Ambedkar's logic considers human value as supreme in social life. However he pointed also towards the destructiveness of evil minded individuals, who had done a great disservice to the human values of equality, liberty, fraternity and justice or the movement of independence by their treacherous acts of siding the enemy camps, at the cost of indigenous enslavement as was witnessed by the acts of villains like Jaychand for Mohammed bin Kasim against his own king Dahir, that of Prithviraj Chauhan's General for Mohammed Gori, that of Marathas for the Moghul against Shivaji, that of Sikh Commanders against their rulers and that of most of the Indian people against the section who revolted against the Britishers in the mutiny of 1857 during pre-independence period.

If the Indian people will keep their creed and party above the national interest then the country may lose its independence once again and perhaps once for all unless the Indians deem themselves as Indians first and Indians last and fight for the cause of egalitarian society till the last drop of blood in their bodies on the side of revolutionary forces against the counteracts of inequalities in Indian society.

However no society can fare better without internal discipline or external organization or state, which will never wither away as long as society is bound together by moral binding and material force. The state has its three organs legislature, executive and judiciary. The last one is the weakest organ of the three as it derives its power from the source of people's representative in Lok Sabha or the House of Commons and depends on the executive organ to enforce its orders or will. As these three are interrelated organs historians, law students and general public are affected by omission or commission of acts on their part in disrespect of their mutual cooperation, coordination and end of their existence. Sometimes out of contumacy or ill-will the executive is liable to neglect the judicial decrees and conversely the latter also might trespass its jurisdiction in carrying justice out of personal interest dominating that of the general public. 34000 crore rupees stamp scam, bakery scam, and other such cases prove such inclinations. However the attorney-General of India Shri Soli Sorabji and his Israel counterpart Mr. Barak differed and viewed judiciary the strongest organ of all under the present circumstances[11].

Prof. Mungekar warned against caste-finding tendency of the Hindu mentality in the name of general fact finding show. Prof. Subhadra Channa gave her critique against projection of India as sectional, and upheld the Dalits, the farmers, the labourers or women or such other backward classes as the real builders of true India[12]. This only shows that the philosophy in right direction will lead nation to right formation of society also. One does not need soothsayers to foretell that wrong creed will create long suffering for the largest democracy of the world. However we should aspire for becoming not only longer survived and larger votaries but worthy successors treading on higher planes of life.

Chattopadhyaya in his book "*What is living and what is dead in Indian philosophy*" discussed that it was very unfortunate that proponents of physics and atomism (Nyaya-Vaishesika) like Vatsyayan and Prasastapada surrendered their principles of philosophy before the pressure of the law-giver and government and thereby reconciled their rightly founded impartial philosophy of all's freedom with traditional social prerogatives of Varnashrama dharmas of general duties for liberation of the Brahmans' souls and everlasting bondage and slavery of the Shudras under prescribed specific duties in Manusmriti. Compared to these Indian atomists their western counterparts like Bacon and Descartes were truer seekers of truth as they never compromised their stand of upholding philosophy of welfare and well-being of the producing and toiling majority masses with traditional religious dogmas of parasite classes.

Dr. D.R. Jatav referred to four kinds of humanism, viz., Santayan's poetic humanism, Bertrand Russell's realistic humanism, John Dewey's pragmatic humanism and Ravindra Nath Tagore's spiritual humanism in his book "Social Philosophy of Dr. B.R. Ambedkar". But Dr. Ambedkar's social humanism, he said, is a blend of Buddhism's morality and universal moral order with modern science or reason. While western minds were found flabby in morals, shallow in sentiments and indecisive in values Ambedkar was positive and progressive in his view of man as supreme end and ideal society as an organization of human beings on the principles of liberty, equality, fraternity or justice. The constitution of India has rightly framed the letters and spirit of Ambedkar's ideal government and society in its preamble in the following terms:

We, the people of India, having solemnly resolved to constitute India into a Sovereign Socialist Secular Democratic Republic and to secure to all its citizens:

> JUSTICE, social, economic and political;
>
> LIBERTY of thought, expression, belief, faith and worship; EQUALITY of status and of opportunity; and to promote among them all
>
> FRATERNITY assuring the dignity of the individual and the unity and integrity of the Nation; In our consitutent assembly this twenty-sixth day of November, 1949, do hereby adopt, enact and give to ourselves this constitution.[13]

In such an Republic of Freedom the national flag carries the Dhamma wheel at its central white strap flanked by vermillion on top and green below and the social objectives are of welfare state as follows:

> *As a welfare State, India is committed to the welfare and development of its people, particularly the vulnerable sections like the Scheduled Castes (SCs), Scheduled Tribes (STs), backward classes, minorities and the handicapped. There are specific articles in the Constitution, which outline this commitment. The strategy adopted for these aims at minimizing inequalities in income, status and opportunities. This section of the society constitutes nearly 85% of the population. The task is gigantic for a country with limited resources.*[14]

Thus indeed the society in which all sections of people long to belong to oneness and togetherness is ideal society. This society has three pillars in the form of three social principles of liberty, equality and fraternity borrowed from Buddhist culture. Politically Dr. Ambedkar wholly went with political thinker John Stuart Mill's ideology, according to which, "If all mankind were of one opinion and one of them were of contrary opinion, the mankind would no more be justified in silencing that one person than he, if he had power, would be justified to silence that mankind[15]".

Was democracy only a political philosophy of Ambedkar? Democracy was defined by Abraham Lincoln as Government of the people, by the people and for the people. According to Bagehot it is a means of bringing socio-economic-political revolution by peaceful method. But Dr. Ambedkar meant by democracy the associated mode of living and it is a personality trait with every individual to act as democrat in all sheres of life. So for him the philosophy of life is to think in terms of the principles of liberty, equality, fraternity and act accordingly so that no man or group of men should be discouraged as unworthy or unfit of improving his present status by striving further.

Why did he embrace Buddhism? He embraced Buddhism because the words of Buddha gave encouragement to the oppressed, depressed and neglected people as much as he gave it to the general public unlike Hinduism. It also gave the teaching of compassion for helping the needy, of understanding for removal of superstition and of equality for annihilation of unnatural differences.

Did the present day Shudras and the Untouchables have the same kind of past? The shudras belonged to the same race as the Aryan and warrior and the Buddhists as military class had their unflinchable faith in the Buddha's religion. Just further north of Gulbarga is a place called Bidar, where the Mahar hero Amrit Nak or Naik saved the chastity of Mughal ruler's queen in the past and in return for his heroic deeds the ruler awarded him as many as fifty-two rights including that of land and collecting remuneration from the villagers. In Koregaon also stands the victory pillar or vijay stambha telling the names and heroic deeds of the Mahars, who sacrificed their lives for ending Brahman-Peshwa rule by siding the British Raj. They fought to win Maratha ruler Shivaji's kingdom also. Thus their past was glorious and shining.

What strategy can unite the disintegrated Dalits in the world? Actually Ambedkar's slogan *Educate, Agitate and Organize* influenced his followers the world over and today we have among us our own intellectuals in every field of life. But they ought to strive for better solidarity by overpowering their differences as well as their enemies before the counter-revolutionary forces defame and destroy their egalitarian philosophy.

Is philosophical aspect distinct and different from practical side? If so then one cannot live as one whole integrated life as is evident in a man of right speech and right action. Experiences consolidate and affirm our principles and principles direct our steps. So there is no contradiction between the two. All men are not on equal level of consciousness. The role of intellectuals is to bring such awareness amongst those masses psychologically and succeed in fulfilling the common goal.

The philosophy and method invented and applied by Buddha in ancient time to reorganize and reconstruct society and remove social ills was selfsome as prescribed and laid down in the constitution of India in modern time by Ambedkar. What was that social ill, that philosophy or that way of life? Released from all snares, both divine and human you and I should go and wander for the bebefit and happiness of many people, out of compassion for the world, for the welfare, benefit and happiness of Devas and men. Two of you are not to go by he same path, Teach the meaning and detail of the doctrine that is good in the beginning, good in the middle, and good in the end, fulfilled in its entirety, wholly pure. Make known the holy life. There are those who have few defilements, who are going to ruin through not hearing the Doctrine They will be the ones who fully understand the Doctrine. And I, Brethren, will go to Uruvela, to Senanigama, to teach the Doctrine. ***Muttaham bhikkhave sabbapasehi ye dibba ye ca manussa. Caratha bhikkhave carikam bahujanahitaya bahujanasukhaya lokanukampaya, atthaya hitaya devamanussanan. Ma ekena dve gamittha. Desetha bhikkhave dhammam adikalyanam majjhekalyanam, pariyosanakalyanam sattham savyanjanam kevalaparipunnam parisuddham brahmacariyam pakasetha. Santi satta pparajakha-jatikaassavanata hammassapannhayanti.bhavissanti dhammassa annataro. Ahampi bhikkhave yena Uruvela yena senanigamo tena upasankamissami dhammadesanaya'ti.***

What should women-folk do under the present circumstances? Is there any remedy in Ambedkar's social philosophy for their existing malady? One thing the womenfolk forgot and for which they cannot be excused according to my opinion is this that they have been ingrate to their own real saviours in the forms of Buddha and Ambedkar by taking refuge to different kinds of gods and hobgoblins, goddesses and supernatural quagmire. Is any lady elevated to such an high status as that of founder of religion in any tradition except in Buddhism and its Pali Tripitakas, in which Theras, Theris and Buddha words are equally weighed and incorporated as parameters of truth the Tathagata himself invented and discovered? Was any woman given freedom of becoming sanyasin to seek spiritual life and liberation in the world as far back as 2549 years hence? Has any philanthropist or world-guru restored and revived Buddhism in India and thereby regained the lost paradise of women and low caste people except one whom we call Babasaheb Ambedkar?

This is the social message of Buddhism hidden in meditational practice that gives hope to you and new builders of India towards better life with the conviction in every heart that "Nature and Nature's laws lay hid in night and let the Ambedkar consciousness come and all will be light".

All political revolutions are preceded by social and religious revolutions. Buddhism set the scene for Asokan Empire; Brahmanism brought the enthronement of Shunga dynasty; Marathi saints prepared ground for Maratha ruler Shivaji; Guru nanak brought change in social set up for the Sikh rule; social marginalization of the Shudras and exclusion of the Untouchables shattered Hindu unity and invited Moghuls to rule India followed by the British Raj till we became independent sovereign socialist secular democratic republic in 1950.

Will this hard won independence be put in jeopardy once again and lost for ever? Dr. Ambedkar worried and warned the various different castes, communities, creeds and political parties against such acts as placing one's own party's interest above national interest and foredooming their independence. For national integrity and ideal mode of associated living Dr. Ambedkar exhorted all to be the Indians first and Indians last by shedding till the last drop of blood of our bodies to keep our self-respect and national integration intact.

Let us refresh us with Ambedkar consciousness expressed in the letters and spirit as follows:

> We must exert ourselves for those among whom we are born. Blessed are those who think and act in this way. In order to end enslavement we shall sacrifice our bodies, minds, wealth and youthfulness and exert ceaselessly in the same manner till each man has secured his manliness or humanity come what may, bearing with suffering and happiness, evil and good, tremor and tempest, cemetery and calamity, success and failure, loss and gain, and praise and dispraise.

Bibliography

1. Rollin Chambliss, Social Thought, New York, 1954, p. 4.
2. R.N. Mukherjee, A History of Social Thought, Second Revised Edition, Saraswati Sadan, Mussoorie, 1964, p. 10 or R.K. Mukherjee, Social Thought—from Comte to Mukerjee, Vivek Prakashan, Delhi, reprint 1989, p. 32.
3. E.S. Bogardus,The Development of Social Thought, Longman Green and Co., New York 1957, p. 3.
4. R.N. Mukherjee, A History of Social Thought, *ibid.*
5. Rollin Chambliss, Social Thought, 1954, p. 399.
6. Slavery, Dhananjay Keer and S.G. Malshe edited Mahatma Phooley Samagra Vangmay, Maharashtra Rajya Sahitya Ani Sanskriti Mandal, Mantralaya, Mumbai, Ist ed. 1969, IInd ed. 1980, pp. 73-74.
7. Free Press, Indore, The Thursday 22nd April 2004, Front Page.
8. Dr. Babasaheb Ambedkar: Writings and Speeches. Education Department, Government of Maharashtra, Mumbai, Vol. 17, p. 446.

9. Raveendra Nath Mukerjee, Social Thought - from Comte to Mukerjee, Vivek Prakashan, Delhi 1989, p.522, footnote no. 12.

10. Talcott Parsons, The Structure of Social Action, McGraw-Hill, New York, 1937, p. 719.

11. The Hindu dated 18th February 2005.

12. Prof. Mungekar and Mrs Channa delivering their presentations during the national seminar on *The Role of Weaker Sections in Democracy and Nation-Building* under the auspices of Dr. Ambedkar Chair at BANISS, Dr. Ambedkar Nagar (M.P.) on the last 6th and 7th February 2004.

13. Constituion of India.

14. Website.

15. The Free Press, Indore, dated 23 April 2004, p. 4.

Chapter - 15

भारत की बौद्ध पहचानः भरहुत

सी. डी. नाईक'

प्रास्ताविक

टी. डब्ल्यू रिस डेविडस की बुद्धिस्ट इंडिया (1971) आज भी भरहुत स्तूप के बारे में अधिकृत ग्रंथ है। उन्होंने अपनी इस ऐतिहासिक रचना में इस बात का उल्लेख किया है कि भरहुत सही नाम नही है, बल्कि उसका सही अभिधान 'भरहतष' है। भरत सिंह उपाध्याय ने भी एक जैन ग्रंथ को उद्धृत करते हुए 'भरहश' कबीले का उल्लेख किया। तथापि डॉ. आंबेडकर ने अपने शोध ग्रंथ *शूद्र कौन थे* में कहा है कि भारतवर्ष का नाम भरत कुल यानी विश्वमित्र, दिवोदास, सुदास के कबीले के प्रभाव से पड़ा है। हालांकि धर्मानंद कोसम्बी जी मानते थे कि वशिष्ठ ऋषि भी दास वंश के थे। यूं तो ऐसे भी पाश्चात्य विद्वान हुए है कि जिन्होंने देवों के प्रिय प्रियदर्शी को अशोक के पहले का सम्राट मानकर इतिहास लेखन किया। दोनों एक ही सम्राट होने का तथ्य बाद में प्रकट हुआ। परंतु प्रश्न है कि क्या भारत की पहचान भरहुत रही है? उत्तर के लिए निम्नांकित आलेख प्रस्तुत है।

भरहुत स्तूप

भरहुत स्तूप प्रथम बार 1873 में जनरल सर अलेक्जेंडर कनिंघम द्वारा खोजा गया। सतीशचंद्र सील के अनुसार (1934) हरप्पा व मोहन्जो–दरो की सिन्धु घाटी की प्राचीन सभ्यता और मौर्य शिल्पावशेष के बाद भरहुत वास्तु व कला का कालानुक्रम है।

भरहुत स्तूप में तोरण के आड़े बीम पर उत्कीर्ण दृश्य बुद्ध चरित्र की सांकेतिक रुपरेखा बताते हैं और उसके तीन आड़े आर्किट्रेव के छोर पर अंकित मकर नीचे जल प्रवाह के अस्तित्व का बोध देते हैं तथा उसके मध्य भाग कष्ट पार कराने वाले सेतु का बोधक हैं। सब से ऊपर त्रिरत्न और धम्म चक्र है, जो क्रमशः सर्वोत्तम शरण स्थान और सेतु की भांति संसार सागर को पार कराने वाला आर्य अष्टांगिक मार्ग के द्योतक हैं।

अर्ध चन्द्राकार पूर्वद्वार पर उकेरे चित्र बुद्ध के जीवन के पांच बड़े प्रसंग अर्थात् जन्म, महाभिनिष्क्रमण, बुद्धत्व, प्रथम धर्मचक्रप्रवर्तन देशना और महापरिनिर्वाण के संकेत हैं।

भरहुत स्तूप का शिल्प कौशल समकालीन और उत्तरकालीन भारतीय और श्रीलंका की मूर्ति कला का आदर्श नमूना रहा है।

उस पर आगरजु के पुत्र धनभूति, शुंगक्षत्रप अग्निमित्र, रेवतिमित्र की पत्नि चापादेवी, धनभूति के पौत्र धनभूति द्वितीय आदि का नामोल्लेख है। शुंगवंश के संस्थापक पुष्यमित्र शुंग ई. स. पूर्व 184–148 में हुये थे।

बोधि वृक्ष

प्रत्येक बुद्ध ने अलग–अलग वृक्ष को बोधि वृक्ष के नाम से विख्यात किया। विपस्सी बुद्ध पाटली (bignonia suoveolens or trumpet-flower), सीखी बुद्ध पुण्डरीक (magnifera Indica or white-mango), वेस्सभू साल (shorea robusta), ककुसन्ध शीरीष (acacia), कोणागमन उदुम्बर (ficus glomereta), कस्सप न्यग्रोध (ficus indica or banyan), और शाक्यमुनि बुद्ध पिपल अथवा अश्वत्थ (ficus religiosa) नामक बोधि वृक्ष के पाद तले बुद्ध बने थे। बोधिवृक्ष को यहां पुरुष, हाथी, सिंह और गरुड़ादि द्वारा पूजित दर्शाया गया है।

वज्रासन

शेधिमण्ड अथवा वज्रासन पाषाणासन है, जो बुद्ध के विजय और लोकोत्तर दृढ़ प्रण का सूचक है। उसका चतुर्भज आकार उस समय के विश्वास यानी पृथ्वी चौकोणी है का ज्यामितीय प्रस्तुतिकरण है।

दिशायें

गंधर्वों के नेता धृतराष्ट्र लोकपाल सूर्य की मदद से पूर्व दिशा के प्रहरी हैं। कुम्भण्ड के नेता विरुढक यम की सहायता से दक्षिण दिशा के पहरेदार हैं। नागनायक विरुपाक्ष वरुण के साथ पश्चिम दिशा के रक्षक हैं और यक्ष नेता कुबेर मणिभद्र से मिलकर उत्तर दिशा के लोकपाल हैं। वे कामलोक के वासी हैं व स्याषी चिन्ह के धारक हैं।

जातक

भरहुत स्तूप पर जो 28 जातक खुदवाये, उनकी संख्या 28 बुद्ध परंपरा से मिलती है। उदाहरण स्वरुप उस पर उत्कीर्ण महाउम्मग्ग जातक का अंश देखिये। यवमज्झकिय जातक के दृश्य को प्रदर्शित करते हुए भरहुत स्तूप में दिखाया गया है कि महोषध पंडित न्यायविद है, जो वस्तुओं के असली स्वामी की पहचान कराने वाला निर्णय देकर झगड़े का निपटारा करते है। इस में यवमध्यक प्रसंग में श्रीवर्धक श्रेष्ठी के पुत्र महौषध किस प्रकार क्लिष्ट समस्या का समाधान देते हैं का वर्णन है। घटना निम्न प्रकार हैः विदेह की राजधानी मिथिला के चारों द्वारों के पास बसी मंडियों को पूर्व, दक्षिण, पश्चिम व उत्तर नगर कहते थे। श्रीवर्धन की पत्नि सुमना ने महोषध को जन्म दिया। बालक का जन्म उसके हस्त में औषधि की वनस्पति के साथ होने से उसका नाम महोषध पड़ा। उसने अपने नागरिकों के विवादों का निपटारा करने हेतु एक भव्य न्याय सभागृह बनवाया था। उसके होते मानो बुद्धप्रिय सुखी व न्यायिक समय का समाज प्रस्थापित हुआ हो का आभास हो रहा था।

एक दिन एक महिला तालाब में स्नान करने गई। उसने अपने हाथ से बनाये सूक्ष्म धागे के गोले को तट पर रख लिया था। तब दूसरी महिला वहां आई और उसने उसे वहां से उठा कर अपनी गोदी में छिपाया व वहां से निकल गई। नहाते हुई महिला ने उसे देख लिया और वह जल से बाहर आकर उसके पीछे दौड़ी और उसे वस्त्र से पकड़ लिया। फिर उसने उसे चिल्लाकर कहा, 'तुम मेरे धागे के गोले को चुरा कर ले जा रही हो। उस पर दूसरी महिला बोली, यह गोला मेरा है, तुम्हारा नही। इस प्रकार झगड़ते–झगड़ते दोनों महिलायें न्याय सभागृह के पास से गुजरी तो

महोशध ने उनका शोर सुन कर पूछा, क्या हो रहा है? जब वे दोनों उनके सामने खडी थीं तभी उन्होंने मुखमुद्रा से चोर महिला को पहचान लिया था और उसे पूछा, तुमने गोला कब बनाया और उसे किस चीज से लपेटा था? चोर महिला ने कहा, मैने गोला बना कर उसे कपास के बीज में लपेटा था। तब महोशध ने दूसरी महिला से पूछा तो उसने तिंबरु बीज में गोले को लपेटा होने की बात कही। तब उस गोले को निकलवाया और देखा तो उस में तिम्बरु बीज ही निकला। उसी से चोर महिला का भेद खुल गया। वहां एकत्रित लोगों ने महोशध के इस न्याय पद्धति की प्रशंसा की।

इस प्रकार महोशध के न्यायप्रियता की प्रसिद्धि चारों ओर फैली। उसकी बुद्धि की परीक्षा करने हेतु विदेहराज ने पूर्व नगर के लोगों के पास नर और मादा पुरुष की दो खोपड़ियां भेज कर उन्हें पहचानने को कहा अन्यथा हजार कार्षापण के दंड का हुक्म दिया। पूर्व नगर के लोगों ने महोषध की मदद ली। महोषध ने खोपड़ियों को जोड़ा फिर उन्हें देख कर ही पहचान लिया था कि कौनसी नर है और कौन सी मादा और उसने लोगों को बताया कि नर की खोपड़ी के जोड़ सीधे होते है तथा मादा के सिर के जोड़ टेढ़े होते है।

तीसरी बार राजा ने आदेश दिया कि पूर्व नगर के लोग ऐसा नया हौद बनवा कर भेजें, जिस में पांच प्रकार के कमल उगे हो। तब पंडित महोषध ने प्रतिप्रश्न से उसका समाधान किया। उस ने कुछ अच्छे बोलने वाले लोगों को बुला कर कहा कि तुम अपनी आंखें लाल होने तक जल में क्रीड़ा करो और गीले बाल व कपड़े के साथ कीचड़ से भरे शरीर से रस्सियां, दण्ड और ढ़ेले हाथ में लिए राजा के पास जाकर कहो कि महाराज! हम ने महातालाब आप की रुचि के अनुसार बनवाया और उसे यहां तक ले आ रहे थे। परंतु जलाशय जंगल के जीवन का आदी होने से नगर की दिवारें, परकोट और पहरा–स्तंभों को देखते ही भयभीत होकर रस्सियों को तोड़ कर जंगल में भाग गया। हम ने हर प्रयास किया परंतु उसे वापस नही ला सके। यदि आप अपना जंगल से लाया हुआ पुराना जलाशय दे तो हम दोनों को इकट्ठा बांध कर वापिस ले आयेंगे। राजा को ऐसा पूछने पर कहना पड़ा कि उसने कोई जलाशय जंगल से कभी नही लाया था। तब पंडित महोशध के मार्गदर्शन के अनुसार उन आदमियों ने कहा,

महाराज! यदि ऐसा ही है तो पूर्व नगर के लोग आप को जलाशय कैसे भेज सकते हैं?

इसी प्रकार भरहुत के स्तूप में कई जातक है। उनमें से उल्लेखनीय एक जातक वृक्षमृग और शाखा मृग के पात्रों को लेकर है, जिसके माध्यम से मानवी जीवन को प्रेरणा देने वाले प्रसंग भरहुत की पाशान वेष्टनियों पर उत्कीर्ण किये गये हैं, जो विधिशासन और मृत्यु पर विजय के मूल्यों पर प्रकाश डालते हैं।

बुद्ध

बौद्ध परंपरा में 28 बुद्धों का उल्लेख है। अट्ठाईसवें शाक्यमुनि बुद्ध के महापरिनिर्वाण के बाद कुशीनगर में उनकी अस्थियां मल्लों ने सुरक्षित रखी थी और उस पर अपना एकाधिकार जमाया। उसमें दूसरों को हिस्सेदार बनाने से इंकार करने पर, परिणामतः मगध–नरेश अजातशत्रु, वैशाली के लिच्छवी, कपिलवस्तु के शाक्य, अल्लकप्प के बुली, रामग्राम के कोलिय, वेठदीप का ब्राह्मण और पावा के मल्लों को बुद्धावशेष की राख के लिए लड़ाई करने तक की नौबत आई। परंतु द्रोण नामक ब्राह्मण के हस्तक्षेप से युद्ध टला और अस्थियों का आठ समान भागों में बंटवारा हुआ। बाद में पिप्पलीवन के मौर्य भी अपनी हिस्सेदारी जताने आये परंतु उनके लिए कुछ भी नही मिला। अतः उन्होंने जले हुए कोयले को ही ले जाकर उन पर एक स्तूप बनवाया था।

सम्राट अशोक ने उपरोक्त आठ हिस्सों पर बने स्तूपों में से सात की अस्थियों को निकाल कर उसके हिस्सों पर 84000 स्तूप बनवाये थे। परंतु रामगाम के स्तूप को नागरक्षकों के अपरिमित विरोध के कारण वे छू न सके। वह स्तूप नागों द्वारा रक्षित था और वे बुद्ध के गहन भक्त थे'।

सांची स्तूप के दक्षिण तोरण पर नेपाल तराई में स्थित रामग्राम के स्तूप को सम्राट अशोक भेंट करते हुए दिखाई देते है। उस पर उत्कीर्ण शिलालेख में अंकित है कि 'यह चैत्य धम्म–देशक आर्य शूद्र आयचूड़ के शिष्य बालमित्र का दान है।

बौद्ध पहचान

भरहुत के चैत्य; 'वचम' में प्रस्तर–वेष्टनी पर कोशल–नरेश प्रसेनजित के रथ के ऊपर धम्म चक्र का प्रदर्शन इस बात की गवाही देता है कि ईसा पूर्व छठी शताब्दी में भी पश्चात् के सम्राट अशोक के साम्राज्य की भांति शासक और जनता के जीवन का प्रतिष्ठा चिन्ह् धम्मचक्र रहा है। भरहुत स्तूप में बुद्ध के प्रतीकात्मक चिन्हों यथा आसन, पद, बोधिवक्ष, चक्र, स्वस्तिक आदि का प्रयोग किया जाना तत्कालीन समाज की मौलिक पहचान बुद्ध या बौद्ध रही को सरलता से माना जा सकता है।

धम्मचक्र

धम्मचक्र के माने हैं विश्व के जीवों की सबसे कठिन समस्या दुख को समझने और उनको सुख देने के मार्ग पर आरुढ़ करने के लिए संकल्पित चिन्ह। यह एक प्रकार से बुद्धकालीन समाज और शासन की अलिखित सांकेतिक उद्‌देशिका थी और वह बौद्ध संघ और नैतिक जीवन की वैश्विक आधारशिला रही।

भरहुत के स्तूप में सोलह, अठारह और चौबीस आरोंवाले चक्रों के डिजाईन मिलते हैं। यूं तो अथर्ववेद में भी चक्र की उपमा देते हुए कहा गया है कि जैसे काट और नाभी आरों से परस्पर जुड़े रहते हुए चक्र को गति देते हैं वैसे ही जीवन के रथ का जूं सब के कंधों से वहन किया जाये।

बौद्ध चक्रों का संदेश जीवन को सुखकर या दुखकर अथवा आगे या पीछे ले जाने के हर व्यक्ति के मानसवृत्ति के यथार्थ को प्रकट करने वाला है और मात्र सुखकर और प्रगत दिशा की ओर जानेवालों के लिए अष्टांगमार्ग के अवलंबन की पद्धति बताना है।

डॉ. आंबेडकर ने भी कौम को आगाह करते हुए कहा था कि मैं भारी पीड़ा सहकर इस सामाजिक जीवन रथ को यहां तक खेंच लाया हूँ, उसे यह पीढ़ी आगे ले जाये। यदि वह वैसा नही कर सकती तो उसे जहां का वहां ही रख दें परंतु उसे पीछे न धकेले। आधुनिक समाज जीवन का धम्मचक्र संदेश बाबासाहेब के इस वचन से बेहतर और क्या हो सकता है? पिटकों में धम्म को भी रथ की संज्ञा दी गई है।

भरहुत स्तूप में धर्म चक्र चार स्थानों पर अंकित है। प्रथम और द्वितीय स्थानों के धम्मचक्र बुद्ध की प्रथम देशना के प्रतीक हैं और तृतीय और चतुर्थ स्थलों पर अंकित धम्मचक्र धम्मचेतिय सुत्त के संकेत हैं। धम्म के चैत्य पर जो चक्र है उसके धम्मिक व वास्तुकलात्मक महत्व हैं। उसके चक्र अलंकृत हैं। उस से बुद्ध का व्यक्तित्व और उपस्थिति जाहिर होते है। उसमें सोलह आरे हैं। उसके शीर्ष पर दो हिरण अंकित हैं। जीवन चक्र व्यक्ति की पांच गतियों अर्थात् नारकीय, पाशविक, मृतात्मक, मानवीय और परम गति को निदेर्शित करता है, जो भरहुत स्तूप में उत्कीर्ण नही है।

सिंह, हाथी व पदचिन्ह

तथापि भरहुत में अंकित चार शीर्षवाले सिंह चार प्रकार के बौद्ध श्रमणों को इंगित करते हैं। स्तूप में उत्कीण्र हाथी राणी महामाया के शिशु के जन्म के द्योतक है। अशोक स्तंभ पर उत्कीर्ण हाथी राजपद का चिन्ह है। उसमें अंकित पदचिन्ह सिद्धार्थ का अस्तित्व, गृहत्याग के लिए अभिनिष्क्रमण, उनका तुशित देवलोक से कौशाम्बी में अवतरण तथा पादवंदना के प्रयोजन से प्रयुक्त हुआ है।

कला

बौद्ध कला और बौद्धेतर कला में सूक्ष्म और स्पष्ट भेद है। 'यत् प्रतिरुपं तत् शिल्पं' अर्थात् जो निसर्ग में उस का प्रतिरुप बनाना शिल्प है यह ब्राह्मण कला का निर्धारण है। परंतु बौद्ध कला में समय, आकाश और मन के संगठन से सामान्य से असाधारण की ओर उभर जाने को कला माना गया है। पतिरुप देसवासो च अर्थात् अनुकुल स्थान में वास करना मंगल सूत्र का वचन है। क्षण–क्षण और बूंद–बूंद क्रमिक भावों को उदात्त में साकार कर कृति के आनन्द को भी पार करना बौद्ध कला का मन्तव्य है। जहां मन वर्तुलाकार संसार चक्र से निर्वाणाकार व निर्विकार धम्म चक्र में गुजर कर असीम में समा जाता है।

मन अपने स्वरुपों से पदार्थ को प्रभावित करता है। स्वरुपों को अपने स्वभाव पर अंकित करता है। उन्हें अपनी कल्पनाओं का आकार देता है। उन्हें अपनी वेदनाओं से सजीव बनाता है। उन्हें अपनी भावनाओं से

गतिमान करता है और उन्हें अपनी चेतना से उत्स्फूर्त बनाता है। अर्थात् कला और रंग को चित्त कहा गया है और कलात्मक रूप निर्मिति को चित्तकत बिंब की संज्ञा दी गई है।

स्तूप

ऐतिहासिक घटना और महापुरुष के स्मरण में निर्मित विशाल कृति को स्तूप (monument) कहते हैं। और किसी महापुरुष के अवशेष पर निर्मित चेतना स्थलि को चैत्य (tope) की संज्ञा दी जाती है। मध्य प्रदेश में विद्यमान सांची और भरहुत के स्तूप 'स्तूप और चैत्य दोनों हैं।

श्री टी. डब्ल्यू. रिस डेविड्स ने भरहत और भरहुत दोनों नामों को एक ही स्थान के पर्याय के रूप में प्रयुक्त किया (इन्डेक्स पृ. 324)। परंतु उनके अनुसार भरहत नाम ही अधिक सही है (पृ. 209)। लेकिन इस आलेख में दोनों नामों का प्रयोग किया गया है। उन्होंने पृ. 9 पर एक आंखें खोल देने वाली सूचना दी कि भरहत स्तूप के प्लेट 13 पर राजा प्रसेनजीत ई. स. 600 ई. पू. अपने रथ में विराजमान हैं और रथ के ऊपर 24 आरेवाला धम्म चक्र प्रदर्शित है। इस से एक बात जाहिर है कि राजा प्रसेनजित न केवल बुद्धानुयायी थे, बल्कि वे सम्राट अशोक के 300 सदियों पहले से ही बुद्ध के धम्म के प्रतीक चक्र को अपने राज्य का गौरव मान कर उसे राज चिन्ह के रुप में अपने वाहन पर प्रदर्शित करते थे। अगले पृष्ठ 10, 82, 198, 209 और 288 पर और उत्कीर्ण मकर नीचे जल प्रवाह के अस्तित्व का बोध देते है तथा उस के मध्यभाग धम्मसेतु के प्रतीक हैं।

संस्कृति

धर्मानंद कोसम्बी जी ने अपने ग्रंथ संस्कृति और अहिंसा में भारतीय आर्य संस्कृति एलाम से प्रवाहित होने का संकेत दिया है। भरहुत के शुंग कालीन कला पर परसेपोलिस के वास्तु शिल्प का प्रत्यक्ष प्रभाव है। यही बात मौर्यकालीन घण्टा शीर्ष के बारे में भी कही गई है। यहां के स्तंभों पर जो पंखयुक्त चतुष्पाद के चित्र हैं यथाः– अश्व, हिरण, बकरे, शेर या हाथी वे सब इरान के युनिकार्न स्तंभों के डिजाईन से मिलते हैं। इरान के स्तंभचित्रों का स्रोत अंततः असिरिया या पश्चिम एशिया ही है। उसमें आख्यायिक वनस्पतियों का सजावट के लिए प्रयोग किया जाना एलाम

अर्थात् हेलेनिक की कला परंपरा से ग्रहण किया गया प्रभाव जान पड़ता है। भरहुत स्तूप में उत्कीर्ण यक्ष और यक्षिणि के परिधान इजिप्ट की कला का अनुकरण लगता है। ऐसा विदेशी प्रभाव, भारतीय कला व जानकारी मिलती है, जो भरहुत स्तूप के उक्त प्रस्तर–वेष्टिनियों का काल ई.पू. 300, कनिंघम द्वारा उसका पुनरोद्धार किया जाना, उन पर उत्कीर्ण बास–रिलिफ उनकी तिथि की गवाही कैसे दे रहे, और बौद्ध जातक ग्रंथों में उपलब्ध 28 जातक की कहानियाँ भरहुत के बास–रिलिफ में लगभग उसी शीर्षक से किस प्रकार दृष्टिगोचर होते हैं से संबंधित है।

पुरातत्वविद् जनरल कनिंघम ने न केवल भरहुत स्तूप का उत्खनन किया बल्कि रीवा रोड पर स्थित रामबन का भी पता लगाया, जिस में बुद्ध के शिष्य और उनके निजी सहायक आनंद की अस्थियां मिली। भरहुत में जो छत्री प्राप्त हुई थी, उसे नगौदा के परिहार कुल के वंशज और विधायक श्री राम प्रतापसिंह के भवन में सुरक्षित रखा गया है।

उपरोक्त स्तूप पर आकृति क्रमांक 21, 22 और 23 परिचक्रों की आकृतियां, शीर्ष के आवरण और अनाथ पिंड़िक का जेतवनाराम का संघदान उल्लेखनीय प्रदर्श हैं।

तोरण

तोरण एक धम्मसेतु है, जिसका सांकेतिक अर्थ सांसारिक नदी के दोनों तीरों पर शिकार के लिए प्रतिक्षित मकर के आघात से बचाव के लिए सुरक्षा कवच के प्रतीकात्मक द्वार है। भरहुत स्तूप में तोरण के आड़े बीम बुद्ध चरित्र की सांकेतिक रुपरेखा बताते है और उसके तीन आड़े आर्किट्रेव के छोर पर वास्तुशिल्प पर पड़ना स्वाभाविक है क्योंकि मौर्य और शुंग कालीन कला रुप, इरान, ग्रीक–यवनादि के साथ सांस्कृतिक संबंध स्थापित होने के बाद विकसित हुए थे और भरहुत के शिल्पी उत्तर–पश्चिम भारत से आये थे, जहां भारतीय, इरान, यवन और पश्चिमी आशिया की संस्कृति परस्पर घुल–मिल चुकी थी।

निस्संदेह भरहुत स्तूप में प्राप्त मिहिर सूर्य देवता का कटिबंध यवनी है। यह उत्तरापथ अर्थात् उत्तर पश्चिम क्षेत्र के सूर्य देवता का अनुकरण है।

राष्ट्र–राष्ट्र को जोड़ना

लगभग 28 बौद्ध लोकप्रिय कहानियों को भरहुत के स्तूप के पाषाण–वेष्टनियों पर उत्कीर्ण किया गया है। स्थविरवादी सूत्र पिटक के पांचवे खुद्दक निकाय के दसवे ग्रंथ जातक की 547 कहानियों में से उपरोक्त को उस स्तूप में अंकित करने के लिए चयनित किया गया। बौद्ध संस्कृति वैश्विक कलह को तोडकर एक राष्ट्र को दूसरे राष्ट्र के साथ जोड़कर भातृत्व पर आधारित समाज के निर्माण के लिए समर्पित है।

विश्व को श्रेष्ठ नैतिक संदेश देना

इसलिए स्तूपों पर उत्कीर्ण पाषाण–वेष्टनियों के माध्यम से नैतिक संदेश के पुंज जातक कहानियों को लोकप्रिय स्थलों यथा स्तूप व चैत्य पर लौकिक कलात्मक और मनमोहक तरीकों से उत्कीर्ण कर जन–जन को नैतिक सबक दिये जाते हैं।

इतिहास बनाना

डॉ. आंबेडकर ने कहा ही है कि जो लोग इतिहास को भूलते हैं वे इतिहास नही बना सकते। अतः बौद्ध जन का गौरवमय ऐतिहासिक संदेश जन–जन को इस बात की चेतना देता है कि भव्य महान संस्कृति बनाये रखने के लिए भव्य और उदात्त विचार संजोये रखना सबसे महान कार्य है।

डॉ. आंबेडकर ने भारत के नाम को उस भरत के नाम पर पड़ा हुआ होने की बात कही, जो श्रीराम के भ्राता, और दुष्यन्त–शकुंतला का बेटा भी नही थे, बल्कि भरत नामक वैदिक जनजाति के प्रभावी जन थे। क्या भरहुत ऐसे भारत को उदात्त पहचान देने का महान प्रतीक नही है?

भारत को आदर्श पहचान दिलाना

दास का अर्थ उदात्त (noble) और देनेवाला होता है। सुदास के उत्तराधिकारी और आज के बुद्ध और आंबेडकर के अनुयायी अपनी गौरवमयी संस्कृति को न भूलें, बल्कि जानें कि वे ही कल के उदात्त भारत के भविष्य हैं। अतः उन्हें चाहिए कि वे अपने इतिहास को जान कर उसकी पहचान भारत को दें।

अबैर से बैर मिटाना

खुद्दक निकाय के एक ग्रंथ धम्मपद की गाथा हैः *'नहि वेरेन वेरानि सम्मंतीध कुदाचनं अवेरेन च सम्मंति एस धम्मो सनन्तनो।'* अर्थात् बैर से बैर कभी शांत नही होता। अबैर से ही बैर शांत होता है। यही कालसिद्ध धम्म है।

उसी प्रकार विधि शासन और मृत्यु विजय के मूल्यों को संजोये रखने वाला मिगजातक का संदेश भरहुत के पाषाण–वेष्टनियों पर उत्कीर्ण है।

जन–जन हिताय, सुखाय के लिए अविरत प्रयास करना

बुद्ध ने अपने शिष्यों को गतिशील बने रहने के लिए जो उपदेश दिया था, जो विनय पिटक के उपसम्पदा कथा में संकलित है, इस प्रकार हैः भिक्षुओं! जितने भी दिव्य और मानुष बन्धन हैं, मैं उन सबों से मुक्त हूँ, तुम भी दिव्य और मानुष बंधनों से मुक्त हो। भिक्षुओं! बहुत जनों के हित के लिए, बहुत जनों के सुख के लिए, लोक पर दया करने के लिए, देवताओं और मनुष्यों के प्रयोजन के लिए, हित के लिए, सुख के लिए विचरण करो। एक साथ दो मत जाओ। हे भिक्षुओं! आदि में कल्याणकारक, मध्य में कल्याणकारक, अन्त में कल्याणकारक इस धर्म का उपदेश करो। अर्थ सहित व्यंजन सहित, केवल; अमिश्रद्ध परिपूर्ण परिशुद्ध ब्रह्मचर्य का प्रकाश करो। अल्प दोषवाले प्राणी भी हैं, धर्म के न श्रवण करने से उनकी हानि होगी। सुनने से वह धर्म के जानने वाले बनेंगे। भिक्षुओं! मैं भी जहां उरुवेला है ना नी ग्राम है, वहां धर्म देशना के लिए जाऊंगा। *ये केचि बंधना देवा वा मानुसा वा सब्बेपि अहं मुत्तस्मिं तुम्हेपि सब्बे ते बंधनानं देवा वा मानुसा वा मुत्ता। चरथ भिक्खवे चारिकं, बहुजन हिताय बहुजन सुखाय लोकानुकम्पाय अत्ताय हिताय देवमनुस्सानं। मा एकेन द्वे गच्छथ। देसेथ भिक्खवे धम्मं आदिकल्याणं मज्झे कल्याणं परियोसान कल्याणं सात्थं सव्यंजनं केवल परिपुण्णं परिसुद्धं ब्रह्मचरियं पकासेथ। सन्ति अयं अप्पदोसा पाणा। तस्स धम्मस्स असवनस्स हानाय भविस्सन्ति। सवनता ते धम्मजानकारो होन्ति।* मतलब यह कि बौद्धों! विश्व में सब के सुख के लिए अविरत प्रयत्न करो।

भरहुत स्तूप किस सामाजिक वर्ण/जाति और जनजाति/वर्ग का प्रतिनिधिक स्मारक है?

इसे जानने के लिए भरहुत स्तूप से प्राप्त व्यवसायिक जनों की सूची पर नजर डालना आवश्यक है, जो निम्नानुसार हैः 1. मोची, 2 कुम्हार, 3. हस्तिदंतशिल्पी, 4. रंगरेज, 5. जौहरी, 6. मछेरे, 7. खटीक, 8. शिकारी, 9. पाककर्मी, 10. हज्जाम, 11. फुलकर्मी, 12. नाविक, 13. हस्तशिल्पी, 14. रंगारी, 15. व्यापारी इत्यादि।

भरहुत कैसे पहुंचें?

बघेलखण्ड का एक प्रमुख भाग और बघेली जनभाषा का केन्द्र सतना जिले से नातिदूर एक प्राचीन व्यापार मार्ग, गंधार–उज्जैयनि का केन्द्र स्थान भरहुत है। सतना–मैहर रोड से 13–14 कि. मी. जाकर पूर्व दिशा में उंचेहरा पार कर 2–3 कि. मी. पर गोबराय के पास की मोड़ से भरहुत पहुंचा जा सकता है। भरहुत नामक गाांव अपने प्राचीन ऐतिहासिक स्थान की स्मृति जीवित रखने हेतु आज भी विद्यमान है। वह नगरगंवा स्टेशन से लगभग दो कि. मी. आगे है। उसके आगे 15 कि. मी. दूरी पर जो पहाडियां हैं, उसके ऊपर गुफायें भी विस्मृत संस्कृति की याद दिलाती हैं। सतना नगर पार करते ही पहाड़ियां दिखने लगती हैं। वही पर भरहुत स्तूप अपने ऐतिहासिक खण्डहर से बिखरा हुआ दिखता है। उसी के समीप एक पहाड़ी पर 10वीं सदी में प्रचलित देवनागरी लिपि में बलाल देव द्वारा उत्कीर्ण एक शिलालेख है। उस के स्तूप पर अंकित अण्डभूत अथवा अन्धभूत जातक का दृश्य भी मिला है। अब यहां के सारे प्राचीन अवशेष कलकत्ता के संग्रहालय में सुरक्षित रखे हैं।

लिपि

भरहुत स्तूप पर अंकित लिपि ब्राह्मी या खरोष्ठी लिपि है। पालि में सात बुद्धों के जो नाम है, वे पालि, भरहुत और दिव्यावदान तथा महावस्तु ग्रंथों में अक्षरभेद से अंकित है। उनमें से तीन के नाम इस प्रकार दिए हैः यथा वेस्सभुस्स, कोणागमणस्स, विपसिस्स (pali), विश्वभुव, कणकमुनेः/ कणकमुनिस्य, विपश्यिनो/ विपश्यिने (divyavadana,mahavastu), वेसभुनो, कोणागमेनस, विपासिनो, (bharahut)।

भरहुत स्तूप में जो प्रसेनजित, विडूडभ, बिंबिसार और अजातशत्रू ठभ है। प्रथम ठभ अथवा स्तंभ विदिशा राजघराने के रेवतिमित्र की राणी चम्पादेवी का है। उसी प्रकार वेनिमित्र की पत्नि वासिठिदेवी का ऋणानुनिर्देश है। धनभूति का दान भी उल्लेखनीय है। भरहुत में प्राप्त वेदिका स्तम्भलेख से उस काल की उत्तर भारत की ब्राह्मी लिपि का नमूना देखिए।

सुगनं रञे रञो गागीपुतस विसदेवस। पौतेण गोतिपुतस आगरजुस पुतेण। वाछिपुतेन धनभूतिन कारितं तोरनां। सिलाकंमंता च उपंण।

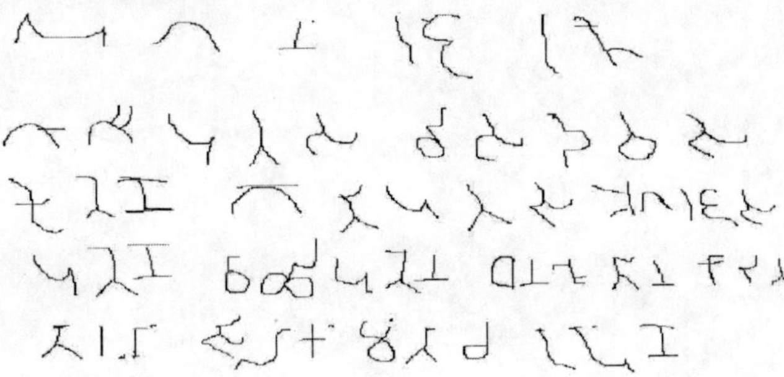

उपरोक्त लिपि का देवनागरी में लिप्यंतर निम्नानुसार होगा।

सुगनं रञे रञो गागीपुतस विसदेवस। पौतेण गोतिपुतस आगरजुस पुतेण। वाछिपुतेन धनभूतिन कारितं तोरनां। सिलाकंमंता च उपंण।

उपसंहार

उपरोक्त सभी बातें भरहुत के स्तूप की वेष्टनियों पर अंकित बौद्ध संस्कृति का सार है। यही भारत को बौद्ध पहचान देने की आगाज थी और यही आज की आवाज है। अस्तु।

संदर्भ

1. टी. डब्ल्यू रिस डेविडस की बुद्धिस्ट इंडिया (1971)
2. भरत सिंह उपाध्याय, प्राचीनकालीन भारतीय भूगोल
3. धर्मानन्द कोसम्बि, संस्कृति व अहिंसा
4. डॉ. आम्बेडकर, हू वेअर द शूद्राज, शूद्र पहले कौन थे, 1946
5. राहुल सांकृत्यायन, दर्शन–दिग्दर्शन, विनय पिटक
6. सी. डी. नाईक, मंथन,
7. गुणाकर मुळे, अक्षर कथा, दिल्ली, 1972
8. Sir John Marshall, A Guide to Sanchi, Delhi, 1936, p. 50, 165-166.

Chapter - 16

वैचारिक आज़ादी और वास्तविकता

प्रो. सी. डी. नाईक'

कमजोर वर्ग

ईसा पूर्व 600 ई. स. में सिद्धार्थ गौतम की जन्म स्थली, लुम्बिनी और बुद्धत्व का स्थल बोध गया दोनों जम्बुद्वीप यानी भारत की धरोहर थे, परंतु बाद में लुम्बिनी वन ही नही, बल्कि उस वन के दो साल वृक्ष जिसके बीच उनका जन्म हुआ था, उनकी माता महारानी महामाया की कुटी और राजा शुद्धोदन की राजधानी कपिलवस्तु नगर (अब पिपरहवा), और उस घटना के तीन सदियों बाद सम्राट अशोक का वहां पर स्थित विशाल स्तंभ, जिस के ऊपर खरोष्ठी लिपि में ''इधो तथागतो जातो'' अर्थात् ''तथागत का जन्म यहीं हुआ'' उत्कीर्ण किया हुआ है और संबंधित सारे पुरातात्विक सबूत भी नेपाल की धरोहर बने है। उसी प्रकार डॉ. आंबेडकर की जन्मस्थली अब मध्यप्रदेश की धरोहर हैं और उन की दीक्षा स्थलि महाराष्ट्र की। हालांकि वे स्थल भोपाल राजधानी वाले आज के मध्य प्रदेश के जन्म (1.11.1956) के पहले नागपुर राजधानी वाले मध्य प्रांत व बेरार (सी. पी. एण्ड बेरार) के थे। परंतु भुखमरी और प्लेग जैसी नैसर्गिक आपदा में कुछ मराठी जन, विशेषतः महार लोग महाराष्ट्र से स्थलांतरित होकर मध्य प्रदेश के इन्दौर, खंडवा, उज्जैन आदि जिलों में जाकर बस गये थे।

भारत का इतिहास गैर भारतीय आर्य, ग्रीक, ईरानी, कुशान, शक, हूण, मुस्लिम और अंग्रेज आदि के आक्रमणों और भारतीय जाति, उपजाति और जमातिओं में सामाजिक दुराव, आपसी बैरत्व और द्वेश का रहा है। गाने के लिये हम गाते हैं कि *'धर्म नही सिखाता आपस में बैर रखना।'* परंतु

प्राचीन भारतीय पराधीनता का बीज धार्मिक दुराव में ही छिपा था इस से इन्कार नही किया जा सकता। डॉ. आंबेडकर ने सन् 1946 में स्वरचित शोध ग्रंथ ''शूद्र पहले कौन थे'' में इस प्रकार वर्णित किया हैः–

''आर्यों से भी ज्यादा पराक्रमी दास या दस्यु लोग थे। वे जंगली आदि–मानव नही थे। वे आर्यों की भांति सभ्य और उन से भी अधिक बहादुर थे। श्री अयंगर ने लिखा है कि ऋग्वेद संहिता के अनुसार दस्यु लोग नगरों में रहते थे और कई लोगों के नाम राजाओं की सूची में आते थे। इन्द्र ने अपने भक्त दिवोदास के लिये दस्युओं के शत–शत शिलाओं से बने महलों पर अतिक्रमण किया था। अग्निदेवता ने आर्यों की खातिर अग्निपूजा के वैरी दस्युओं के नगर तोड़कर उन्हें अग्नि में स्वाहा कर दिया था। जिन शिला–कारागृहों में आर्यों से छिनी हुई गौवें सुरक्षित रखी जाती थीं, उन्हें ही बृहस्पति ने नष्ट कर दिया था। दस्यु लोगों के अपने रथ, और आयुध थे, जिनका प्रयोग वे आर्यों की तरह, युद्ध में करते थे[1]।

आर्यों के साथ दस्युओं का विवाद नस्ल का नही बल्कि धर्म पर आधारित विवाद था। ऊपरोल्लेखित वही लेखक बताते हैं कि दस्यु अव्रत थे यानी वे आर्य के संस्कार से नही चलते थे। वे अपवगत और विभिन्न प्रकार के अन्य व्रत के संस्कार वाले थे। वे अनगनित्र, अग्निविहीन, अयज्यु, अयज्वन या बलिकर्म के विरोधी थे। वे अब्रह्म, वैदिक अर्चना और अर्चक को न माननेवाले, अनरिछः या रिक्विहीन, ब्रह्मद्वेश या ब्रह्मण अर्चना के द्वेष्टा, अनिन्द्र या इन्द्र के शत्रु थे। वे न क्षीर का तर्पण करते थे न किसी ब्राह्मण को चढ़ावा चढ़ाते थे[2]।

स्वाधीनता से वंचित जाति, महार और उनके राष्ट्र, महाराष्ट्र का इतिहास डॉ. आम्बेडकर के जीवन–चरित्र को समझने के लिये आवश्यक है। महाराष्ट्र की उत्पत्ति का एक विचारणीय तर्क यह है कि पूर्व समय में वर्तमान महाराष्ट्र में एक महारट्ठ नामक बौद्ध भिक्षु को प्रचारार्थ भेजा गया था। उस ने वहां के लोगों को बौद्ध धर्म में धर्मांतरित किया था। इस प्रकार बौद्ध धर्म अपनानेवालों को उनके गुरु महारट्ठ के नाम से पहचाना जाने लगा। सब से अधिक महारट्ठ जिस प्रदेश में निवास कर रहे थे, उस प्रदेश का नाम कालांतर में महाराष्ट्र पड़ा। महारट्ठ स्थविर द्वारा नाग लोगों को

बौद्ध धर्म की दीक्षा देने का जिक्र श्रीलंका के प्राचीन इतिहास का ग्रंथ ''महावंस'' में भी मिलता है[3]।

एक दूसरा सिद्धान्त है जिस की मान्यता है कि नाग शब्द नाईक की पर्यायवाची संज्ञा है[4]। इस जाति के लोगों ने समानता की लडाई लड़ने के लिये काफी कुर्बानियां दी थीं।

महार यानी भूमिपुत्र, नाग या नाईक। वह एक लड़ाऊ जाति थी और उनका राज्य महाराष्ट्र था जिस की राजधानी नागपुर थी। उनका धर्म बौद्ध था। वे आज भी महाराष्ट्र और उसके इर्द–गिर्द के प्रदेशों में विद्यमान हैं। ऐतिहासिक काल से उन्हें अपना अस्तित्व कायम रखने के लिये कई दुदम्य युद्धों का सामना करना पडा था। जब उनका सर्वस्व नष्ट हुआ तो उनका सामाजिक–आर्थिक दर्जा भी घटा और उन पर कई सख्त और हानिकारक पाबंदियां लाद दी गईं। हालांकि उनके पास उपजाऊ जोतें, सैनिकी और नागरी प्रशासनिक पद और बस्तीवालों से सभी प्रकार के फसलों का सोलहवां हिस्सा वसूल करने के आय के साधन आदि बावन अधिकार थे। कालान्तर में वे ही अधिकार अहितकर हो गये और वे उनके पैर की बेडियां बन गये, जिसे तुडवाने के लिये वे लड़ते रहे और अन्त में सन् 1956 में बौद्ध धर्म अपना कर सफल हुये।

प्राचीन समय में महार लोग बुद्ध के अनुयायी थे। अस्सी प्रतिशत भारतीय बौद्धों की उत्खनन की सामग्री महाराष्ट्र में और विशेशतः महार बस्तियों के क्षेत्र में पाई गई हैं। बौद्ध गुफाओं में भी महार नाम उत्कीर्ण किया हुआ प्राप्त हुआ है। परंतु गुप्त काल के दौरान, विशेषतः मुगल काल में महारों ने बौद्ध धर्म के संस्कारों का पालन करना छोड़ दिया प्रतीत होता है।

यद्यपि महारों ने मुस्लिम, मराठा, पेशवा, ब्रिटिश और भारतीय सेना में अपनीं सेवायें प्रदान की थीं और उन्होंने वारकरी, महानुभाव, कबीर और लिंगायत जैसे हिन्दू संप्रदायों, मुस्लिम और क्रिश्चियन मजहबों को अपनाया था तथापि उन की सामाजिक प्रगति और प्रतिष्ठा, आर्थिक बढ़ोतरी तथा सांस्कृतिक हिस्सेदारी बौद्ध धर्म अपनाने के बाद भी और आज भी निरन्तर प्रश्न चिन्ह बनी हुई है।

ईस्ट इंडिया कंपनी के प्रत्येक टुकड़ी के लिये स्वतंत्र स्कूल और योग्य शिक्षक की व्यवस्था थी। पुणे में नार्मल स्कूल अध्यापक प्रशिक्षण केन्द्र था। रामजी सकपाल ने इसी नार्मल स्कूल में मास्टर का डिप्लोमा प्राप्त किया था। वे 14 वर्षों तक सैनिक स्कूल में हेडमास्टर रहे और बाद में तरक्की करते हुये सूबेदार मेजर बने थे। सेना में 25 वर्षों की सेवा पूर्ण होने के उपरान्त वे सेवानिवृत्त हुये थे।

उस के एक वर्ष बाद श्री गोपाल विठ्ठल वलंगकर (मृत्यु इ. स. 1940 में) को कंपनी शासन ने महाड़ के लोकल बोर्ड में नियुक्त किया था। उनका जन्म महाड़ जिले के रावदक गांव में हुआ था। वे श्री रामजी मालोजी सकपाल के समकालीन और ब्रिटिश सेना में नौकरी और समाज सेवा करने वाले पहले महार थे। वे महात्मा ज्योतिबा फुले के सानिध्य में लेखन कार्य करते थे। उन्होंने सन् 1886 में सैनिकी सेवा से सेवामुक्त होकर ''विटाळ विध्वंसक'' नामक ग्रंथ लिखा था। उसके चार वर्ष पश्चात उन्होंने ''अनार्य दोष परिहार मंडल'' की स्थापना की। जब अंग्रेजों ने सन् 1892 में महारों को सेना में भर्ती करना बंद कर दिया तो उन्होंने इसके विरुद्ध प्रतिकार किया था। श्री वलंगकर की तरह श्री रामजी भी वारकरी पंथ, कबीर पंथ और ज्योतिराव फुले के भक्त रहे।

दूसरे महार समाज सुधारक श्री शिवराम जानबा कांबळे थे। उनका जन्म पूना में सन् 1875 में हुआ था। सन् 1904 में उन्होंने ''सोमवंशीय हितचिंतक मित्र समाज'' नामक संस्था की स्थापना की थी। उन्हीं का समाचार पत्र ''सोमवंशीय मित्र'' के प्रेरणास्पद वचनों से प्रभावित होकर श्री गणपतराव हनमंत गायकवाड ने उस समय में प्रचलित धार्मिक वेश्या रिवाज में पली जागतीनी, मुरली आदि देवदासियों में से एक शिबूबाई के साथ विवाह कर लिया था।

सन् 1901 में ''सन्मार्ग निराश्रित समाज'' नामक एक सामाजिक संस्था की भी स्थापना और 1910 से 1918 के दरम्यान ''निराश्रित हिन्द नागरिक'', ''विटाळ विध्वंसक'', और ''मजदूर पत्रिका'' नामक समाचार पत्र चलाने वाले श्री किसन फागू बन्सोडे पाटील की धर्मपत्नि श्रीमति तुलसाबाई बन्सोडे पाटील पहली महार समाज कार्यकर्ता महिला थीं। सन 1906 में तीसरे महार श्री विठोबा राव मून उर्फ संत पंडे ने ''अंत्यज समाज कमिटी''

की स्थापना की थी। इस प्रकार उपरोक्त संस्था और उनके नेताओं ने डॉ. आंबेडकर के सामाजिक सुधार कार्य हेतु एक खास पृष्ठभूमि तैयार कर रखी थी।

उसके अनंतर डॉ. आंबेडकर भारत के सामाजिक क्षितिज पर उतरे तो उन्होंने दलितों के राजनीतिक पृथक अधिकार हेतु साउथबरो मताधिकार कमिटी के सम्मुख 1919 में अपनी लिखित साक्ष्य दी थी और बाद में ''बहिष्कृत हितकारिणी सभा (20.7.1924) ''समता सैनिक दल (मार्च 1927)'', स्वतंत्र मजदूर दल (15.8.1936), अखिल भारतीय शिडयुल्ड कास्ट फेडरेशन (19.7.1942) और ''रिपब्लिकन पार्टी ऑफ इंडिया (3.10.1957) जैसी देश सुधारक संस्थाओं की स्थापना की थी।

अपने इंदौर आगमन के दौरान वे अपनी जन्म स्थली महू भी आये थे और यहां आपने अपने कार्यकर्ताओं के साथ यादगार के रुप में एक सामूहिक फोटो भी खिंचवाई थी, जो डॉ. बाबासाहेब आंबेडकर राष्ट्रीय सामाजिक विज्ञान शोध संस्थान के कलेक्शन में भी सुरक्षित है।

आर्य, मुगल और ब्रिटिश आक्रमकों से पराजित और अपनी स्वाधीनता के लिये आक्रामकों के साथ अधिक से अधिक समझौता और आत्मीय लोगों से ज्यादा से ज्यादा नफरत करते हुए अपना वैशिष्ट्य कायम रखनेवाले भारतीय समाज की अपनी एक अलग चर्या रही है।

डॉ. आंबेडकर के अनुसार ''भारतीय इतिहास यानी ब्राह्मणवाद और बौद्धवाद के बीच विद्यमान संहारक संघर्ष है। भारतीय इतिहास के तीन काल खंड अर्थात् ब्राह्मणी भारत, बौद्ध भारत व हिंदु भारत है। ब्राह्मणी भारत की जो समाज रचना थी वह बौद्ध धर्म ने बदल डाली। वह एक विशाल क्रांति थी क्योंकि उस क्रांति से धार्मिक, सामाजिक और राजनीतिक सरंचना में परिवर्तन हुआ है। परंतु हिंदू भारत ने समानताधिष्ठित समाज रचना को क्रमिक असमान जातियों में बदल डाला।

डॉ. आंबेडकर के अनुसार क्रांति के लिये वर्गों में सत्ता संघर्ष होता है जैसा कि वह भारतीय इतिहास में ब्राह्मण और क्षत्रिय वर्गों में रहा है और पराजित क्षत्रिय जाति ही शूद्रों में परिणत हुई है। इस के लिये मूल्य संघर्ष भी आवश्यक है। बदलते समाज में मूल्य में भी निरंतर बदल होते रहना जरुरी है। यदि मनुष्य की कृति का मूल्यांकन करनेवाले मापदण्ड हैं तो

उसमें भी पुनः सुधारना करने की तैयारी उसे रखना चाहिये। चिरस्थायी मूल्यों के निर्देशन में उसे कालस्थायी मूल्यों में परिवर्तन करना चाहिये। क्रांति के लिये महापुरुष और बुद्धिजीवी वर्ग की भी जरुरत होती है। डॉ. आंबेडकर के अनुसार जब समाज संकटावस्था में होता है तो उसे उस से बाहर निकलने के लिये पथ प्रदर्शन का कार्य मानवी बुद्धि करती है। महापुरुष इतिहास का निर्माता है इस बात को मानने या न मानने के बावजूद भी यह बात अमान्य नही की जा सकती है कि प्रत्येक समाज में बुद्धिजीवी वर्ग होता है और वह सत्ताधारी न होने पर भी अधिक प्रभावशाली होता है[5]।

भीम

सन् 1904 में रामजी मुंबई में आये। वहां वे परेल की एक श्रमिक कालोनी में रहते थे। भीम ने मुंबई में एलफिन्स्टोन हायस्कूल में दाखिला लिया था और वहीं से उस ने सन् 1907 में मैट्रिक की परीक्षा उत्तीर्ण की। सन् 1908 में भीम 17 वर्ष के हुये तो उन्होंने 9 वर्षीय रमा के साथ विवाह किया। सन् 1912 में एलफिन्स्टोन कॉलेज से अंग्रेजी और पर्शियन आदि विषयों को लेकर और बड़ौदा महाराज सयाजी राव की वित्तीय सहायता से पढ़ाई कर वे ग्रेज्युएट परीक्षा में उत्तीर्ण हुये। उसके पश्चात् भीम राव की बड़ौदा सैनिक दल में लेफ्टीनेंट के पद पर नियुक्ति हुई। कुछ दिनों के पश्चात् उनके पिताजी का देहांत हुआ।

तथापि सन् 1913 में बड़ौदा नरेश सयाजीराव गायकवाड द्वारा पिछड़े वर्ग के लिये संस्थापित छात्रवृति के हासिल होने पर भीम राव कोलंबिया विश्वविद्यालय, अमेरिका गये और वहां से *ईस्ट इंडिया कंपनी का प्रशासन और वित्त* विषय पर शोधग्रंथ प्रस्तुत कर एम. ए. हो गये। उन्होंने फिर *नेशनल डिविडंडः ए हिस्टारिकल एण्ड अनालिटिकल स्टडी* अर्थात् *राष्ट्रीय लाभः एक ऐतिहासिक तथा विश्लेषणात्मक अध्ययन* पर पीएच.डी. की उपाधि हासिल की। वहीं उनका संपर्क जॉन डिवि, एडविन सेलिग्मन और ए.ए. गोल्डनवेजर जैसे सुविख्यात दार्शनिक और प्रोफेसरों के साथ हुआ। उन्होंने वहीं पर *भारत में जातियाः उनकी सरंचना, व्युत्पत्ति, और विकास* नामक एक शोध पत्र भी लिखा था।

सन् 1916 में डॉ. आंबेडकर ने लंदन स्कूल ऑफ एकानामिक्स एण्ड पोलिटिकल सायंस में प्रवेश प्राप्त किया। वहां पर उनका संपर्क श्री सिडनी वेब, बेट्रिस वेब, एडविन केनन, जे.ए. हाबसन, एल.टी. हाबहाउस प्रभृति विद्वान दार्शनिकों से हुआ। डॉ. आंबेडकर बार–एट–लॉ की उपाधि हेतु ग्रेज इन नामक विधि संस्थान में भी प्रविष्ट हुये थे। परंतु शिष्यवृत्ति की शर्तों के अनुसार छात्रवृत्ति का नियुक्त समय बीत जाने के पश्चात उन्हें अब अपनी सेवा बडौदा राज्य को अर्पित करना लाजमी हो गया था। अतः डॉ. आंबेडकर अपनी पढ़ाई बीच में ही छोडकर सन् 1917 में भारत वापस आ गये और बडौदा में अकाउंटन्ट जनरल के ऑफिस में प्रोबेशनर की हैसियत से काम करने लगे। परंतु दफ्तर के अन्दर और बाहर भी तत्कालीन दकियानूसी समाज ने डॉ. आंबेडकर को इतना पढ़ा–लिखा होने पर भी एक अछूत ही मान कर वैसा ही उनके साथ सलूक भी किया, फलतः उन्हें वह स्थान जल्दी ही छोड़कर वापस बंबई जाना पड़ा।

बंबई लौट कर कुछ दिन डॉ. आंबेडकर को बेरोजगारी में ही काटने पड़े। बाद में वे सिडेहेम कॉलेज में राजनीति–अर्थशास्त्र के प्रोफेसर पद पर नियुक्त हुये।

सन् 1919 में जब मान्टेग्यू–चेम्सफोर्ड सुधार चल रहा था तो मताधिकार के विषय पर डॉ. आंबेडकर ने अपना अभिमत साउथबरो कमिटी के समक्ष रखा था। उनका मत था कि जब 1916 से ही मुसलमानों को पृथक मताधिकार सरकार द्वारा मान्य हो गया था तो सबसे अधिक पिछड़े दलित वर्ग के लिये पृथक मताधिकार क्यों न बहाल किया जाये।

31 जनवरी 1920 को उन्होंने मूकनायक नामक एक मराठी पाक्षिक पत्रिका को आरंभ किया। प्रथम अंक में उन्होंने ऐसे मुख पत्र की आवश्यकता को बयान करते हुये कहा था कि वह अन्याय के खिलाफ मंथन और समीक्षण करने वाला मुखपत्र है। सन 1920 में उन्होंने कोल्हापुर के छत्रपति शाहू महाराज की छत्रछाया में प्रथम अखिल भारतीय दलित वर्ग संस्था का नागपुर में सम्मेलन कराया और वहां यह ऐलान किया कि दलित वर्गों की मुक्ति उनके अपने प्रयासों से ही संभव है।

सितंबर 1920 में उन्होंने अपने लंदन विश्वविद्यालय की पढ़ाई फिर से आरंभ की। अगले ही वर्ष उन्होंने एम. एससी. की उपाधि प्राप्त की, जो

डॉक्टरल शोध के लिये अनिवार्य शर्त थी। उसके बाद उन्होंने उस समय के सर्वश्रेष्ठ अर्थशास्त्र के विद्वान सर एडविन केनन के मार्गदर्शन में *रुपये की समस्या* पर एक बृहद् शोध प्रबंध लिखा, जिसे बाद में लंदन के ही पब्लिशर, पी. एस. किंग एण्ड सन्स ने सन् 1923 में *'रुपये की समस्या', उसकी उत्पत्ति और उसका उपचार'* शीर्षक से प्रकाशित किया और उसी प्रकाशक ने अमरीका के कोलंबिया विश्वविद्यालय से स्वीकृत उनका पहले से ही तैयार *बिट्रीश भारत में प्रांतीय वित्त* नामक पी. एच. डी. की उपाधि का शोध प्रबंध सन 1925 में प्रकाशित किया। सन 1922 में डॉ. आंबेडकर ने बर्लिन में उच्चतर शोधाध्ययन के लिये तीन माह खर्च किये। उसी वर्ष ग्रेज इन के बार का बुलावा आया।

अगले वर्ष वे भारत लौट आये और वहां मुंबई उच्च न्यायालय में वकालत की। इंदौर के तत्कालीन महाराज मल्हार राव होलकर के एक राज घराने के बाहर की महिला के साथ वैवाहिक संबंध के बारे में उपजे विवाद में महाराजा की वकालत करने, और एक अन्य इंदौर निवासी के एक मंदिर के पास की जमीन के मुकदमें में पैरवी करने के सिलसिले में डॉ. आंबेडकर इंदौर आये थे। इंदौर के इन दोनों मामले में उनकी वकालत ने संबंधित पक्षों को जिताकर राहत दिलाई थी।

जून 1925 से मार्च 1928 तक उन्होंने वहां के अकाउन्टंसी की बाटलीबोई प्रशिक्षण संस्थान में अंशकालीन प्राध्यापक की सेवायें प्रदान की। जून 1928 से मार्च 1929 तक वे मुंबई के शासकीय विधि महाविद्यालय के प्राध्यापक रहे।

सन 1924 में उन्होंने *बहिष्कृत हितकारणी सभा* की स्थापना की। उसके तहत उन्होंने सोलापुर में दलित वर्ग छात्रावास खोला। सन् 1927 में उन्होंने महाड़ सत्याग्रह चलाया और अहिंसा के मार्ग से आम लोंगों की तरह अछूतों के अधिकार को भी कुओं, तालाबों आदि पर प्रस्थापित किया। उससे दलितों का हिंदुओं के साथ सीधा संघर्ष छिड़ गया। इतना ही नहीं, बल्कि 25 दिसंबर 1927 के दिन मनुस्मृति का सामुहिक रुप से दहन कर उन्होंने सिद्ध कर दिया कि अब वे हिंदुओं की गुलामी में नही रहेंगे।

सन् 3 अप्रैल 1927 से डॉ. आंबेडकर ने *बहिष्कृत भारत* नामक पाक्षिक चलाया। उनके संघर्ष का यह एक पायदान था। इसी दौरान डॉ. आंबेडकर

ने समाज सुधार और राष्ट्र निर्माण की कटिबद्धता स्वीकार की थी। अतः उन्होंने मुंबई विधान मंडल में सन् 1927 से सन् 1937 तक कुल 10 वर्ष के कार्यकाल में एक सक्रिय सदस्य की भूमिका निभाई। मुंबई विधान मंडल में उन्होंने गरीबों पर लादे जानेवाले बजट के संबंध में प्रशासन की लापरवाही पर कठोर प्रहार किया।

उनका वक्तव्य अनोखा रहता था। उन्होंने 29 मई और अक्टूबर 1928 में सायमन कमिशन में मुंबई विधान मंडल कमिटी से हटकर उसके एक सदस्य की हैसियत से अपना अलग वक्तव्य दिया कि भारत के संवैधानिक प्रजातंत्र में दलित वर्गों का दृष्टिकोण ध्यान में रखा जाना चाहिये। वहां उन्होंने मुंबई पैतृक व्यवसाय अधिनियम 1874 के संशोधन का विधेयक प्रस्तुत किया।

समाज में एकता स्थापित करने के लिये उन्होंने क्रमशः समाज समता संघ और समता सैनिक दल की स्थापना सितंबर और दिसंबर को सन् 1927 में की।

उन्होंने बहिष्कृत हितकारणी सभा की ओर से शिक्षा में दलित वर्गों की स्थिति पर प्रकाश डालते हुये वक्तव्य दिया था कि प्रशासन का आधार सार्वत्रिक वयस्क मताधिकार होना चाहिये। उसी वर्ष उन्होंने दलित वर्ग शिक्षा समाज की स्थापना की और उसके माध्यम से उच्च विद्यालय के दलित छात्रों के लिये पनवेल, ठाने, नासिक, पुणे और धारवाड में छात्रावास खोले।

सन् 1930 में नासिक में ही कालाराम मंदिर प्रवेश सत्याग्रह में उन्होंने दलित वर्ग के धार्मिक हितों की रक्षा के लिये अहम भूमिका निभाई। और उसी वर्ष नागपुर में आयोजित अखिल भारतीय दलित वर्ग कांग्रेस की अध्यक्षता की। उन्होंने ब्रिटिश प्रशासन के प्रतिकूल रवैये, भारतीय उच्च जातियों का रुढ़िवाद तथा गांधी और कांग्रेस की सनातनी नीतियों पर अपनी आलोचना से प्रहार किया और दूसरी गोलमेज परिषद में उन्होंने गांधी से दलित हितों के रक्षणार्थ लडाई मोल ली। उनके विचारों का मायनारिटी पैक्ट पर इतना प्रभाव था कि उनके सुझावों का समावेश 1932 के जातीय समझौता तथा 1935 के भारत अधिनियम में भी है, हालांकि

गांधी के आमरण अनशन से दलितों को पृथक प्रतिनिधित्व के स्थान पर संयुक्त प्रतिनिनिधित्व और आरक्षण से संतोष करना पड़ा।

उन्होंने 24 नवंबर 1930 को जो *जनता* नामक पाक्षिक चलाया था वह एक वर्ष बाद साप्ताहिक के रुप में चलता रहा, और 4 फरवरी 1956 से *प्रबुद्ध भारत* के नाम से प्रकाशित होता रहा।

भारतीय मताधिकार कमिटी अथवा लोथीयन कमिटी के एक सदस्य की हैसियत से डॉ. आंबेडकर ने दलितों की प्रातिनिधिक और मताधिकार की स्थिति का जायजा लेने हेतु पूरे भारत का दौरा कर उसका परीक्षण किया।

पूना पैक्ट के बाद एंटी–अन्टचेबिलिटी लीग की स्थापना भी हुई। परंतु डॉ. आंबेडकर ने पाया कि अछूतों पर हिंदू दमन बरकरार रखनेवाली बलात् अवस्था में हुये पूना पैक्ट और हरिजन सेवक संघ यानी एन्टी अन्टचेबिलिटी लीग के द्वारा अछूतों का आत्म सम्मान दांव पर लगा देख कर डॉ. आंबेडकर ने सन् 1933 में संघ से अपना इस्तीफा दे दिया।

उन्होंने 17 नवंबर 1932 से 24 दिसंबर 1932 तक के दौरान आयोजित गोलमेज परिषद में हिस्सा लिया था।

मुंबई के शासकीय महाविद्यालय में जून 1934 में प्रथम अंशकालीन प्रोफेसर के पद पर कार्य किया और 1 वर्ष पश्चात् वहां के प्राचार्य पद को संभाला।

27 मई 1935 में उनकी धर्मपरायण पत्नी रमाबाई का देहांत हुआ। उन्होंने स्वयं 3 पुत्र और 1 पुत्री के निधन का दुख सह कर और डॉ. आंबेडकर के विदेश में अध्ययन करने के दौरान अपना जीवन एकांत और दरिद्रता में बिताकर अब संसार से विदा ली थी।

13 अक्तूबर 1935 को डॉ. आंबेडकर ने नासिक में येवला की दलित वर्ग की सभा में हिंदू धर्म छोड़ने की बात कही थी। मई 1936 में उन्होंने इस प्रश्न को सुलझाने के लिये एक महार परिषद भी बुलाई। अगले 21 वर्ष तक उन्होंने धर्मों का तुलनात्मक अध्ययन किया।

1936 का उनका अत्यंत प्रखर भाषण जात–पात तोड़क मंडल, लाहौर की सभा के लिये तैयार किया गया था। उसमें व्यक्त विचारों में धर्म पर

की गई समीक्षा पर मंडल के संगठक श्री संत राम व अन्य प्रमुख नेताओं को एतराज होने से वह सभा ही रद्द कर दी गई। अतः उस भाषण को बाद में *जातिभेद निर्मूलन* शीर्षक से एक पुस्तिका की शक्ल में छाप दिया गया। डॉ. आंबेडकर की यह पुस्तिका भारत के मजलूमों के लिये वही कार्य कर रही है, जो काम कार्ल मार्क्स और एंगल्स के कम्युनिष्ट घोषणा पत्र ने विश्व के सर्वहाराओं के लिये किया था। डॉ. आंबेडकर की हिंदू धर्म की समीक्षा पर गांधी जी भी खफा हो गये थे, क्योंकि उनके लिये वर्ण व्यवस्था में कोई बुराई नही थी।

उसी वर्ष डॉ. आंबेडकर ने खेतीहर श्रमिकों की अल्प जोतों से संबंधित खेति पद्धति को मिटाने का विधेयक मुंबई विधान परिषद में प्रस्तावित किया।

इतना ही नही बल्कि 15 अगस्त 1936 में ही उन्होंने स्वतंत्र मजदूर दल की स्थापना कर 1937 के निर्वाचन में 17 सीटों में से 15 सीटों पर निर्वाचन में जीत हासिल की और 1938 में श्रमिकों के हितैषी के नाते श्रमिक आंदोलन को नियंत्रित करने वाले औद्योगिक श्रम विवाद विधेयक का विरोध भी किया। शासन की युद्ध नीति पर भी उनका एक विशेष दृष्टिकोण रहा, जिस के आधार पर उन्होंने शासकीय प्रयासों को सराहा था।

गांधी और कांग्रेस के सामाजिक सुधार के प्रति उदासीन रहने के फलस्वरुप मुस्लिम लीग ने लाहौर में अपने अलग राष्ट्र पाकिस्तान की मांग की। सन् 1940 में डॉ. आंबेडकर ने *पाकिस्तान अथवा भारत का विभाजन* और सन् 1943 में अपने दूसरे भाषण–ग्रंथ *रानडे, गांधी और जिन्ना* के माध्यम से इस खतरे की ओर इशारा किया था। बार–बार चेतावनी देने पर भी सनातनी समाज के कान में जूं तक नही रेंगी। डॉ. आंबेडकर ने भांप लिया कि यहां का समाज राजनीतिक कम और जातिगत अधिक है। अतः जुलाई 1942 में, जब क्रिप्स मिशन की चर्चा चल रही थी, उन्होंने शिडयुल्ड कास्ट फेडरेशन की स्थापना की। भारत के संवैधानिक निर्माण में हिंदु और मुस्लिम राजनैतिक दलों के बीच उस फेडरेशन की भूमिका ऐसी ही अपेक्षित थी जैसी दो बड़े धड़ों के बीच एक संतुलन शक्ति की होती है।

27 जुलाई 1942 में महाराज्यपाल की कार्यकारिणी में पांच साल के लिये श्रम मंत्री के पद पर नियुक्त हो जाने के पश्चात् दिसंबर 1942 में ही

डॉ. आंबेडकर ने पेसिफिक रिलेशन्स कमिटी द्वारा क्युबेक में आयोजित सम्मेलन के लिये *गांधी और अछुतों की मुक्ति* नामक एक शोध पत्र लिखा। इसी समय के दौरान डॉ. आंबेडकर ने दलितों का नौकरी में आरक्षण, श्रम विधियां व श्रम कल्याण तथा श्रमिक–उद्योगपति – सरकार की परस्परावलंबी त्रिसूत्रीय योजना, बहुउद्देशीय विकास योजना अर्थात् दामोदर घाटी तथा महानदी परियोजना की व्यापक नीतियां बना ली थी। संक्षेप में उन्होंने एक कल्याणकारी शासन की नींव रखी हालांकि सन 1951 में पंचवर्षीय योजना विभाग मंत्रालय श्री नेहरु ने उन्हें सौंपने से इंकार किया था।

अवाम के आंबेडकर ने सार्वजनिक जीवन में अपना सर्वस्व समर्पित कर दिया था। 24 अप्रैल 1942 में मुंबई प्रांत के राज्यपाल श्री लुमली ने वायसराय श्री लिनलिथगो को लिखा था कि डॉ. आंबेडकर सार्वजनिक कार्य में अरुचि रखते हैं, यह वक्तव्य डॉ. आंबेडकर की चर्या से असिद्ध हुआ है। भले ही अनुसूचित जाति परिषद दल सन् 1945 के अंत में हुये चुनाव में अयशस्वी रहा, संवैधानिक सभा के लिये भले ही उन्हें बंगाल से निर्वाचित होना पडा, और जब केबिनेट मिशन मार्च 1946 में भारत आया और उसके सदस्य प्रतिनिधियों अर्थात लार्ड पेथिक लॉरेन्स और ए.वी. अलेक्झेंडर और उस समय के ब्रिटेन के प्रधान मंत्री श्री ॲटली ने एस. सी. एफ की पराजय को इंगित कर अनुकुल सलूक नही किया, तथापि डॉ. आंबेडकर ने जून 1946 में दलितों की भावी समय में भूमिका के लिये चलाये गये संघर्ष का नेतृत्व किया, सन् 1945 में *गांधी और कांग्रेस ने दलितों के लिये क्या किया* नामक एक बड़ा ग्रंथ रचा, सन 1946 में हिंदू धर्म के विभाजन और ब्राह्मणवाद के परिणाम को दर्शाने वाला ग्रंथ *'शूद्र पहले कौन थे'* लिखा, और 1948 में अस्पृभयों का मूल बौद्ध बतानेवाला ग्रंथ *अछूत* का निर्माण किया ।

बंगाल का विभाजन होने के पश्चात् वहां से संविधान सभा के लिये डॉ. आंबेडकर द्वारा जीती गई सीट भी निरस्त हुई, अतः कांग्रेस ने मुंबई से उन्हें जिताया। उसके कारण कांग्रेस को उन की सेवाओं को ग्रहण करने का एक अच्छा अवसर मिला और उसका उसने भरपूर फायदा भी उठाया। 3 अगस्त 1947 में डॉ. आंबेडकर से श्री नेहरु की केबिनेट में कानून मंत्री के पद की सेवायें ली गई। 19 अगस्त 1947 में उन्हें मसौदा

समिति का सभापति बनाकर उन से संविधान रचा गया, हालांकि उनकी सेहत सन् 1940 से ही खराब चल रही थी और उस वजह से उन्होंने डॉ. शारदा कबीर से अंतर्जातीय विवाह भी कर लिया था। परंतु जब डॉ. आंबेडकर ने हिंदू परिवार तथा समाज की सीढ़ी–दर–सीढ़ी विभाजक स्तरों को मिटाने के लिये हिंदू कोड बिल की संहिता संविधान सभा में पारित करने की अपेक्षा शासन से की तो कांग्रेस का सनातनी हिंदुत्व आड़े आया। सन् 1951 में सितंबर माह में डॉ. आंबेडकर ने अपने पद से प्रधान मंत्री को इस्तीफा सौंप दिया।

भले ही 1952 के आम चुनाव में अस्पृभय जाति परिषद लोक सभा के निर्वाचन और सन् 1954 में भंडारा निर्वाचन क्षेत्र से लोक सभा के उपचुनाव में वह हार गई थी और भारत के राजनीतिक जीवन में नया प्राण फूंकने वाली रिपब्लिकन पार्टी ऑफ इंडिया की उनकी योजना अधूरी रह गई थी तथापि शिक्षा और बौद्ध वैचारिकी के क्षेत्र में उनके द्वारा विश्व नव निर्माण का बुना हुआ सपना वास्तव में अब साक्षीभूत हो गया और उसकी पूर्णता का अभियान चल रहा हैं।

उन्होंने 8 जुलाई 1945 में पिपुल्स एज्युकेशन सोसायटी की स्थापना कर उसके माध्यम से सिद्धार्थ कॉलेज आफ आर्टस् एण्ड सायंस, 1946; सिद्धार्थ नाइट स्कूल 1947; मिलिंद महाविद्यालय, 1950; सिद्धार्थ कॉलेज ऑफ कामर्स एण्ड एकॉनामिक्स, 1953; मिलिंद मल्टिपरपज हायस्कूल, 1955; और सिद्धार्थ कॉलेज ऑफ लॉ, 1956 इन शैक्षणिक संस्थाओं को खड़ा कर अपने अभियान को फलिभूत किया है। उन्होंने हिंदू धर्म का पर्याय ही नहीं बल्कि विश्व का बेहतर मानवतावादी धर्म को 21 वर्ष अध्ययन के परीक्षण के बाद परख कर उसे भारत के लिये अनुसंशित किया। सन् 1949 में उन्होंने काठमांडू में विश्व बौद्ध परिषद में मार्क्सवाद और बौद्धधर्म पर संबोधन दिया, बुद्ध और उनके धर्म का भविष्य नामक आलेख महाबोधि जर्नल में छपवाया, उन्होंने सन् 1950, 1954 और 1956 में श्रीलंका, रंगून और नेपाल में जाकर वहां आयोजित विश्व बौद्ध सम्मेलन में उद्बोधन ही नही दिया बल्कि व्यवहार में जीवित बौद्ध संस्कारों का अवलोकन भी किया। 14 अक्तूबर 1956 में उन्होंने नागपुर में लाखों जनता के साथ बौद्ध जीवन पद्धति को अपनाया। उनकी अंतिम रचना बुद्ध और उनका धम्म थी।

5 जुलाई 1952 में कोलंबिया विश्वविद्यालय ने उन्हें एलएल.डी. की मानद उपाधि प्रदान की और एक वर्ष पश्चात उस्मानिया विश्वविद्यालस ने उन्हें डी. लिट की उपाधि से विभूषित किया। परंतु डॉ. आंबेडकर ने 6 दिसंबर 1956 को महाप्रयाण किया और विश्व के भावी जीवन की खुशहाली के लिये वे हमारे पास अपने द्वारा प्रदत्त शिक्षा, संस्कार और प्रेरणा ही छोड़ गये, जो हमें कदम–कदम पर मार्गदर्शन करते रहेंगे।

अस्पृश्यता

अब रामजी कोरेगांव में एक निजी कंपनी में कैशियर के पद पर काम कर रहे थे। कोरेगांव में घटित उनके बालपण की मुख्य घटना को डॉ. आंबेडकर ने स्वयं की लेखनी से इस प्रकार बयान किया है। उन्होंने लिखा है:

''हमारा परिवार मूलतः मुंबई प्रेजीडेंसी के रत्नागिरी जिले के दापोली तहसील (अंबावडे ग्राम) से आया था। ईस्ट इण्डिया कंपनी के बिलकुल आरंभ से मेरे पूर्वजों ने अपना पैतृक व्यवसाय त्याग दिया था और कंपनी की सैनिकी सेवा में भर्ती हो गये थे। मेरे पिताजी ने भी परिवार की इस परंपरा का अनुकरण किया और सैनिकी सेवा में भर्ती हुये। अपने कैरियर में वे अधिकारी की श्रेणी तक पहुंचे और मेजर सूबेदार के पद पर (महू से) सेवा निवृत्त हुये। अपने सेवानिवृत्त होने के पश्चात् स्थायी रुप से बसने के इरादे से मेरे पिता अपने कुटुंब को लेकर दापोली आये। लेकिन कुछ कारणों से मेरे पिताजी ने अपना मन बदला। अतः वे दापोली छोड़कर सतारा आये और वहां हम सन् 1904 तक रहे।

पहला प्रसंग जो मैं लिपिबद्ध कर रहा हूं और जिसे मैं याद कर सकता हूं वह सतारा में ही लगभग सन् 1901 में घटित हुआ था। मेरी मां (जिसे मैं *बय* कहता था) शांत हो गई थी। मेरे पिताजी कोरेगांव में कैशियर का काम करते थे। यह गांव सतारा जिले के खाटव तहसील में था। यहीं पर मुंबई सरकार ने हजारों की तादाद में भूख से मर रहे लोगों को आजीविका देने के उद्‌देश्य से तालाब की खुदाई का उपक्रम शुरु किया था। जब मेरे पिताजी कोरेगांव गये तो उन्होंने हम दो भाईयों और हमारे दो भानजों को मेरी बुआ और कुछ दयालु पडोसिओं की निगरानी में छोड़ दिया था।

कैशियर होने के कारण मेरे पिता अवकाश लेकर हमें देखने के लिये सतारा नही आ सकते थे। अतः उन्होंने लिख भेजा था कि हम आगामी ग्रीष्म की छुट्टियां उनके पास गोरेगांव में ही बितायें। हम बच्चे इस सुअवसर को पाकर फूले न समाये, विशेषतः इसलिये क्योंकि हम में से किसी ने भी अभी तक रेलगाड़ी नहीं देखी थी।

बड़ी तैयारियां की गई। अंग्रेजी बनावट के नये शर्ट, चमकीली रत्नजड़ित टोपियां, नये जूते, रेशम की जरी की किनारे वाली नई धोतियां यात्रा के लिये मंगाई गई।

रेलवे स्टेशन हमारे घर से 10 मील की दूरी पर था। रेलगाड़ी से गोरेगांव जाने के लिये सब से नजदीक मसूर स्टेशन पड़ता है। वहां पर हम शाम को 5 बजे पहुंचे। सभी यात्री जा चुके थे। हम चार बच्चे प्लेटफार्म पर पिताजी अथवा उनके नौकर, जिसे वे भेजने वाले थे, का इंतजार कर रहे थे। काफी समय बीत गया पर कोई नही आया। हमारे सुंदर परिधान देखकर स्टेशन मास्टर को लगा कि हम ब्राह्मण लड़के होंगे। अतः उन्होंने पूछा कि हम कौन हैं। मैने महार कह दिया। बंबई प्रेजीडेंसी में महार एक अस्पृश्य जाती होती है। यह बात तांगेवालों तक फैल गई। हमें ले जाने के लिये एक तांगेवाला बडी मुश्किल से तैयार हुआ। वह भी इस शर्त पर कि हम उसे दुगुना भाड़ा देंगे और तांगा हम खुद चलायेंगे और स्वयं तांगेवाला गाडी के पीछे–पीछे पैदल चलेगा।

शाम के लगभग साढ़े छह बज चुके थे जब हम लोगों ने स्टेशन छोड़ा। तांगेवाला कह रहा था कि कोरेगांव पहुंचने के लिये तीन घंटे से अधिक समय नही लगेगा। आगे एक नदी थी। तांगेवाले ने सुझाया कि हम वहीं पर अपना भोजन कर लें क्योकि आगे पानी नही मिल पायेगा। वह स्वयं खाने के लिये पास के किसी गांव में गया जिसके लिये हम ने किराये का कुछ भाड़ा नकद अदा कर दिया था। हम ने भी अपने खाने के डिब्बों की टोकरी खोली और उस में से खाना निकाल कर खाने लगे। हम में से एक पानी लेने नदी में उतर गया परंतु खाली हाथ लौट आया क्योंकि वहां का पानी कीचड और गंदगी से बदबूदार हो चुका था। हम ने अपना खाना लपेट कर टिफिन में बंद कर दिया और गाडीवाले का इंतजार करते रहे।

वह काफी विलंब से आया। जब आया तो यात्रा फिर जारी की गई लेकिन रात के दस भी बज चुके थे पर कोरेगांव नही आया।

मध्य रात्री भी बीत गई जब मात्र चुंगी नाके तक पहुंचे थे। नाके वाला हिंदू था, उसे पानी मांगा तो उस ने साफ इंकार कर दिया। हम वहां भूखे–प्यासे ही सोये। दूसरे दिन सुबह 8 बजे फिर बैलगाड़ी में यात्रा जारी रखी तो कोरेगांव सुबह 11 बजे पहुंचे। हमें देखकर पिताजी को आश्चर्य हुआ। हम ने कहा सूचना भेजने पर भी हमें लेने स्टेशन पर क्यों नही आये तो उन्होंने पता लगाया कि उन्हें इसकी सूचना मिली ही नही थी, जो उनके नौकर की भूल थी।

खैर, इस घटना का मेरे जीवन में खास महत्व है। जब वह घटना हुई तो में 9 साल का बालक था। लेकिन उस ने मेरे मन पर अमिट छाप छोडी है। इस प्रसंग के पूर्व मैं जानता था कि मैं एक अछूत बालक हूं और सभी अस्पृभय कुछ अप्रतिष्ठा और भेद–भाव के शिकार हैं। मिसाल के तौर पर मैं जानता था कि स्कूल में मैं अपने क्रम के अनुसार अपने वर्ग–सहपाठियों के बीच में नही बैठ सकता था और मुझे एक कोने में अकेले ही बैठना पड़ता था। मैं जानता था कि स्कूल में मुझे एक बोरी की चटाई पर अपनी कक्षा से अलग हट कर बैठना पडता था और जो फर्राश स्कूल की सफाई करता था वह भी मेरे द्वारा इस्तेमाल की गई बोरी की चटाई को नही छूता था। बोरी की चटाई भी मैं प्रति दिन घर से अपने साथ ले कर स्कूल में जाया करता था। स्कूल में अन्य बच्चे प्यास लगने पर अध्यापक की अनुमति से पानी के नल के पास जाते, उसे खोलते और अपनी प्यास बुझाते थे। पर मैं पानी का नल छू नही सकता था और जब तक कोई दूसरा स्पृभय प्राणी मेरे लिये उसे खोल नही देता तब तक मैं प्यासा का प्यासा ही रह जाता। अध्यापक ऐसे काम के लिये स्कूल के चपरासी को भेजते पर जब वह उपलब्ध नही होता तो मैं बिना पानी के ही रह जाता था। क्योंकि चपरासी नही तो पानी नही ऐसा नियम बन गया था। मैं जानता था कि घर में कपड़े धोने का कार्य मेरी बहनें करती थीं, इसलिये नही कि सतारा में धोबी नही थे, अथवा हम धुलाई का खर्चा देने योग्य नही थे, बल्कि इसलिये कि हम अछूत थे और कोई भी धोबी अछूत के कपड़े नही धोता था। दाढ़ी बनाने और बाल कटवाने का काम मेरी बड़ी बहन

करती थी क्योंकि सतारा का कोई नाई अछूत की दाढ़ी और बाल नही बनाता था। ये सब मैं जानता था। परंतु इस घटना ने तो मेरे दिल को ऐसी चोट पहुंचाई जिसे मैंने पहले कभी अनुभव नही किया था और उस घटना ने मुझे उस अछूतपन के बारे में सोचने के लिये मजबूर कर दिया जो इस प्रसंग के पूर्व मेरे और अन्य कई स्पृभय और अस्पृभयों के लिये एक आम बात थी और आज भी है[6]''।

डॉ. आंबेडकर के लिये यह घटना मानो सिद्धार्थ द्वारा दुःख दर्शन के सत्य को पाने के समान थी जब वे अपनी आयु के 29 वे वर्ष में चार दृभय अर्थात बुढ़ापा, बीमारी, मृत्यु और संसार त्याग की मानवीय घटनाओं से मजबूरन् लाईलाज गुजरते हुये मनुष्यों को देखकर सर्व दुःख मुक्ति यानी निर्वाण की खोज में घर से बाहर एकान्त में निकल पड़े थे अथवा न्यूटन के उस अनुभव के समान थी। जब किसी खास अवसर पर सेब को दरख्त से जमीन पर गिरते हुये देख कर उन्होंने गुरुत्वाकर्षण सिद्धान्त का आविष्कार किया था हालांकि उन्होंने पहले भी कई बार सेब को गिरते हुये देखा होगा। इसी के अनुरुप डॉ. आंबेडकर को अस्पृभयता के बारे में नई दृष्टि और नया एहसास उक्त मौके पर हुआ हालांकि उन्होंने अस्पृभयता का अनुभव इस घटना के पूर्व भी कई बार किया था।

उनके लेखन में अस्पृश्यता का उल्लेख कई बार हुआ है। अस्पृश्यता का अर्थ है ऐसे सामाजिक संबंध जो एक मनुष्य को दूसरे मनुष्य से तोड़ने वाले हों। जैसे मनुष्यों में स्वाभाविक रुप से एक साथ बैठने, एक साथ विचार करने, एक साथ निर्णय लेने, एक साथ खान–पान करने, एक दूसरे के गोत्र में शादी–ब्याह करने जैसी बातों में कृत्रिम दूरियां पैदा करना अस्पृश्यता है। अथवा सार्वजनिक तालाबो, कुओं, नदियां, पनघटों, स्कूलों, संस्थाओं, धर्मशालाओं अथवा अन्य किसी भी सामूहिक उपभोग की जगहों को किसी वर्ग के लिये प्रतिबंधित कर देना, अथवा जाति–जाति में अंतर्विवाह करने न देना, समाज के समस्त स्त्री–पुरुष सदस्यों में बराबरी की भावना न रखना और समानता, स्वतंत्रता और भाईचारा के सिद्धान्त से सार्वजनिक सार्वभौमिक प्रजातंत्रीय जीवन व्यवस्था को व्यवहार में न अपनाना इत्यादि अस्पृभयता है।

जिस समाज की दैनंदिन की चर्या अस्पृश्यता के संबंध से निश्चित होती है वह समाज अन्गिनत वर्गों और संवर्गों में लिंग, रुप, रंग, वर्ण, भाषा, प्रांत, परंपरा, धर्म आदि के आधार पर विभक्त होता चला जाता है। ऐसे समाज की सरंचना पिरामिड की भांति होती है। सबसे ऊपर मुट्ठी भर लोग, और सब से नीचे आम परिश्रमी लोग। सीढ़ी–दर–सीढ़ी के क्रम से कई श्रेणियों में विभक्त क्षत्रिय, वैश्य और शूद्र जातियों की साहसिक, सांपत्तिक और शारीरिक कमाई पर ऐश करने वाले सर्वोपरी अधिकारी ब्राह्मण होते हैं यद्यपि वे भी कई श्रेणियों में विभक्त होते हैं। इतना ही नही बल्कि हिंदू धर्म शास्त्रोक्त कानून के तहत एक ब्राह्मण मनुष्य कम से कम ब्राह्मणी, क्षत्राणी, वैश्याणी तथा शूद्राणी इन चार–चार महिलाओं के साथ वैधता से यौन संबध रख सकता है और राजनीतिक, धार्मिक और आचार के नियमों का नियन्ता और न्याय कर्ता भी वही होता है। इस आधार पर हम कह सकते हैं कि भले ही कोई अस्पृभय व्यक्ति हो लेकिन वह भी ब्राह्मण का उपभोग्य पदार्थ होता है।

नीचे के सभी वर्ण, वर्ग या जातियां ऊपर की तथाकथित सर्वश्रेष्ठ जाति की तरह आपस में विभक्त तो हैं परंतु उन्हीं की तरह एक होकर कभी अपना संगठित 'समाज' नही बना पाने के कारण पराधीन हैं।

वर्ण–जाति और लिंग के आधार पर बटे समाज की चौखट से परे एक धर्म या नैतिकता की वरिष्ठता पर आधारित लड़ाई की भी परंपरा है, जिस से आहत वर्ग एक साथ विद्यमान राजनैतिक सत्ता; आर्थिक संपन्नता, शैक्षणिक विकास, सामाजिक प्रतिष्ठा और सांस्कृतिक गुणात्मकता के बराबरी के हिस्सेदार नही हैं और न उनके धर्म एक हैं।

समाज

अवाम से अभिप्राय ऐसे बहुसंख्यक श्रमिक, शिल्पकार, बुद्धिजीवी, कृषक और उत्पादक सामाजिक वर्ग से है, जो अपने श्रमाधिक्य से संपूर्ण सामाजिक विलासिता के भार को सहन करते हुये विनष्ट हो रहा है किन्तु अपने परिश्रम का न्यायोचित लाभ उठाने की प्रतीक्षा में निरंतर संघर्षरत है।

अवाम को उनकी इस भयानक लड़ाई में आगे की विकास सीढ़ी पर पहुंचाने के लिये रहबर की भूमिका में योगदान देनेवाली विभूति के रुप में

डॉ. आंबेडकर धन्य हैं और महान हैं उनका जीवन और कृतित्व जिसने उनके संपर्क में आनेवाले हर व्यक्तित्व को उज्वल भविष्य की धरोहर का स्वामित्व प्रदान किया और कर रहा है।

अवाम का भावी विकास डॉ. आंबेडकर के विचार और दर्शन को सही भावार्थ में लेने पर निर्भर है। उनके अभियान को निम्न पंक्तियों में अभिव्यक्त किया जा सकता है:

''शब्द का इंसान लेकर आ गया मैं, अर्थ का ईमान लेकर आ गया मैं
वक्त की परछाईयों को मोड़ देने क्रांति का अभियान लेकर आ गया मैं।''

अवाम की उपलब्धि इसी बात में है कि वे लंबे अर्से के बाद अपने में से किसी एक को रहबर के गुणों से अभिभूत कर अगली सामाजिक विकास सीढी लांघे और जब वे ऐसी शख्शियत पैदा करें तो वह भी लंबे अर्से तक अपनी ऊर्जा का लाभ उन्हें भेंट करता रहें।

अवाम के आंबेडकर जीवन के प्रति उत्साहित करनेवाले दर्शन के समर्थक रहें। उन्होंने अपने शैक्षणिक विचारों से अवाम के सुप्त क्रियाशील भीतरी श्रोतों को अभिव्यक्त कर उन्हें उपयुक्त ऊर्जा में प्रवर्तित किया था।

उन्होंने बताया कि सामाजिक, आर्थिक और राजनीतिक क्रांति का मूलाधार शिक्षा है। डॉ. आंबेडकर के सभी शैक्षणिक विचारों का सार ''सीखो, संगठित हो और संघर्ष करो'' के तत्व में निहित है। शैक्सपियर को उद्धृत करते हुये डॉ. आंबेडकर कहते थे, ''हर मनुष्य के आयुष्य में जब अवसर की लहर आती है तो उसका युक्त प्रकार से उपयोग करने के बाद उसे वैभव प्राप्त होता है''। वे कहते थे, ''माता–पिता संतान को जन्म ही नही बल्कि कर्म भी देते हैं। वे अपनी संतान के जीवन में दिशा दे सकते हैं''। इस बात को ध्यान में रख कर हम सभी को बालकों की शिक्षा के साथ–साथ बालिकाओं की शिक्षा के लिये भी प्रयास करना चाहिये ताकि समाज की प्रगति द्रुत गति से हो सके।

सन् 1986 में भारत सरकार ने नई शिक्षा नीति की घोषणा की थी। उसके अनुसार भारतीय लोगों में साक्षरता का अंतर लिंग भेद और जाति भेद के उच्च और निम्न वर्ग के क्रम में असमान प्रतीत होता था। सवर्ण पुरुष सब से ज्यादा साक्षर, महिला पुरुष से कम साक्षर, अनुसूचित जाति

महिलाओं से कम साक्षर और अनुसूचित जमात सबसे कम साक्षर अर्थात् उनकी साक्षरता का प्रतिशत क्रमशः 36, 24, 22 और 16.1 था। डॉ. आंबेडकर सामुदायिक शिक्षा के प्रणेता थे। वे चाहते थे कि लोगों की प्रभु सत्ता पर संचालित प्रजातन्त्र में अमीर वर्ग के बच्चों के लिये शाही विद्यालय की व्यवस्था होना और गरीब बच्चों के लिये कोई स्कूल ही न होना असह्य दुर्व्यवस्था है।

बुद्ध ने अविद्या में ही सभी मानवीय प्रश्नों के मूल को तलाशा था। फुले ने तो कह दिया था कि ''विद्याविना मति नही, मतिविना नीति नही, नीतिविना गति नही, गति विना वित्त नही, वित्त विना शूद्र गिरा, इतना अनर्थ एक अविद्या ने करा''! लोक शिक्षक गाडगे महाराज और लोक शिक्षिका सावित्रीबाई फुले के शैक्षणिक विचार उक्त कथन से एकदम मिलते–जुलते हैं। गाडगे जी कहते थे कि शिक्षाविहीन मानव पत्थर है। और सावित्रीबाई का वचन थाः *शूदों को बताने योग्य एक ही मार्ग यही कि शिक्षा से है मनुष्यत्व, पशुत्व नहीं*।

डॉ. आंबेडकर के अनुसार शिक्षा के परिणाम स्वरुप स्वाभिमान, स्वावलंबन और आत्मोद्धार से क्रमशः बंधुत्व, समानता और स्वतंत्रता के मूल्य प्राप्त होना चाहिये। शिक्षा यानी परिवर्तन यह उनके शैक्षणिक विचारों का मुख्य सूत्र रहा है। 13 जून 1953 को रावळी कैम्प, मुंबई की सभा में संबोधित करते हुये डॉ. आंबेडकर ने कहा था, ''हम लोग शिक्षित हुये यानी सब कुछ हो गया ऐसी बात नही है। शिक्षा के साथ–साथ मनुष्य का शील भी सुधरना चाहिये। उसके बिना शिक्षा का मूल्य शून्य है। ज्ञान तलवार की भांति है। यदि किसी आदमी के पास तलवार है तो उसका सदुपयोग अथवा दुरुपयोग करना उसके सदाचार पर निर्भर करेगा। वह उस से किसी की जान भी लेगा या किसी की जान बचा भी लेगा। ज्ञान भी ऐसा ही है। इसके अतिरिक्त उन्होंने कहा कि इस से काम नही चलेगाा कि शिक्षित मनुष्य केवल अपने उदर भरण में ही लगा रहे। जिन्हें स्वार्थ के अलावा कुछ दूसरा दिखता ही नहीं है वे किंचित भी परार्थ कर नहीं सकते। ऐसे व्यक्ति मात्र शिक्षित होने से क्या लाभ? समाज का वर्णों में विभाजन व्यवसाय के उद्‌देश्य से हुआ है। परंतु ज्ञान रोजगार का प्रश्न हो ही नही सकता। ज्ञान जीवन के लिये अत्यंत आवश्यक है। उसके बिना

हमारा नुकसान होता है[8]। इस मापदण्ड से वर्तमान भारतीय शिक्षा पद्धति का पीठ किस प्रकार मानवीय चूंचे निर्माण करने का केन्द्र बन गया इस की हम कल्पना कर सकते हैं।

अर्थव्यवस्था

डॉ. आंबेडकर ने एम.ए., पी.एच.डी., एम.एस.सी., और डी.एस.सी. की शैक्षणिक उपाधियां प्राप्त करने हेतु *ईस्ट इड़िया कंपनी का प्रशासन और वित्त (1913), ब्रिटिश भारत में प्रांतीय वित्त का विकास (1915), ब्रिटिश भारत में साम्राज्यीय वित्त का प्रांतीय विकेंद्रीकरण (1917), और रुपये की समस्या, उत्पत्ति तथा विकास (1923)* नामक शोध ग्रंथों को लिखा और प्रकाशित किया।

पहले ग्रंथ में आर्थिक इतिहास बताया गया कि ईस्ट इंडिया कंपनी ने अपने 66 वर्षों के राज में प्रशासन और वित्त व्यवस्थापन किस प्रकार किया। उसे सन 1814 में ब्रिटिश सरकार ने प्रशासन और वित्त व्यवस्थापन में पृथकता बरतने का आदेश दिया था और 24 वर्ष बाद शासन ने उसका व्यापार में विद्यमान एकाधिकार भी बंद करवाया। 1858 में कंपनी को बर्खास्त कर ब्रिटिश सरकार ने स्वयं शासन और व्यापार का संचालन भारत में करना आरंभ कर दिया। ब्रिटिश सरकार के कार्यों का मूल्यांकन करते हुये डॉ. आंबेडकर ने लिखा था कि ''भारत ने इंग्लैंड़ के लिये आर्थिक रुप से जो प्रचंड योगदान किया वह जितना आश्चर्य चकित करनेवाला है, उतना इंग्लैंड ने भारत के लिये जो नगण्य आर्थिक योगदान किया वह विस्मयकारक है''। अर्थात् ब्रिटिश सरकार द्वारा कानून और शिक्षा द्वारा प्रस्थापित पाशविक शांति का आर्थिक रुप से यतीम किये गये भारतीयों के लिये कोई उपयोग नही था। डॉ. आंबेडकर को मरघट और पाशविक शांति नही बल्कि सामाजिक शांति की चाह थी जो आर्थिक गुलामी में अस्तित्वहीन हो जाती है।

उपरोक्त दूसरे ग्रंथ में उन्होंने कहा था कि केंद्रीय, प्रांतीय और स्थानीय शासकों में 1833 से 1921 की कालावधि में आर्थिक संबंध का विकास क्रम–क्रम से होता गया। 1871 तक वित्त व्यवस्था क्रेंद्रीभूत रही। उसके बाद केंद्र और राज्य का स्वतंत्र बजट बनाने की पद्धति आरंभ हुई।

1872 से 1877 में कुछ विशिष्ट केंद्रीय सरकार के विभागों के प्रशासन का भार राज्य सरकार को सौंपा गया। 1878 से 1882 के दरम्यान राजस्व पर आधारित बजट प्रस्तुत करने की पद्धति अपनाई गई। राजस्व के हिस्से के वितरण पर आधारित संतुलनात्मक पद्धति सब से बेहतर सिद्ध हुई। अतः वह 1883 से 1921 तक प्रचलित रही। हालांकि इसी बीच 1919 के कानून सुधार द्वारा जबाबदार सरकार निर्माण करने के ध्येय से स्वयंशासित संस्थाओं को सुरक्षित रखने का सिद्धान्त मान्य हुआ था। इस ग्रंथ का मूल्यांकन करते हुये डॉ. आंबेडकर के मार्गदर्शक प्रो. सेलिग्मन ने कहा था, ''मेरी जानकारी में अबतक कहीं भी भारतीय केंद्र सरकार और घटक राज्य के बीच आर्थिक संबंध की इतनी विस्तृत और गहरी मीमांसा नहीं की गई''।

तीसरे ग्रंथ में भारतीय रुपया चलन में 1800 से 1893 तक किस प्रकार परिमाण और मूल्य का कार्य संपादन करता रहा इसका इतिहास है। पहले भारत में सुवर्ण तथा चांदी का परिमाण के रुप में प्रचलन रहा। 1833 में ब्रिटिश सरकार ने संपूर्ण भारत में अपना आधिपत्य जमाया। 1842 तक भारत के निर्यात पर 50 से 500 प्रतिशत कर लादा जाता था। जब इस कर को घटाया गया तब भारत का निर्यात फिर से बढ़ गया। लेकिन 1853 के कानून द्वारा स्वर्ण का प्रचलन बंद कर दिया गया और एकमात्र चांदी का रुपया प्रचलन में चलने दिया गया। 1864 में भारतीय निर्यात में वृद्धि होने के कारण चांदी के रुपये चलन में अपर्याप्त होने लगे। तब चांदी के रुपयों के पूरक के रुप में कागज के रुपयों को प्रचलित किया गया। 1873 तक भारतीय रुपया और ब्रिटिश पौंड के बीच विनिमय का दर 1 रुपया बराबर 1 शिलिंग, 10/.5 पेन्स के स्तर पर स्थिर था। यानी चांदी का 15/.5 औंस का रुपया सोने के 1 औंस सिक्के के बराबर था। परंतु बाद के समय में सोना और चांदी के दरम्यान यह दर स्थिर रखना कठिन हो गया। 70 वर्ष के पश्चात् आज भी इस ग्रंथ की प्रासंगिकता हैं। 1926 में रिजर्व बैंक के स्थापनार्थ जो हिल्टन यंग कमिशन नियुक्त हुआ था उसके सामने अपनी साक्ष्य देते हुये डॉ. आंबेडकर ने कहा था, ''चलन निर्माण करनेवाली संस्था की चलन निर्माण क्षमता पर परिणाम कारक प्रतिबंध होना आवश्यक है। अनिबार्ध चलन पूर्ति और बेहिसाब मूल्य वृद्धि के कारण आर्थिक स्थिरता खतरे में आ सकती है''[9]।

बौद्ध धर्म तथा मार्क्सवाद नामक शोध आलेख में डॉ. आंबेडकर ने रयत का शोषण केवल वर्ग कलह से होता है इस मार्क्स के सिद्धान्त को नकारते हुये सामाजिक और धार्मिक शोषण भी आर्थिक शोषण के समान ही घातक होता है इस अभिमत को प्रतिपादित किया है। *गांधी और कांग्रेस ने अछूतों के लिये क्या किया* इस ग्रंथ में डॉ. आंबेडकर ने कहा कि ''अस्पृश्यता केवल धार्मिक रचना न होकर वह गुलामगिरी से भी भयानक आर्थिक रचना है। उसी प्रकार *जातिभेद निर्मूलन* में उन्होंने बताया कि जातिभेद में बताई गई व्यवस्था श्रम विभाजन की नही बल्कि श्रमिकों के विभाजन की व्यवस्था थी[10]।

छोटी जोतों की चकबंदी करने हेतु डॉ. आंबेडकर ने फ्रांस और इटली में विद्यमान सामूहिक खेती पद्धति और राष्ट्रीयकरण की प्रक्रिया को अनुकरणीय बताया था। उत्पादन साधनों को सामूहिक स्वामित्व में करने के बाद भी जबतक समाज में जातिभेद की निम्न श्रेणियां और अस्पृभयता हैं तबतक सामूहिक स्वामित्व अर्थशून्य रहेगा। खोति पद्धति (उत्तर भारत की जमींदारी प्रथा की भांति)[10] के कारण छोटे–छोटे जोत धारक या कुलजन जमीनदारों यानी खोतों के अधीन गुलाम होते जा रहे थे और वतन पद्धति (बेगार प्रथा की भांति)[11] के कारण महार लोग स्वाभिमान और स्वावलंब से वंचित हो रहे थे, इसलिये उन्होंने उन दोनों पद्धतियों को समाप्त करने वाले दो विधेयक मुंबई विधान सभा में प्रस्तुत किये थे। खोति पद्धति रयत पद्धति से इस बात में भिन्न थी कि दूसरी में स्वयं भूधारक प्रत्यक्ष रुप से शासन को भू– शुल्क देता था परंतु पहली पद्धति में शासन द्वारा वरिष्ठ खोत भू– शुल्क अदा करने हेतु नियुक्त किये गये थे, जो शासन को निश्चित राजस्व की रकम अदा कर देने के पश्चात कनिष्ठ भूधारकों पर आर्थिक जुल्म ढ़ाते थे। अतः डॉ. आंबेडकर ने खोतों की समाप्ति हेतु एक विधेयक दिनांक 15 सितम्बर 1937 को मुंबई विधान सभा में प्रस्तावित किया था। इस से पहले सन् 1927 में श्री एफ. जी. एच. ॲन्डरसन ने मुंबई विधान सभा में अल्पभूधारक मदद विधेयक प्रस्तुत किया था। परंतु उसका अभिप्राय जमीन का शासकीय स्वामित्व स्थापित करना नही था। अतः इस से जमीनदारों की प्रगल्भता और छोटे जोतोंवालों की दरिद्रता बेहिसाब बढ़नेवाली थी। इस विधेयक में एक निश्चित आकार से

कम जमीन धारणा पर प्रतिबंध और दण्ड की व्यवस्था थी। छोटे किसानों को छोटी जोतों से वंचित कर भूमिहीन मजदूर बनने से मुक्ति दिलाने हेतु उन्होंने सामूहिक कृषि की अनुसंशा की यानी एक से अधिक छोटे किसान मिल कर निश्चित आकार का खेत बनाये रखना और इस प्रकार सामूहिक कृषि कायम करना संभवनीय था।

अर्थशास्त्र के सुप्रसिद्ध विद्वान रॅगनर नर्क्स के प्रछन्न बेरोजगारी और डॉ. आंबेडकर की अतिरिक्त श्रमिक की संकल्पना में अत्यधिक समानता है।

ब्रिटिश भारत में प्रांतीय वित्त का विकास बयान करते समय डॉ. आंबेडकर ने शासन की नीतियों में जो सप्ताह–सप्ताह में सुधार होता गया उस बाबत् टिप्पणी की थी, ''संयुक्त कुटुंब पद्धति में कुटुम्ब प्रमुख जिस प्रकार प्रत्येक सदस्य के नाम से बैंक में खाता खोलता है, उसी प्रकार सरकार की व्यवस्था थी[13]।

आर्थिक जोत से उनका अभिप्राय ऐसे उत्पादक खेत से था जिसकी निवेशित व्यय की पूर्ति हो जाने के बाद शेष उत्पादन की राशी पर एक परिवार अपना खर्च चला सके[14]।

परंतु भारत में डॉ. आंबेडकर द्वारा लिखित *छोटी जोतें और उनके उपाय* नामक शोध आलेख 1918 में प्रकाशित होने के 86 वर्षों के बाद भी भारत में औसतन बोने योग्य जोत का आकार 1.67 हेक्टर, सीमांत जोत का प्रतिशत 56.00, जोत के औसतन टुकडे 4.04 हेक्टर और प्रत्येक टुकडे का औसत आकार 0.41 हेक्टर रहा है। इतना ही नही बल्कि प्रत्येक राज्य में हर दशक में जोत का औसतन आकार घट रहा है। भारत में यह आकार वर्ष 1961, 1971 और 1981 में क्रमशः 2.6, 2.20 और 1.67 हेक्टर तक कम होता गया। तथापि सन 1950 से भूसुधार कानून को भारत के हर राज्य मे लागू करना आर्थिक क्षेत्र में एक बहुत बड़ा परिवर्तन था।

उनका शासकीय समाजवाद शोषितों को न्याय देने के हेतु से आर्थिक, सामाजिक व राजनीतिक जीवन को जोड़नेवाली दर्शन प्रणाली थी। वह सहकारी कृषि, औद्योगिकरण तथा सामुदायिक कृषि से संलग्न रहा। आर्थिक समानता के बिना राजनीतिक स्वाधीनता का अर्थ नहीं था।

इसलिये डॉ. आंबेडकर ने संवैधानिक स्टेट सोशलिज्म के एक अंग के रुप में सामुदायिक कृषि की अनुसंशा की थी। उन्होंने विखंडित और छोटी जोतों के लिये उपाय के रुप में सहकारी कृषि की सिफारिश की थी। उन्होंने भारतीय कृषि सुधार के लिये अर्थात कृषि पर अतिरिक्त पड़े मनुष्य बल के भार को गैर कृषि क्षेत्र में स्थानांतरित करने हेतु औद्योगिकरण का जो उपाय बताया था वह सामाजिक न्याय की दृष्टि से भी उचित था और है, क्योंकि ग्रामीण क्षेत्र में जाति व्यवस्था और अस्पृश्यता थी, है और रहेगी परंतु शहरों में उनकी तीव्रता कम हो रही है।

सन् 1946 में डॉ. आंबेडकर ने अखिल भारतीय अनुसूचित जाति परिषद की ओर से संविधान समिति को एक मसौदा प्रस्तुत किया था, जो *राज्य और अल्पसंख्यंक* नामक ग्रंथ के रुप में प्रकाशित हुआ था। उस में उन्होंने कृषि जमीन को बीमा और मूलभूत उद्योगों की तरह शासन के स्वामित्व में रखने की बात कही थी। इसी मसौदे में उन्होंने निजी मालिकों की हुकुमशाही से समाज और शासन पर पड़नेवाले कुप्रभाव का भी जिक्र किया है। उन्होंने शासन के हस्तक्षेप से मुक्ति को स्वतन्त्रता नही माना है। बल्कि वे शासन द्वारा सामाजिक और आर्थिक मामलों में न्याय के हित में हस्तक्षेप चाहते थे। उनका मानना था कि यदि शासन ने सामाजिक आर्थिक क्रियाकलापों का नियमन नही किया तो वह निजी मालिकों को करना पड़ेगा और ऐसा करते समय वे अपनी आजादी का उपयोग दूसरों पर अधिसत्ता स्थापित करने के लिये भी करेंगे। उस परिस्थिति में जमीनदार भी कुलों पर जबरदस्त जमीन भाड़ा थोपेंगे और पूंजीपति भी कामगारों के काम करने के घंटे बढायेंगे और उनके वेतन कम करेंगे। अर्थात् इस से राजनीतिक प्रजातन्त्र के मूलभूत सिद्धान्त यानी स्वयंभू व्यक्ति, अविछिन्न मूलभूत अधिकार, संवैधानिक अधिकार का बिन शर्त लाभ, और शासन संस्था द्वारा दूसरों पर लादने योग्य सत्ता का निजी व्यक्ति के हाथों में अहस्तांतरण को ही क्षति पहुंचेगी।

खोतों ने अपनी स्वाधीनता का उपयोग छोटे भूधारकों का शोषण करने में किया था और उस से मुंबई प्रांत में अशांति फैल चुकी थी। अतः खोतों का अन्त करना उस समय के भूमि सुधार की मांग थी, जिसे बाबासाहेब ने पूरी करने की चेष्टा की थी[15]।

डॉ. आंबेडकर का समाजवाद व्यक्ति के निम्न भौतिक अधिकारों पर आधारित हैः–

1. व्यक्ति उद्देश्य है।
2. व्यक्ति के कुछ अधिकार अहस्तांतरणीय है। इस की गारंटी संविधान को देनी चाहिये।
3. किसी भी व्यक्ति को अपनी सुख सुविधा का उपयोग करते हुये अपने संवैधानिक अधिकार की तिलांजली देने का अवसर नहीं आना चाहिये। और
4. शासन ने किसी भी निजी व्यक्ति को अन्य व्यक्तियों पर आधिपत्य करने का अधिकार नहीं देना चाहिये।

इस समाजवाद में सामाजिक संघर्ष के कारकों में धन की तरह धर्म पर भी बल दिया गया है। इस बात में डॉ. आंबेडकर का समाजवादी सिद्धान्त औरों से विशेश और अनोखा है।

1917 में रशिया में राज्यक्रांति हुई और उसके 8 वर्ष के बाद भारत में भारतीय कम्युनिस्ट पार्टी की स्थापना की गई। 1926 में स्थापित ''लाहौर नौजवान सभा'' और 1928 में प्रस्थापित ''नौजवान भारत सभा'' जैसे स्वतन्त्र संगठनों के माध्यम से कम्युनिस्ट विचारों का अमल भी किया जा रहा था। तत्कालीन कम्युनिस्ट विचारों के नेता कॉमरेड एम. एन. राय थे। 1934 में आचार्य नरेन्द्र देव और जयप्रकाश नारायण प्रभति मार्क्सवादी; श्री अशोक मेहता जैसे फेबियन समाजवादी; डॉ. राममनोहर लोहिया जैसे गांधीवादी; युसुफ मेहेर अली और संपूर्णानन्द जैसे राष्ट्रवादी और मिनू मसानी जैसे ट्राट्स्कीवादीओं ने अपनी वैचारिक भिन्नता को कायम रख कर समाजवादी आंदोलन को वैश्विक, आर्थिक और राजनीतिक संदर्भ में चलाया था।

कॉ. श्रीपाद अमृत डांगे, बी. टी. रणदिवे, नंबुद्रिपाद, कॉ. श्रीनिवास, कॉ. सरदेसाई प्रभृति विद्वानों के नेतृत्व में अंतर्राष्ट्रीय कम्युनिस्ट आंदोलन ने 1943 तक भारतीय कम्युनिस्ट पार्टी का पथ प्रदर्शन किया।

जनता नामक पाक्षिक में दिनांक 7 नवंबर 1938 को प्रकाशित अपने एक साक्षात्कार में डॉ. आंबेडकर ने कहा था कि वे एक मुक्त समाजवादी

है। जातिभेद निर्मुलन को चाहने वाले समाजवादी डॉ. आंबेडकर ने लिखा था कि ''भारतीय समाजवादी यूरोप के समाजवादियों के कदमों पर कदम रखकर भारतीय परिस्थिति पर भी आर्थिक सिद्धान्त लागू करने की चेष्टा करते हैं। धर्म भी एक बहुत बडी प्रेरक शक्ति है, इसके प्रति समाजवादियों की उपेक्षा दृष्टि रही है।

डॉ. आंबेडकर को प्रजातन्त्र में दो बातें अभिप्रेत थी। पहली बात मानवीय वृत्ती की है। यह वृत्ती समाज के अन्य सदस्यों के प्रति समानता और आदर से देखने की होनी चाहिये। दूसरी बात यह है कि समाज की सरंचना में सख्त बंधन नही होने चाहिये। अन्यथा प्रजातन्त्र अधूरा रहेगा। अलगाववाद और एकाकीपन प्रजातन्त्र व्यवस्था के विसंगत गुण हैं क्योंकि उनकी परिणति विशेषाधिकार संपन्न अल्प और अधिकार विपन्न बहुसंख्य वर्गों में होती है। यही उनके राजनीतिक समाजशास्त्र का प्राण है।

आरक्षण

सदियों से समाज का एक वर्ग सामाजिक प्रतिष्ठा, दण्डविहीन अपराध, शासन में एक वर्ग केंद्रित सत्ता, शिक्षा में एकाधिकार आदि का भोक्ता रहा है। परंतु उसे बर्दाश्त करते हुये जिन जातियों ने अपना खून पसीना बहा दिया उनके प्रति शासक और शोषक वर्ग की हृदय–शून्यता अब तक अवाक रही है। जब से भारतीय संविधान ने जीवन में सबसे अधिक दलित और पीड़ित जनों के लिये आरक्षण की व्यवस्था बहाल की तब से ही आरक्षण के विरुद्ध आंदोलन ने विकराल रुप धारण कर लिया है। आरक्षण विरोधियों की दृष्टि आरक्षितों के प्रति समाज के एक ऋग्ण वर्ग को स्वस्थ बनाने की नही बल्कि उन्हें अधिक से अधिक वंचित रख कर बेमौत मारने की है ऐसा प्रतीत होता है।

जब बिहार के श्री कर्पुरी ठाकुर के नेतृत्व में जनता दल की सरकार ने मुंगेरीलाल आयोग की सिफारिशों के अनुसार शासकीय नौकरियों में अन्य पिछड़ा वर्ग 8 प्रतिशत, अति पिछड़ा वर्ग 12 प्रतिशत, अनुसूचित जाति 14 प्रतिशत, अनुसूचित जमाति 10 प्रतिशत, महिला 3 प्रतिशत, आर्थिक रुप से पिछड़ों के लिये 3 प्रतिशत आरक्षण की घोषणा की थी। उसके 3 वर्ष के बाद गुजरात में वैद्यकीय छात्रों ने अनुसूचित जाति–जमातियों

के छात्रों को पदव्युत्तर वैद्यकीय अभ्यासक्रम में प्रवेशार्थ प्राप्त आरक्षित सीटों के विरुद्ध हिंसक आंदोलन शुरु किया। 1989 में केंद्र में भूतपूर्व प्रधानमंत्री श्री विश्वनाथ प्रताप सिंग के नेतृत्व में राष्ट्रीय फ्रंट की सरकार ने मंडल आयोग के प्रतिवेदन की कुछ सिफारिशों को कार्यान्वित करने के लिये अधिसूचना निकाली थी कि सामाजिक और आर्थिक रुप से पिछड़े हुये वर्गों {एस. ई. बी. सी.} के लिये सरकारी नौकरी में 27 प्रतिशत आरक्षित सीटें हैं। इस दौर में नौकरियों में आरक्षित सीटों के विरुद्ध तर्क दिया जाता था कि इस आरक्षण के कारण सभी दलितों को फटाफट नौकरियां मिल जाती हैं और उस से अन्य जातियों में बेरोजगारी पैदा होती है। शैक्षणिक आरक्षण पर यह एतराज था कि वैद्यकीय और अभियांत्रिकी शाखाओं में दलितों को कम गुणों पर ही प्रवेश मिलता है और उन्हें कम गुणों से ही पास किया जाता है। उस से अधिक गुणवाले और मैरिट के छात्रों की उपेक्षा होती है। और उस से समाज में और व्यावसायिक गुणवत्ता में कोताई आ जाती है। उसी प्रकार राजनीतिक आरक्षण के कारण आरक्षित निर्वाचन क्षेत्र के सवर्ण मतदाताओं को अपने समाज का प्रतिनिधि लड़ाने का अवसर नही मिलता। आरक्षित उम्मीदवार लाद दिया जाता है और निर्वाचन क्षेत्र का विकास रुक जाता है।

1990 के पूर्व और बाद का आरक्षण विरोधी आंदोलन दलितों के विरुद्ध हिंदी भाशाई राज्यों में हुआ था। परंतु इतिहास में आरक्षण के निर्माता सामाजिक असमानता के पुजारी रहे और आज भी हैं।

ऐसे ही एक असमानता के राज, पेशवाई का अन्त 1818 में भले ही हुआ परंतु उसके अवशेश ब्रिटिश–राज में भी विद्यमान थे। 1774 में जिस प्रकार ईस्ट इंड़िया कंपनी का प्रशासन ब्रिटिश संसद ने अपने हाथ में कर लिया था परंतु उसी संसद ने अगले सौ वर्षों से भी अधिक समय तक कंपनी को नये नये कानून के अंतर्गत नई नई सनद देते रहना जारी रखा था। उसी प्रकार भारत में ब्रिटिश शासन ने ब्राह्मणों का एकाधिकार खत्म तो किया था परंतु अपने प्रशासन में सुशिक्षित व्यक्तियों को उच्च पदों पर बिठाने हेतु उन्होंने जो उपक्रम चलाया उस से परिणामतः ब्राह्मणवाद के अवशेश ही नये शासन में ज्यों के त्यों कायम रहे। भारत की दलित और शोषित जनता अपने शासकों से यह उम्मीद बांधे हुई थी कि विद्यमान

सामाजिक ढांचे में बदलाव के लिये हस्तक्षेप किया जायेगा। हस्तक्षेप तो हुआ परंतु स्थिति को जैसी है वैसी ही रखने में। अतः उस बाबत डॉ. आंबेडकर ने एक चीनी दर्जी की मिसाल देते हुये अपनी टिप्पणी में कहा था कि ''एक चीनी दर्जी ने अपने एक ग्राहक का नया कोट सिलते वक्त उसके एक पुराने कोट का उपयोग कोट को सुंदर तरीके से सिलने के लिये ही नही बल्कि उस कोट के पुराने पैबंद भी नये कोट पर ज्यों के त्यों उतार देने में किया था''। उसी प्रकार भारत के नये नये शासकों ने अपने अपने शासन में सदियों से विद्यमान जाति–पांति के पुराने पैबंद को नये सामाजिक ढांचे में ज्यों के त्यों बरकरार रखने में किया है।

श्री तिलक राजनीति में क्रांतिकारी और समाज सुधार में सनातनी थे। 1895 में अंग्रेजों ने एक अस्पृभय श्री नारायणराव लोखण्डे और एक चितपावन ब्राह्मण श्री विश्वनाथ केशव जोगळेकर को ''रावबहादुर'' की उपाधियां बहाल की थीं। इस बाबत् केसरी में छापा गया था कि ''श्री जोगळेकर ऑनरेरी मेजिस्ट्रेट थे। उनको बहाल किया गया सम्मान उचित है परंतु श्री लोखंडे को रावबहादुर की उपाधि बहाल करने में उनकी योग्यता की अपेक्षा उनकी जाति ही विशेष कारक प्रतीत होता है''[16]।

अतः 1882 से 1904 के दरम्यान भारतीय सिविल सेवा में यशस्वी हुये 16 भारतीयों में 15 ब्राह्मणों का होना कोई आश्चर्य जनक नहीं था। हालांकि ज्योतिराव फुले ने इस समय के दौरान ब्राह्मणवाद पर तीखा प्रहार करनेवाली ग्रंथ संपदा प्रकाशित की थी और 19 अक्तूबर 1882 को हंटर शिक्षा आयोग के समक्ष सादर प्रस्तुत निवेदन में बयान किया था कि ''उच्च शिक्षा पद्धति में स्पष्ट झलकने वाली प्रवृत्ति यह है कि उस में वरिष्ठ अधिकारी के पद केवल ब्राह्मणों की बपौति हो चुके हैं। यदि शासन को रैयत के कल्याण की वास्तविक चिंता है तो उस का प्रथम कर्तव्य है कि वह इस पद्धति के कई प्रकार के दुरुपयोग को प्रतिबंधित कर, शासकीय नौकरियों में धीरे धीरे अन्य जातियों के लोगों को प्रवेश के अवसर दिला कर उसी अनुपात में ब्राह्मणशाही का नियमन करें''। उन्होंने शासन से यह भी सिफारिश की कि वे कनिष्ठ जातियों के बच्चों की शिक्षा हेतु स्वतन्त्र विद्यालय की व्यवस्था करें।

फुले के समाज सुधार आंदोलन के कार्यकर्ता श्री भालेकर ने पूना अधिवेशन में सवर्ण बहुल कांग्रेस के रुख के विरुद्ध निदर्शन किया था। श्री वलंगकर ने भी श्री रानडे की मदद से सेना में महारों की भर्ती को प्रतिबंधित करने के आदेश के विरुद्ध ब्रिटिश सरकार से अपील की थी। श्री कांबले ने भी सेना और पुलिस में अस्पृभयों की भर्ती हेतु मांग रखी थी। वर्तमान के मध्य प्रदेश और तत्कालीन मध्य प्रांत और बेरार के समाज कार्य कर्ता गण श्री बन्सोडे, श्री गवई और श्री नंदागवली ने दलित जागरण का अभियान चलाया था। उसी प्रकार श्री शिंदे की भारतीय निराश्रित सहायक मंडल {डिप्रेस्ड क्लासेस मिशन सोसायटी ऑफ इण्डिया} के तत्वावधान में अस्पृभयों के हितों के प्रति संवेदनशीलता को बढाया गया।

उक्त समयावधि के दौरान कोल्हापूर के साहू महाराज ने भी जब देखा कि शासकीय नौकरियों में उच्च पदों पर ब्राह्मणों का प्रतिनिधित्व अतिरेकी है तो उन्होंने अपने रियासत में 26 जुलाई 1902 को घोषणा की थी कि उनकी संस्थान के प्रशासनिक सेवाओं में पिछड़ी जातियों को 50 प्रतिशत आरक्षण बहाल किया जावेगा। इस से लगभग 17 वर्ष पूर्व राष्ट्रीय कांग्रेस की स्थापना हो चुकी थी। लेकिन वह फुले व रानडे के संगठन की तरह सामाजिक आंदोलन न होकर एक शुद्ध राजनीतिक संगठन था। इस के साथ बाद में हिंदु महासभा {1915} और राष्ट्रीय स्वयंसेवक संघ {1925} नामक ब्राह्मणवादी संगठनों की स्थापना हुई और इसी समय विदेशों के प्रख्यात विश्वविद्यालयों से शिक्षा की उच्चतम डाक्टरेट उपाधि से विभूषित होकर प्रतिक्रांति कारी ताकतों के विरुद्ध अकेले ही लड़ने के लिये डॉ. आंबेडकर स्वदेश लौटे थे।

राजनीति

प्रथम महायुद्ध के बाद ब्रिटेन की संसद ने हिन्दुस्तान को जिम्मेदार शासन प्रदान करने हेतु मॉटेग्यू नीति को लागू कराने की घोषणा की थी और कांग्रेस ने अपने कलकत्ता के अधिवेशन में अस्पृश्यता को मिटाने की घोषणा की थी।

मॉटेग्यू योजना का मकसद भारत में प्रजातन्त्र राज पद्धति को बहाल कर ब्रिटिश सत्ता को शिक्षित उच्च जातियों के हाथों में हस्तांतरित करना

था। इस योजना का विरोध कोल्हापूर के शाहू महाराज (1910), पूना के सत्यशोधक समाज, मद्रास के साउथ इंडियन लिबरल फेडरेशन और जस्टीस पार्टी तथा महाराष्ट्र के डेक्कन रैयत समाज ने दर्शाया था।

श्री तिलक के बाद कांग्रेस का नेतृत्व गांधी जी ने सम्भाला। फरवरी 1922 में बारडोली में कांग्रेस वर्किंग कमिटी ने दलित वर्ग की शैक्षणिक दशा को सुधारने का नया कार्यक्रम अमल में लाने का निर्णय लिया। उधर डॉ. आंबेडकर ने मुंबई में मूकनायक नामक पाक्षिक पत्रिका चलाई और नागपुर में अखिल भारतीय बहिष्कृत समाज की स्थापना की। मुंबई में सिडेनहेम शासकीय महाविद्यालय में प्रोफेसर होते हुये भी डॉ. आंबेडकर ने दिनांक 27 जनवरी 1919 के दिन साउथबरो कमिटी के समक्ष दलितों के लिये पृथक निर्वाचन अधिकार की मांग के पक्ष में अपनी साक्ष्य दी थी। सन् 1928 में उन्होंने उक्त मांग को संयुक्त निर्वाचन और आरक्षण अधिकार के रुप में सायमन कमिशन के सम्मुख प्रस्तुत किया था।

1928 से 1930 तक उन्होंने महाड और नासिक के सार्वजनिक तालाब और मंदिर पर पानी और पूजा के संबंध में समानता का अधिकार स्थापित करने हेतु अपने नेतृत्व में सफल आंदोलन चलाया था।

परंतु 1930–32 के दौरान चले बर्तानिया के गोलमेज परिषद ने भारतीय राजनीति की दिशा ही मोड दी। इस गोलमेज परिषद के अधिवेशन में जब गांधी जी मुसलमान, क्रिश्चन, सिख, ईसाई, पारसी, ॲंग्लो–इंडियन आदि के स्वतंत्र राजनीतिक अस्तित्व को मान्य कर रहे थे तब वे अस्पृभय के ऐसे स्वतंत्र राजनीतिक अस्तित्व को मानने से इंकार क्यों कर रहे थे यह समझ में नही आ रहा था। आखिर गांधीजी भी श्री तिलक के नक्शे–कदम पर ही चल रहे थे।

ब्रिटेन के प्रधान मंत्री श्री मेक्डोनल्ड द्वारा दलितों को बहाल किया गया स्वतन्त्र निर्वाचन अधिकार निरस्त करने हेतु सन 1932 में गांधी जी ने पूना के येरवडा कारागृह में आमरण अनशन आरंभ किया था।

सन 1935 में नासिक के येवला में डॉ. आंबेडकर ने घोषणा की थी कि वे हिंदू धर्म में पैदा हुये लेकिन वे हिंदू के रुप में नहीं मरेंगे।

सन 1936 में डॉ. आंबेडकर का ''जातिभेद निर्मूलन'' नामक भाषण उस के आयोजकों को इतना क्रांतिकारी लगा कि लाहौर के ''जात–पांत–

तोडक–मंडल ने डॉ. आंबेडकर की अध्यक्षता में होने वाली उस सभा को ही भंग कर दिया। आखिर उस भाषण को समाज हित में एक लघु ग्रंथ की शक्ल में प्रकाशित करने के पश्चात् ही लोगों तक पहुंचाया गया। उस पर गांधी जी की टिप्पणी यह थी कि ''हिंदू धर्म के प्रति अपनी नफरत दर्शानेवालों में अकेले आंबेडकर ही नही है, बल्कि उन लोगों में वह सब से अधिक दृढ़ और योग्यतम व्यक्ति है''।

द्वितीय महायुद्ध की पृष्ठभूमि में भारतीय राजनीति के घटनाक्रमों में प्रचंड उलट–पुलट हो रही थी। उनमें भारत छोड़ो आंदोलन, क्रिप्स–व्हेवल योजना, केबिनेट मिशन इत्यादि के साथ साथ धर्म और जातियों का उभार अधिक विस्फोटक रहा, कहना अतिशयोक्ति नही होगा। इसी बदलाव के कारण डॉ. आंबेडकर ने 1936 में एक व्यापक नींव पर स्थापित स्वतन्त्र मजदूर दल नामक राजनीतिक पक्ष के स्थान पर चार वर्ष के बाद मात्र अनुसूचित जातियों पर केंद्रित शिडयुल्ड कास्ट फेडरेशन नामक पार्टी की स्थापना की। उन्होंने मनमाड की दलित वर्गीय रेल्वे मजदूर परिशद को उदबोधन दिया था कि वे मनुष्यत्व को गिरानेवाले पूंजीवाद से सावधान रहें।

1942 में नागपूर के दलित जाति परिषद के सम्मेलन में दलितों के अधिकारों को भारत के भावी संविधान में अंतर्भूत करने का निर्णय सर्व सम्मति से पारित किया गया।

1945 में पीपल्स एज्युकेशन सोसायटी के तत्वावधान में मुंबई और औरंगाबाद में उच्च शिक्षा के प्रचार और प्रसार हेतु बुद्ध और मिलिंद नामक दो बौद्ध ऐतिहासिक महापुरुषों के नाम पर दो महाविद्यालय शुरु किये गये। डॉ. आंबेडकर ने भिन्न–भिन्न जाति और धर्मों को अविभाजित भारत की राजनीति में युक्त प्रतिनिधित्व प्रदान करने हेतु ''*जातीय गुत्थी और उसे सुलझाने का उपाय*' नामक योजना एक लिखित पुस्तक की शक्ल में प्रस्तुत की थी। परंतु विभाजित भारत की बदलती परिस्थिति को देखते हुये उन्होंने ''*राज्य और अल्पसंख्यक*'' नामक योजना को भी एक पुस्तिका के रुप में ही देशवासियों के विचारार्थ रखा।

श्रम मंत्री के पद पर 5 वर्ष तक उन्होंने महा–राज्यपाल की कार्यकारिणी में श्रमिक कल्याण और प्लानिंग का कार्यभार संभाला था। 1947 से उन्होंने

श्री नेहरु की केबिनेट में कानून मंत्री का भार वहन कर संविधान का मसौदा तैयार करने और और राष्ट्रीय जीवन में स्वाधीनता के संविधान को मूर्त बनाने के लिये स्वयं को खपाया। 26 जनवरी 1950 के अपने संबोधन में उन्होंने भारतीय राजनीतिक जीवन और सामाजिक–आर्थिक लोक चर्या में विद्यमान विसंगति की तरफ इशारा करते हुये उसे मिटाने का देशवासियों को आवाहन किया।

इस विसंगति को मिटाने का एक उपाय आरक्षण पद्धति भी है। परंतु जब तक भारत में मनुष्य और मनुष्य के बीच के संबंध जातिव्यवस्था से निश्चित करने वाली ब्राह्मणी परंपरा चालू रहेगी तब तक सामाजिक, सांस्कृतिक और आर्थिक जीवन में पिछडे हुये वर्गों के लिये ''समान अवसर के लिये विशेष अवसर' के सिद्धान्त पर निर्भर आरक्षण की सीटें रखना ही पड़ेगी क्योंकि समान मनुष्यों में ही समानता हो सकती है और असमान लोगों को समान मानना यानी असमानता को कायम रखना है।

पूंजीवाद और ब्राह्मणवाद की ताकतों और उभरती साम्यवादी शक्तियों के बीच का निरंतर सत्ता संघर्ष विश्व के देशों को दो प्रतिस्पर्धी वर्गों में विभक्त कर रहा है।

जो राष्ट्र अभी तक प्रजातन्त्र शासन के अधीन स्थापित नही हुए वे उक्त दोनों शक्तियों में से किसी भी एक में शामिल हो सकते है। नेपाल में अब तक लोकतन्त्र शासन की स्थापना नही हो सकी है तो उस दशा का उपयोग ब्रिटेन व अमेरिका, भारत तथा कम्युनिस्ट चीन सुगमता के साथ कर सकते हैं[17]।

हालांकि नेपाल, तिब्बत, चीन और भारत के सांस्कृतिक संबंध बौद्ध धर्मीय थे क्योंकि नेपाल नरेश अंशुवर्मा की बेटी भृकुटी ने तिब्बत के तत्कालीन शक्तिशाली राजा स्रोंङ–त्सान–गैम्पो से विवाह किया था। अंशुवर्मा के समकालीन भारतीय राजा हर्शवर्धन और चीनी सम्राट ताओ–त्सुंग थे। उस सम्राट की राजकुमारी ने भी स्रोंङ–त्सान–गैम्पो से विवाह किया था[18]।

समाज परिवर्तन

समाज परिवर्तन के दो मुख्य साधन हैं – कानून और शिक्षा।

भारतीय संविधान ने शासन को 14 वर्ष तक की उम्र के बालक–बालिका को मुफ्त और सख्ती से शिक्षा प्रदान करने का आदेश दिया है। और अस्पृश्यता जैसे सामाजिक कुरीतियों के व्यवहार को दण्डनीय अपराध करार दिया है।

कानून की दृष्टि से भारतीय प्रजातन्त्र में दो त्रुटियां हैं। एक, उस में ब्रिटिश संसदीय प्रणाली की प्रभावशीलता नहीं है और उस में अमेरिका की न्यायपालिका की निर्णायकता का अभाव है। उदाहरणार्थ 1896 में प्लेसी बनाम फर्ग्युसन नामक मशहूर मामले में अमेरिका के सर्वोच्च न्यायालय ने काले वर्ग के लोगों के लिये पृथक सुविधाओं की व्यवस्था पर अपना फैसला सुनाते समय कहा था कि ऐसे विशेष वर्ग की विशेष सुविधा की व्यवस्था से समानता के तत्व का उल्लंघन नही होता है। परंतु 67 वर्ष के बाद भारत में बालाजी बनाम मैसूर के मामले में सर्वोच्च न्यायालय ने व्यवस्था दी थी कि आरक्षण व्यवस्था के रहते समानता के तत्व का अमल तभी होगा जब दो शर्तों अर्थात् 1. आरक्षण का मापदण्ड जात न हो तथा 2. आधे से अधिक पदों का आरक्षण न हो का पालन किया जायेगा।

कानून समाज परिवर्तन के साधनों में से एक साधन है। परंतु हिंदू कानून इस का अपवाद है। ई. स. 1772 से पूर्व और 1772 के बाद के हिंदू कानून को मिताक्षर तथा दायभाग इन दो परंपराओं में वर्गीकृत किया जा सकता है।

ईस्ट इंडिया कंपनी ने अपने प्रशासन में रेग्युलेशन अधिनियम, के ठीक एक सदी बाद तलाक की व्यवस्था देनेवाला पंजीयन विवाह अथवा विशेष विवाह अधिनियम, और 1856 में हिन्दू विधवा पुनर्विवाह अधिनियम सम्मत कर लिया था। 1929 में बाल विवाह निरोध अथवा शारदा अधिनियम के अंतर्गत वधू और वर की विवाह योग्य आयु क्रमशः 14 और 18 वर्ष निश्चित की गई थी। परंतु इस अधिनियम का बड़े–बड़े नेताओं ने विरोध किया।

1935 में आर्य विवाह विधिग्राह्ता अधिनियम से अंतर्जातीय और अंतर्धमीय विवाहों का प्रचलन आसान हो गया था। सन् 1942 में तत्कालीन कानून मंत्री सर सुल्तान अहमद ने विवेदन किया था कि बिना मृत्यु पत्र उत्तराधिकार और विवाह के संबंध के दो विधेयकों को एक मसौदा समिति ने तैयार किया और उन्हें लोकमत का समर्थन प्राप्त करने हेतु राजपत्र में प्रकाशित

किया गया है। 1946 में एक ही गोत्र के व्यक्तियों के विवाह को वैध बनानेवाला कानून और 1949 में हिंदू विवाह निःसमर्थता निर्मूलन अधिनियम के सम्मत हो जाने से हिंदू धर्म की भिन्न–भिन्न जाति–उपजातियों को ऐसे विवाह करने का परवाना मिल गया। 9 अप्रैल 1948 में हिंदू संहिता विधेयक को संविधान समिति के सम्मुख डॉ. आंबेडकर ने प्रस्तुत किया था। परिणाम स्वरुप 1955 में हिंदू विवाह अधिनियम, हिंदू उत्तराधिकार अधिनियम, भरणपोषण और दत्तक ग्रहण अधिनियम सम्मत किये गये।

सामाजिक परिवर्तन का दूसरा साधन शिक्षा में डॉ. आंबेडकर का काफी योगदान रहा है। उन्होंने दलितों के प्राथमिक व माध्यमिक शिक्षा के प्रचलनार्थ बहिष्कृत हितकारणी सभा और दलित वर्ग शिक्षा समाज को क्रमशः 1924 और 1928 में स्थापित कर दलित छात्रों के लिये छात्रावास, खेल क्लब, ग्रंथालय, बोर्डिंग आदि की व्यवस्था की थी और दलितों की उच्च शिक्षा हेतु उन्होंने पिपुल्स एज्युकेशन सोसायटी (8 जुलाई, 1945), को संस्थापित कर उसकी छत्रछाया में सन 1946 में मुंबई में सिद्धार्थ कला, विज्ञान, व विधि महाविद्यालय और 1953 में सिद्धार्थ वाणिज्य और अर्थशास्त्र महाविद्यालय तथा 1950 में औरंगाबाद में मिलिंद कला व विज्ञान महाविद्यालय की शैक्षणिक सेवायें उपलब्ध कराईं।

डॉ. आंबेडकर का राजनैतिक विचार दर्शन उनके समकालीन चिंतक आचार्य नरेन्द्र देव और एम. एन. राय के वैज्ञानिक तथा नैतिक समाजवाद से काफी नजदीक रहा है, अपितु उनका मानना था कि मार्क्स और बकल ने इतिहास के निर्माण में मनुष्य की भूमिका शून्य बताकर भारी भूल की है। उन्हों ने कहा[19] कि बुद्ध द्वारा लाये गये धार्मिक और सामाजिक सुधार के बाद चंद्रगुप्त ने राजकीय क्रांति की। महाराष्ट्र में संतों द्वारा किये गये धार्मिक और सामाजिक सुधारणा के पश्चात् ही शिवाजी ने राज्य क्रांति की थी। सिक्खों के राजनीतिक परिवर्तन के पूर्व गुरु नानक द्वारा धार्मिक–सामाजिक क्रांति की गई थी।

श्री रसेल ने कहा है कि शिक्षा का झुकाव समाज की स्थितिशीलता कायम रखने के लिये होता है, तथापि स्वभाव और मत निर्माण करने की उसकी क्षमता बहुत अधिक होती है। डॉ. आंबेडकर के अनुसार क्रांति के तीन घटक (1) समाज के दोष का संज्ञान, (2) उस दोष से पीड़ित वर्ग की

उपस्थिति का एहसास और (3) शस्त्रार्थ हैं। उनमें से पहले दो घटक शिक्षा पर निर्भर है। इस प्रकार शिक्षित वर्ग ही संगठित होकर संघर्ष की बुनियाद बनाता हैं। डॉ. आंबेडकर के अनुसार बुद्ध द्वारा बताई गई सबसे बड़ी बात यह थी कि मनुष्य और जगत में सुधार किये बगैर संसार में सुधार नही किया जा सकता। परंतु इस का भावार्थ यह नही है कि मनुष्य के मन में बदल होने के साथ ही समाज में अपने आप परिवर्तन हो जाता है। उदाहरणार्थ पूंजीपति और गरीब वर्ग पहले वर्ग के लोभ–लालच के कारण नही पैदा होते। अतः उनका खात्मा पहले वर्ग के संपत्ति त्याग से नहीं होगा। बल्कि उनका नियमन किसी की व्यक्तिगत इच्छा के बाहर की बात है।

डॉ. आंबेडकर ने कहा है कि किस समाज में किसने जन्म लेना चाहिये और उसको किस ढंग से रखना चाहिये यह मनुष्य के काबू में नहीं है। परंतु एक बार किसी मनुष्य का अस्पृभय के रुप में किसी हिंदू समाज में जन्म हुआ तो उस के भीतर विद्यमान जातियों के संबंध और सामाजिक नियम उस के ऊपर नियत हो जाते है। उस के अनुसार आचरण करना उसकी मजबूरी हो जाती है। इस परिस्थिति में यदि ब्राह्मणों ने अस्पृशयों को समानता के नाते से सलूक करने के मत को परिवर्तित किया तो उस से अधिक से अधिक व्यक्तिगत रुप में अस्पृशय की अन्याय से मुक्ति हो सकती है, परंतु सामाजिक रुप में कदापि नही हो सकती। उसके लिये उन वर्गों में विद्यमान सामाजिक संबंध को बदलना जरुरी होता है। यह संबंध यदि धर्म संस्था नियंत्रित करती है तो धर्म संस्था में परिवर्तन करना पड़ेगा, यदि वह धार्मिक, सामाजिक, आर्थिक और राजनीतिक संरचना से जुडी समस्या है तो उस प्रकार से परिवर्तन करना लाजमी हो जायेगा।

आज विश्व में भारत के सपूत डॉ. भीमराव आंबेडकर के विचार–दर्शन ने समानता–स्वतंत्रता–बंधुत्व पर आधारित अवाम की जीवन पद्धति के प्रजातंत्र की ऐसी पहचान बनाई कि कई विभूतियों की वैचारिकियां विस्मृत हो चुकी हैं। डॉ. आंबेडकर द्वारा रोपित यह पहचान आज उनके आलोचकों के सिर पर चढ़कर बोल रही है। श्री अरुण शौरी ने कहा ही हैः 'गत पचास वर्षों का शुद्ध परिणाम यह है कि फिर एक बार भारत में आज वही क्रम शुरु हुआ है। लोकमान्य विस्मृत से हो गये। नारायन गुरु को केरला के

बाहर कोई नही जानता है। स्वामी दयानंद, रामकृष्ण परमहंस, श्री औरोबिंदो, रमन महर्षि, कांची के परमाचार्य इत्यादियों ने हमें अपने पैरों पर खड़ा करने के लिये क्या किया इसे भक्तों के एक संकुचित दायरे के सिवाय और कोई नही जानता। स्वामी विवेकानंद को धूल झाड कर कुछ अवसर पर बाहर निकाला जाता है और उनको ठीक ऐसे संप्रदाय–निरपेक्ष के पहनावे में दर्शाया जाता है, जिसे वे स्वयं तीव्र रुप से फटकार देते। गांधीजी की तो प्रति दिन छंटनी हो ही रही है– एक दिन पहले से चली आ रही विकास की प्रतिक्रिया के कारण तो दूसरे दिन मुसलमान नेताओं को पाकिस्तान का आग्रह धरने में प्रवृत्त कराने के कारण यह छंटनी की जा रही है और आंबेडकर जैसे व्यक्तियों की देवता की भांति पूजा हो रही है[20]।

क्या डॉ. आंबेडकर देवता थे? नही। वे एक साधारण आम आदमी की तरह थे। तथापि उन्होंने अपने व्यक्तित्व को इतना ऊपर उठाया, उसे इतना निखारा और जनता की सेवा में उसे इतना समर्पित किया कि लोग उन्हें कृतज्ञतावश सचमुच अपने भगवान मानने लगे। सैम्युअल जानसन ने भी कहा है कि ''कृतज्ञता महान उद्यम का फल है, जाहिल लोगों में आप इसे नही पाते''।

संविधान

अंबेडकर ने क्या किया ग्रंथ के लेखक और मध्य प्रदेश शासन द्वारा वर्ष 2002–3 में डॉ. बाबासाहेब आंबेडकर स्मृति पुरस्कार के विजेता श्री बाली ने बताया है, ''1927 में लार्ड बर्कन हैड ने भारतीयों को चुनौती दी थी कि वे अपना संविधान बनाकर दिखायें। एक संविधान बनाया गया जिसे 'नेहरु–संविधान' कहा गया, चूंकि संविधान निर्माण समिति के अध्यक्ष पंडित मोतीलाल नेहरु थे इसलिये उसे यह नाम दिया गया किन्तु उस को भारतीयों ने नकारा समझ रद्दी की टोकरी में डाल दिया। 1930 में गोलमेज सम्मेलन द्वारा संविधान बनाने का यत्न किया गया किन्तु भारतीय लोग इस में विफल रहे। सप्रू कमेटी द्वारा संविधान बनाने का तीसरी बार यत्न किया गया मगर कोई सफलता न मिली। दिसंबर 1946 में गठित संविधान सभा में सर तेज बहादूर सप्रू, के. एम. मुंशी, ठाकुरदास भार्गव, सरदार पटेल आदि कितने ही वकील थे। उनमें से किसी को संविधान के निर्माण का काम नहीं सौंपा गया। यह काम डॉ. आंबेडकर ही के जिम्मे

सौंपा गया। यह इसलिये कि वह संविधानिक–कानून में कुशल व निपुण थे और एक सच्चे देश प्रेमी थे।"[21]

डॉ. आंबेडकर कैसे देशप्रेमी थे? मुंबई से सन् 1943 में प्रकाशित ग्रंथ, रानडे, गांधी और जिन्नाह की भूमिका में उसके लेखक स्वयं डॉ. आंबेडकर ने कहा है:

> "यदि मैं श्री गांधी तथा श्री जिन्नाह से घृणा करता हूं, मैं उन से घृणा नही करता। मैं उन्हें नापसंद करता हूँ, तो उसका कारण यह है कि मैं भारत से अधिक प्रेम करता हूँ। यह एक राष्ट्रवादी की सच्ची निष्ठा है। मुझे आशा है कि मेरे देशवासी किसी न किसी दिन यह सीख लेंगे कि देश व्यक्ति से कही महान होता है। श्री गांधी या श्री जिन्नाह की पूजा और भारत की सेवा में आकाश–पाताल का अन्तर है और वह परस्पर विरोधी भी हो सकती है।"

डॉ. आंबेडकर अवाम का एक ऐसा राष्ट्र, एक ऐसा आदर्श समाज और एक ऐसा कारगर प्रजातंत्र बनाना चाहते थे कि जिस में ऐसे जीवन भवन के चारों स्तंभ – विधिपालिका, कार्यपालिका, न्यायपालिका और मीडिया अपनी योग्यता की वेश्यावृत्ति न करें। डॉ. आंबेडकर "कमीनगी को अत्याचार से बदतर" मानते थे[22]। सन 1942 में उन्होंने कहा था:

> "विश्व युद्ध संसार के क्षेत्रों यानी प्रदेशों के बटवारे के लिए नहीं है बल्कि वे एक ऐसी क्रान्ति है जो इन्सान व इन्सान और राष्ट्र व राष्ट्र के मध्य मेल मिलाप में मूल–परिवर्तनों का तकाजा करता है। ये क्रांति सहचारी जीवन को रद्द कर के, समाज के पुनः गठन के लिये है। मजदूरों को इसलिए नाज़ीवाद पर विजय पाने हेतु लड़ना चाहिए क्योंकि ये जीत गया तो ऐसी नाज़ी व्यवस्था स्थापित हो जाएगी जिस से स्वतन्त्रता का दमन हो जाएगा, समता से इन्कार होगा और भातृत्वभाव को घातक सिद्धान्त कह कर मिटा दिया जायेगा। नाजीवाद पर विजय के फल होंगे: आजादी और नई सामाजिक व्यवस्था। केवल सवतंत्रता काफी नही, स्वतंत्रता की उपयुक्तता तो इस बात में है कि उस से किस प्रकार की सरकार गठित होती है और कैसे समाज का निर्माण होता है। इसलिए कामकरों को 'क्विट इण्डिया के बजाय 'न्यू इण्डिया' पर ज्यादा बल देना चाहिए। हिंसा की शक्तियों के सामने

घुटने टेक कर प्राप्त की गई शान्ति, अमन नही हुआ करता। ये तो एक घातक कृति होगी और अच्छे मानवीय जीवन को बनाए रखने के लिए जो कुछ भी उत्तम व अनिवार्य है, उसे बहशी व बर्बर शक्तियों के सामने कुर्बान कर देने जैसा होगा। जब हमला किया गया हो तो युद्ध करने से इन्कार कर युद्ध को समाप्त नही किया जा सकता। युद्ध की समाप्ति के लिए आपको जंग जीतना होगा और न्यायी अमन स्थापित करना होगा[23]।''

डॉ. आंबेडकर ऐसा न्यायी अमन चाहते थे कि शांति के समय अवाम में ऐसी बातें या घटनायें अपनी पुनरावृत्ति न कर पायें। संविधान सभा द्वारा गठित 'अल्पसंख्यक कमिटी' को अपने स्मरण पत्र में डॉ. भीमराव आंबेडकर ने बताया थाः

''भारत में प्रशासन पूर्णतः हिंदुओं के हाथों में है। प्रशासन पर उनकी इजारादारी है। ऊपर से नीचे तक उनका नियंत्रण है। कोई विभाग ऐसा नही जिस पर उनका प्रभुत्व न हो! पुलिस पर उनका प्रभुत्व है। मैजिस्ट्रेसी व राजस्व सेवाओं पर उनका प्रभुत्व है। वास्तव में प्रशासन की हरेक शाखा पर उन्हीं का प्रभुत्व है। अगली बात याद रखने की यह है कि प्रशासन में हिंदुओं का अछूत के प्रति समाज–विरोधी व शत्रुआना रुख उसी प्रकार का स्पष्ट व्यवहार है जैसा कि प्रशासन से बाहर के हिंदुओं का बर्ताव है। उनका एक ही मकसद है और वह है अछूतों के विरुद्ध पक्षपात व भेदभाव करना। नतीजा यह होता हैः अछूत हिन्दू आबादी और हिन्दू प्रभुत्व वाले प्रशासन के बीच स्थान पाते हैं। हिन्दू अछूतों पर जुल्म जबर ढाता है और प्रशासन उत्पीडितों की सहायता करने के बजाए अत्याचारी ही की सुरक्षा करता है[24]।''

राष्ट्रीयता और राष्ट्रवाद

राष्ट्रीयता के बारे में अलबर्ट आइन्स्टाइन और डॉ. आंबेडकर के विचार एक समान ही नही अपितु वैज्ञानिक दूरदृष्टि से भी ओतप्रोत हैं। आन्स्टाइन ने कहा था, ''राष्ट्रीयता एक भयानक रुप से संक्रामक बीमारी के समान है''[25]।

डॉ. आंबेडकर ने भारत में सन् 1940 में जिस राष्ट्रीयता के दावानल में हिंदू और मुसलमान जल रहे थे उस संक्रामक बिमारी के प्रति देश को सजग करने हेतु उन्होंने अपना राजनीतिक विज्ञान का ग्रंथ "*पाकिस्तान अथवा भारत का विभाजन*" लिखा था। उस में उन्होंने दो विदेशी शासनों का उदाहरण देकर उनसे सीख लेने की भारतीयों से विनम्र अपील की थी। उन्होंने कहा था कि इ.स. 1230–1240 के बीच मंगोलों ने तुर्कों को अपने निवास स्थान मध्य एशिया से बाहर खदेड़ दिया था। परिणामतः वे उत्तर–पश्चिम के अनातोलिया में जाकर बस गये। तुर्की साम्राज्य बनाने का उनका कार्य सन् 1326 में ब्रूसा की विजय के साथ ही आरंभ हुआ। एजियन से काला समुद्र तक फैले थ्रेस के साथ–साथ बिजन्टाइन शासक, बल्गेरिया, मेसेडोनिया, कान्स्टनटिनोपल, सर्विया, सलोनिया, ट्रेबिझोण्ड, कुरामान, काफा और टाना, मोसुल, सिरिया, इजिप्ट, हियाज और यमन, बेलग्रेड, हंगेरी, और बगदाद ने इ.स. 1360 से इ. स. 1639 तक उस्मान तुर्कों का आधिपत्य स्वीकार कर लिया। यदि वियना को भी परास्त करने में तुर्क सफल हो जाते तो उनका साम्राज्य विस्तार युरोप की सीमाओं को भी लांघ जाता। तथापि सन 1789 के फ्रेंच क्रांति के समय तक तुर्की साम्राज्य की सीमा के भीतर बाल्कन, दक्षिण का दानुब, एशिया मायनर, लेवन्त और सायप्रस आदि उनके पड़ोसी द्वीप समूह, सिरिया, पॅलेस्टाइन, इजिप्त और मोरोक्को तक के उत्तर अफ्रिकन देश आते थे। परंतु इतना विशाल तुर्की साम्राज्य धीरे–धीरे खण्ड–खण्ड हो गया। क्योंकि वहां के नागरिक जनों में राष्ट्रीयता की भावना इतनी घर कर गई थी कि एक तरफ ख्रिश्चन यवन, सर्व, बल्गेरियन तथा बाल्कन टर्की से अलग हुये तो दूसरी तरफ स्वयं अरब मुसलमान भी टर्की के अपने सहधर्मीयों के साथ न रह कर अपना पृथक अरब राष्ट्र बनाने पर अडिग रहे। क्योंकि उन्हें तुर्की प्रजा बने रहने की अपेक्षा अरब राष्ट्र बनना अधिक पसंद था। अरब राष्ट्रीयता ने इस्लाम के बंधन को तोड़ा और अपने साथी मुस्लिम तुर्क के विरुद्ध अपनी स्वाधीनता के लिये लड़ाई लड़ी। उसकी विजय हुई परंतु टर्की का पूर्णतः विभाजन हुआ।

चेकोस्लोवाकिया ने भी चेकों और स्लोवाक दोनों एक ही जन है की स्वीकृति से शुरुआत की थी। कुछ वर्षों के भीतर ही स्लोवाकों ने पृथक राष्ट्र का दावा किया। वे यहां तक स्वीकार करते थे कि वे चेकों के एक

वंश की शाखा हैं। उनकी राष्ट्रीयता ने चेकों को यह तथ्य स्वीकार करने पर मजबूर किया कि वे एक अलग प्रकार के जन थे। चेकों ने स्लोवाकों की राष्ट्रीयता को शांत करने के लिये एक हायफन (–) चिन्ह को दो नामों के बीच रख कर उन की भिन्नता को मान्यता दे दी। और एक संयुक्त संज्ञा चेकोस्लोवाकिया की जगह चेको–स्लोवाकिया नामाभिधान को स्वीकृति दे दी। परंतु इस पृथकता की परिचायक हायफन के बावजूद स्लोवाकी राष्ट्रीयता असंतुश्ट रही। क्योंकि हायफन के चिन्ह की स्वायततता की कृति दो बातों की सूचक थी – चेकों से अलगांव तथा चेकों से मिलाप। अलगांव सूचक हायफन का स्लोवाकियों ने स्वागत किया परंतु मिलाप सूचक हायफन से वे बेचैन थे। उन्हें उस के स्थान पर बार (/) चिन्ह चाहिये था। अतः जैसे ही हायफन को प्रस्तुत किया गया तो चेक और स्लोवाकों के बीच बार स्थापित करने की लड़ाई आरंभ हुई। इस हेतु किस प्रकार के साधनों का प्रयोग हो इस के प्रति वे चिंतित नही थे। उनकी राष्ट्रीयता इतनी बेकाबू और तीव्र हो गई थी कि जब उनका विभाजन का प्रयत्न असफल हुआ तो उन्होंने अपने ध्येय की पूर्ति हेतु जर्मनी की मदद मांगने से भी परहेज नही किया।

स्लोवाकियों को संवैधानिक सुरक्षा, आनुपातिक प्रतिनिधित्व, संसद में विटो पावर और प्रशासन और सेवाओं में पृथक प्रतिनिधित्व की बहाली इतनी दी गई थी कि कोई भी यह कल्पना आसानी से कर सकता था कि भविष्य में चेक और स्लाव दोनों एक दूसरे में इतने घुल–मिल जायेंगे कि उनको एक ही जाति–प्रजाति के लोग हैं ऐसा माना जा सकेगा। परंतु नही इतिहास को ऐसा विलयन मंजूर न था और स्लावों को अपनी राष्ट्रीयता में झुलसकर अपना पृथक देश बनाना अधिक पसंद था। अतः उस का भी हश्र वही होना था जो 1947 में हिंदू–मुसलमान कौमों का भारतवर्ष में हुआ।

इस प्रकार टर्की और चेकोस्लोवाकिया के गहन अध्ययन से ज्ञात होता है कि एक बार राष्ट्रीयता की शक्ति गतिशील हो जाये तो न स्थानीय स्वायत्तता और न ही धार्मिक बाध्यता उसका सामना करने में सक्षम होती है।

अखण्ड भारत के हिंदू और मुसलमानों में कई सदियों की सामाजिक व सांस्कृतिक एकता होने के बावजूद भी सन् 1947 में भारत के विभाजन

को कोई ताकत रोक न सकी। आज भी नूतन वर्ष की पावन बेला दिनांक 4 जनवरी 2004 पर इस्लामाबाद में दक्षिण एशिया के देशों की शिखर बैठक संपन्न होने के बावजूद भारत देश के उत्तर में पाकिस्तान, उत्तर–पश्चिम में खालिस्तान, भूटान में उल्फादि संगठन और श्रीलंका में दक्षिण के लिट्टे (एल.टी.टी.ए.) आतंकवाद से विभाजन का इतिहास दोहराना चाहते हैं।

उक्त तथ्यों के प्रकाश में भारतीय हिंदुओं को अपने आप से यह प्रश्न पूछना चाहिये कि यदि ग्रीक, बाल्कन तथा अरब राष्ट्रीयवाद ने तुर्की राज्य को ध्वस्त कर दिया और यदि स्लोवाक के राष्ट्रीयवाद ने चेकोस्लोवाकिया को विभक्त कर दिया है परंतु बाद का टर्की और चेकोसलोवाकिया आंतरिक रुप से एक हो गया और इतना ही नही बल्कि चेकोस्लावाकिया के राज्य प्रमुख श्री हॉवेल को भारत सरकार ने गांधी शांति पुरस्कार से भी इसी माह में नवाजा है, तो फिर मुस्लिम राष्ट्रीयवाद से विभक्त भारत को आंतरिक रुप से एक होने में अब क्या अड़चन है? क्या भारत अपरिवर्तनशील जाति के समान शरीर और कुटस्थ आत्मा की भांति चेतना तो नही बन गया? क्योंकि ये दोनों असाध्य रोग के लक्षण हैं।

डॉ. आंबेडकर जानते थे कि देश में संगठन की चेतना सभी जाति–वर्गों में एक जैसी नही रहती और भारतीय समाज में संकुचित मानसिकता उनका एक राष्ट्र बनने में बाधक थी। जिस प्रकार विकास के दौर में प्राचीन समाज उपयोगितावाद से उभरकर आधुनिक समय के दौरान वह न्याय तत्व के आधार पर संगठित हुआ। फलस्वरुप विकासनशील देश अपने हितों के प्रति इतने सजग हो गये कि वे अब पहले की तरह विकसित देशों की हाँ– में– हाँ मिलाकर चलने वाले नही हैं, जिस की प्रतीति कानकुन के विश्व शिखर सम्मेलन में चीन और भारत आदि देशों द्वारा सम्मेलन के विकसित राष्ट्र के प्रस्ताव के विरुद्ध अपना पृथक अभिमत रखने से सिद्ध हुआ है।

दूसरी बात यह है कि यूरोपीय संघ अपना आर्थिक संगठन और युरो मुद्रा को कायम करने में फिलहाल जितना सक्षम है उतना आगे भी होगा या नही यह समय ही बता पायेगा। पश्चिम एशिया में संबंधित देशों का आर्थिक संगठन खड़ा कर उसे टिकाना उस प्रदेश के युद्ध और अशांति की परिस्थितियों पर निर्भर है, जो उसका इतिहास रहा है। परंतु जी–21 नाम

से परिभाषित देश अपना ''आसियन'' नामक संगठन खड़ा कर आर्थिक विकास में पश्चिमी संगठन की बराबरी और प्रतियोगिता करेगा इस उम्मीद में जान लग रही है क्योंकि उनका अतीत और वर्तमान ऐतिहासिक रक्तपात और बैरत्व का न होकर अमन, चैन और बौद्ध संस्कृति की मैत्री से अभिभूत रहा है।

आज विश्व का धर्म राज्य किसी एक जाति, भाषा, रंग, पेशा, लिंग, वंश, और नस्ल के ऊपर निर्भर नही है। तथापि भौतिक शक्ति और हथियार लैस भयभीत मनोवृत्ति से कुछ ऐसी ही चेष्टा विश्व मंच से की जा रही है। अमेरिका प्रधान क्रिश्चन संस्कृति के वैश्विक धर्मराज्य का टर्की प्रमुख अरब शक्तियां इस्लाम के धर्मराज्य का झंड़ा हाथ में थामे किसी भी तरीके से प्रतिकार कर रहा है। जी–21 की ताकतें जापान, चीन और भारत के नेतृत्व में बौद्ध संस्कृति के ध्वज में एकत्रित होकर शायद जो भी रुप और आकार वे विश्व को देंगे वह डॉ. आंबेडकर के स्वप्न का प्रारुप होगा ऐसा लग रहा है[26]।

वैसे कहा जाता है कि विश्व में ब्रिटेन का शासन वहां तक फैला था जहां कभी सूर्य नही डूबता। परंतु ऐसा होने पर भी जो ब्रिटेन का सामाज्य फैला उसका उद्‌देश्य राजनीतिक और आर्थिक तो रहा पर सामाजिक न्याय और विश्व कल्याण कदापि नही था। आंबेडकर पूर्व काल के राजनीतिक साम्राज्य और आंबेडकरोत्तर आर्थिक साम्राज्य में यही फर्क है कि पहले यूरोपियन व्यापार कंपनियां अपने राजनीतिक शासकों से मिलकर अलग–अलग होकर व्यवसाय करते थे और आज बहुराष्ट्रीय कंपनिया एकजुट होकर अपने अधिशासक के राजनीतिक बलबूते पर सहकारी और सामुहिक पद्धति से विकासनशील देशों में अपनी वस्तुओं के लिये बाजार खोल रहे है। और जिधर वरिष्ठ शक्तिमान राष्ट्र उधर अधिकतर आर्थिक लाभ का सिद्धान्त साकार हो रहा है। वाणिज्य, राजनीति, बाजार और वस्तुयें धर्म और संस्कृति पर भी अपना असर डालती हैं। इस मायने में डॉ. आंबेडकर का यह कथन कि संस्कृति व्यापार की पिछलग्गू होती है बड़ा मार्मिक है। इस से निष्कर्ष में यही कहा जा सकता है कि बलिष्ठ राष्ट्र अपने बाजार में वस्तुओं के साथ अपने धर्म और संस्कारों का भी जाने–अनजाने आदान प्रदान करते हैं।

क्या आजाद भारत में क्रूरता, दासता, गरीबी और असभ्य जीवन आज भी विद्यमान है? क्या यहां आज भी स्कूलों में दलित बालक–बालिकाओं को घड़े में से पानी पाने के लिए अपनी आंख फुटवानी पड़ती है और दलित स्त्री–पुरुषों को अपने सिर पर मैला ढोना, बंधक मजदूरी करना, घरेलू नौकरी व सफाई करना, पत्थर तोड़ना, खेतों व खानों में सेवा रत रहना इत्यादि की मजबूरी विद्यमान है? अर्थात् क्या फैज अहमद फैज के निम्नांकित पंक्तिओं द्वारा वर्णित किया जा सकनेवाला संवर्ग हमारे बीच मौजूद है?

अर्थात् ''जा–ब–जा बिकते हुए कूच–ओ–बाजार में जिस्म
खाक में लिथड़े हुए खून में नहलाये हुए,
जिस्म निकले हुए अमराज के तन्नूरों से

पीब बहती हुई गलते हुए नासूरों से। ''यदि हाँ तो ऐसी परिस्थितियों में अवाम को क्या करना चाहिये? क्या उन्हें चुप रहना चाहिये?

नैतिकता खतरे में पड़ने पर भी यदि कोई व्यक्ति मौन धारण करता है तो उसे मानवी जीवन पद्धति के अधःपतन की निशानी माना जाना चाहिये। मजलूमों के दुःखों पर अवाम की एक बडी जमात चुप्पी साधे तो यह शर्म की बात है और स्वयं मजलूम भी कुछ न करे तो यह कौम के मौत की निशानी है। डॉ. आंबेडकर ने ऐसी घड़ी में आम लोगों और विशेषतः शोषित व पददलित वर्गों का जो नेतृत्व किया उसका बखान साहिर लुधियानवी के शब्दों में निम्न प्रकार बताया जा सकता है:

सितम के दौर में हम अहल–ए–दिल ही काम आए
जबां पे नाज था जिन को वो बेजबां निकले।

प्रजातन्त्र का चौथा स्तंभ मिडिया है, उस बाबत् डॉ. आंबेडकर का कथन है: ''पत्रकारिता भारत में एक समय व्यवसाय था। अब यह व्यापार बन गया है। इस में साबुन तैयार करने से अधिक नैतिक कार्य नही है। यह अपने आपको जनता का एक जिम्मेवार सलाहकार नही समझती। भारत में पत्रकारिता इसे अपनी सर्वप्रथम और महत्वपूर्ण दायित्व नही समझती कि जो समाचार वह दे उन में सच्चाई की रंगत हो। सरकारी नीति के किसी दृष्टिकोण को इस ढंग से प्रस्तुत करे जिसे वह जन कल्याण के हित में

बगैर किसी भय के अच्छा समझती है। वह सब को दुरुस्त और ठीक करे, जो गलत और निष्फल रास्ते पर पड़े हों चाहे ऐसे आदमी बड़े हों या छोटे। किसी को अपना नायक मान लेना और उस की पूजा करना इस का प्रमुख कर्तव्य बन गया है। इस व्यवस्था के अधीन समाचारों का स्थान सनसनीदार बातों ने, विवेकात्मिक विचारों का बेतुकी उत्कंठा ने, जिम्मेवार लोगों के अन्तकरणः छूने का गैर–जिम्मेवार लोगों की भावनाओं को भड़काने ने लिया है[27]"।

अवाम

अवाम के डॉ. आंबेडकर ने अवाम की आदर्श जीवन पद्धति को प्रजातन्त्र का नामाभिधान देकर उसके खतरों से भी सावधान कराया। उन्होंने कहा, "प्रजातन्त्र के मुख्य दो शत्रु हैं। पहला – हुकुमशाही या तानाशाही और दूसरा मानवभेद नीति अर्थात् मानव–मानव में भेदभाव रखने वाली नीति। हुक्मशाही से उत्पन्न सामाजिक संगठन हमेशा कायम नही रह सकते। क्योंकि उसका आधार मजबूत नही होता। हुक्मशाही की प्रेरणा स्थिर नही है और यह प्रेरणा निकल जाने के पश्चात् उस से प्राप्त संगठन शिथिल हो जाता है। यही कारण है कि कम्युनिस्ट शासन की नींव कमजोर है। उसी तरह मनुष्य–मनुष्य में भेदभाव रखनेवाली नीति, सामाजिक, आर्थिक भेद–बुद्धि को प्रेरणा देनेवाली संस्कृति इन दोनों से प्रजातन्त्र को बहुत जबरदस्त खतरा है।

ऐसे खतरों से निजात पाने के लिए ही उन्होंने अवाम को अपनी स्वतन्त्रता के प्रति समर्पित कर्तव्य का एहसास दिलाने हेतु कहा था, "यदि लोग अपने–अपने पथ और पक्ष को अपने देश की अपेक्षा अधिक महत्व देने लगे तो उस से अपने भारत की स्वतन्त्रता समूल नष्ट हो जायेगी। इस प्रकार का समय न आवे इस के लिए हम सब अत्यधिक सजग रहें। अपनी स्वतन्त्रता की रक्षा हेतु अपने शरीर के अंतिम रक्त–बूंद के बहने तक तैयार रहना चाहिये। इतना ही नही बल्कि समाज का ऐसा संगठन हो कि यदि इस के चालक नेता चले भी गये तो भी समाज कार्य निरन्तर चालू रहते हुए चिरकाल तक टिका रहे। इस प्रकार की कार्य योजना होने पर ही समाज विश्व में वैभवशाली हो सकता है।

प्रजातन्त्र और धर्म का संबंध बताते हुये डॉ. आंबेडकर ने कहा था – "मानव समाज को धर्म की दो प्रकार की देन प्राप्त है। प्रथम मानव जीवन में एकता प्राप्त करा देनेवाली मानसिक प्रेरणा का निर्माण करना। धर्म के ही कारण एक विशिष्ट प्रकार का मानसिक वातावरण निर्माण होता है, जो मनुष्य की एकता का पोषक है। दूसरा, मानव समाज में समानता का निर्माण करना। धर्म से ही मानव समाज में समानता का संचार होता है। इन्हीं दो महत्वपूर्ण बातों के कारण आज की स्थिति में प्रजातन्त्र को बनाये रखा जा सकता है और प्रजातन्त्र को बनाये रखना है तो धर्म निहायत जरुरी है।

धर्म की ऐसी आवश्यकता होने पर भी लक्ष्य धर्म नहीं है बल्कि मनुष्य है और धर्म एक साधन है। साधन एक समान नही होते, न ही वे समान रुप से अच्छे होते हैं। अतः जरुरी है कि धर्मरुपी साधन को मनुष्यत्व पाने के उद्देश्य से अपनाते समय ऐसी सावधानी बरतें कि जो धर्म अपनाया जाय वह समाजद्रोही न हो, पाखण्डी न हो, विडम्बन या सजा न हो, रोग या पागलपन न हो बल्कि वह मानवता, संगठन, सामर्थ्य, समता, स्वतन्त्रता और संसार को इसी जीवन में सुखी बनाने वाला धर्म होना चाहिये।

जिस प्रकार रत्नों में अच्छे रत्न की परख के लिये पारखी की जरुरत होती है उसी प्रकार प्रजातन्त्र, धर्म और देश के परस्पर सम्बन्धों को समझने के लिये भी प्रज्ञादृष्टि की आवश्यकता होती है। इस बात को डॉ. आंबेडकर ने मणी भवन मुंबई में दिनांक 14 अगस्त 1931 के दिन महात्मा गांधी जी के साथ वार्तालाप में स्पष्ट रुप से बताया था। जब गांधी जी ने तारीफ करते हुये डॉ. आंबेडकर से कहा कि "विदेश में तुम्हारे कार्यों की जो मुझे जानकारी प्राप्त हुई उस से मालूम होता है कि तुम एक महान देशभक्त भी हो" तो बाबासाहब ने बताया, "गांधी जी! मेरी कोई मातृभूमि नही है। जिस धर्म और देश में हमें कुत्ते और बिल्ली से भी नीच माना जाता है, जहां हमें सार्वजनिक स्थानों में पानी भी पीने नही दिया जाता, उस देश को मैं अपना देश, उस धर्म को मैं अपना धर्म कैसे कहूँ?"

"आपके कथनानुसार यदि मेरे द्वारा कोई देश सेवा हुई है तो वह देश सेवा की जानकारी होने के कारण नही, बल्कि मेरी सद्विवेक बुद्धि के कारण हुई है। इस देश को घातक ऐसा कोई भी कृत्य मेरे हाथ से नहीं हुआ यह मेरी सद्विवेक बुद्धि का फल है"।

डॉ. आंबेडकर कहते थे, ''जिस प्रकार पुरुषों को शिक्षा की आवश्यकता होती है वैसे ही स्त्रियों को भी होती है। यदि तुम्हें लिखना–पढ़ना आ गया तो तुम्हारी बहुत उन्नति होगी। जैसे तुम वैसी तुम्हारी संतान भी होगी''।

स्त्री–पुरुष समानता

मनुस्मृति के श्लोक ''स्त्री हमेशा पराधीन रहे और बचपन में अपनी सुरक्षा पिता के अधीन, जवानी में पति, और बुढ़ापे में पुत्र के अधीन रहकर करें'' और राम चरित मानस की चौपाई ''ढोर, गंवार, शूद्र, पशु, नारी ये सब ताड़न के अधिकारी'' को जब हम पढ़ते हैं तो लगता है कि भारत में नारी शर्म की बात बन गई है। परंतु डॉ. आंबेडकर द्वारा प्रस्तुत स्त्री स्वतन्त्रता का बौद्ध स्त्री का आदर्श चरित्र, और पुरुष के बराबर समान अधिकार के लिये उन्हें विवाह, तलाक, गोद लेना, संपत्ति अधिकार आदि में सशक्त बनाने की हिंदू कोड़ बिल की योजना को देखते हैं तो लगता है कि भले ही उसे कार्यान्वित करने की दृढ़ शक्ति तत्कालीन राजनीतिक संगठन में नहीं थी और न समाज उतना वैचारिक रुप से प्रगल्भ था, परंतु डॉ. आंबेडकर ने स्त्री स्वतंत्रता, सम्मान और मुक्ति के प्रश्न पर प्रतिकारी ताकतों से समझौता न कर प्रधानमंत्री श्री जवाहरलाल नेहरु जी को अपने कानून मंत्री के पद से इस्तीफे का पत्र प्रस्तुत किया और तब से लेकर अपने आयु के अन्तिम क्षण तक विपक्ष में रह कर समानता की लड़ाई के लिये संघर्ष करते रहे। फलतः उनके इस संघर्ष के पचास वर्ष बाद ऐसा लग रहा है कि जो स्त्री पहले भारत की शर्म थी वह आज उस की शान बन गई है।

प्रथम महिला प्रधानमंत्री श्रीमती इंदिरा गांधी, प्रथम महिला आई. पी. एस. ऑफिसर किरण बेदी, प्रथम मिस यूनीवर्स सुष्मिता सेन, प्रथम अंतरिक्ष यात्री कल्पना चावला इत्यादि के उदाहरण हम विश्व के सामने बड़े गर्व से प्रकट कर सकते हैं जो स्वर्णिम बौद्ध अतीत और वर्तमान एशियन युग के उज्वल भविष्य की याद दिलाता है।

भारतीय इतिहास में तथागत गौतम बुद्ध ही ऐसे पहले व्यक्ति थे, जिन्होंने शूद्र–अतिशूद्रों और दलित महिलाओं को अपनी धर्मशक्ति का हिस्सेदार ही नही, बल्कि अधिकारी भी बनाया था। विद्यमान विश्व व्यवस्था को बदलने के लिये आंबेडकर ने एक हाथ में शिक्षा, संघर्ष और संगठन

सूत्र तो दूसरे हाथ में स्वतंत्रता, समानता और बंधुत्व के त्रयी सिद्धांत का हथियार अवाम के लिये बहाल किया।

संतति नियमन

सन 1936 में भारत में जन्म दर प्रति हजार 35 थी, जो विदेशी राष्ट्र इटली, जर्मनी और इंग्लैंड के जन्म दर से अधिक थी। सन 1938 में डॉ. आंबेडकर ने मुंबई विधान सभा में संततिनियमन विषयक विधेयक प्रस्तुत किया था। परंतु उस का अवलंब सन 1951 में प्रथम पंचवार्षिक योजना में 70 लाख रुपयों की शासकीय सहायता प्रदान कर किया गया। सातवीं पंचवार्षिक योजना में कुटुंब कल्याण की योजना को अमल में लाने हेतु राशि रु. 3,256 करोड़ का इंतजाम था।

इस से पूर्व जब स्वतन्त्र मज़दूर दल के विधान सभा के सदस्यों की ओर से श्री पी. जे. रोहम ने दिनांक 10 नवंबर 1932 को संतति नियमन और जनसंख्या नियंत्रण से संबंधित प्रस्ताव को मुंबई प्रांत विधान परिषद में रखा था, जिसे किसी अन्य सदस्यों का समर्थन नही मिलने से निरस्त किया गया था।

उन्नीसवी सदी के आरंभ में ब्रिटिश अर्थशास्त्रज्ञ माल्थस का जनसंख्या वृद्धि का सिद्धान्त यह था कि कृषि उत्पादन मंद गति से बढ़ता है परंतु जनसंख्या द्रुत गति से बढ़ती है। इसका प्रमाण अन्य देशों की अपेक्षा भारत में अधिक प्रतीत हो रहा था। सन 1871 से जनगणना के आंकडों का अवलोकन भी इस कथन की पुष्टि कर रहा था। 1921 से भारत की जनसंख्या अति शीघ्र गति से बढ़ रही थी। प्रा. र. धे. कर्वे, अमेरिकन बर्थ कंट्रोल लीग, मार्गरिट सॅगर और महात्मा गांधी के संतति नियमन और जनसंख्या वृद्धि के नियंत्रण पर प्रचार कार्य चलाये जाने के बावजूद भी परिवार नियोजन भारत में असफल रहा था और इस के दो मुख्य कारण थेः (1) लोगों में धार्मिक भावना का दृढ़ होना और (2) आधुनिक उपायों के प्रति आम असहमति।

प्रजातन्त्र

प्रजातन्त्र में जनता की संप्रभुता के बारे में डॉ. आंबेडकेर की यह सोच रही कि ''प्रजातन्त्र के मूल को सामाजिक संबंधों में खोजना पडता है। प्रजातन्त्र

सहजीवन की एक पद्धति है। जो लोग उस समाज का गठन करते हैं, उनके सहजीवन के संदर्भ में उस पद्धति के मूल को खोजना पडता है।

ऊपर वर्णित व्यक्ति प्राधान्यता को संवैधानिक कर्तव्य परायणता से निम्न चार प्रकारों से जोड़ा गया:– (1) व्यक्ति की स्वतन्त्रता कानून व सुव्यवस्था, नैतिकता और स्वास्थ्य के संदर्भ में निष्पन्न कल्पनाओं से सुसंगत होगी। (2) यह स्वतन्त्रता इस ढंग से अमल में लाई जाये कि उस से अन्य मूलभूत अधिकारों का संकुचन न हो। (3) लौकिक बातों से संलग्न धार्मिक आचरण को नियंत्रित करने का अधिकार शासन के अधीन होगा और (4) धर्म विषयक स्वतन्त्रता कानून अथवा जाति के कारण हिंदू मंदिर में प्रवेश निषेध न होने हेतु किये गये विधान से सुसंगत होनी चाहिये।

बिरले ही पुरुष युग प्रवर्तक होते हैं। जो लोग गरीबी और गुलामी में पैदा होकर गरीबी और गुलामी की जंजीर तोड़ देते हैं वे धन्य हो जाते हैं। बीसवीं सदी के आरम्भ और मध्य में जो राजनैतिक पराधीनता थी उस से मुक्त होने मात्र से सामाजिक स्वाधीनता के ख्वाब पूर्ण नही हुये हैं।

विश्व मे आज आर्थिक विषमता के साथ–साथ मुक्त बाजार व्यवस्था के जरिये विकसित देशों के द्वारा अविकसित देशों के हित–साधन को बढ़ाने की अपेक्षा उनके शोषण और दमन को और अधिक उग्र किया जा रहा है। नब्बे के दशक में नई आर्थिक नीतियां भारतीय समाज में कार्यान्वित की गई और उसी के अनुसार बहुराष्ट्रीय निजी कंपनियों ने यहां के उपभोक्ताओं को प्रभावित, यहां के उत्पादकों को प्रताड़ित और यहां के शासन कर्ताओं को दिग्भ्रमित करना आरंभ किया।

परंतु अगतिक हुई विश्व व्यवस्था को सार्वभौमिक हिताय और सार्वभौमिक सुखाय के उद्‌देश्य से नई जीवन व्यवस्था में प्रवर्तित करने के लिये जिस नैतिक, मानव केंद्रित वैचारिकी और युग प्रवर्तक की जरुरत है, और जिस की कमी सबको खल रही है, उस पूर्ति हेतु डॉ. आंबेडकर जैसे कर्मठ रहबर और सम्यक युगद्रष्टा के दर्शन–ज्ञान को आत्मसात करना होगा। क्योंकि विश्व के हर देश की भांति भारत में भी इस दृष्टा के युग प्रवर्तक वैचारिकी से सबसे खतरनाक मानवता मारक मानसिक कोढ़ अस्पृश्यता की बीमारी खत्म होने जा रही है।

अतः एक आवाज से ऐसी प्रार्थना करना चाहिये जिस से लोगों के उद्धार की भावना जागृत हो और ऐसा दृढ़ निश्चय करना चाहिये कि "जिन लोगों में अपना जन्म हुआ है उनका उद्धार करना अपना कर्तव्य है, यह जिन्हें मालूम हैं वे धन्य हैं। परतन्त्रता पर आक्रमण करने के लिये जो अपना तन, मन, धन और यौवन कुर्बान कर देते हैं वे धन्य हैं। मनुष्य को अपनी मानवता पूर्ण रुप से मिलने तक जो अच्छाई–बुराई, सुख–दुःख, संकट–संघर्ष, मान–अपमान, इत्यादि की परवाह न कर सतत संघर्ष करते रहे हैं वे धन्य हैं"।

अमर संदेश

अपने पचासवें जन्मदिवस समारोह पर अवाम को संदेश देते हुये डॉ. आंबेडकर ने कहा था, "मैं प्रजातन्त्र का कट्टर अनुयायी हूँ। व्यक्तिगत पूजा प्रजातन्त्र की विरोधी है। अपने इस भारत में राष्ट्रीय नेता को अवतारी पुरुषों के जैसा आदर का स्थान दिया जाता है। भारत के बाहर अन्य देशों में केवल महापुरुषों की ही जयंतियां मनाई जाती है। अगर नेता योग्य हुआ तो उस की प्रशंसा, प्रेम और आदर करना कोई हरकत नही और उतने में ही उस नेता एवं उस के अनुयायियों का समाधान होना चाहिए, परंतु नेता की देव स्वरुप पूजा करना मुझें कतई पसन्द नहीं। इस से नेता के साथ–साथ उस के अनुयायिओं का भी अधःपात होता है। मेरा व्यक्गित जन्मदिन मनाया जाना मुझे बिलकुल पसंद नहीं"।

"परन्तु यहां यह सब बताने से कोई लाभ नहीं। संदेश की बजाय मेरे भाईयों को ग्रीक पुराण में लिखित स्रोत की एक कहानी बताऊंगा, जो ग्रीक देवता पर है, जिसे होमर ने लिखा है। प्रसंग इस प्रकार है –

> "ग्रीस में एक डिमेटर नाम की देवी थी। वह अपनी पुत्री की खोज में घूमते–घूमते केलिओस के राज्य में पहुंची। उस ने दाई का वेश धारण किया था। इसलिए उसे कोई पहचान न सका। रानी मेटोनेरा ने अपने छोटे बच्चे डेमोफून की देखभाल के लिए उस को अपने घर रख लिया। डिमेटर देवी प्रति दिन रात के समय राज महल में सब के सो जाने पर द्वार बन्द करके उस बच्चे को झूले से धीरे–धीरे बाहर निकालती और उसे वस्त्र विहीन कर जलते अंगारों पर रखती थी।

शायद श्रोताओं को यह कृत्य क्रूर सा लगेगा। परन्तु यह वास्तव में वैसा नही था। बड़े प्रेम से वह देवी उसे देवता बनाने में लगी थी। क्रमशः उस बालक में जलते अंगारों की ज्वाला सहन करने की शक्ति एवं सामर्थ्य उत्पन्न हो गई। उस का बल बढ़ने लगा। उस में कुछ तेज, दिव्यत्व एवं असाधारणता के अंश विकसित होने लगे। परन्तु एक रात उस बालक की मां अचानक उस कमरे में पहुंच गई और अपने पुत्र को देवता बनाने का वह प्रयोग देखते ही डिमेटर देवी को धकेल अंगारों में से बालक को शीघ्र उठा लिया। उस का पुत्र उसे मिल तो गया परन्तु साधारण मनुष्य–बालक को असाधारण रुप में न पा सकी''।

यह कहानी बताती है कि अपना भविष्य उज्वल करने हेतु मनुष्य को वर्तमान सुख एवं आवश्यकताओं का भी त्याग करना चाहिये। ऐसा क्यों होता है कि जीवन की दौड़ में भाग लेने का आमंत्रण सब को आता है परन्तु बहुत थोड़े लोग सफल होते है? इस का कारण यह है कि भविष्य की आवश्यकता की पूर्ति हेतु वर्तमान की विलासिताओं का त्याग करने में लगने वाला धैर्य या निर्धारण मनुष्य के पास नहीं रहता। इसलिये जीवन की दौड़ में इन्हें बड़प्पन नही मिलता[28]।''

यही दर्शन अवाम को जीने की दृष्टि दे सकता है।

इसके अलावा डॉ. आंबेडकर के कुछ अनमोल वचन यहां उद्धृत किये गये हैं, जो अवाम के जीवन में हर मोड़ पर पथ प्रदर्शक बने रह सकेंगे।

1. दुःखियों के आंसू पोंछने के लिये तुम्हारे नयन तरसने चाहिये। दीन–दुःखियों की सेवा के लिये तुम्हारा हृदय पसीजना चाहिये। संकट ग्रस्त लोगों की रक्षा के लिये तुम्हारी भुजायें फड़कना चाहिये।
2. नीचे सिर झुकाकर चलनेवाले हजारों भेड़ों के विशाल समूह की अपेक्षा वीरता की वृत्ति रखनेवाला सिंह का समूह बेहतर होता है।
3. निष्प्रभ सुशिक्षितों के झुण्डों की अपेक्षा सुसंस्कृत मन से व्यवहार करनेवालों का मेला ही निःसंशय उपकारक होता है।

4. सदाचार का सत्व साथ में रख जीवन में मंगलत्व निर्माण करो।
5. पुस्तकों के सहवास में शांत जीवन बिताने जैसा दूसरा आनंद कहीं नहीं है।
6. मानव जीवन का तत्वज्ञान हमें आज अधिक प्रभावी ढंग से समझ में आ रहा हैं।
7. जिस गांव में अभिमानशून्य जीवन व्यतीत करना पड़ता है वह गांव किस काम का।
8. यद्यपि मैं हिन्दू धर्म में जन्मा हूँ फिर भी हिन्दू धर्म में रहकर मरुंगा नहीं।
9. देश का संविधान कितना भी अच्छा क्यों न हो लेकिन उसको उपयोग में लाने वाले मनुष्य यदि अच्छे नही हों तो संविधान निश्चित ही बुरा सिद्ध होगा।
10. केवल मेरा नाम लेकर जयजयकार करने की अपेक्षा जो चीज मेरी दृष्टि में अनमोल है उसे करने के लिये प्राणपण से जूझो।
11. देश के राजनैतिक दलों ने यदि देश हित की अपेक्षा अपने दल हित को प्राधान्य दिया तो देश फिर एक बार संकट में गये बिना नही रहेगा और तब फिर अपना सर्वस्व हमेशा के लिये नष्ट हो जायेगा।

संदर्भ ग्रंथः

1. श्री अयंगर, ''मन्त्र युग के प्राचीन भारत में जीवन'' पृ. 13 और ऋ. वे. 1.53.8; 103.3, ऋ. वे. 4. 30. 20, ऋ. वे. 7. 5. 3, ऋ. वे. 4. 67. 3, ऋ. वे. 8. 24. 27; 30.5; 5.11.4; आं: 110; डॉ. बी. आर. आंबेडकर, हू वेअर द शूद्राज, ठक्कर, मुंबई 1946, पुमु 1947, 1970, प . 110.
2. ऋ. वे. 1. 51.8,9; 1.1.32 4; 4.41.2; 5.14.3.
3. मुंशी एन. एल. खोब्रागडे, मध्य प्रांत मे दलित आंदोलन का इतिहास, मध्य प्रदेश दलित साहित्य अकादमी, बालाघाट, 1999 पृ. 40–41.
4. एम. डी. कांबले, डिप्राइब्ड कास्टस् एण्ड देअर स्ट्रगल फॉर इक्वालिटी, आशिश पब्लिशिंग हाउस, नई दिल्ली 1983, मुख पृष्ठ।
5. डॉ. बाबासाहेब आंबेडकर रायटिंग्ज एण्ड स्पीचेज, वाल्युम 1, पृ. 44 और एस. एस. गायकवाड, डॉ. आंबेडकर यांची समाजरचनेची सैद्धांतिक मांडणी, डॉ. बाबा साहेब आंबेडकर गौरव ग्रंथ, महाराष्ट्र राज्य साहित्य आणि संस्कृति मंडळ, मुंबई 1993, पृ. 27.
6. डॉ. आंबेडकर, *वीसा की प्रतिक्षा में* , 1942–46, पृ. इस शीर्षक से अपने श्रम मंत्रीत्व के कार्यकाल के दौरान विदेशी पाठकों के सूचनार्थ आत्म–चरित्र की विधा में डॉ. आंबेडकर का लेखन।

7. रोड़रिग्ज, एसेनशियल रायटिंग्ज ऑफ डॉ. बी. आर. आंबेडकर, नई दिल्ली, 2002.
8. डॉ. बी. आर. आंबेडकर, रायटिंग्स एण्ड स्पीचेस, खण्ड 1 मुंबई 1979 पृ. 227.
9. प्रो. बी. एच. कल्याणकर, डॉ. आंबेडकरांचा शैक्षणिक दृष्टिकोण, डॉ. बाबासाहेब आंबेडकर गौरव ग्रंथ, महाराष्ट्र राज्य साहित्य आणि संस्कृति मंडळ, मुंबई 1993, पृ. 419–425.
10. डॉ. भालचंद्र लक्ष्मण मुणगेकर, डॉ. आंबेडकर यांचे भारतीय शेतीविशयक विचार, डॉ. बाबासाहेब आंबेडकर गौरव ग्रंथ, मुंबई 1993, पुनर्मुद्रण 1999, पृ. 393–394.
11. डॉ. भदन्त आनन्द कौसल्यायन, यदि बाबा न होते, नागपूर, 1981, पृ.
12. डॉ. भदन्त आनन्द कौसल्यायन, वही
13. डॉ. नरेन्द्र जाधव, डॉ. आंबेडकरांचे अर्थशास्त्रीय लेखन, डॉ. बाबासाहेब आंबेडकर गौरव ग्रंथ, महाराष्ट्र राज्य साहित्य आणि संस्कृति मंडळ, मुंबई 1993, पृ. 362–372.
14. डॉ. नरेन्द्र जाधव, वही, पृ. 362–391.
15. श्री गोविंद तळवलकर, डॉ. आंबेडकर यांचे आर्थिक विचार, डॉ. बाबासाहेब आंबेडकर गौरव ग्रंथ, मुंबई 1993, पुनर्मुद्रण 1999, पृ. 399–400.
16. डॉ. एस. डी. तुपे, डॉ. बाबासाहेब आंबेडकर आणि जमीनधारणा, वही, पृ. 400–404.
17. विसाव्या शतकातील महाराष्ट्र 1910–1914 खंड 1, पृ. 214 और शांताराम पंदेरे, डॉ. आंबेडकर आणि राखीव जागांचा प्रश्न, डॉ. बाबासाहेब आंबेडकर गौरव ग्रंथ, मुंबई 1993 पुनर्मुद्रण 1999, पृ. 307.
18. लेखक के विचार
19. सत्यकेतु विद्यालंकार, एशिया का आधुनिक इतिहास, सरस्वति सदन, मसूरी, उ. प्र., 1964 तृतीय संस्करण, पृ. 896.
20. डॉ. बी. आर. आंबेडकर, रानडे, गांधी और जिन्नाह, मुंबई 1943 भूमिका से।
21. श्री अरुण शौरी, वरशिपिंग फाल्स गॉड़, एएसए प्रकाशन, नई दिल्ली 1997, पृ.ग।
22. एल. आर. बाली, शौरी का शोर, सम्यक साहित्य, नई दिल्ली 1997, पृ. 15.
23. एल. आर. बाली, वही,
24. डॉ. बी. आर. आंबेडकर, आकाशवाणी मुंबई का भाषण दिनांक 13.11.1942.
25. डॉ. बी. आर. आंबेडकर, स्मरण पत्र, साप्ताहिक मेनस्ट्रीम, नई दिल्ली, वार्शिक नवंबर 1993, पृ. 45.
26. दैनिक भास्कर, दिनांक 2 दिसंबर 2003, सुविचार में, संपादकीय पृष्ठ।
27. लेखक की कल्पना।
28. एल. आर. बाली, शौरी का शोर, सम्यक साहित्य, नई दिल्ली 1997, पृ. 15।
29. प्रो. एन. जी. मेश्राम, डॉ. आंबेडकर का दिव्य संदेश, मुंबई (प्रथम आवृत्ति 1968), (दूसरी आवृत्ति 1995) पृ. 1–70.
30. सी. डी. नाईक, थॉटस् एण्ड फिलासफी ऑफ डॉ. बी. आर. आंबेडकर, सरुप एण्ड सन्स, नई दिल्ली 2003, बुद्धिस्ट ड़ेवलपमेन्ट इन इस्ट एण्ड वेस्ट नामक अध्याय, पृ.
31. डॉ. धनंजय कीर, डॉ. आंबेडकरः जीवन तथा कार्य, प्रकाशन पुणे, 1976, पृ.
32. डॉ. बी. आर. आंबेडकर, रायटिंग्स एण्ड स्पीचेस, खण्ड 1 मुंबई 1979 पृ. 54.
33. डॉ. बी. आर. आंबेडकर, थॉटस् ऑन पाकिस्तान, ठक्कर एण्ड कंपनी, मुंबई, 1945, विदेशियों से सबक नामक अध्याय, पृ.

Chapter - 17

बौद्ध तत्वज्ञान और भारतीय संविधान

डॉ. प्रीति नाईक

प्रस्तावना

अगर सिद्धार्थ गौतम राजा ही बनकर रह जाते, घर छोड़ के उनको ज्ञान प्राप्त न होता, प्रचार नहीं करते तो उनको ज्ञान प्राप्त न होता, प्रचार नहीं करते तो उनका कोई महत्व नहीं था।

हिन्दुस्तान में हजारों राजे हुए, उनके नाम हम अभी जानते भी नहीं, वैसे ही एक महाराजा होकर सिद्धार्थ गौतम के नाम से मर जाते। हिन्दुस्तान के बहुत से लोग कहते हैं कि भगवान बुद्ध की पूरी भक्ति हुई। भगवान बुद्ध ने किसी की भक्ति नहीं की। तो बुद्ध को क्या प्राप्त हुआ? संक्षिप्त में उनको चार आर्य सत्य का ज्ञान हुआ। आमतौर से दूसरे धर्म इस बात से शुरू होते है कि दुनिया किस ने बनाई है। यह दुनिया कैसे शुरू हुई, यह नदी, पहाड़ किस ने बनाये। भगवान ने बुद्ध ने कहा है कि हमारा मसला यह नहीं है कि पहाड़ किस ने बनाये। यह जो हमारे अन्दर जो दुख है, हमें अपने मन के बारे में कुछ पता नहीं कि मैं कौन हूँ। मुझे दुःख क्यों होता है, समाज के अन्दर यह लड़ाईयां क्यों, अपने मन के अंदर ये लड़ाईयाँ क्यों हैं, अपने मन के अन्दर क्या बात हो रही है, उनका खुद को पता नहीं तो पहाड़, आसमान के बारे में क्या बात करते हो पी. एच. डी. करके उनको दुःख का ज्ञान नहीं हुआ। सारा का सारा बुद्ध धर्म आदमी के अंदर है। सवाल है इस शरीर को कैसे पढ़े ? कैसे समझे? उस के लिए भगवान बुद्ध ने

> ''वेदियमानस्स अहं भिक्खवे दुक्खडच पञ्ञापेमि
> दुक्ख समुदयत्र्च, दुक्ख निरोधत्र्च पटिपदा।''

अर्थातः– जो आदमी अपनी वेदना के प्रति जागरूक है उस के लिए भिक्षुओं, मैं कहता हूँ, यह दुःख है, यह दुःख समुदय है, यह निरोध है, यह दुक्ख निरोध गामिनी परिपदा है। आप लोग भगवान बुद्ध की आमिष यानि वस्तुओं से पूजा करते हैं, लेकिन उन्होंने प्रतिपत्ति की पढ़ाई की और कही।

यदि आप भगवान बुद्ध के प्रति श्रद्धा रखते हैं तो कम से कम आज एक दिन शराब मत पियो।

बुद्ध

आज हम उस महान पुरुष को याद कर रहे हैं, जिन्होंने इस संसार को शांति के प्रकाश से प्रकाशित किया, प्रज्ञा की आभा से प्रज्वलित किया, भयानकता को मैत्री से शांत करने का उपदेश दिया। अनाथों के नाथ, दलितों के दुःखहर्ता, महान करूणा से स्त्रोत, जिन्होंने प्राणियों के हित के लिए, कल्याण के लिए, विभिन्न प्रकार से अनेक दुःख, अनेक पीड़ा सहकर के भी पारमिता गुण धर्मों को पूर्ण करके सम्बोधि लाभ किया। आज हम उन को उमझने का प्रयास कर रहे हैं। भगवान बुद्ध दो हजार और दो सौ सैंतीस वर्ष भारत के सीमान्त प्रदेश नेपाल की अपत्य का लुम्बिनी में जन्मे। उनका यौवन बहुत ही सुखमय बीता था। एक दिन बहुत से विचारों ने उनके ह्रदय को छुआ। आतंकित जनता को देखकर वह रोने लगे और सत्य के खोजने के लिए उन्होंने अपना राज सुख पाठ त्याग दिया। इस प्रकार उन्होंने 29 वर्ष की आयु में गृहत्याग किया, महाभिनिष्क्रमण किया। छः साल की कठिन चर्या के बाद बुद्धत्व लाभ किया। उस सुख को बोधि वृक्ष के नीचे रहकर सात हफ्ते तक अनुभव किया और उसके बाद प्राणियों के दुःख दर्द और पीड़ाओं को मिटाने के लिए सर्वप्रथम सारनाथ में पांच ब्राह्मण ऋषियों को उपदेश दिया, अपने ज्ञान को फैलाया उनके संघ में सब से नामी प्रकांड भिक्षु के रूप में निकलने वाले सभी भिक्षु ब्राह्मण ही थे। किन्हीं व्यक्तियों का विचार है, भगवान बुद्ध का धर्म हिंदू धर्म का एक अंश है। यदि ऐसा है तो हिन्दु धर्म के प्रतिष्ठाता ब्राह्मण लोग बौद्ध धर्म में क्यों प्रतिष्ठित हुए ? अगर वो ही धर्म महान था तो ब्राह्मण के पुत्रों को बौद्ध भिक्षु बनने की कोई जरूरत नहीं थी। लेकिन ब्राह्मण लोग बुद्ध धर्म में आकार आत्मशांति का अनुभव करते थे। उसका थेरगया वथेरीगाथा में

विवरण है। जिससे हमें मालूम होता है कि बौद्धों की अपनी ही एक मौलिकता है और अगर हिन्दू धर्म से बौद्ध धर्म का प्रादुर्भाव हुआ तो भारत के बौद्ध धर्म का अन्त करने के लिए हिन्दू धर्म ने क्यों प्रयास किया। आदि प्रश्न हमारे सामने आते हैं। आज यह सब प्रश्न हल करने के लिए हम तर्क वितर्क नहीं कर रहे हैं। लेकिन जिस बुद्ध ने आज तक भारत को, एशिया को या विश्व को जो दिया है, उस संदेश के मुताबिक हम कह सकते है कि वह व्यक्ति जो व्यक्ति जिन्होंने बुद्ध धर्म का आविष्कार किया, प्रचार किया, वह अवश्य महान–महान होंगे, थे और महान रहे हैं। पैंतालिस वर्ष तक बुद्ध ने अपने प्रयास से बौद्ध धर्म को भारत भूमि में स्थापित किया। उनके दो सौ वर्ष बाद अशोक ने उसे एशिया, अफ्रीका और कहीं यूरोप में भी फैलाया। यह सम्राट अशोक का बहुत बड़ा योगदान है।

आज तक विभिन्न घात और अघातों के होने के बावजूद बुद्ध धर्म जी रहा है। उसका मुख्य कारण है उनके उपदेशों की सच्चाई जो शांति की आभा से प्राणियों के मर्म समझााने की शक्ति धारण किये हुये है। उसी तत्व के कारण आज यूरोप के लोग भी बुद्ध धर्म में आकर्षित होने लगे हैं।

हमारे भारत में बाबासाहब डाक्टर भीमराव अम्बेडकर ने भी इसे अपनाकर कुण्टित्र अवस्था, दबाव खत्म किया और कष्ट व वेदना सहकर जातियों का उत्थान किया। उन्होंने कहा था, मैं भारत को बौद्धमय बनाऊंगा काश! ऐसा होता।

सिंह के जैसे दृश्य वाले अम्बेडकर को भी मृत्यराज ने अपने हाथ में समेट कर इस जीवन से अन्त कर दिया। उस महान पुरुष के संदेश को जो उन्होंने बुद्ध से प्राप्त किया था आप लोग इंग्लैण्ड में रहकर भी नहीं भूले हैं और उनके स्मरण में आज यहां बुद्ध जयंती मना रहे हैं। ऐसे आप लोग सौभाग्यशाली हैं।

बौद्ध तत्वज्ञान

भारतीय संविधान के निर्माण के पहले भारत में हिंदुत्ववाद, बुद्धवाद, गांधीवाद, एवं मार्क्सवाद जैसे तत्वज्ञान मौजूद थे। लेकिन भारतीय संविधान पर गहरा प्रभाव बुद्ध तत्वज्ञान का ही दिखाई देता है। भारतीय संविधान की उद्देशिका संविधान का हृदय है। यह यह उद्देशिका अत्यंत महत्वपूर्ण है। इस

उद्देशिका में 'सम्पूर्ण प्रभुत्व संपन्न समाजवादी पंथ निरपेक्ष लोकतंत्रात्मक गणराज्य' स्थापना करने का जिक्र किया है और सभी नागरिकों को सामाजिक, आर्थिक और राजनैतिक न्याय, विचार, अभिव्यक्ति, विश्वास, धर्म और उपासना की 'स्वतंत्रता' प्रतिष्ठा और अवसर की समता प्राप्त करने के लिए अभिवचन दिया गया है और व्यक्ति की गरिमा और राष्ट्र की एकता और अखण्डता सुनिश्चित करने वाली बंधुता बढ़ाने के लिए दृढ़ संकल्प करते हुए यह संविधान भारत के लोगों ने स्वयं को अर्पित किया है।

संविधान की इस उद्देशिका के गहराई में अगर हम जाये तो हमें यहां भगवान बुद्ध के प्रतीत्य समुवाद सिद्धांत का (परस्परावलम्बी सहवर्धन) एहसास होता है। किसी भी घटना के पीछे कार्यकारण भाव (cause & effect) होता है। इस उद्देशिका में स्वतंत्रता समता, बंधुता एवं न्याय प्राप्त करने का उद्देश्य क्यों रखा गया है ? उसका कारण था, जिसका परिणाम उद्देशिका इस तरह की हुई ?

कारण यह थाः— समाज में सामाजिक आर्थिक और राजनैतिक न्याय नहीं था। सामाजिक आर्थिक राजनैतिक समता नहीं थी। स्वतंत्रता नहीं थी। उच्च – नीच भाव था। विषमता थी। यह सब क्यों था ? इसकी जड़ तक जाना जरूरी है।

ऋग्वेद के पुरूषसुक्त के निर्माता और मनुस्मृति के निर्माता दोनों प्राचीन काल के बहुत बड़े सोशल इंजिनियर थे। बुद्ध कहते हैं मन ही सब मानसिक क्रियाओं में प्रधान है। धम्मपद की पहली गाथा में बुद्ध ने मन पर प्रकाश डाला है और कहा है, भलाईयों और बुराईयों का स्त्रोत मन ही है। मन अच्छा सोचे तो अच्छा होता है। बुरा सोचने के कारण परिणाम बुरा होता है। वेद निर्माता और मनु इन सोशल इंजिनियरों ने प्राचीन समाज की वास्तु की संकल्पना को जन्म दिया और वह हकीकत में लायी। इन्होंने कहा बृहमदेव के मुख से हमारे ब्राह्मण बंधु का जन्म हुआ। बाहू से क्षत्रिय बंधुओं का जन्म हुआ। जांघों से वैश्व बंधुओं का जन्म हुआ और पैरों से शूद्र बंधुओं ने जन्म लिया।

ये सामाजिक अभियंता बड़े चालाक थे। उन्होंने यह वर्णव्यवस्था निर्माण करके उसको धर्म का रूप दिया। ऐसा उन्होंने क्यों किया? स्वार्थ

के कारण और हमारे ब्राह्मण बंधुओं के विशेषाधिकार रखने के लिए किया। इस वर्ण व्यवस्था ने सत्ता का विषय विभाजन किया है। ब्राह्मण बंधुओं के पास ज्ञान सत्ता, क्षत्रिय बंधुओं के पास राजसत्ता, वैश्य बंधुओं के पास केवल सेवाभाव।

इसका मतलब है कि शूद्रों का जानबूझकर ज्ञानसत्ता, राजसत्ता अर्थसत्ता एवं सम्मान से दूर रखा गया। मुख से लेकर पैर तक ब्राह्मण, क्षत्रिय, वैश्य शूद्र यह समाज पुरुष की अवधारणा दोनों अभियंताओं ने की लेकिन समाज की इस अवधारणा में अस्पृश्यता कहां है ? आदिवासी कहां है? धुमन्तू कहां है? इन अभियंताओं ने समाज रूपी इस वास्तु से अस्पृश्यों को गांव के बाहर निकाल दिया। आदिवासीयों बंधुओं को जंगल में निकाल दिया और घुमनतुओं का न जंगल न जमीन न जल न मकान दिया। इन्हें घूमते रहो का आदेश दिया। तीनों को गांव से बहिष्कृत किया गया।

संविधान निर्माण के पहले जो सामाजिक, आर्थिक, राजनैतिक, व्यावसायिक विषमता थी। यह उन्हीं सोशल इंजिनियरों की देन है। स्त्री पुरूष विषमता को भी उन्होंने जन्म दिया। ज्ञान के प्रकाश से शुद्र, अतिशुद्र एवं नारी को दूर रखा। इस पुरानी सामाजिक वास्तु के बोझ के नीचे उन्होंने न्याय, समता, स्वतंत्रता, बंधुता इन मूल्यों को कुचल दिया था।

संविधान निर्माता के सामने सबसे बड़ा आव्हान यही था कि, इस विषमता रूपी सामाजिक वास्तू को कैसे ध्वस्त किया जाय ? क्योंकि यह वास्तु की सामाजिक भेदभाव की जड़ थी, जो देश की एकता और अखण्डता को खतरा था। इसके बारे में प्रज्ञा सम्राट बाबासाहेब आंबेडकर ने उसे अंग्रेजी में twer tight compartment कहा है। बाबासाहेब कहते थे यह समाज रचना एक मीनार की तरह है। इस एक दूसरे के ऊपर खड़ी हुई मीनार में क्रमशः ऊपर से प्रथम में ब्राह्मण है। इसके नीचे क्षत्रिय है। उसके भी नीचे तृतीय कमरे में वैश्य है और अंतिम जमीन पर के कमरे में शूद्र है। इस मीनार की एक विशिष्टता है कि इस पर पहुँचने के लिए कोई सीढ़ी नही है। प्रत्येक वर्ण स्वतंत्र है। उनके कार्यो का विभाजन है लेकिन आपस में कोई समन्वय नहीं। परन्तु यदि इस महल की नींव शूद्र बगावत कर दे और खिसक जाये तो यह मीनार अपने आप लड़खड़ा कर गिर पडेगी।

समय का करिश्मा तो देखो, इस मीनार में भी जिसका स्थान नहीं था। ज्ञान की प्यास पूरी करने के लिए जिसे विद्यार्थी दशा में तड़पना पड़ा उसी अछूत के हाथ में संविधान निर्माण का कार्य सौंपा गया। विद्यार्थी अवस्था में जिनके हाथों में केकुस्कर गुरूजी ने बुद्धचरित दिया था, उसी 'प्रबुद्ध' हाथों को संविधान निर्माण का कार्य सौंपा गया। डॉ. बाबासाहेब आम्बेडकर केवल राजनीतिज्ञ नहीं थे, वे विधिज्ञ थे, समाजशास्त्रज्ञ थे। जो भी कलकृति कोई साकार करता है तो उसके व्यक्तित्व का प्रभाव उस कृति पर पड़ता है। बाबासाहेब आंबेडकर बोधिसत्व थे। उनकी बोधिप्रथ भारतीय संविधान में यमकती हमें दिखाई देती है। संविधान की मसौदा समिति का अध्यक्ष डॉ. बाबासाहेब आम्बेडकर को चुना गया। धनंयज कौर ने लिखा है–

> वह अछूत, जिसे छकड़ों से धकेला गया, जिसे लड़कपन में स्कूल में एक और अलग कर बैठाया गया, जिसे प्राध्यापक के रूप में अपमानित किया गया, जिस युवावस्था में घृण्यमहार कहकर होटलों, होस्टलों, सभा मंडपो और मन्दिर से निकाला गया"। की आगे लिखते हैं वही अब स्वतंत्र भारत का प्रथम विधि मंत्री बना और वही भारत के लोगों की इच्छा, लक्ष्य और सपनों को परिभाषित करने वाले संविधान का मुख्य रूप से निर्माता बना। भारत के इतिहास की यह एक बहुत बड़ी उपलब्धि भी है और हैरानी भी। भारत ने अपने युगयुगान्तरों से चले आ रहे अछूत पन के पाप को दूर करने के लिए अपना शासनकार, नया मनु, अपना नया स्मृतिकार उस जाति से चुना जिसे युगों से पशु के समान कर दिया गया था। जिसका मनोबल क्षीण कर दिया गया था और जिसकी शक्ति नष्ट कर दी गयी थी नवभारत ने अपना संविधान बनाने का कार्य उस व्यक्ति को सौंपा जिसने कुछ वर्ष पहले हिन्दुओं के संविधान मनुस्मृति को अग्नि में भस्मसत् किया था।

आधुनिक भारत के निर्माताः– डॉ. आम्बेडकर

डॉ. बाबासाहेब आम्बेडकर आधुनिक काल के बहुत बड़े 'सोशल इंजिनियर' थे। अकुशल मन से बनाए हुए उस सामाजिक वास्तु को उन्होंने देखा। उसका गहरा अध्ययन किया। उसमें परिवर्तन की जरूरत महसूस की।

मा. भगवान सिंह रावत लिखते हैं, चूंकि बाबासाहेब अतिशूद्र और भुक्तभोगी होने के कारण छुआछुत एवं ब्राह्मणवाद के थपेड़ों के कटु अनुभवी थे, इसलिए उन्होंने सर्वप्रथम मनु के काले कानूनों को दफनाया और ब्राह्मणों के विशेषधिकारों को समाप्त किया। उन्होंने संविधान की धारा 13(3) में कहा इस संविधान के प्रारंभ होने से ठीक पहले राज्य क्षेत्र में प्रवृत विधियां उस मात्रा तक शून्य होंगी, जिस तक कि वे इस भाग के उपबंधों से असंगत हैं। ''धारा 13 (3) में कहा है'' विधि के समान प्रभावी को अध्यादेश, आदेश, उपविधी, नियम, विनियम, अधिसूचना, रूढ़ी अथवा प्रथा विधि के अन्तर्गत होगी।

भारतीय संविधान में अनुच्छेद 13 (1) बहुत बड़ा क्रांतिकारी है। उसमें बारूद की शक्ति है। इस अनुच्छेद का बारूद पुरानी वर्णप्रधान सामाजिक वास्तु को बाबासाहेब ने लगाया और उसको ध्वस्त किया।

डॉ. बाबासाहेब आम्बेडकर की प्रागतिक सामाजिक अभियांत्रिकी

प्रतीत्य समुत्पाद सिद्धांत के अनुसार कारण से परिणाम या कार्य घटित होता है। और यह परिणाम या कार्य पूर्णतः नया होता है। मनुष्य को कुरूप बनाने वाली वर्णव्यवस्था को नकार देने के साथ इस संविधान के माध्यम से डॉ. बाबासाहेब आम्बेडकर जैसे सर्वश्रेष्ठ सामाजिक अभियंता ने आधुनिक भारत के नवनिर्माण की नींव रखी। जिसका अपना एक मानवतावादी रूप सौंदर्य है। मानवीय मूल्यों को रौंदनेवाली जो वास्तू वर्ण एवं जाति की दीवारों पर और उच्च नींच भाव के छोटे – बड़े स्तंभों पर खड़ी थी उसको उन्होंने ध्वस्त करते हुए स्वतंत्रता, समता, बंधुता, न्याय एवं धर्म निरपेक्षता के पंचस्तभों पर एक नयी वास्तू खड़ी कर दी। संविधान की उद्‌देशिका के पीछे वर्ण एवं वर्गव्यवस्था की कुरूपता 'कारण' रहा और उद्‌देशिका में अभिव्यक्त सम्यक संकल्प उसका नया, सुरूप एवं सुन्दर परिणाम रहा।

बौद्ध काल में संसदीय शासन प्रणाली

डॉ. बाबासाहेब आम्बेडकर ने 28 अक्टूबर 1951 में दयानंद ऐंग्लों वैदिक कॉलेज जालंधर में गंभीर एवं विचारपूर्ण भाषण दिया। बाबासाहेब आम्बेडकर ने कहाः ''आज हम पालमेंटरी शासन पद्धति से अपरिचित हैं। लेकिन एक समय था, जब भारत में पार्लमेंटरी ढंग की संस्थाऐं थी। प्राचीन समय में

भारत दुनिया के दूसरे देशों से बहुत आगे बढ़ा हुआ था। यदि आप पाली 'दीघ निकाय' के महापरिनिर्वाण सूत्र को पढ़ें, तो वहां आपको मेरे कथन के पक्ष में काफी सामग्री मिलेगी। उस सूत्र में लिखा है कि, जिस समय कुशीनगर में भगवान बुद्ध का परिनिर्वाण होने जा रहा था, तो मल्ल जनपद के लोगों को, जो उस समय अपनी बैठक कर रहे थे, उसकी सूचना भिजवाई गई। मल्ल लोग पार्लमेंटरी पद्धति के भक्त थे। जब उन्हें भगवान बुद्ध के बारे में समाचार मिला, तो उन्होंने तय किया कि वे अपना अधिवेशन बंद नहीं करेंगे, कार्यवाही जारी रखेंगे और अपनी पार्लमेंट का कार्य समाप्त करके ही कुशीनगर जायेंगे। हमारे साहित्य में ऐसे अगणित उल्लेख हैं, जिनसे सिद्ध किया जा सकता है कि हम पार्लमेंटरी शासन – पद्धति से अपरिचित नहीं रहे हैं।

मल्ल लोगों का बर्ताव किसी को अजीब लग सकता है, मुझे नही। क्योंकि भगवान बुद्ध ने सभी को 'अनित्यबोध' की शिक्षा दी थी। उसी का एहसास मुझे उनके निर्णय में होता है। अनित्य बोध जीवन का एक सत्य है। इसी कारण 'शोक' करना, देशहित का कामकाज रूकवाना व्यर्थ है। इसी कारण तो चक्रवर्ती सम्राट, बौद्ध सम्राट का नाम था अशोक।

भारतीय संविधान के अन्तर्गत आज लोकसभा में कोई प्रस्ताव रखता हो तो चौदह दिन पहले सूचना देनी पड़ती है। तभी वह प्रस्ताव स्वीकृत होता है। लेकिन यह प्रथा बुद्धकारक की संसदीय शासन प्रणाली में हमें दिखायी देती है। बाबासाहेब डॉ. आम्बेडकर ने इस बारे में कहा था, "पार्लमेंटरी शासन पद्धति के बहुत नियम हैं, एक नियम जिसका अनिवार्य रूप से सभी जगह पालन किया जाता है, यह हैं कि बिना प्रस्ताव उपस्थित किये, किसी भी विषय पर चर्चा नहीं हो सकती। प्राचीन समय में हमारे देश में यह पद्धति प्रचलित थी। इस समय जो 'गुप्त मत' देने की प्रथा प्रचलित है, यह भी हमारे लिए नहीं है। बौद्ध ग्रंथों से यह पता चलता है कि ऐसे मत पत्रों को शलाका कहते थे। दुर्भाग्य से हमने अपनी यह सारी वंश परंपरा से प्राप्त मूल्यवान सम्पत्ति गवॉ दी। भारत के इतिहास वीरों को इस प्रश्न का उत्तर देने का प्रयास करना चाहिए कि हमारे देश से ये पार्लमेंटरी संस्थाएँ क्यों लुप्त हो गयी। लेकिन मुझे लगता है कि हमारे देश के इतिहास–लेखक या तो इस प्रश्न का उत्तर खोज नहीं सकते या

जान–बूझकर खोजना नहीं चाहते। प्राचीन भारत संसार का गुरू था। प्राचीन भारत में ऐसी मानसिक स्वतन्त्रता थी, जैसी अन्यत्र कहीं नहीं थी। फिर यह प्राचीन सभ्यता इस प्रकार छिन्न–भिन्न होकर नष्ट क्यों हो गई? भारत को निरंकुश शासकों की अधीनता क्यों स्वीकार करनी पड़ी ? हम पार्लमेंट की शासन पद्धति से परिचित थें। हम छन्द (वोट), छन्द प्रदान तथा तत् सम्बंधी कमेटियों से परिचित थे।

भारतीय लोकतंत्र का पंचशील

शाक्यमुनी, शांतिसागर भगवान बुद्ध ने व्यक्ति और समाज को पंचशील का ऐसा प्रकाश दिया जो हमें सदाचार के बलबूते पर खड़ा करके प्रगति की ओर ले जाता है। डॉ. बाबासाहेब आम्बेडकर ने भारतीय संविधान में हमें लोकतांत्रिक पंचशील प्रदान किये। 1. न्याय, 2. समता, 3. स्वतंत्रता, 4. बंधुता और 5. धर्मनिरपेक्षता। यही है वह पंचशील। यह पंचशील समाज के हर तबके के लोगों का जीवन प्रकाशमान करने वाला है। यह पंचशील का पालन अगर प्रत्येक नागरिक प्रामणिकता से करे तो समाज सामाजिक, आर्थिक एवं राजनैतिक नीतिमत्ता के बलबुते पर खड़ा होने के कारण विश्व में कल्याणकारी महासत्ता बन सकता है। बाबासाहेब का दिया हुआ यह पंचशील हमारे भारतीय राष्ट्र–पुरुष को, जो जातिवाद धर्मांधता, भ्रष्टाचार, दहशतवाद के जो रोग हुए है उसकी गुणकारी दवा है।

भारतीय संविधान ने स्वतंत्रता, समता एवं बंधुता इन लोकतांत्रिक मूल्यों को अपनाया है। इस संदर्भ में संविधान के प्रमुख निर्माता डॉ. बाबासाहेब आम्बेडकर ने 3 अक्टूबर 1954 में दिल्ली आकाशवाणी पर दिये हुए भाषण में कहा "स्वतंत्रता, समता एवं सहभाव यही मेरा जीवन विषयक तत्वज्ञान है। फ्रेंच राज्यक्रांती से मैने मेरा यह तत्वज्ञान लिया है ऐसा किसी ने समझना नहीं चाहिए। मैं पूरे विश्वास के साथ कहता हूॅ कि मैंन ऐसा किया नहीं। मेरे तत्वज्ञान का मूलाधार राजनीति में नही, धर्म में है। मेरे गुरू भगवान बुद्ध की शिक्षा से यह तत्वज्ञान मैने हासिल किया है।

संघ में 'न्याय–व्यवस्था' के सिद्धान्त

भारतीय संविधान की उद्देशिका में सबसे बड़ा महत्त्व 'न्याय' तत्व को दिया है। यह लोकतंत्र का ऐसा मूल्य है, जिससे शोषित एवं पीड़ित का दुःख

और दर्द दूर हो जाता है। अन्याय के दर्द भरे शिकंजे से उसे छुटकारा मिलता है। लोकतंत्र के पंचशील का यह एक महत्वपूर्ण शील है और जो कोई इसे पैरों तले रौंदना चाहे भारतीय कानून उसे माफ नहीं करता।

भगवान बुद्ध सामाजिक, आर्थिक एवं राजनीतिक न्याय के प्रबल पक्षधर थे। अन्याय के खिलाफ आवाज उठाने वे बोलते हैं, ''एक आदमी यदि जोर–जबरदस्ती किसी से कोई काम करा लेता है तो उससे वह 'न्यायी' नहीं माना जाता। ऐसा नही, जो 'धर्म' और 'अधर्म' की पहचान रखता है, जो बुद्धिमान है जो बुद्धिमान है और जो जोर–जबरदस्ती नहीं बल्कि धर्मानुसार दूसरों का मार्गदर्शन करता है ऐसे विज्ञ धर्मरक्षक को ही 'न्यायीट' कह सकते हैं।'' दुबारा संघर्ष होने से कैसे रोका जा सके इसी हेतु बुद्ध के वरिष्ठ शिष्यों और कौशाम्बी में हुए संघर्ष के प्रमुख नेताओं की बैठक मान्य मोद्गल्यायन के सुझाव के अनुसार, मान्य महाकाव्य की अध्यक्षता में हुई। इस समय बुद्ध ने जो सौहार्द्धपूर्वक रहने के जो छः नियम वेणुवन में प्रवास के दौरान बताए थे, उस पर चर्चा हुई और काफी विचार विमर्श के बाद वे सात सिद्धान्त निर्धारित किए गए कि यदि कहीं झगड़े के कारण किसी प्रकार के विवाद उठे तो इन सिद्धान्तों के अनुसार उनका निवारण किया जाए। उन्होंने इसका नाम 'सप्ताधिकरण' शमथ' रखा। उसे ही हम न्याय व्यवस्था के 'सप्त सिद्धान्त' कह सकते है।''

प्रथम सिद्धान्त था – ''समुख विनय'' अर्थात उपस्थिति/इसके अनुसार आरोपितों को संघ के सामने उपस्थित किया जाता था। आरोपन करने वाले भी वहाँ उपस्थित रहते थे। उसके बारे में अनुपस्थित गवाहों का बयान भी प्रस्तुत किया जाता था क्योंकि इससे उपस्थित गवाहों को इस बाबत् कोई आक्रोश नहीं होता। अतः उसे 'सम्मुख विनय' कहते थे।

दूसरा सिद्धान्त 'उदवाहिका' था। इससे विवाद का निपटारा करने हेतु एक कमिटी गठित की जाती थी। उसमें दस गुणों से युक्त व्यक्तियों का सदस्य के रूप में चयन किया जाता था। सदस्य में (1) सदाचार, (2) विद्वान, (3) स्त्री या पुरुष, (4) वादी या प्रतिवादी को मनवाने में समर्थ, (5) दृढ़ निश्चयी, (6) झगड़े के कारण को शांत करने में सक्षम, (7) विवाद को शांत करने में समर्थ, (8) विवाद का जानकार, (9) विवाद का शमन

करने में सक्षम और (10) विवाद को शमन की ओर ले जाने वाले तरीके का ज्ञाता ये गुण होने चाहिए।

हम देखते हैं कि वर्तमान न्याय प्रणाली प्रमाणों एवं गवाहों के आधार पर ही खड़ी है और यह व्यवस्था बुद्धकाल में भी विद्यमान थी।

तीसरा सिद्धान्त "अमूढ़ विनय" था। यह शास्तिका एक प्रकार है। इसके अन्तर्गत बेहोशी या मूढ़ता में किए गए दाशों की आरोपित से स्वीकृति मिलने के बाद उन्हें दोषमुक्त करने हेतु यह अनुशासन दिया जाता था।

चौथा सिद्धान्त 'प्रतिज्ञात–करण' अर्थात् स्वीकृति कहलाता था। यह भी दोषमुक्त व्यक्ति को दिया जाने वाला एक दण्ड का प्रकार था। इसे प्रतिदेराना या कबूल करना भी कहते थे। उसमें दोषी व्यक्ति को भविष्य में पहले की हुई गलती न दोहराने की हिदायत दी जाती थी।

पांचवाँ सिद्धान्त 'यद भूयसिक' अर्थात निर्णय की स्वीकृति था। इसमें तीन तरह के मत दिए जाते थे। गुप्त मत, मुक्त मत और न–गुप्त व न–मुक्त मत। तीसरे प्रकार का मत कानों में कहीं जाने वाली बातों जैसा होता था। यदि कोई विवाद 'उद्वाहिका' से शांत नहीं होता था तो उसे 'यदभूयसिका' से शांत करने के लिए संघ के सम्मुख प्रस्तुत किया जाता था। इस प्रकार इसमें धर्मवादी सदस्यों के बहुमतों से झगड़े का निपटारा किया जाता था।

छठवाँ सिद्धान्त "तत्पापीयसिक" अर्थात् शास्ती की प्रक्रिया कहलाता था। इसके अनुसार जानबूझकर झूठ बोलने वाले दोषी को अपना दोश कबूल करने का अवसर दिया जाता था। दोषी अपनी बड़ी गलती स्वीकार करने के लिए पर्याप्त अवसर प्रदान कर अपना बयान दे सकता था और तदानुसार ही उसे दण्डित किये जाने का प्रावधान था।

सांतवाँ सिद्धान्त "तिठावस्थारक" अर्थात् श्रृंग से आच्छादित करने जैसा अनुशासन का एक प्रकार था। इसमें में दोषी से अपनी गलती का एहसास करवा कर उसे निणवस्थारक प्रक्रिया के अनुसार शास्ति दी जाती थी।

इन सात प्रकार के अधिकरण शमथों के बारे में राहुल सांस्कृत्यायन ने अपनी 'बुद्धचर्या' (लखनऊ 1995: 4492–452) में लिखा है कि बुद्ध ने अपने शिष्यों को इस प्रकार संबोधित किया था।

''विवाद निपटाने के ये सात सिद्धान्त सही अर्थ में किसी को अन्याय से बचाते हुए न्यायदान करने के ही सप्त सिद्धान्त थे। भारतीय संविधान की न्याय प्रणाली पर इसी का प्रभाव दिखायी देता है। यह सप्त सिद्धान्त और हमारी न्याय प्रणाली का सूक्ष्म एवं तुलनात्मक अध्ययन अगर हम करेंगे तो कुछ समान बिन्दू हमें मिलते हैं। इससे हमें एहसास होता है कि बुद्ध तत्वज्ञान आज भी कितना प्रासंगिक एवं कालसंगत है।

''हमारे संविधान का उद्देश्य व्यक्तिगत न्याय के साथ–साथ जन सामान्य हेतु भी न्याय प्रदान कराना है और इसी परिप्रेक्ष्य में नीति निर्देशक सिद्धान्तों को संविधान में सम्मिलित किया गया है। संविधान के अनुच्छेद 38, 39, 44 एवं 46 में व्यक्तिगत न्याय एवं जनसामान्य को न्याय प्रदान करने के प्रावधान है।''

भगवान बुद्ध ने लोगों से कहा कि, ''यदि तुम अपने दुःख का अन्त करना चाहते हो, तो हर किसी को दूसरे के साथ न्याय संगत, धर्म संगत व्यवहार करना होगा। तभी यह पृथ्वी 'धर्म का राज्य' बन सकेगी।'' बुद्ध का न्याय संदेश विश्वमानव के कल्याण के लिए हैं।

बुद्ध तत्वज्ञान में स्वतंत्रता

भगवान बुद्ध विश्व के पहले ऐसे विचारक है जिन्होंने विचारों की स्वतंत्रता दे दी है। 'लोकतंत्र' का जो 'स्वतंत्रता' तत्व है जो संविधान की उद्देशिका में सम्मिलित है, उसकी आधारशिला 'कालामसुल' है। इस सुत्र में आई है किसी बात को केवल इसलिए मत मानों कि वह परम्परा से प्राप्त हुई है, किसी बात को केवल इसलिए मत मानो कि बहुत से लोग उसके समर्थक है, किसी बात को इसलिए मत मानो की वह धर्मग्रंथों में लिखी है, किसी बात को इसलिए मत मानो की वह तर्क (शास्त्र) के अनुसार है, किसी बात को इसलिए मत मानो कि वह न्याय (शास्त्र) के अनुसार है, किसी बात को इसलिए मत मानो कि वह ऊपरी तौर पर मान्य प्रतीत होती है, किसी बात को इसलिए मत मानो कि वह अनुकूल विश्वास, अनुकूल दृष्टि की है,

किसी बात को इसलिए मत मानो कि वह ऊपरी तौर पर सच्ची प्रतीत होती है, किसी बात को केवल इसलिए मत मानो वह किसी आदरणीय आचार्य की कही हुई है। ''केवल जब तुम आत्मानुभव से ही यह जानो कि ये बातें अहितकर हैं, ये बातें निन्दनीय हैं, ये बातें विज्ञ पुरुष द्वारा निशिक है, ये बातें करने से कष्ट होता है, दुःख होता है–हे कालामों तब तुम्हें उनका त्याग कर देना चाहिए।''

बुद्ध तत्वज्ञान में समता

भारतीय संविधान में सम्मिलित 'समता' के तत्व का मूलाधार बुद्ध तत्वज्ञान ही है। एक दिन गंगा तट पर भिक्षा मांगते समय बुद्ध ने एक व्यक्ति को मल–मूत्र ले जाते देखा। उसका नाम सुनीत था। समाज की निगाहों में वह अस्पृश्य था। बुद्ध और भिक्खू अपवित्र न हो जाए इसलिए वह डर रहा था। लेकिन करूणासागर बुद्ध उसके पास जाते है और कहते है, ''हमारे सद्धर्म में जाति–पाति का कोई भेद भाव नहीं है। तुम भी हमारे भांति मानव हो। हमें अपवित्र होने का भय नहीं है।'' आगे वे कहते हैं, ''जिस प्रकार गंगा, यमुना, अचिरावती, माही और रोहिणी नदियाँ समुद्र में मिल जाने पर अपना पृथक अस्तित्व छोड़ देती हैं, ऐसे ही जो व्यक्ति गृह त्यागकर संद्धर्म का मार्ग अपना लेता है उसकी जन्म–जाति छूट जाती है, भले ही वह ब्राह्मण, क्षत्रिय, वैश्य, शूद्र अथवा अस्पृश्य जाति में क्यों न जन्मा हो।''

भगवान बुद्ध ने शुद्र, अतिशूद्र एवं नारी वर्ग को अपने धम्म में समान स्थान दिया। यह वर्णव्यवस्था के असमानता के सिद्धान्तों पर बड़ी और कड़ी चोट थी। संविधान के अनुच्छेद 94 में अस्पृश्यता को हटाया गया है। ''संविधान के अनुच्छेद 14, 15, 16, 17 तथा 51(क) (झ) में भारत के हर नागरिक को समानता के अधिकार दिये गये है जिनके अनुसार किसी भी रूप में किसी भी प्रकार की असमानता संविधान विरोधी घोषित की गयी है।''

बुद्ध तत्वज्ञान में बंधुता

संविधान की उद्देशिका में बंधुता को सम्मिलित किया गया है, जो लोकतंत्र का बहुत ही महत्वपूर्ण शील है। भगवान बुद्ध ने सारनाथ में अपने प्रवचन में शील मार्ग की शिक्षा दी। शक्ति के पथ का पथिक होने के लिए उन्होंने दस सद्‌गुण बताये है, उसमें से एक है मैत्री। ''मैत्री'' का मतलब होता है

कि सभी प्राणियों के प्रति भ्रातृभावना हो, मित्रों के प्रति ही नहीं, शत्रुओं तक के प्रति, आदमियों के प्रति ही नहीं, सभी विश्वशेष प्राणियों के प्रति''।

बौद्ध तत्वज्ञान में भ्रातृभाव याने 'लोकतंत्र' का बंधुता भाव लबालब भरा हुआ है। अगर यह बुद्ध का मेत्ता भाव याने मैत्रीभाव का हम अनुसरण करे तो जातिभेद, धर्मभेद, भाषाभेद, पथ भेद, की दिवारे गिरने में देर नहीं लगेगी। बुद्ध ने दिया हुआ यह मेत्ता भाव हमें संविधान की उद्देशिका में दिखायी देता है। वर्ण व्यवस्था के कारण समाज में जो एक दूसरे के प्रति तिरस्कार का माहौल है वह भ्रातृभाव से ही दूर हो सकता है। ''संविधान के अनुच्छेद–51(क) (50) के अनुसार प्रत्येक नागरिक में भ्रातृत्व की भावना की अवधारणा होनी चाहिए जो एकता, भाई–चारे, अपनापन एवं गाढ़े प्रेम का प्रतिक है और विभिन्न भाषा, धर्म, सम्प्रदाय, विश्वासों, परम्पराओं आदि के होने पर भी विभिन्नता में एकत्व का सिद्धान्त आदर्श प्रस्तुत करती है। संविधान में भ्रातृत्व का यह सिद्धान्त मानवतावादी है।''

भारतीय संविधान ने भारतीय नागरिकों को पेशे की स्वतंत्रता बहाल की है। लेकिन वर्णव्यवस्था के तहत दूसरों का पेशा करने की बंदी थी। बुद्ध ने इस पेशाबंदी पर कड़ा प्रहार किया। मज्झिम निकाय के एसुकारी सुत्र में बुद्ध ने कहा, ''यदि किसी सेवा (पेशे) के करने से आदमी की स्थिति अच्छी न होती हो, खराब होती हो तो वह सेवा (पेशा) नहीं करना चाहिए, यदि किसी सेवा (पेश) के करने से आदमी की स्थिति खराब होने की बजाए बेहतर होती हो वह सेवा (पेशा) की जानी चाहिए। इसी एक कसौटी पर क्षत्रियों, ब्राह्मणों, वैश्यों, शूद्रों – सभी की सेवा करनी चाहिए, हर व्यक्ति को ऐसी सेवा (पेशा) करने से इंकार करना चाहिए, जो उसकी स्थिति को अच्छा न बनाती हो।''

संविधानः प्रवर्तनीय और अप्रवर्तनीय

भारतीय संविधान की विशेषता यह है कि वह लिखित परिसंघ संविधान को लचीलापन प्रदान करता है। भावी शासन पर अंकुश लगाने हेतु कुछ महत्वपूर्ण मूलभूत अधिकार एवं संविधान का प्राण जिसमें है ऐसा भाग अपरिवर्तनीय रखा गया है।

ठीक यही भूमिका भगवान बुद्ध ने भिक्खू संघ के संविधान में इससे पहले ही ली है। बाबासाहेब कहते है, ''महापरिनिर्वाण सूत्र में आनंद को संबोधित कर उन्होंने बताया है कि उनका धम्म तर्कसंगत और अनुभव पर आधारित है। और उनके अनुयायियों को चाहिए कि वे इस शिक्षा को केवल इस कारण सही और स्वीकरणीय माने कि वह उन (बुद्ध) से प्राप्त हुई है। यह शिक्षा तर्कसंगत और अनुभव पर आधारित होने से यदि किसी समय और किसी विशेष स्थिति में वह लागू नहीं होती हो, तो वे (अनुयायी) चाहे तो उस में सुधार कर सकते हैं, या तो गैर लागू शिक्षा को त्याग भी सकते हैं।'' वे चाहते थे कि उनके धम्म पर भूतकाल के मुर्दा बोझ डाले न जाऐ। वे चाहते थे की उनका धम्म सदाबहार रहे। और सभी समय काम आएं। यही कारण था जरूरत पड़ने पर अपने अनुयायियों को उन्होंने अपनी शिक्षा में समयानुकूल काट–छाँट करने की स्वतंत्रता दे रखी है। ऐसा करने का साहस अन्य किसी धर्म संस्थापक ने नही दिखाया है। वे ऐसी स्वतंत्रता देने से डरते थे। कारण उन्हें इस बात का डर थ कि अनुयायियों को अपनी शिक्षा में सुधार करने की स्वतंत्रता देने सेकहीं वे उसका इस्तेमाल अपने बने–बनाये ढाँचे को गिराने में न करें। बुद्ध को ऐसा डर नहीं था। उनको अपनी शिक्षा की नींव पर पूरा भरोसा था। वे भलीभाँती जानते थे कि सबसे भयंकर मूर्तिभंजक भी उनके धम्म के आंतरिक हिस्से को नष्ट नही कर पाएगा।''

संविधान के प्रधान निर्माता डॉ. बाबासाहेब आम्बेडकर का यह विश्लेषण, चिंतन बहुत ही महत्वपूर्ण है। बुद्ध के इस विचार का प्रभाव बाबासाहेब आंबेडकर के व्यक्तित्व पर पड़ा होगा।'' इसी कारण उन्होंने भारतीय संविधान को लचीला बना दिया।

संदर्भ सूची

1. डॉ. आंबेडकर और पिछड़ा वर्ग – स्वरूप चन्द्र 'धम्मदर्पण' शताब्दी विशेशांक पृ–41 दिल्ली।
2. डॉ. आम्बेडकर और भारतीय संविधान पृ. – 109, 'धममदर्पण' वही पृ. 19.
3. शुद्रों की अस्मिता एवं बाबासाहेब अम्बेडकर भगवान सिंह रावत – 'धममदर्पण' वही पृ. 19.
4. बाबासाहेब की भविष्य वाणी – संकलनकार्त पंडित चन्द्रिका प्रसाद जिज्ञासु – बहुजन कल्याण प्रकाशन लखनऊ – पृ. 21.
5. बाबासाहेब की भविष्य वाणी, वही – पृ. 22.
6. राहुल सांकृत्यायन (अनु.) चुल्लवग्ग, विनय पिटक, महाबोधि सभा, सारनाथ 1935 पृ. 411.

7. भगवान बुद्ध और उनका धर्म डॉ. बाबासाहेब आंबेडकर – अनुवाद डॉ. भदन्त आनंद कौसल्यायन पृ. 289.
8. जहं जहं चरन परे गौतम के – तिक न्यात द्वन्द गव जू ग्गू म्त्दले का हिन्दी रुपांतर डॉ. रामचंद्र तिवारी पृ. 314.
9. जहं जहं चरन परे गौतम के, वही – पृ. 315.
10. जहं जहं चरन परे गौतम के, वही – पृ. 315.
11. जहं जहं चरन परे गौतम के, वही – पृ. 315, 316.
12. भारतीय संविधान बनाम रामचरित मानत के एम. संत, दालित हुडे प्रकाशन लखनऊ पृ. 249.
13. भगवान बुद्ध और उनका धर्म वही – 223.
14. कॉटर बौद्ध धम्म की लाईन पर बदलों की बार सांपला पृ. 65.
15. जहं जहं चरन परे गौतम के वही– पृ. 284.
16. भारतीय सविधान बनाम रामचरित मानव वही – पृ. 248.
17. भगवान बुद्ध और उनका धम्म – वही प्राण।
18. भारतीय संविधान बनाम वही – पृ. 249.
19. कॉटः बौद्धधम्म की लाईन पर बदलो वही – पृ. 43.

Chapter - 18

सामाजिक न्याय

सी. डी. नाईक'

प्रास्ताविक

नवंबर 26, 2017 भारत के एकमेव गरीमामय गणवेश ''संविधान'' की यादगार तिथि है। इस अवसर पर डॉ. बी. आर. अम्बेडकर ने स्वरचित राष्ट्रीय डॉक्यूमेंन्ट को तत्कालीन राष्ट्रपति डॉ. राजेन्द्र प्रसाद को संविधान सभा में सौंप दिया था, जिसे राष्ट्र ने स्वयं अंगीकार कर दो माह पश्चात् आत्मार्पित किया था।

भारत के आजादी के सात दशकों बाद भी इस घटना को याद करने में नागरिकों की चेतना तरोताजा होनी चाहिए। आज देश अंतराष्ट्रीय राजनीतिक दूरदृष्टि, सामाजिक भाईचारा, और आर्थिक स्वनिर्धारण की चुनौतियों से गुजर रहा है। इतने अंतराल के बाद पहले से प्राप्त सांस्कृतिक और वैचारिक विरासत को छोड़ने, बिछुड़ने और परिमार्जित करते–करते कुछ कष्ट तो होगा ही परंतु वह न्याय हित में जरुरी है।

समाजिक न्याय के प्रर्वतक डॉ. अम्बेडकर

सितंबर 1920 में डॉ. अम्बेडकरने अपने लंदन विश्वविद्यालय की पढाई फिर से आरंभ की। इसी वर्ष गांधीजी ने लोकमान्य तिलक की राजनीतिक धरोहर का चोला पहन लिया। डॉ. अम्बेडकर ने अगले ही वर्ष एम. एससी. की उपाधि प्राप्त की, जो डॉक्टरल शोध के लिये अनिवार्य शर्त थी। सन 1922 में उन्होंने बर्लिन में तीन माह उच्चतर शोधाध्ययन किया। उसी वर्ष ग्रेज इन के बार–एट–लॉ की उपाधि का ऐलान हुआ। उसके बाद उन्होंने

उस समय के सर्वश्रेष्ठ अर्थशास्त्र के विद्वान सर एडविन केनन के मार्गदर्शन में *रुपये की समस्या* पर एक बृहद् शोध प्रबंध लिखा, जिसे बाद में *रुपये की समस्या, उसकी उत्पत्ति और उसका उपचार* शीर्षक दिया गया, जिसे लंदन में पी. एस. किंग एण्ड सन्स द्वारा सन् 1923 में और पहले से तैयार उनकी पी. एच. डी. उपाधि का शोध प्रबंध *ब्रिटिश भारत में प्रांतीय वित* सन 1925 में प्रकाशित किया गया।

वर्ष 1924 में डॉ अम्बेडकर भारत लौट आये और वहां मुंबई उच्च न्यायालय में वकालत की। उन्होंने इंदौर के तत्कालीन महाराज मल्हार राव होलकर और अमेरिकन देवी के विवाह से उपजे विवाद में महाराजा के पक्ष में वकालत की और वहीं एक शिव मंदिर के पास की जमीन के मुकदमे में पैरवी की। इन दोनों मामले में उन्होंने संबंधित पक्षों को जीताकर राहत दिलाई थी। जून 1928 से मार्च 1929 तक वे मुंबई के शासकीय विधि महाविद्यालय के प्राध्यापक और बाद में प्राचार्य भी रहे।

न्यायाधिष्ठित संविधान

''1927 में लार्ड बर्कन हैड ने भारतीयों को चुनौती दी थी कि वे अपना संविधान बनाकर दिखायें। एक संविधान बनाया गया जिसे 'नेहरु–संविधान' कहा गया, चूंकि संविधान निर्माण समिति के अध्यक्ष पंडित मोतीलाल नेहरु थे इसलिये उसे यह नाम दिया गया किन्तु उस को भारतीयों ने नकारा समझ रद्दी की टोकरी में डाल दिया। 1930 में गोलमेज सम्मेलन द्वारा संविधान बनाने का यत्न किया गया किन्तु भारतीय लोग इस में विफल रहे। सप्रू कमेटी द्वारा संविधान बनाने का तीसरी बार यत्न किया गया मगर कोई सफलता न मिली। दिसंबर 1946 में गठित संविधान सभा में सर तेज बहादूर सप्रू, के. एम. मुंशी, ठाकुरदास भार्गव, सरदार पटेल आदि कितने ही वकील थे। उनमें से किसी को संविधान के निर्माण का काम नहीं सौंपा गया। यह काम डॉ. आंबेडकर ही के जिम्मे सौंपा गया। यह इसलिये कि वह संविधानिक–कानून में कुशल व निपुण थे और एक सच्चे देश प्रेमी थे।''[1]

न्यायप्रिय देशभक्ति

देशप्रेमी आंबेडकर कहते थे, ''यदि मैं श्री गांधी तथा श्री जिन्नाह से घृणा करता हूँ, मैं उन से घृणा नही करता। मैं उन्हें नापसंद करता हूँ, तो उसका

कारण यह है कि मैं भारत से अधिक प्रेम करता हूँ। मुझे आशा है कि मेरे देशवासी किसी न किसी दिन यह सीख लेंगे कि देश व्यक्ति से कही महान होता है। श्री गांधी या श्री जिन्नाह की पूजा और भारत की सेवा में आकाश–पाताल का अन्तर है और वह परस्पर विरोधी भी हो सकती है।''

डॉ. आंबेडकर ''कमीनगी को अत्याचार से बदतर'' मानते थे[2]। ''विश्व युद्ध संसार के क्षेत्रों यानी प्रदेशों के बंटवारे के लिए नही है बल्कि वे एक ऐसी क्रान्ति है जो इन्सान व इन्सान और राष्ट्र व राष्ट्र के मध्य मेल मिलाप का तकाज़ा करता है। ये क्रांति सहचारी जीवन को ध्वस्त कर सामाजिक पुनर्गठन के लिये है। मजदूरों को नाज़ीवाद पर विजय पाने हेतु लड़ना चाहिए क्योंकि ये जीत गया तो ऐसी नाज़ी व्यवस्था स्थापित हो जाएगी जिस से स्वतन्त्रता का दमन हो जाएगा, समता से इन्कार होगा और भातृत्वभाव को मिटा दिया जायेगा। नाजीवाद पर विजय के फल होंगेः आजादी और नई सामाजिक व्यवस्था। केवल स्वतंत्रता काफी नही है, स्वतंत्रता का उपयोग कल्याणकारी सरकार का गठन और न्यायप्रिय समाज के निर्माण में होना चाहिए। इसलिए कामगरों को 'क्विट इण्डिया के बजाय 'न्यू इण्डिया' पर ज्यादा बल देना चाहिए। हिंसा की शक्तियों के सामने घुटने टेक कर प्राप्त की गई शान्ति, अमन नही हुआ करती। ये तो एक घातक कृति होगी और अच्छे मानवीय जीवन को बनाए रखने के लिए जो कुछ भी उत्तम व अनिवार्य है, उसे वहशी व बर्बर शक्तियों के सामने कुर्बान कर देने जैसा होगा। जब हमला किया गया हो तो युद्ध करने से इन्कार कर युद्ध को समाप्त नही किया जा सकता। युद्ध की समाप्ति के लिए आपको जंग जीतना होगा और न्यायी अमन स्थापित करना होगा[3]।''

संविधान सभा द्वारा गठित 'अल्पसंख्यक कमिटी' को डॉ. भीमराव आंबेडकर ने बताया थाः कि ''प्रशासन किसी एक धर्मीयों के हाथों में नही होना चाहिए, न उस पर उनकी इजारादारी हो या ऊपर से नीचे तक उनका नियंत्रण हो या हर विभाग पर उनका प्रभुत्व हो! चाहे पुलिस हो, मैजिस्ट्रेसी हो या राजस्व सेवा विभाग हो। यदि प्रशासन में विशिश्ट धर्मियों का अन्य धर्मियों के प्रति समाज–विरोधी व शत्रुआना रुख होगा तो वह प्रशासन से बाहर के बर्ताव से कतई अलग न होगा। उससे एक ही मकसद सिद्ध होगा और वह होगा गैरधर्मीय के विरुद्ध पक्षपात व भेदभाव

करना। नतीजा यह होता है कि एक बहुसंख्यक आबादी और उसके प्रभुत्व वाला प्रशासन के बीच यदि कोई गैर स्थान पाता है तो एक तरफ उस पर वह आबादी जुल्म जबर ढाती है और प्रशासन उत्पीड़ितों की सहायता करने के बजाए अत्याचारी ही की सुरक्षा करता है[4]।"

संविधानिक न्याय

भारत के संविधान के प्राक्कथन में ही हम भारतीय लोग संकल्प करते हैं कि अपने देश को एक संप्रभुता सम्पन्न समाजवादी धर्मनिरपेक्ष प्रजातांत्रिक गणतंत्र बनाकर लोगों के लिए सामाजिक, आर्थिक और राजनीतिक न्याय सुनिश्चित करेंगे। प्राप्त भौतिक और आर्थिक विरासत को लोगों में न्यायिक ढंग से वितरित करेंगे। नागरिकों के निजी प्रयास को प्रोत्साहित कर स्वतंत्रता को व्यावहारिक बनायेंगे। सामाजिक सरंचना को सुदृढ़ और लचीली परंतु जबाबदेही बनाने में बंधुत्व का अंगीकार करेंगे और आवश्यक सुधारों से विद्यमान असमानता, हिंसक तथा बुरे प्रभावों और रुकावटों को जड़ से उखाड़ फेकेंगे। ये हम लोगों के कुछ संकल्प हैं, जिसे सदा स्मृति में रखने और आगे बढ़ने के लिए प्रत्येक नागरिक कटिबद्ध है।

न्याय के लिए आरक्षण

सदियों से समाज का एक वर्ग सामाजिक प्रतिष्ठा, दण्ड़विहीन अपराध, शासन में एक वर्ग केंद्रित सत्ता, शिक्षा में एकाधिकार आदि का भोक्ता रहा है। परंतु उसे बर्दाश्त करते हुये जिन जातियों ने अपना खून पसीना बहा दिया उनके प्रति शासक और शोषक वर्ग की हृदय–शून्यता अबतक अवाक रही है। जब से भारतीय संविधान ने जीवन में सबसे अधिक दलित और पीड़ित जनों के लिये आरक्षण की व्यवस्था बहाल की तब से ही आरक्षण के विरुद्ध आंदोलन ने विकराल रुप धारण कर लिया है। आरक्षण विरोधियों की दृष्टि आरक्षितों के प्रति समाज के एक ऋग्ण वर्ग को स्वस्थ बनाने की नही बल्कि उन्हें अधिक से अधिक वंचित रख कर बेमौत मारने की है ऐसा प्रतीत होता है।

जब बिहार के श्री कर्पुरी ठाकुर के नेतृत्व में जनता दल की सरकार ने मुंगेरीलाल आयोग की सिफारिशों के अनुसार शासकीय नौकरियों में अन्य पिछड़ा वर्ग 8 प्रतिशत, अति पिछड़ा वर्ग 12 प्रतिशत, अनुसूचित जाति

14 प्रतिशत, अनुसूचित जमाति 10 प्रतिशत, महिला 3 प्रतिशत, आर्थिक रुप से पिछड़ों के लिये 3 प्रतिशत आरक्षण की घोषणा की थी तो उसके 3 वर्ष के बाद गुजरात में वैद्यकीय छात्रों द्वारा अनुसूचित जाति–जमाति के छात्रों के पदव्युत्तर वैद्यकीय अभ्यासक्रम में प्रवेशार्थ प्राप्त आरक्षित सीटों के विरुद्ध हिंसक आंदोलन शुरु किया गया। जब 1989 में केंद्र में भूतपूर्व प्रधान मंत्री श्री विश्वनाथ प्रताप सिंग के नेतृत्व में राष्ट्रीय फ्रंट की सरकार ने मंडल आयोग के प्रतिवेदन की कुछ सिफारिशों को कार्यान्वित करने के लिये अधिसूचना निकाली और सामाजिक और आर्थिक रुप से पिछड़े हुये वर्गों {एस. ई. बी. सी.} के लिये सरकारी नौकरी में 27 प्रतिशत आरक्षित सीटों का ऐलान किया तो देश के अन्य भागों में नौकरियों में आरक्षित सीटों के विरुद्ध तर्क दिया गया कि इस आरक्षण के कारण सभी दलितों को फटाफट नौकरियां मिल जाती हैं और उस से अन्य जातियों में बेरोजगारी पैदा होती है। वैद्यकीय और अभियांत्रिकी शाखाओं में शैक्षणिक आरक्षण के तहत दलितों को कम गुणों पर ही प्रवेश मिलता है और उन्हें कम गुणों से ही पास किया जाता है और उस से अधिक गुणवाले और मैरिट के छात्रों की उपेक्षा होती है और उस से समाज में और व्यावसायिक गुणवत्ता में कोताई आ जाती है। उसी प्रकार राजनीतिक आरक्षण के कारण आरक्षित निर्वाचन क्षेत्र के सवर्ण मतदाताओं को अपने समाज का प्रतिनिधि लड़ाने का अवसर नही मिलता, आरक्षित उम्मीदवार लाद दिया जाता है और निर्वाचन क्षेत्र का विकास रुक जाता है। ऐसा आरक्षण विरोधी आंदोलन हिंदी भाषाई राज्यों में हुआ।

''एक चीनी दर्जी के माफिक, जिसने अपने एक ग्राहक का नया कोट सिलाते वक्त उसके एक पुराने कोट का उपयोग पुराने पैबंद नये कोट पर ज्यो के त्यों उतार देने में किया था'', भारत के नये नये शासकों ने अपने अपने शासन का उपयोग सदियों से विद्यमान जाति–पांति के पुराने पैबंद नये सामाजिक ढांचे में ज्यों के त्यों बरकरार रखने में किया हैं। श्री तिलक ने कहा ही था कि 1895 में अंग्रेजों द्वारा एक अस्पृश्य श्री नारायणराव लोखण्डे को बहाल की गई ''रावबहादुर'' की उपाधि दया थी और एक चितपावन ब्राह्मण श्री विश्वनाथ केशव जोगळेकर को बहाल की गई ''रावबहादुर'' की उपाधि उचित थी''[5]। अतः 1882 से 1904 के दरम्यान भारतीय सिविल सेवा में यशस्वी हुये 16 भारतीयों में 15 ब्राह्मणों का होना

कोई आश्चर्य जनक नही था। ज्योतिराव फुले ने 19 अक्तूबर 1882 को हंटर शिक्षा आयोग के समक्ष सादर प्रस्तुत किया था कि ''उच्च शिक्षा पद्धति में स्पष्ट झलकने वाली प्रवृत्ति यह है कि उस में वरिष्ठ अधिकारी के पद केवल ब्राह्मणों की बपौति हो चुके हैं। यदि शासन को रैयत के कल्याण की वास्तविक चिंता है तो उस का प्रथम कर्तव्य है कि वह इस पद्धति के कई प्रकार के दुरुपयोग को प्रतिबंधित कर, शासकीय नौकरियों में धीरे धीरे अन्य जातियों के लोगों को प्रवेश के अवसर दिला कर उसी अनुपात में ब्राह्मणशाही का नियमन करें''। वे कनिष्ठ जातियों के बच्चों की शिक्षा हेतु स्वतन्त्र विद्यालय की व्यवस्था करें।

इसीलिए श्री भालेकर ने पूना अधिवेशन में सवर्ण बहुल कांग्रेस के रुख के विरुद्ध निदर्शन किया, श्री वलंगकर ने श्री रानडे की मदद से सेना में महारों की भर्ती को प्रतिबंधित करने के आदेश के विरुद्ध ब्रिटिश सरकार से अपील की, श्री कांबले ने सेना और पुलिस में अस्पृश्यों की भर्ती हेतु मांग रखी, श्री बन्सोडे, श्री गवई और श्री नंदागवली ने दलित जागरण का अभियान चलाया, उसी प्रकार श्री शिंदे की भारतीय निराश्रित सहायक मंडल {डिप्रेस्ड क्लासेस मिशन सोसायटी ऑफ इण्डिया} के तत्वावधान में अस्पृश्यों के हितों के प्रति संवेदनशीलता को बढ़ाया गया।

कोल्हापूर के साहू महाराज ने भी जब देखा कि शासकीय नौकरियों में उच्च पदों पर ब्राह्मणों का प्रतिनिधित्व अतिरेकी है तो उन्होंने अपने रियासत में 26 जुलाई 1902 से अपने संस्थान के प्रशासनिक सेवाओं में पिछड़ी जातियों को 50 प्रतिशत आरक्षण बहाल किया। इस से लगभग 17 वर्ष पूर्व राष्ट्रीय कांग्रेस की स्थापना हो चुकी थी और उसके 13 वर्ष और 23 वर्ष बाद फुले व रानडे के सामाजिक आंदोलन के विरुद्ध हिंदू महासभा {1915} और राष्ट्रीय स्वयंसेवक संघ {1925} नामक ब्राह्मणवादी संगठनों की स्थापना हुई।

न्याय और अर्थव्यवस्था

ईस्ट इड़िया कंपनी का प्रशासन और वित्त (1913) ग्रंथ में आर्थिक इतिहास बताया गया कि ईस्ट इंडिया कंपनी ने अपने 66 वर्षों के राज में प्रशासन और वित्त व्यवस्थापन किस प्रकार किया। उसे सन् 1814 में ब्रिटीश

सरकार ने प्रशासन और वित्त व्यवस्थापन में पृथकता बरतने का आदेश दिया था और 24 वर्ष बाद शासन ने उसका व्यापार में विद्यमान एकाधिकार भी बंद करवाया। 1858 में कंपनी को बर्खास्त कर ब्रिटीश सरकार ने स्वयं शासन और व्यापार का संचालन भारत में करना आरंभ कर दिया। ब्रिटीश सरकार के कार्यों का मूल्यांकन करते हुये डॉ. आंबेडकर ने लिखा था कि ''भारत ने इंग्लैंड़ के लिये आर्थिक रुप से जो प्रचंड योगदान किया वह जितना आश्चर्य चकित करनेवाला है, उतना इंग्लैंड ने भारत के लिये जो नगण्य आर्थिक योगदान किया वह विस्मयकारक है'' ब्रिटीश सरकार के कानून और शिक्षा द्वारा प्रस्थापित पाशविक शांति का आर्थिक रुप से यतीम किये गये भारतीयों के लिये कोई उपयोग नही था। यह मरघट और पाशविक शांति आर्थिक गुलामी थी। डॉ. अम्बेडकर को सामाजिक शांति की तलाश थी।

ब्रिटिश भारत में प्रांतीय वित्त का विकास (1915) तथा ब्रिटीश भारत में साम्राज्यीय वित्त का प्रांतीय विकेंद्रीकरण (1917) ग्रंथों में उन्होंने कहा था कि केंद्रीय, प्रांतीय और स्थानीय शासकों में 1833 से 1921 की कालावधि में आर्थिक संबंध का विकास क्रम–क्रम से होता गया। 1871 तक वित्त व्यवस्था केद्रीभूत रही। उसके बाद केंद्र और राज्य का स्वतंत्र बजट बनाने की पद्धति आरंभ हुई। 1872 से 1877 में कुछ विशिष्ट केंद्रीय सरकार के विभागों के प्रशासन का भार राज्य सरकार को सौंपा गया। 1878 से 1882 के दरम्यान राजस्व पर आधारित बजट प्रस्तुत करने की पद्धति अपनाई गई। राजस्व के हिस्से के वितरण पर आधारित संतुलनात्मक पद्धति सब से बेहतर सिद्ध हुई। अतः वह 1883 से 1921 तक प्रचलित रही। हालांकि इसी बीच 1919 के कानून सुधार द्वारा जबाबदार सरकार निर्माण करने के ध्येय से स्वयंशासित संस्थाओं को सुरक्षित रखने का सिद्धान्त मान्य हुआ था। इस ग्रंथ का मूल्यांकन करते हुये डॉ. आंबेडकर के मार्गदर्शक प्रो. सेलिग्मन ने कहा था, '' मेरी जानकारी में अब तक कहीं भी भारतीय केंद्र सरकार और घटक राज्य के बीच आर्थिक संबंध की इतनी विस्तृत और गहरी मीमांसा नहीं की गई''।

रुपये की समस्या, उत्पत्ति तथा विकास (1923) में भारतीय रुपया चलन में 1800 से 1893 तक किस प्रकार परिमाण और मूल्य का कार्य

संपादन करता रहा इसका इतिहास है। पहले भारत में सुवर्ण तथा चांदी का परिमाण के रुप में प्रचलन रहा। 1833 में ब्रिटीश सरकार ने संपूर्ण भारत में अपना आधिपत्य जमाया।1842 तक भारत के निर्यात पर 50 से 500 प्रतिशत कर लादा जाता था। जब इस कर को घटाया गया तब भारत का निर्यात फिर से बढ गया। लेकिन 1853 के कानून द्वारा स्वर्ण का प्रचलन बंद कर दिया गया। और एकमात्र चांदी का रुपया प्रचलन में चलने दिया गया। 1864 में भारतीय निर्यात में वृद्धि होने के कारण चांदी के रुपये चलन में अपर्याप्त होने लगे। तब चांदी के रुपयों के पूरक के रुप में कागज के रुपयों को प्रचलित किया गया। 1873 तक भारतीय रुपया और ब्रिटिश पौंड के बीच विनिमय की दर 1 रुपया बराबर 1 शिलिंग, 10 / .5 पेन्स के स्तर पर स्थिर था। यानी चांदी का 15 / .5 औंस का रुपया सोने के 1 औंस सिक्के के बराबर था। परंतु बाद के समय में सोना और चांदी के दरम्यान यह दर स्थिर रखना कठिन हो गया। 70 वर्ष के पश्चात् आज भी इस ग्रंथ की प्रासंगिकता हैं। 1926 में रिजर्व बैंक के स्थापनार्थ जो हिल्टन यंग कमिशन नियुक्त हुआ था उसके सामने अपनी साक्ष्य देते हुये डॉ. आंबेडकर ने कहा था, ''चलन निर्माण करनेवाली संस्था की चलन निर्माण क्षमता पर परिणाम कारक प्रतिबंध होना आवश्यक है। अनिर्बंध चलन पूर्ति और बेहिसाब मूल्य वृद्धि के कारण आर्थिक स्थिरता खतरे में आ सकती है''[6]।

बौद्ध धर्म तथा मार्क्सवाद नामक शोध आलेख में डॉ. आंबेडकर ने सामाजिक और धार्मिक शोषण भी आर्थिक शोषण के समान ही घातक होता है के अभिमत को प्रतिपादित किया है। *गांधी और कांग्रेस ने अछूतों के लिये क्या किया* इस ग्रंथ में डॉ. आंबेडकर ने कहा कि ''अस्पृश्यता केवल धार्मिक रचना न होकर वह गुलामगिरी से भी भयानक आर्थिक रचना है। उसी प्रकार *जातिभेद निर्मूलन* में उन्होंने बताया कि जातिभेद में बताई गई व्यवस्था श्रम विभाजन की नही बल्कि श्रमिकों के विभाजन की व्यवस्था है[7]।

छोटी जोतों की चकबंदी करने हेतु डॉ. आंबेडकर ने फ्रांस और इटली में विद्यमान सामूहिक खेती पद्धति और राष्ट्रीयकरण की प्रक्रिया को अनुकरणीय बताया था। उत्पादन साधनों को सामूहिक स्वामित्व में करने के बाद भी जब तक समाज में जातिभेद की निम्न श्रेणियां और अस्पृश्यता

हैं तब तक सामूहिक स्वामित्व अर्थशून्य रहेगा। छोटे किसानों को छोटी जोतों से वंचित कर भूमिहीन मजदूर बनने से मुक्ति दिलाने हेतु उन्होंने सामूहिक कृषि यानी एक से अधिक छोटे किसान मिल कर निश्चित आकार का खेत बनाये रखने और इस प्रकार सामूहिक कृषि कायम करने की अनुसंशा की।

अर्थशास्त्र के सुप्रसिद्ध विद्वान रॅगनर नर्क्स के प्रछन्न बेरोजगारी और डॉ. आंबेडकर के अतिरिक्त श्रमिक की संकल्पना में अत्यधिक समानता है।

आर्थिक जोत से उनका अभिप्राय ऐसे उत्पादक खेत से था जिसकी निवेशित व्यय की पूर्ति हो जाने के बाद शेष उत्पादन की राशी पर एक परिवार अपना खर्च चला सके[14]।

परंतु भारत में औसतन बोने योग्य जोत का आकार 1.67 हेक्टर, सीमांत जोत का प्रतिशत 56.00, जोत के औसतन टुकडे 4.04 हेक्टर और प्रत्येक टुकडे का औसत आकार 0.41 हेक्टर होने पर भी प्रत्येक राज्य में हर दशक में जोत का औसतन आकार घटता रहा, जो वर्ष 1961 में 2.6 हेक्टर, 1971 में 2.20 हेक्टर और 1981 में 1.67 हेक्टर तक कम होता गया। तथापि सन 1950 से भूसुधार कानून को भारत के हर राज्य मे लागू करना आर्थिक क्षेत्र में एक बहुत बड़ा परिवर्तन था।

उनका शासकीय समाजवाद सहकारी कृषि, औद्योगिकरण तथा सामुदायिक कृषि से संलग्न रहा। आर्थिक समानता के विना राजनीतिक स्वाधीनता को अर्थ नही था। इसलिये डॉ. आंबेडकर ने संवैधानिक स्टेट सोशलिज्म के एक अंग के रुप में सामुदायिक कृषि की अनुसंशा की, उन्होंने विखंडित और छोटी जोतों के लिये उपाय के रुप में सहकारी कृषि की सिफारिश की, और उन्होंने भारतीय कृषि सुधार के लिये अर्थात कृषि पर पड़े अतिरिक्त मनुष्य बल के भार को गैर कृषि क्षेत्र में स्थानांतरित करने हेतु औद्योगिकरण का उपाय बताया।

सन् 1946 में *राज्य और अल्पसंख्यंक* नामक ग्रंथ में उन्होंने कृषि जमीन को बीमा और मूलभूत उद्योगों की तरह शासन के स्वामित्व में रखने की बात कही। उन्होंने निजी मालिकों की हुकुमशाही से समाज और शासन पर पड़नेवाले कुप्रभाव का भी जिक्र किया। उन्होंने शासन के हस्तक्षेप से

मुक्ति को स्वतन्त्रता नही माना। बल्कि वे शासन द्वारा सामाजिक और आर्थिक मामलों में न्याय के हित में हस्तक्षेप चाहते थे। उनका मानना था कि यदि शासन ने सामाजिक व आर्थिक क्रियाकलापों का नियमन नही किया तो वह निजी मालिकों को करना पड़ेगा और ऐसा करते समय वे अपनी आजादी का उपयोग दूसरों पर अधिसत्ता स्थापित करने के लिये भी करेंगे। उस परिस्थिति में जमीनदार भी कुलों पर जबरदस्त जमीन भाड़ा थोपेंगे और पूंजीपति भी कामगारों के काम करने के घंटे बढायेंगे और उनके वेतन कम करेंगे। अर्थात् इस से राजनीतिक प्रजातन्त्र के मूलभूत सिद्धान्त यानी स्वयंभू व्यक्ति, अविछिन्न मूलभूत अधिकार, संवैधानिक अधिकार का बिन शर्त लाभ, और शासन संस्था द्वारा दूसरों पर लादने योग्य सत्ता का निजी व्यक्ति के हाथों में अहस्तांतरण को ही क्षति पहुंचेगी। अतः खोतों का अन्त करना उस समय के भूमि सुधार की मांग थी, जिसे बाबासाहेब ने पूरी करने की चेष्टा की थी[8]।

डॉ. आंबेडकर का समाजवाद व्यक्ति के निम्न भौतिक अधिकारों पर आधारित है:

1. व्यक्ति उद्‌देश्य है।
2. व्यक्ति के कुछ अधिकार अहस्तांतरणीय है। इस की गारंटी संविधान को देनी चाहिये।
3. किसी भी व्यक्ति को अपनी सुख सुविधा का उपयोग करते हुये अपने संवैधानिक अधिकार की तिलांजली देने का अवसर नहीं आना चाहिये। और
4. शासन ने किसी भी निजी व्यक्ति को अन्य व्यक्तियों पर आधिपत्य करने का अधिकार नही देना चाहिये।

इस समाजवाद में सामाजिक संघर्ष के कारकों में धन की तरह धर्म पर भी बल दिया गया है। इस बात में डॉ. आंबेडकर का समाजवादी सिद्धान्त औरों से विशेष और अनोखा है।

1917 में रशिया में राज्यक्रांति हुई और उसके 8 वर्ष के बाद भारत में भारतीय कम्युनिस्ट पार्टी की स्थापना की गई। 1926 में स्थापित ''लाहौर नौजवान सभा'' और 1928 में प्रस्थापित ''नौजवान भारत सभा'' जैसे

स्वतन्त्र संगठनों के माध्यम से कम्युनिस्ट विचारों का अमल भी किया जा रहा था। तत्कालीन कम्युनिस्ट विचारों के नेता कॉमरेड एम. एन. राय थे। 1934 में आचार्य नरेन्द्र देव और जयप्रकाश नारायण प्रभृति मार्क्सवादी; श्री अशोक मेहता जैसे फेबियन समाजवादी; डॉ. राममनोहर लोहिया जैसे गांधीवादी; युसुफ मेहेर अली और संपूर्णानन्द जैसे राष्ट्रवादी और मिनू मसानी जैसे ट्राट्स्कीवादीयों ने अपनी वैचारिक भिन्नता को कायम रख कर समाजवादी आंदोलन को वैश्विक, आर्थिक और राजनीतिक संदर्भ में चलाया था।

कॉ. श्रीपाद अमृत डांगे, बी. टी. रणदिवे, नंबुद्रिपाद, कॉ. श्रीनिवास, कॉ. सरदेसाई प्रभृति विद्वानों के नेतृत्व में अंतर्राष्ट्रीय कम्युनिस्ट आंदोलन ने 1943 तक भारतीय कम्युनिस्ट पार्टी का पथ प्रदर्शन किया।

जनता नामक पाक्षिक में दिनांक 7 नवंबर 1938 को प्रकाशित अपने एक साक्षात्कार में डॉ. आंबेडकर ने कहा था कि ''भारतीय समाजवादी यूरोप के समाजवादियों के कदमों पर कदम रखकर भारतीय परिस्थिति पर भी आर्थिक सिद्धान्त लागू करने की चेष्टा करते है। धर्म भी एक बहुत बडी प्रेरक शक्ति है, इसके प्रति समाजवादियों की उपेक्षा दृष्टि रही है।

डॉ. आंबेडकर को प्रजातन्त्र में दो बातें अभिप्रेत थी। पहली बात मानवीय वृत्ती की है। यह वृत्ती समाज के अन्य सदस्यों के प्रति समानता और आदर से देखने की होनी चाहिये। दूसरी बात यह है कि समाज की सरंचना में सख्त बंधन नही होने चाहिये। अन्यथा प्रजातन्त्र अधूरा रहेगा। अलगाववाद और एकाकीपन प्रजातन्त्र व्यवस्था के विसंगत गुण है। क्योंकि उनकी परिणति विशेशाधिकार संपन्न अल्प और अधिकार विपन्न बहुसंख्य वर्गों में होती है। यही उनके राजनीतिक समाजशास्त्र का प्राण है।

न्याय के लिए राजनीति

प्रथम महायुद्ध के बाद ब्रिटेन की संसद ने हिन्दुस्तान को जिम्मेदार शासन प्रदान करने हेतु मॉटेग्यू नीति को लागू कराने की घोषणा की थी और कांग्रेस ने अपने कलकत्ता के अधिवेशन में अस्पृश्यता को मिटाने की घोषणा की थी।

मॉटेग्यू योजना का मकसद भारत में प्रजातन्त्र राज पद्धति को बहाल कर ब्रिटिश सत्ता को शिक्षित उच्च जातियों के हाथों में हस्तांतरित करना था। इस योजना का विरोध कोल्हापूर के शाहू महाराज (1910), पूना के सत्यशोधक समाज, मद्रास के साउथ इंडियन लिबरल फेडरेशन और जस्टीस पार्टी तथा महाराष्ट्र के डेक्कन रयत समाज ने दर्शाया था।

श्री तिलक के बाद कांग्रेस का नेतृत्व गांधी जी ने सम्भाला। फरवरी 1922 में बारडोली में कांग्रेस वर्किंग कमिटी ने दलित वर्ग की शैक्षणिक दशा को सुधारने का नया कार्यक्रम अमल में लाने का निर्णय लिया। उधर डॉ. आंबेडकर ने मुंबई में मूकनायक नामक पाक्षिक पत्रिका चलाई और नागपूर में अखिल भारतीय बहिष्कृत समाज की स्थापना की। मुंबई में सिडेनहेम शासकीय महाविद्यालय में प्रोफेसर होते हुये भी डॉ. आंबेडकर ने दिनांक 27 जनवरी 1919 के दिन साउथबरो कमिटी के समक्ष दलितों के लिये पृथक निर्वाचन अधिकार की मांग के पक्ष में अपनी साक्ष्य दी थी। सन 1928 में उन्होंने उक्त मांग को संयुक्त निर्वाचन और आरक्षण अधिकार के रुप में सायमन कमिशन के सम्मुख प्रस्तुत किया था।

1928 से 1930 तक उन्होंने महाड और नासिक के सार्वजनिक तालाब और मंदिर पर पानी और पूजा के संबंध में समानता का अधिकार स्थापित करने हेतु अपने नेतृत्व में सफल आंदोलन चलाया था।

परंतु 1930–32 के दौरान चले बर्तानिया के गोलमेज परिषद ने भारतीय राजनीति की दिशा ही मोड दी। इस गोलमेज परिशद के अधिवेशन में जब गांधी जी मुसलमान, क्रिश्चन, सिख, ईसाई, पारसी, ॲग्लो–इंडियन आदि के स्वतंत्र राजनीतिक अस्तित्व को मान्य कर रहे थे तब वे अस्पृश्य के ऐसे स्वतंत्र राजनीतिक अस्तित्व को मानने से इंकार क्यों कर रहे थे यह समझ में नही आ रहा था। आखिर गांधीजी भी श्री तिलक के नक्शे–कदम पर ही चल रहे थे।

ब्रिटेन के प्रधान मंत्री श्री मेक्डोनल्ड द्वारा दलितों को बहाल किया गया स्वतन्त्र निर्वाचन अधिकार निरस्त करने हेतु सन 1932 में गांधी जी ने पूना के येरवडा कारागृह में आमरण अनशन आरंभ किया था।

सन 1935 में नासिक के येवला में डॉ. आंबेडकर ने घोषणा की थी कि वे हिंदु धर्म में पैदा हुये लेकिन वे हिंदू के रुप में नहीं मरेंगे।

सन 1936 में डॉ. आंबेडकर का ''जातिभेद निर्मुलन'' नामक भाषण उस के आयोजकों को इतना क्रांतिकारी लगा कि लाहौर के ''जात–पांत–तोडक–मंडल ने डॉ. आंबेडकर की अध्यक्षता में होने वाली उस सभा को ही भंग कर दिया। आखिर उस भाषण को समाज हित में एक लघु ग्रंथ की शक्ल में प्रकाशित करने के पश्चात् ही लोगों तक पहुंचाया गया। उस पर गांधी जी की टिप्पणी यह थी कि ''हिंदू धर्म के प्रति अपनी नफरत दर्शानेवालों में अकेले आंबेडकर ही नही है, बल्कि उन लोगों में वह सब से अधिक दृढ और योग्यतम व्यक्ति है''।

द्वितीय महायुद्ध की पृष्ठभूमि में भारतीय राजनीति के घटनाक्रमों में प्रचंड उलट–पुलट हो रही थी। उनमें भारत छोडो आंदोलन, क्रिप्स–व्हेवल योजना, केबिनेट मिशन इत्यादि के साथ साथ धर्म और जातियों का उभार अधिक स्फोटक रहा कहना अतिशयोक्ति नही होगा। इसी बदलाव के कारण डॉ. आंबेडकर ने 1936 में एक व्यापक नींव पर स्थापित स्वतन्त्र मजदूर दल नामक राजनीतिक पक्ष के स्थान पर चार वर्ष के बाद मात्र अनुसूचित जातियों पर केंद्रित शिडयुल्ड कास्ट फेडरेशन नामक पार्टी की स्थापना की। उन्होंने मनमाड की दलित वर्गीय रेल्वे मजदूर परिषद को उदबोधन दिया था कि वे मनुष्यत्व को गिरानेवाले पूंजीवाद से सावधान रहें।

1942 में नागपुर के दलित जाति परिषद के सम्मेलन में दलितों के अधिकारों को भारत के भावी संविधान में अंतर्भूत करने का निर्णय सर्व सम्मति से पारित किया गया।

1945 में पीपल्स एज्युकेशन सोसायटी के तत्वावधान में मुंबई और औरंगाबाद में उच्च शिक्षा के प्रचार और प्रसार हेतु बुद्ध और मिलिंद नामक दो बौद्ध ऐतिहासिक महापुरुषों के नाम पर दो महाविद्यालय शुरु किये गये। डॉ. आंबेडकर ने भिन्न भिन्न जाति और धर्मों को अविभाजित भारत की राजनीति में युक्त प्रतिनिधित्व प्रदान करने हेतु *''जातीय गुत्थी और उसे सुलझाने का उपाय'* नामक योजना एक लिखित पुस्तक की शक्ल में प्रस्तुत की थी। परंतु विभाजित भारत की बदलती परिस्थिति को देखते हुये उन्होंने *''राज्य और अल्पसंख्यक''* नामक योजना को भी एक पुस्तिका के रुप में ही देशवासियों के विचारार्थ रखा।

श्रम मंत्री के पद पर 5 वर्ष तक उन्होंने महा–राज्यपाल की कार्यकारिणी में श्रमिक कल्याण और प्लानिंग का कार्यभार संभाला था। 1947 से उन्होंने श्री नेहरु की केबिनेट में कानून मंत्री का भार वहन कर संविधान का मसौदा तैयार करने और और राष्ट्रीय जीवन में स्वाधीनता के संविधान को मूर्त बनाने के लिये स्वयं को खपाया। 26 जनवरी 1950 के अपने संबोधन में उन्होंने भारतीय राजनीतिक जीवन और सामाजिक–आर्थिक लोक चर्या में विद्यमान विसंगति की तरफ इशारा करते हुये उसे मिटाने का देशवासियों को आवाहन किया।

इस विसंगति को मिटाने का एक उपाय आरक्षण पद्धति भी है। परंतु जब तक भारत में मनुष्य और मनुष्य के बीच के संबंध जातिव्यवस्था से निश्चित करने वाली ब्राह्मणी परंपरा चालू रहेगी तब तक सामाजिक, सांस्कृतिक और आर्थिक जीवन में पिछडे हुये वर्गों के लिये "समान अवसर के लिये विशेष अवसर' के सिद्धान्त पर निर्भर आरक्षण की सीटें रखना ही पडेगी क्योंकि समान मनुष्यों में ही समानता हो सकती है। और असमान लोगों को समान मानना यानी असमानता को कायम रखना है।

पूंजीवाद और ब्राह्मणवाद की ताकतों और उभरती साम्यवादी शक्तियों के बीच का निरंतर सत्ता संघर्ष विश्व के देशों को दो प्रतिस्पर्धी वर्गों में विभक्त कर रहा है।

जो राष्ट्र अभी तक प्रजातन्त्र शासन के अधीन स्थापित नही हुए वे उक्त दोनों शक्तियों में से किसी भी एक में शामिल हो सकते है। नेपाल में अब तक लोकतन्त्र शासन की स्थापना नही हो सकी है तो उस दशा में ब्रिटेन व अमेरिका उसका उपयोग पूंजीवादी बनाने, भारत उसका उपयोग ब्राहमणवादी बनाने तथा कम्युनिस्ट चीन उसका उपयोग साम्यवादी बनाने में सुगमता के साथ कर सकते है[17]। क्योंकि इतिहास गवाह है कि जब राजा स्रोंङ–त्सान–गैम्पो के नेतृत्व में तिब्बत शक्तिशाली था तो उसके साथ सांस्कृतिक संबंध नेपाल, चीन और भारत ने अपने सम्राट अंशुवर्मा, हर्षवर्धन और ताओ–त्सुंग के जरिए मधुर बनाये रखे थे[9]।

सेवायें और संघर्ष

सन 1924 में स्थापित *बहिष्कृत हितकारणी सभा* द्वारा उन्होंने सोलापूर में

दलित वर्ग छात्रावास खोला। आम लोगों की तरह अछूतों के अधिकार को भी कुओं, तालाबों आदि पर प्रस्थापित करने के लिए उन्होंने सन् 1927 में महाड सत्याग्रह चलाया और 25 दिसंबर 1927 के दिन मनुस्मृति का सामूहिक दहन किया। सन 3 अप्रैल 1927 से उन्होंने *बहिष्कृत भारत* नामक मराठी पाक्षिक चलाया। उन्होंने मुंबई विधान मंडल में सन 1927 से सन 1937 तक कुल 10 वर्ष के कार्यकाल में एक सक्रिय सदस्य की भूमिका में उन्होंने गरीबों पर लादे जाने वाले बजट के संबंध में प्रशासन की लापरवाही पर कठोर प्रहार किया। वहां उन्होंने मुंबई पैतृक व्यवसाय अधिनियम 1874 के संशोधन का विधेयक प्रस्तुत किया। उन्होंने एक सदस्य की हैसियत से 29 मई और अक्टूबर 1928 को सायमन कमिशन के समक्ष अपना एक अलग वक्तव्य दिया था कि भारत के संवैधानिक प्रजातंत्र में दलित वर्गों का दृष्टिकोण ध्यान में रखा जाना चाहिये। उन्होंने सन 1927 के सितंबर में समाज समता संघ और दिसंबर को समता सैनिक दल स्थापित किया। उसी वर्ष उन्होंने दलित वर्ग शिक्षा समाज की स्थापना की और उसके माध्यम से उच्च विद्यालय के दलित छात्रों के लिये पनवेल, ठाने, नासिक, पुणे और धारवाड़ में छात्रावास खोले।

उन्होंने वक्तव्य दिया था कि प्रशासन का आधार सार्वत्रिक वयस्क मताधिकार होना चाहिये। सन 1930 में उन्होंने नासिक में कालाराम मंदिर प्रवेश सत्याग्रह किया। उसी वर्ष नागपुर में आयोजित अखिल भारतीय दलित वर्ग कांग्रेस की अध्यक्षता की। उन्होंने 17 नवंबर 1932 से 24 दिसंबर 1932 तक के दौरान आयोजित गोलमेज परषिद में हिस्सा लिया था। उन्होंने ब्रिटीश प्रशासन के प्रतिकूल रवैय के साथ साथ, भारतीय उच्च जातियों का रुढिवाद तथा गांधी और कांग्रेस की सनातनी नीतियों पर भी आलोचना की। दूसरी गोलमेज परिषद में उन्होंने दलित हितों के रक्षणार्थ गांधीजी से लोहा लिया। उनके विचारों का प्रभाव न केवल मायनारिटी पैक्ट बल्कि 1932 के जातीय समझौता तथा 1935 के भारत अधिनियम पर भी है। उनके निर्णयात्मक दृढ़ता में दब कर ही गांधीजी को दलित पृथक प्रतिनिधित्व के खिलाफ आमरण अनशन करना पडा। उनके विचारों की अभिव्यक्ति पाक्षिक/साप्ताहिक मूकनायक, बहिष्कृत भारत, जनता (24 नवंबर), समता, प्रबुद्ध भारत (4 फरवरी 1956) में अनवरत होती रही।

भारतीय मताधिकार कमिटी अथवा लोथीयन कमिटी के एक सदस्य की हैसियत से डॉ. आंबेडकर ने दलितों की प्रातिनिधिक और मताधिकार की स्थिति का पूरे भारत का दौरा कर जायजा लिया। उन्होंने एंटी-अन्टचेबिलिटी लीग अर्थात् हरिजन सेवक संघ से सन 1933 में अपना इस्तीफा दे दिया क्योंकि डॉ. आंबेडकर ने पाया कि हिंदू दमन बरकरार रखनेवाली बलात् अवस्था में अछूतों का आत्म सम्मान दांव पर लगा था।

डॉ. आंबेडकर के विदेश अध्ययन के दौरान 3 पुत्र और 1 पुत्री के निधन का दुख सह कर और अपना जीवन एकांत और दरिद्रता में बिताकर उनकी धर्मपरायण पत्नि रमाबाई 27 मई 1935 में चल बसी। 13 अक्तूबर 1935 को डॉ. आंबेडकर ने नासिक में येवला दलित वर्ग सभा और मई 1936 में एक महार परिषद बुलाकर जिस धर्म में हम पैदा हुये उसमें नही मरेंगे की घोषणा की और अगले 21 वर्ष तक वे धर्मों का तुलनात्मक अध्ययन किया।

1936 का उनका अत्यंत प्रखर भाषण पढ़ कर लाहौर की जात पात तोडक मंडल ने अपनी अखिल भारतीय सभा ही रद्द कर दी थी। वही भाषण *जातिभेद निर्मूलन* शीर्षक से प्रकाशित है। डॉ. आंबेडकर का यह जातिभेदक विचार भारत के मज़लुमों के लिये वही कार्य कर रहा है, जो कार्ल मार्क्स और एंगल्स का कम्युनिष्ट घोषणा पत्र विश्व के सर्वहारा वर्ग के लिये कर रहा था। इस आधार पर गांधी और गांधीवादी भी अपने नकाब के खरोंचे जाने पर वर्ण व्यवस्था प्रेमी ही सिद्ध हुए।

उसी वर्ष खोति पद्धति को मिटाने का विधेयक मुंबई विधान परिषद में प्रस्तावित कर उन्होंने 15 अगस्त 1936 को स्वतंत्र मजदूर दल की स्थापना की और 1937 के निर्वाचन में 17 सीटों में से 15 सीटों पर जीत हासिल की और 1938 में श्रमिक आंदोलन को नियंत्रित करने वाले औद्योगिक श्रम विवाद विधेयक का विरोध भी किया। शासन की युद्ध नीति पर भी उनका एक विशेष दृष्टिकोण रहा।

न्याय के लिए शिक्षा

सामाजिक, आर्थिक और राजनीतिक क्रांति का मूलाधार शिक्षा है। सभी शैक्षणिक विचारों का सार "सीखो, संगठित हो और संघर्ष करो" के तत्व

में निहित है। ''हर मनुष्य के आयुष्य में जब अवसर की लहर आती है तो उसका युक्त प्रकार से उपयोग करने के बाद उसे वैभव प्राप्त होता है'' के वचनानुसार डॉ. अम्बेडकर कहते थे, ''माता–पिता संतान को जन्म ही नहीं बल्कि कर्म भी देते हैं। वे अपनी संतान के जीवन में दिशा दे सकते हैं''। इस बात को ध्यान में रख कर हम सभी को बालकों–बालिकाओं की शिक्षा के लिये प्रयास करना चाहिये ताकि समाज की प्रगति द्रुत गति से हो सके।

सन् 1986 में भारत सरकार ने नई शिक्षा नीति की घोषणा की थी। उसके अनुसार भारतीय लोगों में साक्षरता का अंतर लिंग भेद और जाति भेद के उच्च और निम्न वर्ग के क्रम में असमान प्रतीत होता था। सवर्ण पुरुष सब से ज्यादा साक्षर (36 प्रतिशत), सवर्ण महिला सवर्ण पुरुष से कम साक्षर (24 प्रतिशत), अनुसूचित जाति सामान्य महिलाओं से कम साक्षर (22 प्रतिशत), और अनुसूचित जमात सबसे कम साक्षर (16.1 प्रतिशत) थे। सामुदायिक शिक्षा के प्रणेता डॉ. आंबेडकर चाहते थे कि लोगों की प्रभु सत्ता पर संचालित प्रजातन्त्र में अमीर वर्ग के बच्चों के लिये शाही विद्यालय और गरीब बच्चों के लिये कोई स्कूल ही न होना असह्य दुर्व्यवस्था है।

इसी अव्यवस्था का दूसरा नामाभिधान हैः ''विद्याविना मति नही, मतिविना नीति नही, नीतिविना गति नही, गति विना वित्त नही, वित्त विना शूद्र गिरा, इतना अनर्थ एक अविद्या ने करा''! लोक शिक्षक गाडगे महाराज कहते थे कि शिक्षाविहीन मानव पत्थर है और लोक शिक्षिका सावित्रीबाई फुले का वचन थाः *शूद्रों को बताने योग्य एक ही मार्ग यही कि शिक्षा से है मनुष्यत्व, पशुत्व नही*।

शिक्षा यानी परिवर्तन यह उनके शैक्षणिक विचारों का मुख्य सूत्र रहा है। 13 जून 1953 को रावळी कॅम्प, मुंबई की सभा में संबोधित करते हुये डॉ. आंबेडकर ने कहा था, ''हम लोग शिक्षित हुये यानी सब कुछ हो गया ऐसी बात नही है। शिक्षा के साथ–साथ मनुष्य का शील भी सुधरना चाहिये। उसके बिना शिक्षा का मूल्य शून्य है। ज्ञान तलवार की भांति है। यदि किसी आदमी के पास तलवार है तो उसका सदुपयोग अथवा दुरुपयोग करना उसके सदाचार पर निर्भर करेगा। वह उस से किसी की जान भी लेगा या किसी की जान बचा भी लेगा। ज्ञान भी ऐसा ही हैं।

इसके अतिरिक्त उन्होंने कहा कि इस से काम नही चलेगा कि शिक्षित मनुष्य केवल अपने उदर भरण में ही लगा रहे। जिन्हें स्वार्थ के अलावा कुछ दूसरा दिखता ही नही है वे किंचित भी परार्थ कर नही सकते। ऐसे व्यक्ति मात्र शिक्षित होने से क्या लाभ? समाज का वर्णों में विभाजन व्यवसाय के उद्देश्य से हुआ है। परंतु ज्ञान रोजगार का प्रश्न हो ही नही सकता। ज्ञान जीवन के लिये अत्यंत आवश्यक है। उसके बिना हमारा नुकसान होता है[8]।

डॉ. आंबेडकर के अनुसार शिक्षा के परिणाम स्वरुप स्वाभिमान, स्वावलंबन और आत्मोद्धार प्राप्त होते है और उससे क्रमशः बंधुत्व, समानता और स्वतंत्रता के मूल्य प्राप्त होना चाहिये। इस मापदण्ड से वर्तमान भारतीय शिक्षा पद्धति का पीठ किस प्रकार मानवीय चूंजे निर्माण करने का केन्द्र बन गया इस की हम कल्पना कर सकते हैं।

न्याय के लिए समाज परिवर्तन

समाज परिवर्तन के दो मुख्य साधन हैं – कानून और शिक्षा।

भारतीय संविधान ने शासन को 14 वर्ष तक की उम्र के बालक–बालिका को मुफ्त और सख्ती से शिक्षा प्रदान करने का आदेश दिया है और अस्पृश्यता जैसे सामाजिक कुरीतियों के व्यवहार को दण्डनीय अपराध करार दिया है।

कानून की दृष्टि से भारतीय प्रजातन्त्र में दो त्रुटियां हैं। एक, उस में ब्रिटिश संसदीय प्रणाली की प्रभावशीलता नही है और उस में अमेरिका की न्यायपालिका की निर्णायकता का अभाव है। उदाहरणार्थ 1896 में प्लेसी बनाम फर्ग्युसन नामक मशहूर मामले में अमरिका के सर्वोच्च न्यायालय ने काले वर्ग के लोगों के लिये पृथक सुविधाओं की व्यवस्था पर अपना फैसला सुनाते समय कहा था कि ऐसे विशेष वर्ग की विशेष सुविधा की व्यवस्था से समानता के तत्व का उल्लंघन नही होता है। परंतु 67 वर्ष के बाद भारत में बालाजी बनाम मैसूर के मामले में सर्वोच्च न्यायालय ने व्यवस्था दी थी कि आरक्षण व्यवस्था के रहते समानता के तत्व का अमल तभी होगा जब दो शर्तों अर्थात् 1. आरक्षण का मापदण्ड जात न हो तथा 2. आधे से अधिक पदों का आरक्षण न हो का पालन किया जायेगा।

कानून समाज परिवर्तन के साधनों में से एक साधन है। परंतु हिंदू कानून इस का अपवाद है। ई. स. 1772 से पूर्व और 1772 के बाद के हिंदू कानून को मिताक्षर तथा दायभाग इन दो परंपराओं में वर्गीकृत किया जा सकता है।

ईस्ट इंडिया कंपनी ने अपने प्रशासन में रेग्युलेशन अधिनियम, के ठीक एक सदी बाद तलाक की व्यवस्था देनेवाला पंजीयन विवाह अथवा विशेष विवाह अधिनियम, और 1856 में हिन्दू विधवा पुनर्विवाह अधिनियम सम्मत कर लिया था। 1929 में बाल विवाह निरोध अथवा शारदा अधिनियम के अंतर्गत वधू और वर की विवाह योग्य आयु क्रमशः 14 और 18 वर्ष निश्चित की गई थी। परंतु इस अधिनियम का बड़े बड़े नेताओं ने विरोध किया।

1935 में आर्य विवाह विधिग्राह्ता अधिनियम से आंतर्जातीय और आंतर्धर्मीय विवाहों का प्रचलन आसान हो गया था। सन 1942 में तत्कालीन कानून मन्त्री सर सुल्तान अहमद ने विवेदन किया था कि बिना मृत्यु पत्र उत्तराधिकार और विवाह के संबंध के दो विधेयकों को एक मसौदा समिति ने तैयार किया और उन्हें लोकमत का समर्थन प्राप्त करने हेतु राजपत्र में प्रकाशित किया गया है। 1946 में एक ही गोत्र के व्यक्तियों के विवाह को वैध बनानेवाला कानून और 1949 में हिंदू विवाह निःसमर्थता निर्मूलन अधिनियम के सम्मत हो जाने से हिंदू धर्म की भिन्न भिन्न जाति–उपजातियों को ऐसे विवाह करने का परवाना मिल गया। 9 अप्रैल 1948 में हिंदू संहिता विधेयक को संविधान समिति के सम्मुख डॉ. आंबेडकर ने प्रस्तुत किया था। परिणाम स्वरुप 1955 में हिंदू विवाह अधिनियम, हिंदु उत्तराधिकार अधिनियम, भरणपोषण और दत्तक ग्रहण अधिनियम सम्मत किये गये।

सामाजिक परिवर्तन का दूसरा साधन शिक्षा में डॉ. आंबेडकर का काफी योगदान रहा है। उन्होंने दलितों के प्राथमिक व माध्यमिक शिक्षा के प्रचालनार्थ बहिष्कृत हितकारणी सभा और दलित वर्ग शिक्षा समाज को क्रमशः 1924 और 1928 में स्थापित कर दलित छात्रों के लिये छात्रावास, खेल क्लब, ग्रंथालय, बोर्डिंग आदि की व्यवस्था की थी। और दलितों की उच्च शिक्षा हेतु उन्होंने पिपुल्स एज्युकेशन सोसायटी (8 जुलाई, 1945), को संस्थापित कर उसकी छत्रछाया में सन 1946 में मुंबई में सिद्धार्थ कला, विज्ञान, व विधि महाविद्यालय और 1953 में सिद्धार्थ वाणिज्य और अर्थशास्त्र

महाविद्यालय तथा 1950 में औरंगाबाद में मिलिंद कला व विज्ञान महाविद्यालय की शैक्षणिक सेवायें उपलब्ध कराई।

डॉ. आंबेडकर का राजनैतिक विचार दर्शन उनके समकालीन चिंतक आचार्य नरेन्द्र देव और एम. एन. राय के वैज्ञानिक तथा नैतिक समाजवाद से काफी नजदीक रहा है, अपितु उनका मानना था कि मार्क्स और बकल ने इतिहास के निर्माण में मनुष्य की भूमिका शून्य बताकर भारी भूल की है। उन्हों ने कहा[18] कि बुद्ध द्वारा लाये गये धार्मिक और सामाजिक सुधार के बाद चंद्रगुप्त ने राजकीय क्रांति की। महाराष्ट्र में संतों द्वारा किये गये धार्मिक और सामाजिक सुधारणा के पश्चात् ही शिवाजी ने राज्य क्रांति की थी। सिक्खों के राजनीतिक परिवर्तन के पूर्व गुरु नानक द्वारा धार्मिक–सामाजिक क्रांति की गई थी।

श्री रसेल ने कहा है कि शिक्षा का झुकाव समाज की स्थितिशीलता कायम रखने के लिये होता है, तथापि स्वभाव और मत निर्माण करने की उसकी क्षमता बहुत अधिक होती है। डॉ. आंबेडकर के अनुसार क्रांति के तीन घटक (1) समाज के दोश का संज्ञान, (2) उस दोश से पीडित वर्ग की उपस्थिति का एहसास और (3) शस्त्रार्थ हैं। उनमें से पहले दो घटक शिक्षा पर निर्भर है। इस प्रकार शिक्षित वर्ग ही संगठित होकर संघर्ष की बुनियाद बनाता हैं। डॉ. आंबेडकर के अनुसार बुद्ध द्वारा बताई गई सबसे बडी बात यह थी कि मनुष्य और जगत में सुधार किये बगैर संसार में सुधार नही किया जा सकता। परंतु इस का भावार्थ यह नही है कि मनुष्य के मन में बदल होने के साथ ही समाज में अपने आप परिवर्तन हो जाता है। उदाहरणार्थ पूंजीपति और गरीब वर्ग पहले वर्ग के लोभ–लालच के कारण नही पैदा होते। अतः उनका खात्मा पहले वर्ग के संपत्ति त्याग से नही होगा। बल्कि उनका नियमन किसी की व्यक्तिगत इच्छा के बाहर की बात है।

व्यक्तिगत न्याय

डॉ. आंबेडकर ने कहा है कि किस समाज में किसने जन्म लेना चाहिये और उसको किस ढंग से रखना चाहिये यह मनुष्य के काबू में नही है। परंतु एक बार किसी मनुष्य का अस्पृश्य के रुप में किसी हिंदू समाज में जन्म

हुआ तो उस के भीतर विद्यमान जातियों के संबंध और सामाजिक नियम उस के ऊपर नियत हो जाते है। उस के अनुसार आचरण करना उसकी मजबूरी हो जाती है। इस परिस्थिति में यदि ब्राह्मणों ने अस्पृश्यों को समानता के नाते से सलूक करने के मत को अंगीकार किया तो उस से अधिक से अधिक व्यक्तिगत रुप में अस्पृश्य की अन्याय से मुक्ति हो सकती है, परंतु सामाजिक रुप में कदापि नही हो सकती। उसके लिये उन वर्गों में विद्यमान सामाजिक संबंध को बदलना जरुरी होता है। यह संबंध यदि धर्म संस्था नियंत्रित करती है तो धर्म संस्था में परिवर्तन करना पडेगा, यदि वह धार्मिक, सामाजिक, आर्थिक और राजनीतिक संरचना से जुड़ी समस्या है तो उस प्रकार से परिवर्तन करना लाजमी हो जायेगा।

भगवान अम्बेडकर

आज विश्व में भारत के सपूत डॉ. भीमराव आंबेडकर के विचार–दर्शन ने समानता–स्वतंत्रता–बंधुत्व पर आधारित अवाम की जीवन पद्धति के प्रजातंत्र की ऐसी पहचान बनाई कि कई विभूतियों की वैचारिकियां विस्मृत हो चुकी है। डॉ. आंबेडकर द्वारा रोपित यह पहचान आज उनके आलोचकों के सिर पर चढकर बोल रही है। श्री अरुण शौरी ने कहा ही हैः "गत पचास वर्षों का शुद्ध परिणाम यह है कि फिर एक बार भारत में आज वही क्रम शुरु हुआ है। लोकमान्य विस्मृत से हो गये। नारायन गुरु को केरला के बाहर कोई नही जानता है। स्वामी दयानंद, रामकृष्ण परमहंस, श्री औरोबिंदो, रमन महर्षि, कांची के परमाचार्य इत्यादियों ने हमें अपने पैरों पर खडा करने के लिये क्या किया इसे भक्तों के एक संकुचित दायरे के सिवाय और कोई नही जानता। स्वामी विवेकानंद को धूल झाड़ कर कुछ अवसर पर बाहर निकाला जाता है और उनको ठीक ऐसे संप्रदाय–निरपेक्ष के पहनावे में दर्शाया जाता है, जिसे वे स्वयं तीव्र रुप से फटकार देते। गांधीजी की तो प्रति दिन छंटनी हो ही रही है– एक दिन पहले से चली आ रही विकास की प्रतिक्रिया के कारण तो दूसरे दिन मुसलमान नेताओं को पाकिस्तान का आग्रह धरने में प्रवृत्त कराने के कारण यह छंटनी की जा रही है और आंबेडकर जैसे व्यक्तिओं की देवता की भांति पूजा हो रही है[10]। सैम्युअल जानसन ने भी कहा है कि "कृतज्ञता महान उद्यम का फल है, जाहिल लोगों में आप इसे नही पाते"।

शिक्षा, दीक्षा और प्रेरणा

8 जुलाई 1945 में स्थापित पिपुल्स एज्युकेशन सोसायटी, सिद्धार्थ कॉलेज आफ आर्टस् एण्ड सायंस, 1946; सिद्धार्थ नाइट स्कूल 1947; मिलिंद महाविद्यालय, 1950; सिद्धार्थ कॉलेज आफ कामर्स एण्ड एकॉनामिक्स, 1953; मिलिंद मल्टिपरपज हायस्कूल, 1955; और सिद्धार्थ कॉलेज ऑफ लॉ, 1956 उसकी गवाह है। 21 वर्ष अध्ययन और परिक्षण के बाद उन्होंने भारत के लिये विश्व का बेहतर मानवतावादी धर्म अनुसंशित किया। 14 अक्टूबर 1956 में उन्होंने नागपुर में लाखों जनता के साथ बौद्ध जीवन पद्धति को अपनाया। उनकी अंतिम रचना बुद्ध और उनका धम्म ही थी।

डॉ. आंबेडकर ने 6 दिसंबर 1956 को महाप्रयाण किया और विश्व के भावी जीवन की खुशहाली के लिये वे हमारे पास अपने द्वारा प्रदत्त शिक्षा, संस्कार और प्रेरणा ही छोड गये, जो हमें कदम–कदम पर मार्गदर्शन करते रहेंगे।

संदर्भ ग्रंथः

1. श्री एल. आर. बाली, *आंबेडकर ने क्या किया, जलंधर* 2002.
2. श्री अरुण शौरी, वरशिपिंग फाल्स गॉड़, एएसए प्रकाशन, नई दिल्ली 1997, पृ. ग।
3. श्री अरुण शौरी, वही।
4. श्री अरुण शौरी, वही।
5. डॉ. नरेन्द्र जाधव, डॉ. आंबेडकरांचे अर्थशाास्त्रीय लेखन, डॉ. बाबासाहेब आंबेडकर गौरव ग्रंथ,महाराश्ट्र राज्य साहित्य आणि संस्कृति मंडळ, मुंबई 1993, पृ. 362–372.
6. डॉ. बाबासाहेब आंबेडकर रायटिंग्ज एण्ड स्पीचेज, वाल्युम 1, पृ. 44 और एस. एस. गायकवाड, डॉ. आंबेडकर यांची समाजरचनेची सैद्धांतिक मांडणी, डॉ. बाबासाहेब आंबेडकर गौरव ग्रंथ, महाराश्ट्र राज्य साहित्य आणि संस्कृति मंडळ, मुंबई 1993, पृ. 27.
7. डॉ. बाबासाहेब आंबेडकर रायटिंग्ज एण्ड स्पीचेज, वही।
8. डॉ. बी. आर. आंबेडकर, रायटिंग्स एण्ड स्पीचेस, खण्ड 1 मुंबई 1979 पृ. 227.
9. डॉ. बी. आर. आंबेडकर, वही।
10. डॉ. भालचंद्र लक्ष्मण मुणगेकर, डॉ. आंबेडकर यांचे भारतीय शेती विशयक विचार, डॉ. बाबासाहेब आंबेडकर गौरव ग्रंथ, मुंबई 1993, पुनर्मुद्रण 1999, पृ. 393–394.
11. डॉ. भालचंद्र लक्ष्मण मुणगेकर, वही।
12. डॉ. धनंजय कीर, डॉ. आंबेडकरः जीवन तथा कार्य, प्रकाशाान पुणे, 1976.
13. डॉ. बी. आर. आंबेडकर, रायटिंग्स एण्ड स्पीचेस, खण्ड 1 मुंबई 1979 पृ. 54.
14. डॉ. बी. आर. आंबेडकर, थॉटस् ऑन पाकिस्तान, ठक्कर एण्ड कंपनी, मुंबई, 1945, विदेशियों से सबक नामक अध्याय।
15. सी. डी. नाईक, थॉटस् एण्ड फिलासफी ऑफ डॉ. बी. आर. आंबेडकर, सरुप एण्ड सन्स, नई दिल्ली 2003, बुद्धिस्ट ड़ेवलपमेन्ट इन इस्ट एण्ड वेस्ट नामक अध्याय।

Chapter - 19

Buddhism

Inrtroduction

Tathagata Buddha, as early as 6th century B. C., was an historical, incomparable universal personality, who detected the existing inequalities of his time and prescribed remedy in principle and practice. He organized the world's first commune –the Order of worthy monks, in which there was no discrimination as to caste, race, region, language, culture etc. He taught the populace of every region the art of living in accordance with equality as he discovered the medicine of equality for the disease of inequality. He administered the same and brought the life of brotherly love among human beings of the world. Considering the fact that the society then was fraught with foulfold caste system this was an unique and marvelous revolution.

Buddha

About the 2500 years later another unique personality appeared on this land and at his one clarion call tens of thousands of people spurned their traditional religion and embraced Buddhism. This was an equally marvelous revolution of peace, dhamma and equality. This revolution took place at the capital land of the Nagas, the former disciples of the Buddha, Nagpur on 14th October 1956, to be recognized as the Dhammacakkanupavattana i.e. the turning the wheel of Law after the Buddha. The hero of this dhamma revolution was Dr. Babasaheb Ambedkar, who had earlier established the Welfare Society for the Excluded, Equality Soldiers Force, Peoples' Education Society and the Buddhist Society of India.

World

This is true that at present the world is under the grip of diverse types of inequalities. There is this the greatest issue, there is discrimination, it is under the grips of materialistic pigism and immaterialistic hallucinations, which has deepened the valley of fratricidal ignorance between man and man, nation and nation, communities and communities, there is crass materialist corporate greed on the one hand and there is utter intimidating poverty under which the world has been carpingly groping. This is an imminent threat. Let us come and see how the Buddha and Babasaheb laid down the path leading to the eradication of inequality and foundation of love, peace, fraternity and justice.

Buddhism

Buddha expounded that after entering the Buddhist Dispensation caste, race, group, scope dissolve and all become one Association, In this way there were in the Order of the Disciples of the Buddha, the elder Upali (barber), the elder Angulimala (robber), royal members, wealthy man's son like Yasha, Brahmins like Sariputta, Moggallana and Mahakassapa as well as the scavenger like Sunita.

Kalama Sutta

The people of Kalama asked the Buddha who to believe out of all the ascetics, sages, venerables, and holy ones who, like himself, passed through their town. They complained that they were confused by the many contradictions they discovered in what they heard. The Kalama Sutta is the Buddha's reply.

- Do not believe anything on mere hearsay.
- Do not believe in traditions merely because they are old and have been handed down for many generations and in many places.
- Do not believe anything on account of rumors or because people talk a a great deal about it.
- Do not believe anything because you are shown the written testimony of some ancient sage.
- Do not believe in what you have fancied, thinking that, because it is extraordinary, it must have been inspired by a god or other wonderful being.
- Do not believe anything merely because presumption is in its favor, or because the custom of many years inclines you to take it as true.
- Do not believe anything merely on the authority of your teachers and priests.

- But, whatever, after thorough investigation and reflection, you find to agree with reason and experience, as conducive to the good and benefit of one and all and of the world at large, accept only that as true, and shape your life in accordance with it.

The same text, said the Buddha, must be applied to his own teachings.

- Do not accept any doctrine from reverence, but first try it as gold is tried by fire.

One Taste

"Just as in the great ocean there is but one taste — the taste of salt — so in this Doctrine and Discipline *(dhammavinaya)* there is but one taste — the taste of freedom": with these words the Buddha vouches for the emancipating quality of His doctrine.

Whether one samples water taken from the surface of the ocean, or from its middling region, or from its depths, the taste of the water is in every case the same — the taste of salt. And again, whether one drinks but a thimble-full of ocean water, or a glass-full, or a bucket-full, the same salty taste is present throughout. Analogously with the Buddha's Teaching, a single flavor — the flavor of freedom *(vimuttirasa)* — pervades the entire Doctrine and Discipline, from its beginning to its end, from its gentle surface to its unfathomable depths. Whether one samples the Dhamma at its more elementary level — in the practice of generosity and moral discipline, in acts of devotion and piety, in conduct governed by reverence, courtesy, and loving-kindness; or at its intermediate level — in the taintless supramundane knowledge and deliverance realized by the liberated saint, in every case the taste is the same — the taste of freedom.

Babasaheb

In the same way Dr. Ambedkar had a faith in equality from his childhood, his culmination of love towards equality is reflected in the preamble of the constitution of India as under:

> **WE, THE PEOPLE OF INDIA**, having solemnly resolved to constitute India into a **SOVEREIGN SOCIALIST SECULAR DEMOCRATIC REPUBLIC** and to secure to all its citizens:
>
> **JUSTICE**, Social, Economic and Political;
>
> **LIBERTY** of thought, expression, belief, faith and worship;
>
> **EQUALITY** of status and of opportunity; and to promote among them all

FRATERNITY assuring the dignity of the individual and the unity and integrity of the Nation;

IN OUR CONSTITUENT ASSEMBLY this 26th day of November, 1949, do HEREBY ADOPT, ENACT AND GIVE TO OURSELVES THIS CONSTITUTION.

Protection of Civil Rights Act

In our society there is another evil of treating other human brothers as lower than cats and dogs and treat them inhumanly and for this purpose Dr. Ambedkar introduced in 1955 the Protection of Civil Rights Act to safeguard the interests of the marginalized classes of society.

Prevention of atrocities Act

These days we see that out national newspapers and electronic media channels daily flash the news of rapes, corruption, murder, child abuse, domestic violence, inhumanity, injustice and failure of law and order situation engendering public health and morality. In 1989 the Prevention of atrocities against scheduled caste and scheduled tribe members by the savarna fellow members, who have been exploiting them economically, socially and psychologically also, was enforced for safety of the unfortunate brethren in the country. This Act was further complemented by Rules and in 2016 it was amended and was accompanied by Indian Penal Code sections of punishment for the culprits convicted. This was another means of eradicating hatred from the minds of people and establish friendship and living together among them.

Hindu Code Bill

In addition to that Dr. Ambedkar saw the age-long inequality prevalent in our society, which was that of gender disparity, in which woman cannot enjoy civil rights of marriage, divorce, adoption, inheritance, at par with man. While our constitution speaks about parity and equality in principle, our society is under the grips of practice of discrimination in terms of caste, untouchability, gender and class disparity. The the Hindu Code Bill, which is the heart of equality levelling all human beings equal and at par in respect of all facilities of life such as education, employment, social status, pursuit of happiness, freedom of thought, speech, migration, association, religion, worship, faith and enjoyment of life and progressing at higher levels.

This in nutshell, my friends of the dhamma, is the message of Buddha and Babasaheb on parity or equality and peace in the world. May you all be well and happy by the blessings of the Triple Gem- the Buddha, Dhamma, Sangha and Babasaheb.

Buddhism

Buddhism is spreading westward these days. While it has been established in the Eastern nations it is now dealing with western life and governments with successful results. The whole world is facing the imminent problem of terrorism and disquietitude. This needs to be investigated from the perspective of externality and mentality both. Buddhism has strived to help mankind on both individual and social level from the very ancient times.

Most of the counties in the globe are having the democratic form of governments with its regional-specific culture. Those which do not subscribe to this set up of life are inclined to establish socialism in other than Marxist way. Both the world government of righteousness and democracy presuppose society of the world nations based on the fundamental principles of life, to reproduce the terminology of the Indian Constitution and its principal architect Dr. Ambedkar: Liberty, Equality, Fraternity and Justice. The last one is to pervade social, economic and political spheres and the former three principles in combination import right understanding (Samma Ditthi) and Compassion (Karuna) to get correct vision of understanding the present status of the world life and to help the erring and misdirected humanity.

This noble mission is the motto of the Buddha, who exhorted to his Sangha of preachers in his day in the words as laid down in the Buddhism's constitution called Vinayapitaka-Bahujana Hitaya Bahujana Sukhaya, lokanukampaya atthaya hitaya devamanussanam, desetha bhikkhave dhammam adikalyanam majjhe kalyaynan pariyosana kalyanan satthakam savyanjana paripunnam brahmachariyam pakasetha, ma eken dve gacchatha i.e. to mean that O Brothers go round each in different direction to preach with compassion of world and its dwellers the message pure in the start, middle and end, which is meaningful in right terminology and perfect with highest attainment.

In this paper I attempt to put forward that the Buddhism is the only way for the purification of social and personal lives on global scale as history stands evident from ancient, medieval to modern times.

Points

What is Buddhism, is it a method, a medicine, a social life way? What is Peace? Is it a deadman's abode or a living heaven. Is it external or internal? How Mind affects matter and matter mind? Which is a lasting peace? What is present situation of the world, What is happening in Burma, in Tibet, in Cuba, South Korea, India, Iraq, Iran, Israel? What is the loss of breaking Buddha statues in Bamiyan, in Afghanistan and Pakistan? How Buddhism is relevant today, What is the social message of Buddhism, why Dr. Ambedkar embraced Buddhism?

> Nahi verena verani sammatidhakudachanam averena cha sammanti esa dhammo sanantano. — **Dhammapada**

> kumbhupamam kayamimam viditva nagarupam chittamidam thapitva yodhetha maram pannayudhena jitancha rakkhe anuvesino siya.
> — **Dhammapada**

Peace prevailed and preceded Buddhism. How peace was maintained earlier? What changes Buddhism brought about in peace method, modality in social life?

Buddhism of Pakistan

There are various historical and cultural Buddhist sites in Pakistan worth visiting and getting educated namely (1) Taxila, (2) Peshawar, (3) Uddiyana (Sawat) (4) Mansehra, (5) Shahbaz Garhi, (6) Takht Bai and so on to name a few. While Taxila was the then oldest university of ancient Bharat Peshawar was the native place of both the Buddhist philosophers of Yogachara and Madhyamika, Asanga and Vasubandhu, who were Pathan brothers before they had become the Buddhist monk scholars and reputed Acharyas.

World Order of Righteousness

World Order of Righteousness is prescribed by Dr. Ambedkar for establishment of peace in the world. It goes well along Ven. Thich Minh Chau's Five Principles for a New Global Moral Order, viz.

The law of kamma is redefined by Dr. Ambedkar by removing its adventitious parts coming from Hinduism and restoring its rationality from original Buddhism. Accordingly character of man influences and gets influenced by environment surrounding him. No former life has capacity to affect the future of man and no independent agency like soul is real to coexist with past and future during present status of man. In fact denial of soul automatically rejects ground for past deed as determinant of present status irrelevant to surrounding and parents give to their offspring not only body but karmic conditions and sanskaras or mind also.

Mind in fact influences matter and the latter the former and co-existence of mind and matter is recognized by science and social sciences as palpable forces to determine conditions of man's life during his existence.

The middle path is nirvana consisting of moral foundation of verbal and bodily acts including livelihood and mental exercise of thoughtfulness moving on focused area of research to attain right understanding and compassion to remove superstition and supernaturalism to commit oneself for helping society as selfless servants and elevating mental heights to be the guiding elites of society and form the world order of democracies based on the principles of liberty, equality and fraternity with justice and human and fundamental rights for life, living and happiness.

So the world order of Ambedkar's conception is righteous cosmic order dynamic to flow goodness and happiness from one end to the other in the human association of man, women and children besides loving animals, plants and enemies by way of persuasion and conviction.

Five Principles

First, dedication of our life to the welfare of all sentient beings, and to work for peace, disarmament and international brotherhood. Second, the living of a frugal, healthy and contented life so as to devote more time and energy to peace and to the welfare of all living beings. Third, abstinence from any action which leads to disputes and wars; performance of any action which leads to peace, harmony and international understanding. Fourth, respect for the life of all sentient beings, for the life of our planet, and for the purity of our environment! Fifth, peaceful coexistence and mutual spiritual cooperation[1].

Non-Self

Further he expressed how the doctrine of non-self can help found a new moral world order thus: We think that one of the greatest contributions Buddhism can make to a new world moral order is its theory of "no self." This theory plays an important positive role towards building up a moral way of life for the person of our times. The sickly psychic tendency of the modern person is to seek sensual pleasures and the accumulation of wealth. In order to guarantee individual enjoyment one tries to secure as much material property for oneself as possible. However, material property is limited while the greed of humans is unfathomable. That is why there is no way to escape from disputes and fights between human and human, between nation and nation, between people and people. And in this lies the root cause of war. With the theory of "no self," we can say that Buddhism has dug up the very root of wars, conflicts and contentions. With an insight into "no self" a Buddhist once enlightened will escape the grip of both greed (lobha) and anger (dosa). One is greedy of something for oneself, but when the self is not there greed loses its target and has no incentive to exist. The same goes for anger. When the self is contradicted unsatisfied anger will arise. But when the self is not there anger will automatically disappear[2].

Interbeing

Thich Nhat Hanh revised the traditional five precepts to address issues of mind, speech and body:

> First, do not kill. Do not let others kill. Find whatever means possible to protect life. Do not live with a vocation that is harmful to humans and nature. Second, do not steal. Possess nothing that should belong to others. Respect the property of others, but prevent others from enriching themselves from human sufferings and the sufferings of other species on earth. Third, sexual expression should not take place without love and commitment. Be fully aware of the sufferings you may cause others as a result of your misconduct. To preserve the happiness of yourself and others, respect the rights and commitments of others. Fourth, do not say untruthful things. Do not spread news that you do not know to be certain. Do not criticize or condemn things that you are unsure of. Do not utter words that cause division and hatred, that can create discord and cause the family or the community to break. All efforts should be made to reconcile and resolve all conflicts. Fifth, do not use alcohol and any other intoxicants. Be aware that your fine body has been transmitted to you by several previous generations and your parents. Destroying your body with alcohol and other intoxicants is to betray your ancestors, your parents and also to betray the future generations[3].
> The Order of Interbeing is designed explicitly to address social justice and peace issues, sensitizing the participant to test his/her behavior in relation to the needs of the larger community, while freeing him/her from limiting patterns. Even the way we take refuge in the Triple Gems is explained simply and beautifully:

I take refuge in the Buddha,
the one who shows me the way in this life,
Namo Buddhaya
I take refuge in the Dharma,
the way of understanding, and love,

Namo Dharmaya
I take refuge in the Sangha,
the community of mindful harmony,
Namo Sanghaya[4]

I believe that every individual has a responsibility to help guide our global family in the right direction[5].

Leadership crisis

The *Cullavagga* records that Puraana Thera and his disciples expressed their disapproval in clear-cut words. Thus the position in the Order was such that nobody could command the respect of all the factions in the Order. Hence, the Buddha's reluctance to name anybody as his successor. But on the other hand, the leadership which emerged after his death was capable enough to silence and liquidate all the rest. But the problem remained, and, in course of time, it appeared in much graver form. The Second Council was the culmination of the same. Confusion prevailed. The so-called faithful and orthodox monks of the Order were standing face to face with those who wanted to revise the principles and practices according to convenience. The socio-economic and political conditions had changed. These gave rise to new interpretations of the words of the Master, and new Vinayic practices in the Order, and thereby new methods of checks and balances. This led to a split and the monolith was completely shattered. **This is what** Prof. Sanghasen Singh referred to in his write up entitled **'The problem of leadership in Early Buddhism'. This is corroborated with words of Dalai lama when he said, "** First, I should mention that I do not believe in creating movements or espousing ideologies. Nor do I like the practice of establishing an organization to promote a particular idea, which implies that one group of people alone is responsible for the attainment of that goal, while everybody else is exempt. In our present circumstances, none of us can afford to assume that somebody else will solve our problems; each of us must take his or her own share of universal responsibility. In this way, as the number of concerned, responsible individuals grows, tens, hundreds, thousands or even hundreds of thousands of such people will greatly improve the general atmosphere. Positive change does not come quickly and demands ongoing effort. If we become discouraged we may not attain even the simplest goals. With constant, determined application, we can accomplish even the most difficult objectives[6]."

A Buddhist View of Women

A Comparative Study of the Rules for *Bhiksu.niis* and *Bhiksus* Based on the Chinese *Praatimok.sa by* In Young Chung reminded of Ambedkar's view on equality of gender. The former mentioned that "Equality of *bhik.su.nii* and *bhik.su*, men and women, can be inferred in several of the rules groupings. The penalties for offenses against those *aniyata dharmas* written only for *bhik.sus*, for example, point up a landmark of female-male equality. Here, in a gesture of trust in women most unusual for the time, a trustworthy female lay follower can bring a charge against a *bhik.su* based only on her personal eyewitness testimony, in order to force an investigation of that *bhik.su*'s conduct. Additionally, equal abilities of men and women are presumed in the regulations for settlement of disciplinary matters in the seven *adhikara.na-"samatha Dharmas dharmas*, which are exactly the same, in both numbers and contents, for both the *Bhik.su* and the *Bhik.su.nii Sa"nghas*. However the "Eight Rules" present a thorny problem. These "Eight Rules" are so different in character and tone from the rest of the body of the *Bhik.su.nii Praatimok.sa* that I believe they can be disregarded as later additions, appended by the compilers, and not indicative of either the intentions of Gautama Buddha himself, or of the Buddhist traditions as a whole.

Law of Change

In dwelling upon modern world condition Dr. Malasekere said, "In any case, we cannot stop the world; it will go on changing, for change, says the Buddha, is the fundamental fact of life. No revolution can put an end to change itself. That is the beauty of change. Without constant change, yesterday's revolution becomes today's convention and today's convention is tomorrows tyranny".

"Our very survival is tied up with change. This is where modern man must find Buddhism to be particularly relevant to his age. Buddhism accepts change; in fact, it is built on the truth of constant change and flux. We must learn to take the rivers as they flow".

"We must cultivate the quality of resilience, the ability to adopt, adapt and be flexible. The moment we come to rigid conclusions and refuse to consider different points of view, we cease to be intelligent. Our views tend to harden into dogmas and dogmas make us mulish in our obstinacy. New challenges call for new responses. If each individual takes care to avoid dogmas, the entire community becomes an open society which makes the good life possible"[7].

Rational manifesto

It was a time when various religious teachings were in a ferment and India of the 6th century B. C. was one of the most interesting places to be.

Religious teachers propounding various types of doctrines were vying with each other to have more and more converts. Besides these new teachings, there were religious systems that were deep rooted. In all these religious systems, the theory was: "We have found a way." This is the correct path." "You come, you will be saved." Into their midst comes the Buddha who says: "Do not believe what your book says. Do not believe what your teachers would say. Do not believe what your tradition says. Do not take anything merely because it comes to you with the authority of somebody else. Make it a personal experience. Think for yourself. Be convinced. And once you are convinced act accordingly." Now this was a very refreshing manner in which man was given one of the greatest freedoms that he is fighting for, the freedom to think for himself. If under feudalism, before the present advances were made, we were not able to assert so much of our light to think for ourselves, as these advances take place we will be asserting that right more and more. We will be wanting to feel that we are convinced, after our own investigations, after we have been able to go through the principles, the facts, the pros and cons. This we consider an inviolable right This is the second doctrine, whose applicability to modern times, and future times, would continue[8].

Age-long-cause and effect

Human beings in the twentieth century have created much bad *kamma*, which is going to exert an influence on humanity of the twenty-first century. It is a legacy of problems with which the citizens of the twenty-first century will have to deal. In order to help solve these problems and ensure that the twenty-first century will be a safe one, we must discuss ways of addressing the problems right now. If we can adapt our views as I have mentioned here, there is a possibility that we will be able to solve them successfully.[9]

Who has peace?

Only the really happy person has real peace, and only the person who has peace can be really happy. The person who has happiness radiates happiness, and the person who has peace diffuses peace. People who have no peace of mind tend to destroy peace — in their family, among neighbors or wherever they happen to be. Those who are at peace with themselves naturally and automatically live in peace with everyone. They are happy and peaceful in the full sense of the terms. Their peace and happiness are true to life; and it is this truly happy and peaceful person who is the fully developed and educated human being. The development that creates this free, peaceful and happy person is entitled to the term *Peace Education*[10].

Why Buddhism?

The consequence of all this is that, in the context of contemporary western culture, scientists, psychologists, and philosophers have found in Buddhism a tradition in harmony with some of the most basic principles of western thought. In addition, they find Buddhism particularly interesting because, although the principal methods and conclusions of the western scientific tradition often closely resemble those of Buddhism, western science has thus far suggested no practical way of achieving an inner transformation, whereas in Buddhism such a way is clearly indicated. While science has taught us to build better cities, expressways, factories, and farms, it has not taught us to build better people. Therefore people in the contemporary world are turning to Buddhism, an ancient philosophy that has many features in common with the western scientific tradition but that goes beyond the materialism of the West, beyond the limits of practical science as we have known it thus far[11].

Let us turn to Ambedkar and dicuss how Sankhya philosophy was mutilated to give the dead Bhagavadgita creed a new lease of life and how Patanjali's atheism was turned into traditionalism.

Samapatti

The word Samapatti is a Buddhist term which has occurred in Patanjali's Yoga Sutra also in the same sense as is understood in Buddhist meditation. It was used in the sense of (1) clean-stainless-unblemished precious stonelike consciousness's enjoyer, enjoyment and enjoyable formlike realisation, (2) discursive thought mixed of word, meaning and knowledge, (3) state of consciousness purified of memory, devoid of receiving nature and merely meaning revealing is samapatti.

क्षीणव त्तेरभिजातस्येव मणेर्ग्रहीतग्रहणग्राह्येषु तत्स्थतदञ्जनता समापत्तिः | |41 | |

Kshinavritterabhijatasyeva man+ergrahi+trgrahan+agrahyeshu rntatsthatadaòjanatâ samapatti%/

तत्र शब्दार्थज्ञानविकल्पैः संकीर्णा सवितर्का समापत्तिः | |42 | | स्मृतिपरिशुध्दौ स्वरुपशून्यवार्थमात्रनिर्भासा निर्वितर्का | |43 | |[12]

Patanjali

According to Indian philosophers like B. Chattopadhyay Patanjali Yoga is not a philosophical treatise. Kautilya refers to yoga in his Arthashastra to mean not Patanjali's Yoga but Nyaya-Vaisheshika school of thought based on atomism, logic and also subordinated to religious authority and law code of Manu.

Sankhya

Dr. Ambedkar said in his My Philosophy of Life that (AIR broadcast of Speech , Delhi, 3rd October 1954) "I reject the Hindu Social Philosophy propounded in the Bhagavat Geeta based as it is, on the Triguna of the Sankhya philosophy which is in my judgement a cruel perversion of the philosophy of Kapil, and which had made the Caste System and the System of Graded Inequality the law of Hindu Social Life."

My philosophy has a mission. I have to do the work of conversion; for, I have to make the followers of Triguna theory to give it up and accept mine. Indians today are governed by two different ideologies. Their political ideal set out in the Preamble to the Constitution affirms a life of Liberty, Equality, and Fraternity. Their social ideal embodied in their religion denies them."[13]

Bhagavadgita

Highlighting the role of Bhagavad Gita in Indian History Prem Nath Bazaz exposed that (p. 490) "Like Sri Krishna in the Gita who after praising Pure Reason of the Sankhya in the beginning finally plumps for the Vedanta, Aurobindo subordinates reason to religious faith."

Findings

In contrast to Debiprasad Chattopadhyaya, who blames Mahayana schools of Madhyamika and Yogachara for inculcating idealism and make Nyaya-Vaisheshika and Kumaril Bhatt to swerve from the path of materialism (1976) Dr. Kausalyayan put forth that all four schools of Buddhist philosophy viz., Sautrantika, Vaibhashikla, Yogachara and Madhyamika are extramentalitic or externalistic schools, which vary in emphasising materialism from absolute point to relative position (20. 7. 1978).

Suggestions

Be it Mahayana or Theravada, the global world peace and international interfaith dialogue can be fraternally carried out under the blameless and stainless proven historical role of Buddhism as spring of peace and science, rationality and humanity.

References

1. Thanks to Dr. Binh Anson for providing us with this article. Source: Buddhism and Global Nonviolent Problem Solving - Ulan Bator Explorations (August 989), *Edited by Glenn D. Paige and Sarah Gilliatt, University of Hawaii (1991)*, http://www.hawaii.edu/uhip/buddhism. html.
2. Ibid, as above.
3. Thanks to Dr. Binh Anson for providing us with this article. Source: Buddhism and Global Nonviolent Problem Solving - Ulan Bator Explorations (August 989), *Edited by Glenn D. Paige and Sarah Gilliatt, University of Hawaii (1991)*, http://www.hawaii.edu/uhip/buddhism.html
4. *Ibid,* **Global Problem-Solving: A Buddhist Perspective** by Sulak Sivaraksa.
5. The Global Community and The Need for Universal Responsibility His Holiness the Fourteenth Dalai Lama © Tenzin Gyatso, the Fourteenth Dalai Lama 1990.
6. *Ibid,* as above.
7. Buddhism and Problems of the Modern Age by Dr. G. P. Malalasekera.
8. Buddhism in Modern Life by Dr. Ananda Guruge with *special thanks to Phramaha Somnuek Saksree for transcription of this article.*
9. Buddhist Solutions for the Twenty-First Century by P. A. Payutto, translated and compiled by Bruce Evans, **[*]** Address to the 1993 Parliament of the World's Religions in Chicago.
10. Buddhist Solutions for the Twenty-First Century by P. A. Payutto, translated and compiled by Bruce Evans (**On Peace)**
11. Buddhism: A Modern Perspective by Dr. Peter Della Santina, [Taken from Peter Della Santina., *The Tree of Enlightenment.* (Taiwan: The Corporate Body of the Buddha Educational Foundation, 1997), pp. 3-12]. Sincere thanks to Ti.nh Tue^. for transription of this article.
12. Swami Ramdeo, Samadhipada, Yogadarshan, Yogasandesha, Hindi, February 2007, p. 36.
13. DBAWAS, vol. 17, part three, Mumbai 2003, p. 503.

Chapter - 20

Rising of Marginals

Awaken the enslaved

India is a home of inequality. Hindu society is just like a tower which 0had several storeys without a ladder or an entrance. One was to die in the storey in which one is born. Hindu society consisted of three parts: the Brahmins, the non-Brahmins and the untouchables. He pitied the souls of those persons who said that according to their philosophy there existed God in animals as well as in animate things and yet treated their co-religionist as Untouchables! He lamented that not the spread of knowledge and literacy but accumulation and monopoly was the aim of the Brahmins. In his view the backwardness of the non-Brahmins was due to lack of education and power. In order to save the Depressed Classes from perpetual slavery, poverty and ignorance, herculean efforts must be made, he asserted, to awaken them to their disabilities. – Dr. Ambedkar.

Graded Inequality

Babasaheb Ambedkar differentiated between inequality and graded inequality of the kind we have in India due to the caste system. Examples of inequality are – inequality or slavery faced by the black people in USA, South Africa, etc against which the sufferers of inequality, black people, have revolted against their oppressors and exploiters.

Graded inequality is entirely found only in an Indian subcontinent and it is the product of caste system. The very important characteristic of Graded inequality which differentiates it from pure inequality is – graded inequality divides the sufferers themselves based on unequal burden and benefits.

That means under graded inequality, the middle castes (Kshatriyas, Vaishyas, Shudras) are sufferers on one hand and beneficiaries on the other hand of the graded inequality i.e. caste system. Benefits and burden being unequal from caste to caste, it is only the highest caste of Brahmins who is the absolute beneficiary and the lowest castes of Ati-shudras i.e. untouchables are absolute sufferers of graded inequality.

"The right of a Brahmin to take a woman from the classes below him but not to give a woman to them is inequity. But Kshatriya, Vaishya and Shudra will not combine to destroy it. The Kshatriya resents this right of the Brahmin. But he will not combine with the Vaishya or the Shudra and that is for two reasons. Firstly, because he is satisfied that if the Brahmin has the right to take the women of three communities, the Kshatriya has the right to appropriate the women of two communities. He does not suffer so much as the other two.

Secondly, if he joins in a general revolution against this marriage-inequity, in one way he will rise to the level of the Brahmin, but in another way all will be equal, which to him means that the Vaishyas and the Shudras will rise to his level i.e. they will claim Kshatriya women – which means he will fall to their level. Take any other inequity and think of a revolt against it. The same social psychology will show that a general rebellion against it is impossible.

One of the reasons why there has been no revolution against Brahmanism and its inequities is due entirely to the principle of graded inequality. It is a system of permitting a share in the spoils with a view to enlist them to support the spoil system. It is a system full of low cunning, which man could have invented to perpetuate inequity and to profit by it. For it is nothing else but inviting people to share on inequity in order that they may all be supporters of inequity." (Jayant Pathri).

Marginals Rising or Falling?

The way BSP's candidate was defeated in RS polls exposes the Manuvadi power structure in India. BJP used all the immoral weapons in its armour, misusing state machinery, including courts and the anti-bahujans manuwadi media.

The most interesting fact that has emerged from this election is the cross-voting of 3 MLAs of SP/BSP in favour of BJP. These include Singh a Thakur, Agrawal a Baniya and Mishra a Bramhin. This shows that these Bramhin, Baniya and Thakur MLAs had their allegiance to their caste first and therefore they chose to vote BJP, the party of Brahmin-Baniya-Thakurs. For them, the ideology of the party they belong to was not important, their caste was. This should be an eye-opener for Akhilesh Yadav and Mayawati. On the other hand, BSP-SP alliance is getting stronger each day.

Interestingly, one of the Scheduled Caste MLA of BJP has voted BSP candidate, acknowledging that BSP only can safeguard the interests of SC/ST/OBCs. What about the rest of the SC MLAs in BJP? Just like the Bramhin-Baniya-Thakur trio who voted BJP's candidate, why couldn't the SC MLAs in BJP vote the BSP candidate? The answer is simple. These SC/ST MLAs are products of Poona Pact. They are not true representatives of SC/ST communities. The political reservation elects the stooges and agents of manuvadi parties from SC/STs to the Parliament and the state legislature. They are there to further their individual interests and not the interests of the communities they are supposed to represent. It is time for the SC/STs to get back their lost rights of the separate electorate so that the true representatives of these communities are elected to parliament and state legislatures. Author – Jayant Pathri.

Problem of India

Indian psyche is not changing when it comes to the caste system which has fractured the country beyond repair and in the absence of the strong sense of community which gets fractured with the sense of purity of one human compared to another, no progress is possible. And therefore the nations like Bangladesh are rising up in all different aspects, but India despite so many comparative advantages over other countries is failing and it is failing badly: thanks to India's caste system.

Our neighboring countries have better socioeconomic indicators and the people in Pakistan are happier than the Indians is now attested by the studies. Author – Mangesh Dahiwale, Human Rights Activist.

Hindu ideas and Buddhist thought

"Let a female child be born somewhere else; here let a male child be born" -Atharva Veda 6. 2. 3.

"The nature of women is like that of the hyena" -Rig Veda X. 95.10.

"Women have no right to study Vedas" -Manu Smriti IX 3.

"It is the highest duty of the woman to immolate herself after her husband" -Brahma Puran. 80.75.

"If a wife, proud of the greatness of her relatives or (her own) excellence, violates the duty which she owes to her lord, the king shall cause her to be devoured by dogs in a place frequented by many" - Manu Smriti VIII 371.

"In childhood a female must be subject to her father, in youth to her husband, when her lord is dead to the sons; a woman must never be independent." -Manu Smriti V. 148.

"Shudra dhol pashu nari ye hai sub tadan ke adhikari (Eng. Shudras, drum, animal and women deserve beating)" – Ram Charita Manas.

Gautam Buddha was the first master who gave women, status equal to men. Secondly he provided women access to knowledge and learning by providing them entry into the Buddha's order. He considered women capable of attaining spirituality. Many women under the Buddhist Order attained very high level of learning and intellect; so much so that their contribution in the name of "Therigathas" (The songs of the Buddhists Sisters) occupies a prominent place in the Buddhist Canonical Scriptures.

He said, "Itthi bhi pandita honti" i.e. women too are learned persons. – Buddha

AI

AI predication of caste violence by zip code, or caste group can provide tools to develop preventive measures to stop caste violence, according to Ambedkar followers.

Marginals

Do Depressed Classes desire Temple Entry ? 15/03/2008

N. B. :- Gandhi requested Dr. Ambedkar to lend his support to Dr. Subbarayan's Temple entry Bill and that of Ranga Iyer-when both met on 4th Feb. 1934 at Yeravada Prison. Dr. Ambedkar declined in person, and later issued a statement on 14th Feb, 1933. He outlined the impracticability of the bill, crticised it for not making Untouchability illegal and outlined why he would not prefer just temple entry-this part is reproduced here.

The main question is : Do the Depressed Classes desire Temple Entry or do they not ? This main question is viewed by the Depressed Classes by two points of view. One is the materialistic point of view. Starting from it, the Depressed Classes think that the surest way of elevation lies in education, higher employment and better ways of earning a living. Once they become well placed in the scale of social life, they would become respectable the religious outlook of the orthodox towards them is sure to undergo change, and even if it didn't happen, it can do no injury to their material interest. Proceeding on these lines the Depressed Classes say that they will not spend their resources on such an empty things as Temple Entry. There is another reason why they do not care to fight for it. Their argument is the argument of self-respect.

Not very long ago there used to be boards on club doors and other social resorts maintained by Europeans in India, which said "Dogs and Indians" are not allowed. The temples of Hindus carry similar boards today, the only difference is that the boards on the Hindu temples practically say: "All Hindus and all animals including gods are admitted, only Untouchables are not admitted". The situation in both cases is of parity. But Hindus never begged for admission in those places form which the Europeans in their arrogance had excluded them. Why should an Untouchable beg for admission in a place from which he has been excluded by the the arrogance of the Hindus? This is the reason of the Depressed Class man who is interested in material welfare. He is prepared to say the Hindus, "to open or not to open your temples is a question for you to consider and not for me to agitate. If you think, it is bad manners not to respect the sacredness of human personality, open your temple and be a gentleman. If you rather be a Hindu than a gentleman, then shut the doors and damn yourself for I don't care to come."

I found it necessary to put the argument in this form, because I want to disabuse the minds of men like Pandit Madan Mohan Malaviya of their belief that the Depressed Classes are looking forward for their patronage.

The second point of view is the spiritual one. As religiously minded people, do the Depressed Classes desire temple entry or do they not ? That is the question. From the spiritual point of view, they are not indifferent to temple entry as they would be, if the material point of view alone were to prevail. But their final answer must depend upon the reply which Mahatma Gandhi and the Hindus give to the questions namely : What is the drive behind this offer of temple entry ? Is temple entry to be the final goal of the advancement in the social status of the Depressed Classes in the Hindu fold ? Or is it only the first step and if it is the first step, what is the ultimate goal ? Temple entry as a final goal, the Depressed Classes can never support. Indeed they will not only reject it, but they would then regard themselves rejected by Hindu Society and free to find their own destiny elsewhere. On the other hand, if is only to be a first step they may be inclined to support it. The position would then be analogous to what is happening in India today. All Indians have claimed dominion status for India. The actual constitution will fall short of Dominion status and many Indians will accept it. Why ? The answer is that as the goal is defined, it does not matter much if it is to be reached by steps and not in one jump. But if the British had not accepted the goal of Dominion status, no one would have accepted the partial reforms which many are now willing to accept. In the same way, if Mahatma Gandhi and the reformers were to proclaim what the goal which they have set before themselves is for the advancement of the social status of the Depressed Classes in the Hindu fold, it would be easier for the Depressed Classes to define their attitude towards Temple entry. The goal of the Depressed Classes might as well be stated here for the information and consideration of all concerned. What the Depressed Classes want is a religion,, which will give them equality of social status. To prevent any misunderstanding,I would like to elaborate the point by drawing a distinction between social evils are which are the result of secular causes and social evils which are founded upon doctrine of religion. Social evils can have no justification whatsoever in a civilised society. But nothing can be more odious and vile than that admitted social evils should be sought to be justified on the ground of religion. The Depressed Classes may not be able to overthrow inequalities to which they are being subjected. But they have made up their mind not to tolerate a religion that will lend its support to the continuance of these inequalities.

If the Hindu religion is to be their religion, then it must become a religion of Social Equality. The mere amendment of Hindu religious code by the mere inclusion in it of a provision to permit temple entry for all, cannot make it a religion of equality of social status. All that it can do is to recognize as nationals not aliens, if I may use the common terms which have become so familiar in politics. But that cannot mean that they would thereby reach a position where they would be free and equal, without being above and below any one else, for the simple reason that the Hindu religion does not recognise the principle of equality of social status : on the other hand it fosters inequality by insisting upon grading people as Brahmins, Kshatrias, Vaishyas and Shudras, which now stand toward one another in an ascending scale of hatred and descending scale of contempt. If the Hindu Religion is to be a religion of social equality then an amendment of its code to provide temple entry is not enough. What is required is to purge it of the doctrine of chaturvarna. That is the root cause of all inequality and also the parent of the Caste system and Untouchability, which are merely forms of inequality. Unless it is done not only will the Depressed Classes reject the temple entry, they will also reject the Hindu faith. Chaturvarna and the Caste system are incompatible with the self-respect of the Depressed Classes. So long as they stand to be its cardinal doctrine, the depressed classes must continue to be looked upon as low. The Depressed Classes can say that they are Hindus only the theory of Chaturvarna and Caste system is abandoned and expunged from the Hindu shastras. Do the Mahatma and the Hindu reformers accept this as their goal and will they show the courage to work for it ? I shall look forward to their pronouncements on this issue, before I decide upon my final attitude. But whether Mahatma Gandhi and the Hindus are prepared for this or not, let it be known once and for all that nothing short of this will satisfy the Depressed Classes and make them accept temple entry. To accept temple entry and be content with it, is to temporise with evil and barter away the sacredness of human personality that dwells in them.

There is, however, one more argument which Mahatma Gandhi and the reforming Hindu may advance against the position I have taken. They may say : "acceptance by the Depressed Classes of Temple entry now, will not prevent them from agitating hereafter for the abolition of Chaturvarna and Caste. If that is the view, I like to meet the argument right at this stage so as to clinch the issue and clear the road for future developments. My reply is that it is true that the my right to agitate for the abolition of Chaturvarna and Caste system will not be lost, if I accept Temple entry now. But the question is on what side will Mahatma Gandhi be when the question is put. If he will be in the camp of my opponents, I must tell him I cant be in in camp now. If he will be in my camp he ought to be in it now.

(Almost all the Depressed Classes leaders of Dr. Ambedkar's persuasions, endorsed the view of their leader. Srinivasan, Permtai and Malik upheld views of their leader.

Gandhi issued a statement in reply in which he stated : "I am a Hindu, not merely because I am born in the Hindu fold, but I am one by conviction and choice. There is no superiority or inferiority in Hinduism of my conception. But when Dr. Ambedkar wants to fight Varnashram itself, I cannot be in his camp, because I believe Varnashram to be an integral part of Hinduism.)

Temple entry wont make equals 15/03/2008

N.B :- This is the content of the letter written by Dr. Ambedkar to Mr. Bhaurao Gaikwad on 3rd March 1934, regarding the KalaRam Temple Entry Satyagraha-which stated on 2nd March 1930 , but whose preparation was underway for months. It started "with" the leadership of Dr. Ambedkar. His inaugural speech remained consistent with the conviction in which the Satyagraha was withdrawn. It was stopped immediately after the reciept the the said letter.

….. It is very kind of you to have asked me my views on the propriety of the Depressed Classes launching upon a Satyagraha at the Kala Ram Temple in Nasik on the coming Ram Navami Day. I have no position in saying that such a move would be quite uncalled for and should not merely be suspended but stopped altogether. This may appear strange and surprising coming as it does from one who was the author of the Satyagraha. But I am afraid to declare this change of front. I didn't launch the temple entry movement because I wanted the Depressed Classes to become worshipers of idols which they were prevented from worshiping or because I believed temple entry would make them equal members in and an integral part of the Hindu Society. So far as this aspect of the case is concerned I would advise the Depressed Classes to insist upon a complete overhauling of Hindu Society and Hindu theology before they consent to become an integral part of Hindu Society. I started temple entry Satyagraha only because I felt that was the best way of energizing th Depressed Classes and making them conscious of their position. As I believe I have achieved that purpose I have no more use for temple entry. I want the Depressed Classes to concentrate their energy and resource on politics and education and I hope that they will realise the importance of both.

Moral Equality 4/08/2007

"Why is Equality essential? The best exposition of the subject is by Prof. Beard in his essay on 'Freedom in Political Thought' and I shall do no more than quote him. Says Prof. Beard: —

> "...It (moral equality) is asserted against inequalities in physical strength, talents, industry, and wealth. It denied that superior physical strength has a moral right to kill, eat, or oppress human beings merely because it is superior. To talents and wealth, the ideal of moral equality makes a similar denial of right. And indeed few can imagine themselves to have superior physical strength, talents and wealth will withhold from inferiors all moral rights. In such circumstances government and wealth would go to superior physical strength; while virtue and talents would serve the brute man, as accomplished Greek slaves served the whims, passions and desires to Roman conquerors. When the last bitter word of criticism has been uttered against the ideal of moral equality, there remains something in it which all, except things, must accept and in practice do accept, despite their sheers and protests. A society without any respect for human personalities is a band of robbers."

Prerequisites of a Democracy 16//07/2007

A democratic form of Government presupposes a democratic form of society. The formal framework of democracy is of no value and would indeed be a misfit if there was no social democracy. The politicals never realized that democracy was not a form of Government. It was essentially a form of society. It may not be necessary for a democratic society to be marked by unity, by community of purpose, by loyalty to public ends and by mutuality of sympathy. But it does unmistakably involve two things. The first is an attitude of mind, an attitude of respect and equality towards their fellows. The second is a social organization free from rigid social barriers. Democracy is incompatible and inconsistent with isolation and exclusiveness, resulting in the distinction between the privileged and the unprivileged.

Question to A Socialist 16/07/2007

Is it enough for a Socialist to say, "I believe in perfect equality in the treatment of the various classes ?" To say that such a belief is enough is to disclose a complete lack of understanding of what is involved in Socialism. If Socialism is a practical programme and is not merely an ideal, distant and far off, the question for a Socialist is not whether he believes in equality. The question for him is whether he minds one class ill-treating and suppressing another class as a matter of system, as a matter of principle and thus allow tyranny and oppression to continue to divide one class from another.

If Liberty is the Ideal…. 16/07/2007

Religion, social status and property are all sources of power and authority, which one man has, to control the liberty of another. One is predominant at one stage; the other is predominant at another stage. That is the only difference. If liberty is the ideal, if liberty means the destruction of the dominion which one man holds over another then obviously it cannot be insisted upon that economic reform must be the one kind of reform worthy of pursuit. If the source of power and dominion is at any given time or in any given society social and religious then social reform and religious reform must be accepted as the necessary sort of reform.

N.B :- This is said in through discussion, if economic reform could be brought upon without social reform in India, as socialists' economic interpretation of history contented.

Karl Marx Fails Here… 14/07/2007

To excite the proletariat to bring about an economic revolution, Karl Marx told them : "You have nothing to lose except your chains." But the artful way in which the social and religious rights are distributed among the different castes whereby some have more and some have less, makes the slogan of Karl Marx quite useless to excite the Hindus against the Caste System. Castes form a graded system of sovereignties, high and low, which are jealous of their status and which know that if a general dissolution came, some of them stand to lose more of their prestige and power than others do. You cannot, therefore, have a general mobilization of the Hindus, to use a military expression, for an attack on the Caste System.

Are All Men Equal ? 13/07/2007

The objections to equality may be sound and one may have to admit that all men are not equal. But what of that ? Equality may be a fiction but nonetheless one must accept it as the governing principle. A. man's power is dependent upon (1) physical heredity, (2) social inheritance or endowment in the form of parental care, education, accumulation of scientific knowledge, everything which enables him to be more efficient than the savage, and finally, (3) on his own efforts. In all these three respects men are undoubtedly unequal. But the question is, shall we treat them as unequal because they are unequal ? This is a question which the opponents of equality must answer. From the standpoint of the individualist it may be just to treat men unequally so far as their efforts are unequal. It may be desirable to give as much incentive as possible to the full development of every one's powers. But what would happen if men were treated unequally as they are, in the first two respects ? It is obvious that those individuals also in whose favour there is birth, education, family name, business connections and inherited wealth would be selected in the race. But selection under such circumstances would not be a selection of the able. It would be the selection of the privileged. The reason therefore, which forces that in the third respect we should treat men unequally demands that in the first two respects we should treat men as equally as possible. On the other hand it can be urged that if it is good for the social body to get the most out of its members, it can get most out of them only by making them equal as far as possible at the very start of the race. That is one reason why we cannot escape equality. But there is another reason why we must accept equality. A Statesman is concerned with vast numbers of people. He has neither the time nor the knowledge to draw fine distinctions and to treat each equitably i.e. according to need or according to capacity. However desirable or reasonable an equitable treatment of men may be, humanity is not capable of assortment and classification. The statesman, therefore, must follow some rough and ready rule and that rough and ready rule is to treat all men alike not because they are alike but because classification and assortment is impossible. The doctrine of equality is glaringly fallacious but taking all in all it is the only way a statesman can proceed in politics which is a severely practical affair and which demands a severely practical test.

Ideal society 13/07/2007

What is your ideal society if you do not want caste is a question that is bound to be asked of you. If you ask me, my ideal would be a society based on Liberty, Equality and Fraternity. And why not ? What objection can there be to Fraternity ? I cannot imagine any. An ideal society should be mobile, should be full of channels for conveying a change taking place in one part to other parts. In an ideal society there should be many interests consciously communicated and shared. There should be varied and free points of contact with other modes of association. In other words there must be social endosmosis. This is fraternity, which is only another name for democracy. Democracy is not merely a form of Government. It is primarily a mode of associated living, of conjoint communicated experience. It is essentially an attitude of respect and reverence towards fellowmen. Any objection to Liberty ? Few object to liberty in the sense of a right to free movement, in the sense of a right to life and limb. There is no objection to liberty in the sense of a right to property, tools and materials as being necessary for earning a living to keep the body in due state of health. Why not allow liberty to benefit by an effective and competent use of a person's powers ? The supporters of caste who would allow liberty in the sense of a right to life, limb and property, would not readily consent to liberty in this sense, inasmuch as it involves liberty to choose one's profession. But to object to this kind of liberty is to perpetuate slavery. For slavery does not merely mean a legalized form of subjection. It means a state of society in which some men are forced to accept from other the purposes which control their conduct. This condition obtains even where there is no slavery in the legal sense. It is found where, as in the Caste System, some persons are compelled to carry on certain prescribed callings which are not of their choice. Any objection to equality ? This has obviously been the most contentious part of the slogan of the French Revolution. The objections to equality may be sound and one may have to admit that all men are not equal. But what of that ? Equality may be a fiction but nonetheless one must accept it as the governing principle. A. man's power is dependent upon (1) physical heredity, (2) social inheritance or endowment in the form of parental care, education, accumulation of scientific knowledge, everything which enables him to be more efficient than the savage, and finally, (3) on his own efforts. In all these three respects men are undoubtedly unequal. But the question is, shall we treat them as unequal because they are unequal?

This is a question which the opponents of equality must answer. From the standpoint of the individualist it may be just to treat men unequally so far as their efforts are unequal. It may be desirable to give as much incentive as possible to the full development of every one's powers. But what would happen if men were treated unequally as they are, in the first two respects? It is obvious that those individuals also in whose favour there is birth, education, family name, business connections and inherited wealth would be selected in the race. But selection under such circumstances would not be a selection of the able. It would be the selection of the privileged. The reason therefore, which forces that in the third respect we should treat men unequally demands that in the first two respects we should treat men as equally as possible. On the other hand it can be urged that if it is good for the social body to get the most out of its members, it can get most out of them only by making them equal as far as possible at the very start of the race. That is one reason why we cannot escape equality. But there is another reason why we must accept equality. A Statesman is concerned with vast numbers of people. He has neither the time nor the knowledge to draw fine distinctions and to treat each equitably i.e. according to need or according to capacity. However desirable or reasonable an equitable treatment of men may be, humanity is not capable of assortment and classification. The statesman, therefore, must follow some rough and ready rule and that rough and ready rule is to treat all men alike not because they are alike but because classification and assortment is impossible. The doctrine of equality is glaringly fallacious but taking all in all it is the only way a statesman can proceed in politics which is a severely practical affair and which demands a severely practical test.

Ills of Graded Inequality 6/06/2007

Students of social organization have been content with noting the difference between equality and inequality. None have realized that in addition to equality and inequality there is such a thing as graded inequality. Yet inequality is not half so dangerous as graded inequality. Inequality carried within itself the seeds of its own destruction. Inequality does not last long. Under pure and simple inequality two things happen. It creates general discontent which forms the seed of revolution. Secondly it makes the sufferers combine against a common foe and on a common grievance. But the nature and circumstances of the system of graded inequality leave no room for either of these two things to happen. The system of graded inequality prevents the rise of general discontent against inequity. It cannot therefore become the storm centre of revolution. Secondly the sufferers under inequality becoming unequal both in terms of the benefit and the burden there is no possibility of a general combination of all classes to overthrow the inequity. To make the thing concrete the Brahmanic law of marriage is full of inequity. The right of Brahmana to take a woman from the classes below him but not to give a woman to them is in inequity. But the Kshatriya, Vaishya and Shudra will not combine to destroy it. The Kshatriya resents this right of the Brahmana. But he will not combine with Vaishya or the Shudra and that for two reasons. Firstly because he is satisfied that if the Brahman has the right to take the right of three communities, the Kshatriya has the right to appropriate the women of two communities. He does not suffer so much as the other two. Secondly if he joins in a general revolution against this marriage-inequity in one way he will rise to the level of the Bramhins but in another way all will be equal which to him means that the Vaishyas and the Shudras will rise to his level i.e. they will claim Kshatriya women-which means he will fall to their level. Take any other inequity and think of a revolt against it. The same social psychology will show that a general rebellion against it is impossible.

Warning

Political equality as enshrined in our constitution cannot coexist with widening social and economic inequality.

Dr Bhimrao Ambedkar and Mohandas Gandhi are two of the tallest personalities in India's struggle for freedom. Their influence on modern India will be long lasting. It would be inadequate to describe them merely as political leaders or social reformers. Their thinking has had a deep, abiding impression on large sections of Indian society. Even to this day they continue to inspire us, and also arouse strong and passionate criticism from some sections. Love them, hate them, but you cannot ignore them.

Interestingly, even though both Ambedkar and Gandhi worked toward a vision of India free from caste divisions, they had fundamental differences. Their differences became almost irreconcilable after the episode of the Temple Entry Bill of 1933. Prior to this in 1932, Gandhi had vehemently opposed a separate electorate for untouchables in the Legislature, as demanded by Ambedkar. Gandhi opposed it, even though he had accepted this for Muslims, Christians, Sikhs and Anglo-Indians. Gandhi even threatened to fast unto death. Finally, Ambedkar had to back down and compromise (the famous Poona Pact of 1932).

Ambedkar refused to support the bill Temple Entry Bill, which was to be introduced in Legislative Councils of various provinces. This bill had proposed to throw open the doors of Hindu temples to untouchables, which according to Gandhi would give dignity to the outcastes. He said that the untouchables were not begging to be let in. In fact it was a side issue. The real issue was the complete eradication of untouchability, nay the caste system. He said that untouchability is sinful and immoral, even if it is acceptable to majority of Hindus. The surest salvation for the untouchables was in higher education, higher employment and better ways of earning a living, not in getting a right to entering temples. To open their temple doors to outcastes, was for (caste) Hindus to consider, not for untouchables to agitate, said Ambedkar. If the Temple Entry Bill was passed it would entrench the caste system, and confer symbolic capital to high caste Hindus. The untouchables were determined not to be a part of a religion which tried to defend or rationalise social inequality. After 1933 the schism between Gandhi and Ambedkar widened, leading the latter to walk away from the Congress Party. Ambedkar also grew suspicious of all majoritarian politics because of this episode.

Ambedkar dreamt of an India based on ideas of liberty, equality and fraternity. He made a prophetic speech on November 25, 1949 in the Constituent Assembly. This was when most of the debates on the Constitution were over, and India was on the verge of adopting the final version. His fight for eradication of the caste system was not so much to gain rights for the downtrodden outcastes, but much more to reach the ideal of social equality. It is worth reproducing that part of this speech:

> "On the January 26, 1950, we are going to enter into a life of contradictions. In politics we will have equality and in social and economic life we will have inequality. In politics we will be here cognizing the principle of one man, one vote and one vote one value. In our social and economic life, we shall, by reason of our social and economic structure, continue to deny the principle of one man, one value. How long shall we continue to live this life of contradictions? How long shall we continue to deny equality in our social and economic life? If we continue to deny it for long, we will do so only by putting our political democracy in peril. We must remove this contradiction at the earliest possible moment or else those who suffer from inequality will blow up the structure of political democracy which is Assembly has to laboriously built up."

Ambedkar Logic

Ambedkar contended that caste system is graded inequalities. The four varnas are not only different but also unequal in status – one stands above the others and accordingly the distribution of social benefits are unequal.

The occupants of the higher status get more benefits than the lower status occupants and the lowest- the untouchable get nothing.

Secondly, the occupation of a person is prescribed for a caste is graded from highest to the lowest. The priestly occupation is the highest assigned to the Brahmins and the manual and the most filthy and degrading occupation to the lowest, that is to the Shurdas and the untouchables.

Thirdly, restriction on inter-dinning between and among the castes is a design to keep the higher caste exclusive to its own group and to avoid inter mixing with the low castes.

Ambedkar viewed Varna system as class. Because an individual is not treated on his or her merit but as class like a member of a Brahmin or Shudra or Dalit etc. even in family, as man or woman. So it was a great injustice to a merit of an individual. So, he questioned "Does the Hindu Social order recognize equality?"

On the genesis of caste system Ambedkar refutes all the theories of caste origin put forward by different thinkers. In his view the caste system has either been imposed upon the docile population of India by a lawgiver as divine dispensation or it has developed according to some law of social growth to the Indian people.

Ambedkar says that the caste system assigns task to individuals on the basis of social status of the parents- and not on merit or aptitude of the individual. It is predestined by birth; and unchangeable. This is against the principle of division of labour. This is an artificial device to keep some people to serve other. Therefore Ambedkar wanted annihilation of caste system. In his view caste divides men into separate communities and it places, the communities in a graded order- one above the other. The higher the grade of a caste, the greater is the member of religious and social rights. This is not only inequalities but also injustice. Therefore Ambedkar wanted annihilation of caste system at all.

Having analyzed the exploitative nature of Hindu social order born out a varnas, caste and sub caste Ambedkar gave his own vision of an ideal social order based on liberty, equality, fraternity. Accordingly he incorporated the provisions which do away the casteism and ensure the fundamental rights to citizens of India irrespective of caste, creed and sex. The right guarantees the equality of all Indians in social life.

Literature

The impact of Life and Mission of Dr Ambedkar on Literature is as follows:

Dr. Ambedkar also fought for the dignity of Dalits. He considered the Book of Hindu law Manu Smriti as a source of the caste system and discrimination against Dalits in India. On December 25, 1927, a Satyagraha at Mahad in Maharashtra was launched by him for the human rights of Dalits. He burnt, with thousands of supporters, Manu Smriti which was considered as the valorizing document of Brahmanical social order and source of discrimination. Dr. Babasaheb Ambedkar was thus a humanitarian and truly an emancipation of Dalits.

Dr. Babasaheb Ambedkar became India's most despised writer for the orthodox social system because of his merciless attack on the hidden agenda of Brahminical Social Order. Dr. Babasaheb has displayed the guts to attack Caste hegemony in India though he suffered a series of setbacks in his lifetime because of the Brahmanical media barons. At one stage, all determined to blackout Dr.Babasaheb Ambedkar's literature, writings and speeches but his struggle for the rights of Dalits through his writings continued. This research proposes to make a close reading of his work and its impact on literature to assess the views on discrimination of Dalits.

Rajshekar's book Caste – A Nation within the Nation (2007) marks a deciding change in the literary career of Rajshekar as it switches his basic tone from protest to more mature analysis. It also explains the marginalisation of certain communities that happens within the framework of a nation-state. Rajshekar begins the book with the statement that caste is still an uneasy topic in India though casteism is practised in all the social institutions. He points out that one will have to examine the institution of marriage to see how deep routed is casteism in India. He indicates that the matrimonial columns found in the newspapers are clearly casteist and they resist assimilation of caste which should logically happen in a democracy.

Rajshekar points out that an understanding of a nation without the understanding of its castes and sub-castes is basically incomplete. He argues that people do not even understand that Indian society is not homogeneous society but a collection of castes and communities. According to Rajshekar, the caste system is the brainchild of upper caste hegemony which had generated rigid social classification which eventually generated a structure that could give rise to conflicts. He looks at caste system primarily as a class conflict.

Rajshekar also dismisses the word 'Caste' and prefers the word 'Jati' which seems to be more appropriate in the Indian context. He locates jati as a shaping factor in marriage, a social institution. He indicates that marriage as an institution has been largely responsible for perpetuating caste hegemony. He remembers Dr. Ambedkar on this point:

> According to Dr. Babsaheb Ambedkar, it is mainly the custom of endogamy that has preserved the castes and prevented one caste from fusing into another. Almost all the writers and scholars conform to this view of Dr. Babsaheb Ambedkar. (CNWN: 4)

Rajshekar declares that Dalits of the present day India have seen through the hypocrisy of Gandhi gimmicks, social activism and that of Socialist Brahmins. He argues that the Bahujans have clearly understood the power politics that creates caste system:

> The Bahujans, particularly the Ambedkarites, have correctly understood that the caste system is a power structure resulting in an ascending scale of reverence and a descending degree of contempt. They know that the feeling of superiority among the ruling upper castes and the inferiority feeling (self-hatred) among the servile castes are the exact symptoms of the pernicious caste system. (CNWN: 12)

Rajshekar analysis of the relationship between caste and power is similar to that of Dr. Ambedkar who had identified Hinduism as a Brahminical religion with its own clear power politics Dr. Ambedkar had observed:

> The root of untouchability is the caste system; the root of the caste system is religion attached to varnashram, and the root of varnashram is the Brahminical religion, and the root of the Brahminical religion is authoritarianism or political power. (Dr. Ambedkar; 1980:30)

Rajshekar also points out that the Bahujans have been enlightened by Dr. Ambedkar and that they believe that they need political power to counter the adverse power of casteism. Dr. Ambedkar had pointed out that the untouchability should be taken as a site of resistance by Dalits to acquire political power. Rajshekar defends strongly reservation by arguing that reservation is an empowerment of the deprived people. He also links reservation to the issue of human Rights and condemns all those righting which critique caste based reservation:

> Reservation is nothing but our human rights. All deprived people in the world have reservations. When their human rights are restored, the deprived automatically gain power, and power helps them become rich. That is why the Hindus hate caste-based reservations and every day we read articles and reports criticising reservations. (CNWN: 12-13).

Rajshekar also considers the Bahujan political movement as an assertion of the ethnic identities of the Schedule Caste and the Schedule Tribes.

According to him, the Bahujan movement resists the hegemony and monopoly of the upper caste identities.

Rajshekar is in favour of caste identity and he argues that only by strengthening castes, Brahminism can be attacked. He also argues that this was the very agenda of Dr. Ambedkar who had pointed out that more than castes, Hindu religion is harmful. Rajshekar reminds that Hindu caste system and not the caste is truly dangerous. Dr. Ambedkar had also mentioned that religion kills caste identity.

Rajshekar explains how Buddhism tried to compensate the lives of Dalits by providing them with sacred places for worship. He also argues that Buddhism and Dr. Ambedkar helped Dalits in consolidating their jati identity. Rajshekar also considers the impact of caste consolidation and the political alignment of sub-caste in the interest of the nation. He points out that both communists and Brahmins against caste identity as they believe that such identities will go against nationality. However, Rajshekar reminds that national unity is the slogan of Hindu Nazis and for Dalits, caste identity is as much important as the national identity. It is important to remember Dr. Ambedkar's argument on nationalism in the context of casteism in India. **Nationalist discourse, according to Rajshekar, is controlled by Brahminical Social Order. According to him, nationalism is a strategy used by the Brahmins to divert the attention of Bahujans.** If nationalism is a part of one's identity, defining one's fellowship to kith and kin, it is a matter of tie of kinship. In this regard, Rajshekar believes that caste comes closest to this definition of nation. He argues that the notion of the nation cannot be confined a territory but rather to the patterns of kinship and fellowship. Hence, he believes that **India is the country of several nations with several kinship patterns emerging out of different caste identities** of the untouchables. Dr. Ambedkar had also defended such a caste-based movement and identity of the untouchables. He had made an attempt to deconstruct the idea of the nation from the perspective of different caste based communities:

> First of all, there is no nation of Indians in the real sense of the word. The nation does not exist, is to be created, and I think it will be admitted that the suppression of a distinct and a separate community is not the method of creating a nation. (Dr. Ambedkar: 1944:168).

Rajshekar is also of the opinion that the foundation of the caste system in India is the fear that the lower castes develop. He indicates that this fear is controlled by religion and hence it is unreal.

Rajshekar's notion of caste identity is similar to that of Dr. Ambedkar who had stated that the untouchable need to develop cast pride and cast consolidation to battle the evils of casteism. Rajshekar also argues that it is very difficult to eliminate over eight thousands castes as compare to ending three percent of Brahmins castes. He points out that elimination of caste identity is nearly impossible. According to Rajshekar, casteism is founded on the privileges of certain groups. Hence he maintains that unless these privileges are attacked. Casteism will never be eliminated.

Rajshekar also believes that Hinduism is a kind of imperialism and the Bahujan will have to realized that Hinduism not a religion but a political game plan drawn by Brahmins. Such an idea was also upheld by Dr. Ambedkar who had explained the politics of Hinduism and how it is tilted in favour of upper caste Hindus:

> To put it in plain language, what the Hindus call religion is really Law or at best legalized class ethics. Frankly, I refuse to call this code of ordinances, as religion. The first evil of such a code of ordinances, misrepresented to the people as Religion, is that it tends to deprive moral life of freedom and spontaneity and to reduce it (for the conscientious at any rate) to a more or less anxious and servile conformity to externally imposed rules. (Dr. Ambedkar: 1944:68).

Rajshekar also indicates that like Dr. Ambedkar, Buddha too very particular in acknowledging his caste identity. He also reminds the readers that Buddha was not against tribal identity even as he taught Dhamma. According to Rajshekar, Hinduism tries to curb the minds of Dalits and other Bahujan by propagating the idea of predetermination. He points out that Hinduism deprives the social under class of any freedom of thought. Dr. Ambedkar too had pointed out rigidity and class structure found in Hinduism. While explaining his version of caste identity thesis, Rajshekar considers the questions whether strengthening of caste will destroy Dalits unity and create sub-caste rivalry. His argument is that abolition of sub-caste will only strengthen Hinduism and Brahminical hegemony. He also points the fact that sub-caste is a social reality and it does not inhibit Dalits unity. Rajshekar is of the opinion that Dalits in India are made of different communities, tribes and linguistic backgrounds. He explains that Dalits community is based on the philosophy of equality in differences.

Rajshekar's argument that Hinduism cannot provide a political identity or national identity for all the communities is similar to the view of Romila Thapar. Thapar explains that Hinduism has foundation on Brahminism and hence, it can be viable model for political identity. She says:

> The call to unite under Hinduism as a political identity is if anything, anachronistic. Social and economic inequality whether one disapproves of it or condones it, was foundational to Brahmanism. To propagate the texts associated with this view and yet insist that it is an egalitarians philosophy is hardly acceptable. (Thapar: 2010:26).

Rajshekar argues that sociologist in India talk about class struggle where as what India is witnessing, is a caste struggle. He observes that the study of social classes in India is misleading if it cannot take into account the factor of caste and ethnicity. He also talks about the political reason for identitifing the caste struggle. Rajshekar reminds a reader that the whole world is caught in discourse of identity politics and in this debate on identity ethnicity has a significant role. Dr. Babasaheb Ambedkar condemned the systematic suppression of the Dalits and saw the solution to this in the removal of the social structure that supported the discrimination against them. He was only partly successful in his venture, facing in fighting centuries of unquestioned abuse of the caste system. His influence on the post-Ambedkar Dalit movement and literature however, lives on in the unifying nature of his inspirational writings.

Ruling voters

Malaysia (10-11 October, 98): Addressing the First International Dalit Conference at Kuala Lumpur as a Chief Guest in the inaugural session, Manyawar Kanshiramji said,-"My heartiest congratulations to you all for organizing this international conference which is a big step towards our supreme goal of forming a casteless society in India".

(1) I will not merely sit quite in anticipation that some day or the other caste will be annihilated automatically ; but as long as the "caste" is alive, I will continue to use it in the interest of my society.

(2) What is more important? To become MLA/MP or to run the movement of Babasaheb? According to me it was more important to run the movement of Babasaheb than to become MLA/MP. Therefore I chose to run the movement. For a moment a thought came to my mind that to run the movement effectively we should make our people MLAs/MPs. But the important question was which is the party that will give us MLAs/MPs who will also run the movement of Babasahab. After a lot of thought I reached to a conclusion that such MLAs/MPs can be elected only through our own party.

(3) I have learned a lot from the people from Maharashtra. I have learned my half lesson for running the Ambedkarite movement from Dr Babasaheb Ambedkar. The other half lesson I have learnt from the Mahars of Maharashtra. I have learnt from Babasahab how to run the movement. And from Mahars of Maharashtra I have learned how not to run the movement. To successfully run any movement it is not only sufficient to know how to run the movement but also it is necessary to know how not to run the movement. If you do not know how not to run the movement then you will never be able to know how to run it.

(4) I do not like to talk much even though I have to talk very frequently. I do not like to tell about my work in words but I want my work and the results emanating from that work to speak for themselves. I want to tell all those fellow activists in the movement who do not agree to my work – "I may be wrong, but why don't you analyze the results that I have achieved, what you have to say about those results ?".

(5) Our intellectuals often think that the solution to all our problems is in Marxism, Socialism and Communism. I strongly believe that in the country where Manuvad is present no other ism can become successful. The reason being no other ism is ready to accept the reality of the caste.

(6) Who is capable of giving reservations? Only the ruling class of people can give reservations to others. Even to make your own society capable of reaping the benefits and to protect your interests , you have to become a ruling class. Therefore we have to prepare ourselves in the direction of becoming a ruling class in India. We have to become the rulers…It is the solution on most of our problems.

Annihilation of Caste by ruling

Kanshiramji said – In 1936 Dr Babasaheb Ambedkar was invited by the "Jat Pat Todak Mandal, Lahore" to present his essay on the subject of caste. But the organizers of the conference did not allow Babasaheb to present the essay. Later on Babasaheb published the essay in a form of book titled as "Annihilation of Caste". When I first read this book in 1962-63, I felt that annihilation of caste is certainly possible. But later on when I started thinking deeply and began to study the subject of castes, caste system and behavioural patterns associated with the caste system, my understanding of caste began to change. My study of Caste is not merely based on reading books but it has emanated from my real life experience with the castes. There are millions of people who leave their villages and migrate to metro cities like Mumbai, Delhi, Kolkata and other big cities. These people do not bring anything else with them; the only thing they bring with them is their caste. They leave behind in their villages their small huts, small plot of land, etc. But they can not leave behind their caste in the village, the caste invariably accompanies them to the cities where they begin to stay in dirty shanties along the side of railway tracks and nallahs. If the caste is so dear to the people then how can we annihilate the caste? Therefore I have stopped thinking in the direction of annihilation of caste.

You have organized this convention as a precursor to march ahead in the direction of forming a casteless society. Even my aim is to form a casteless society. But caste is not something that can be annihilated just by your noble thoughts about annihilation of caste. Annihilation of caste is almost impossible. Then what should we do to form a casteless society?

Causes of castes

The castes were not born without any purpose. There is a specific purpose and selfish interests hidden behind the formation of castes. As long as this specific purpose and the selfish interests exist , the caste can not be annihilated. You will never find Bramhins and other Savarna caste people organizing such conventions for "reformation of casteless society". This is because the castes were formed by these same people with an ill intention to secure their self interests. Formation of castes has brought benefits to minuscule few savarna castes but on other hand the generations after generations of the 85 % Bahujan Samaj have been at the receiving end of this oppressive caste system. The Bahujan Samaj has been subjugated to the beastly oppression and inhuman humiliations. If the caste system has been beneficial to the Savarna Caste people then why would they vouch for it's annihilation ? The debates, convention and conferences of these kind can be organized only by we people who have been victims of the oppressive caste system. The beneficiaries of the caste system would never be interested in the annihilation of caste. On the contrary they would work towards strengthening the caste system so that they continue to reap the benefits arising from caste system for the ages to come.

The audience sitting in this conference hall may not have been direct victims of the caste system but we have certainly been born among the people or society that has been victim of the caste system and therefore we all need to necessarily think towards formation of casteless society. But when we talk of annihilation of caste then first of all we need to accept the existence of caste system. We can never annihilate the caste by ignoring it's presence or by undermining it's relevance in the contemporary India.

It may be true that lot of us still nurture a feeling of formation of a casteless society but simultaneously it is also true that the urge for forming a casteless society is dwindling by passage of time. So what do we do till the time the caste is not annihilated completely? I believe that until the time we are not able to form a casteless society, we need to use caste to annihilate caste. If Bramhins can use caste for the benefit of their society then why can not we use it for the benefit of our society?

Two-edged sword

Caste is like a sword with two edges which can attack from both sides. If you use it from one side it cuts enemy from that side; if you use it from other side it cuts from the other side. Therefore I have begun to use this two edged sword of caste system in such a way that it benefits the people of Bahujan Samaj and it takes away the benefits that the savarna castes have been reaping from caste system. Dr Babasaheb Ambedkar has given the political and social rights to the Scheduled castes and Scheduled tribes based on the castes. He has used the very basis of caste to secure the political rights of separate electorate from the Britishers. But he had to forgo those hard earned rights on the adamant insistence of Mohandas Gandhi who used his cheap tactics of fast unto death to blackmail Babasahab.

Separate Electorate

Many people ask me as to why I do not start an agitation for separate electorate just like what Dr Babasaheb Ambedkar did. So far I have never wasted even single minute on the issue of separate electorate. If the right to separate electorate could not be obtained during the time when Britishers were in rule in India then how can I secure those rights when the Manuwadis are the rulers of India. Today this is totally impossible.

Specialist on Caste

Dr Babasaheb Ambedkar taught the SC/STs how to make use of the weapon of caste. Therefore he was able to secure many constitutional rights for our people from the Britishers. But after the departure of Britishers there are just three people who succeeded in using the weapon of caste. The first person was Jawaharlal Nehru, second was Indira Gandhi and third person is Kanshiram.

Nehru applied the weapon of caste like a skilled warrior and succeeded in it. Nehru was an expert in the art of using castes for maintaining the

Manuvadi dominance and Bramhnical hegemony. After him Indira Gandhi became expert in exploiting the weapon of caste so that the Bramhnical Social Order is continuously benefited. But today if you ask any Congressman in Delhi whether he receives any benefits from the caste, he will answer in negative. He will say that he does not know how to get benefited from the caste and that only Kanshiram knows how to make use of caste for the benefits of his people (Laughter).

If you can stop Bramhins from using caste for their own selfish interests then he will think twice before he uses the sword of caste against us. I have learned how to make use of this two wedged sword of caste in the interest of my society. Castes which today to us seem to be a problem, can become, if used tactically, a solution to our problems. The thing which is today our problem can become an opportunity for us provided we learn to make appropriate use of it for our own benefits.

Indian Refugees

We must always be ready to learn a lesson from history. We have to accelerate our work of taking ahead the Ambedkarite movement. In 1932 Dr Babasaheb Ambedkar asked for separate electorate for Dalit/Adivasis. But in 1942 he raised a demand for separate settlements because he wanted that the Dalits should not be dependent on the hindus in any way. They should live their lives with full independence. But what is the real picture in India today ? Today there is 45 lakh hectare tilled agricultural land. Our people toil in the fields and produce crops. But in the field they toil they do not have any property rights. They become victims of exploitation and injustice of Manuvadi landlords. To escape from the exploitation and oppression of the land lords our people leave villages and migrate to big cities in search of respectable life. In the process they end up living in the dirty shanties , under the bridges , along side of railway tracks, on bank of nallahs and at many other dirty places where they are forced to live a life which is worse than that of animals. Such Distress Migration has resulted into nearly 10 Cr people leaving behind their villages, their tiny plots of land , their small huts and their meager belongings, to leave in cities. Ten years ago the number of people who stayed in cities was 5 Crores. Today this number has risen to 16 Cr. 10 Cr people in big cities stay in dirty slums, on roads and at other filthy places. I call these people "Indian Refugees". Who will address the problems faced by these people? The Rural development Ministry and Urban development Ministry of Government of India should be addressing the multitude of problems faced by the Indian refugees. Barring these 10 Cr Indian refugees, the Government of India makes some plan or the other for the development of the other people. But no one looks into the problems faced by these Indian refugees. No budgetary provisions are made in our annual budget for these 10 Cr people. There is no separate department or ministry for such a large number of people. The Indian government has formed separate department and ministry for the Pakistani refugees who came to India in 1947, the refugees from Kashmir and refugees from other places. Government of India spends Crores of rupees on the welfare of such foreign refugees; but no government ever has paid attention to the problems of these 10 Cr Indian refugees.

Since these 10 Cr Indian refugees have left behind their villages, land and other belongings , bringing only their castes to the cities, my work has become very easy. These 10 Cr refugees are considered as a big problem by the Manuvadi rulers. But for us these Indian refugees are a big strength, they are the vehicles of our empowerment. The very "caste"on the basis of which Crores of such people have been living a degraded , humiliated lives and thrown in the gallows of backwardness, we will use the same "caste" to free these crores of people from the injustice and exploitation meted out to them. After the forthcoming state assembly elections in Delhi, Rajasthan and Madhya Pradesh, we will carry out a "Indian refugees' agitation". I will not merely sit quite in anticipation that some day or the other caste will be annihilated automatically; but as long as the "caste" is alive, I will continue to use it in the interest of my society.

Let me now tell you about my experience of using the caste in the interest of our society. Today by organizing the people who have been the victims of the draconian caste system(Bahujan Samaj), I am training these people to make use of caste for the betterment of our society. I am inspiring them to carry forward the mission of Dr Babasaheb Ambedkar. I am preparing and enabling my society which comprises of the victims of the "caste" to make use of this double edged sword of "caste" in their own interests. Today every Manuvadi party and their leaders are afraid of my use of "caste". All these Manuvadi parties are trying to stop this "Kanshiram magic". First Rajiv Gandhi tried then V. P. Singh , Narsimharao, etc tried to stop me. Today the similar efforts are being made by the BJP. But all these people are playing their own games and I am playing my own (claps).

Recognition of Bahujan Samaj Party

The Manuvadis beneficiaries of the 'caste' have formed 'caste' so that they can perpetually rule over Bahujan Samaj. They have been protectors and saviours of 'caste system' to ensure their perpetual monopolistic rule over Bahujan Samaj. The creation of any system is more difficult than it's retention. Once you build a system , keeping the system up and running is not very difficult task.

If you want to annihilate 'caste' then you have to prevent the Manuvadis from reaping the benefits of 'caste'. As long as the Manuvadi beneficiaries of 'caste' are left scot-free to use the 'caste' to their own benefits , the Bahujan victims of 'caste' will continue to suffer from 'caste'. Therefore you will have to learn to use 'caste' in the interest of the Bahujan Samaj and you will have to prevent the Manuvadis from reaping the benefits of 'caste'. You should not ignore the presence of the 'caste' in the Indian society; whereas you should accept the existence of 'caste' as a naked truth. BSP has emerged has 4th largest national party in India by successfully making use of 'caste'. In India there are about 70 recognized political parties. We are ahead of 66 of these political parties. Today only Congress, BJP and CPI (M) are ahead of us. When we formed BSP in the year 1984, the other parties used to say that BSP would remain as a regional party within UP. But today BSP has secured recognition not only in UP but also in MP, Punjab, Jammu and Kashmir and Haryana. Seeing this success of BSP all the savarna hindu castes (Manuvadi samaj) has become very sad. And even I am also not happy. They are sad because BSP is speedily gaining strong ground in other states; whereas I am sad because BSP has not been able to become a recognized party in all the states of India. I want BSP to become recognized party in all the states, and even in Maharashtra.

Ticket Printing Machine?

In the year 1997, the manuvadi ruling class in India decided to celebrate the golden jubilee of India's independence. There may be many reasons for them to celebrate; but the 85 % Bahujan Samaj which continues to remain dependent on others even after 50 years of independence, has no reason to celebrate. Even today our people in the villages do not possess their own land, they work as farm labour in the land of manuvadi landlords. 10 Cr people have migrated to cities because in the villages they were dependent on others. When we established Bahujan Samaj Party, the Dalits, backwards were dependent on manuvadi parties for tickets. They used to run behind these parties for getting tickets. The political parties, if not anything else are the tickets printing machines. We thought as to why we should not possess one such machine and therefore we established Bahujan Samaj Party on 14th April, 1984.

Tickets in Demands

In March 1985 we distributed 237 tickets for the Uttar Pradesh assembly polls. That time I told all our candidates that our tickets are merely platform tickets and that you will not be able to reach Lucknow with help of these tickets. That time there wasn't any quarrel for getting our ticket. But today our tickets are in great demand. Today in UP every BSP candidate secures more than 1 lac of votes. Today our tickets are no more just the platform tickets but one can reach not just Lucknow but also Delhi with the help of our tickets. Today why are our tickets in so much demand?

BSP

On basis of 1984 Loksabha elections in Uttar Pradesh, Congress had won 410 assembly seats out of 425. But in the 1985 assembly elections they won just 265 seats. Congress had to lose 145 seats because of the presence of BSP. Congress got frustrated because of these losses and they carried out a campaign calling BSP a "party of Chamars". This campaign indeed helped BSP to consolidate our ground in UP. Our party became very popular among the Chamar community of Uttar Pradesh. In 1985 election we secured merely 2 % votes. Our vote percentage went on rising in every subsequent elections. In 1989 it went on to 9%, in 1991 – 11%, in 1993 – 20. 6 %. In 1996 Loksabha elections we got 29% votes. We achieved this success not by ignoring the 'caste' but by accepting the existence of 'caste' and by utilizing it in our interests. Today Congress is unable to get benefited by making use of 'caste' whereas we have increased our strength manifold by appropriately using the caste reality; we will continue to strengthen ourselves in future to come.

Maharashtra

Today here many people from Maharashtra are present. I have learned a lot from the people from Maharashtra. I have learned a half lesson for running the Ambedkari movement from Dr Babasaheb Ambedkar. The other half lesson I have learnt from the Mahars of Maharashtra. I have learnt from Babasahab how to run the movement. And from Mahars of Maharashtra I have learned how not to run the movement. To successfully run any movement it is not only sufficient to know how to run the movement but also it is necessary to know how not to run the movement. If you do not know how not to run the movement then you will never be able to know how to run it.

Mahars have not been able to appropriately use the double edged sword of caste. They say that now they have become Buddhists and they are no more Mahars. But simultaneously they kept on fighting for the benefits of reservations in capacity of being Mahars. They began to demand reservations for the people who have become Buddhists. Mahars carried the 'caste'- a bad breath of Hinduism to Buddhism. 'Caste' is that bad breath of Hinduism which has polluted the whole world.

Reservations

On 26th July 1902, the Maharaja of Kolhapur- Chatrapati Shahuji Maharaj implemented reservations in jobs in his kingdom for the Dalits and backwards. On 26th July 2002 we will complete 100 years of reservations. 100 years of reservations is sufficient. Now I consider it my responsibility to empower my people so that they will not ask for reservations but they will become capable to give reservations to others. It is easy to understand and say this thing but it is not easy to make it happen.

Who is capable of giving reservations ? Only the ruling class of people can give reservations to others. Even to enable your own society capable of reaping the benefits and to protect their interests, you have to become a ruling class. Therefore we have to prepare ourselves in the direction of becoming a ruling class in India. We have to become the rulers...It is the solution on most of our problems.

But the question is how the victims of the 'caste' can become the rulers? Should we become MLA/MP or should we run the Ambedkar movement? I have nither seen Dr Babasaheb Ambedkar nor have I heard him when he was alive. I have learned Ambedkarism from the leaders of Maharashtra. Mr Bajirao Kamble who was wearing a blue cap and sitting in front of me was one of those people who gave me lessons in Ambedkarism. When the Ambedkarite leaders from Maharashtra began to crawl behind the Congress for tickets, it resulted into many skirmishes between me and them. They were saying that if they stick to Ambedkarism then they can not become MLAs and MPs. I asked them what is more important ? To become MLA/ MP or to run the movement of Babasaheb? According to me it was more important to run the movement of Babasaheb than to become MLA/MP. Therefore I chose to run the movement. For a moment a thought came to my mind that to run the movement effectively we should make our people MLAs/MPs. But the important question was which is the party that will give us MLAs/MPs who will also run the movement of Babasahab. After a lot of thought I reached to a conclusion that such MLAs/MPs can be elected only through our own party. And therefore I left Mumbai and came back to Lucknow.

Which castes supported Babasaheb?

Having studied deeply the 'caste' as reality in the Indian society Manyavar Kanshiram said, "Babasaheb's movement was supported by the Mahars of

Maharashtra, Pariahs of Tamilnadu, Malas of Andhra Pradesh, Jatavs of Uttar Pradesh and Chandals (Namo shudras) of Bengal. But when Babasaheb himself could not win the election in 1952 and 1954 , his supporters began to think if Babasaheb himself can not win then how can we win and become MLAs/MPs" ?

He further told that he even delved into electoral victories of Babasaheb. In 1946 Babasaheb had won from the Jaisor and Khulna seats from Bengal. How did this happen? In both these constituencies the population of Chandals was 52%. They thought rather than sending anyone else, it is better to send Babasaheb to the constituent assembly. Babasaheb was able to win because the Chandals had majority votes with them. Mahar, Pariah, Jatav, Mala, etc castes did not have numbers as large as the Chandals and therefore these castes did not win elections and thus they began to leave the movement of Babasaheb.

The fight of Babasaheb was for all the castes that were victims of the 'caste system'. But were only Mahars, Pariahs, Malas, Jatavs, etc.castes, the victims of the 'caste' ? Were only these castes the victims of the Manuvadi social order ? The answer is No. These castes were not the only victims of 'caste'. 6000 castes are the victims of 'caste'.

According to Mandal Commission report, there are nearly 1500 castes among the SCs, 1000 castes among the STs and 3743 castes among the OBCs. The number of such castes is more than 6000. These are all such castes which have been victims of the Manuvadi social order. Some of them have been victimized less and some have been victimized more. But the truth is that all these 6000 castes have been victims of the manuvadi social order. Should not all these castes organize together to fight against the exploitative 'caste system' ? Among these castes some castes are bigger and some are smaller in terms of population. If all these castes remain divided among themselves then they will remain as minorities. But if these castes organize among themselves by creating a feeling of fraternity, they can become a majority – Bahujans. These people are 85 % of country's population and thus they constitute of a very big strength in the country.

Fraternity among the Bahujans

When Bahujan Samaj Party was established in 1984, at that time Bahujan Samaj had not been formed in the country. Bahujan Samaj Party can become successful only if the Bahujan Samaj is formed. Therefore we have began to organize the 6000 Bahujan Castes by creating a fraternity among them in order to form a Bahujan Samaj. In last 10 years we have been able to connect together just 600 castes which forms just 10 % of the total number of castes that we want to reach to.

Just by bringing together 600 castes, our party has become 4th largest party in India. If we add 400 more castes then the number of castes that we have brought together will go up to 1000. And if we succeed in adding 400 more castes in our fold then we will become the number one party in the country. I do not like to talk much even though I am compelled to talk very frequently. I do not like to tell in my words but I want my work and the results emanating from that work to speak for themselves. I want to tell all those fellow activists in the movement who do not agree to my work – "I may be wrong, but why don't you analyze the results that I have achieved, what you have to say about those results ?".

Bringing together so many castes on one platform was a mammoth task in itself. Lot of people have been engaged in making severe criticism of those people who have been instrumental in bringing the 600 castes together. Many have advised not to undertake such an impossible task in hand. But when the people who started the noble work of bringing together the divided castes, no force in the world was able to stop them from doing so. The people that carried out the task of joining together people from different castes ; did their work with all the sincerity and dedication at their command. If we have succeeded in bringing together 600 castes then why won't we succeed in bringing many more castes together ? We will certainly succeed. By bringing together all the victim castes, we can capture the political power and become the ruling class.

Capturing the Master Key

Babasaheb has said that "political power is the master key using which you can open all the doors of your progress and self respect".

Our friends from Maharashtra had been fighting since 25 years for changing the name of Marathwada university. They had to do this because they do not have the political master key. In 1989 Rajiv Gandhi came to Lucknow and he laid down the foundation stone for the Dr Ambedkar University. On one hand the Congress party is refusing to change the name of Marathwada university in Maharashtra and on the other hand the same Congress party is laying down a stone for the Dr Ambedkar University at Lucknow. Why this has happened ? The people of Uttar Pradesh have never raised a demand for Dr Ambedkar Univesity at Lucknow. This was the demand of people from Maharashtra.Then why is this demand of people from Maharashtra being fulfilled in Uttar Pradesh ? Why was congress so eager to start a Dr Ambedkar University at Lucknow ? This had happened because the people of Uttar Pradesh were extending their hand towards the political master key. Therefore the ruling class wanted to hide the master key in guise of the university.

By capturing the power in UP we have formed not just one university but many universities for which the people from Maharashtra have been fighting for long time. In 1994 we laid a foundation stone for Shahu Maharaj university at Kanpur. In 1996 we formed Mahatma Phule university and Dr Babasaheb Ambedkar university. Apart from this we acquired 200 acre land at Noida for Gautam Buddha Univesity. We created 17 new districts to fasten the process of development and more importantly to honour our heroes by giving their names to these newly formed districts. It becomes very clear from this that you can use 'caste' to acquire political master key and make use of this master key to secure a life of self respect and take them along the path of progress.

Shed away their "Dalit mentality"

I have so far talked at length about the 'caste'. Now I want to talk something about the Dalits. I rarely go out of India. My party men and other friends were thinking that I may not go to attend the convention at Kuala Lumpur because I am so much overburdened by the vows of Dalits in India. But I get more upset by looking at the Dalit mentality of the people. Dalit mentality is the biggest weakness of the dalits. Dalit mentality has become a sort of a feeling of destitution. A person with a mentality of a beggar can never become a ruler. Similarly without shedding away the Dalit mentality, no society can become a ruling class. The hands which are used to ask/beg have to strive to become the ones which will give, i.e. they have to become a ruling race. If we can not become the ruling class then there can not be any other shorter and easier solution to all our problems. So how you can become ruling class without shedding away your Dalit mentality ? Therefore you have to shed away your Dalit mentality. If you become rulers then you yourselves can find the solution to all your problems.

Inequality can destroy all other isms.

Our intellectuals often think that the solution to all our problems is in Marxism, Socialism and Communism. I strongly believe that in the country where Manuvad is present no other ism can become successful. The reason being no other ism is ready to accept the reality of the caste.

It is the responsibility of these intellectuals as well as mine that we evolve our own ism keeping in mind the presence of Manuvad and accepting the 'caste' as reality of Indian society. Manuvadis often talk about the problem of unemployment in India. They are worried about the unemployment of 1 Cr unemployed youth belonging to the "upper" castes. But these people have no worries about the multiple problems faced by the 10 Cr Indian refugees who are illiterate and unskilled.

No party is worried about the plight of these 10 Cr people. But these 10 Cr people are our people. Therefore only our party is worried about the plight of these 10 Cr people. Only our party can find a solution on the problems of these people. We can easily solve the problems of the Bahujan Samaj by becoming the ruling class.

We have become 4th largest party in India by bringing together 600 castes and by creating a fraternity among these castes. By reaching to 1000 castes and by bringing them in our fold we can become the ruling class in this country. I have a strong belief that in next 3 years we will become the rulers and the political master key will be in our hands.

Vision of Ruling Race

I do not support the idea of imposing my thoughts on others. I am just narrating my experience to you. It is up to you whether you want to take advantage of it or not.

By becoming rulers you can march ahead effectively towards formation of a casteless society. I can tell this one solution to all your problems. Why would the beneficiaries of 'caste' want to destroy it ? The people who are victims of 'caste' and who have suffered because of it will have to take this task of destroying the 'caste'. The caste system can be destroyed only by the rulers themselves provided they have a will to do.

You will think that I am talking about some impossible and unachievable things. But in my life I have always taken seemingly impossible tasks in my hand and have achieved a success in those tasks. This is what is called 'Kanshiram magic'. Today this 'Kanshiram magic' has began to occupy a national form.

Therefore my only message to you all is that you should march ahead in the direction of formation of casteless society by means of right thinking. At the end I would like to tell you that you can form a casteless society by capturing the political master key because only the ruling class can form a new social order.

BRAUSS Vision

According to the Act of University (Article 4) published in Madhya Pradesh Gazette dated 13 January 2016 the University's vision is reflected through its aim and objectives as follows:

Aim

The aim of the BRAUSS is the socio-economic development of Marginals such as SCs, STs, OBCs and to excel in higher education, research, extension and training in social sciences and other subjects through constructive approach with unification of social science perspective with progressive scientific and technological input for such excellence.

Under this aim the university laid down 12 objectives namely (1) to propagate rising ideology and its understanding and sensitize the functionaries to enforce policies and programmes for the marginal, 1(2) promote such branches of knowledge as fulfill the objectives of university, through provisions of institutional and research facilities, (3) to establish network in collaboration with national and international universities, institutions and organizations for exposure of students and faculty with existing evils and advanced nations' technology and techniques, modern means and methods, models and measures, strategy and view, plans and projects for higher education, (4) to organize integrated prospectus on PG and higher level in due programmes of social sciences and other technical subjects including engineering, medical, management, agricultural technology and rural crafts to expedite socio-economic progress of the neglected, (5) to study thought and philosophy of such social thinkers and reformers, who have contributed in socio-economic, educational development and empowerment of the deprived as dreamt of by Dr. B. R. Ambedkar, (6) to study caste system, socio, economic and educational disparities, disabilities and discriminatory facts to explore remedial measures necessary for them, (7) to discover innovative strategies by synthesizing technical know-how with scientific outlook of social sciences centred on elimination of poverty and social evil, inequalities and injustice, (8) to promote awareness and understanding towards social needs among students, faculty and citizens and prepare them to fulfil those needs, (9) to specially facilitate education, research, extension and training with integrated syllabus in social sciences, humanities and technology of university, (10) to advise and suggest state and central govt. and other agencies working on developing and empowering the socially deprived classes, (11) to create, publish and propagate activities undertaken by the university and other literature of like nature in accordance with the objectives of the university and (12) to pursue other such all activities as are conducive to fulfil all or certain objectives of the university.

Bibliography

1. Ambedkar B. R., Annihilation of castes. Vol. I, Dr. Babasaheb Ambedkar Writing and Speeches. SECTION XXI.
2. Ambedkar B. R., CHAPTER-1, The Hindu Social Order: It's Essential Principles, India and The Pre-requisites of Communism.
3. Ambedkar B. R., SECTION-IV Kalaram Temple entry Satryagraha, Nasik and Temple entry movement, Volume-XVII. Dr. Babasaheb Ambedkar Writing and Speeches.
4. Ambedkar B. R., ibid.
5. Ambedkar B. R., CHAPTER-7 The Triumph of Brahmanism : Regicide or the birth of Counter-Revolution, part-III. Revolution and Counter-Revolution in Ancient India, Volume-III. Dr. Babasaheb Ambedkar Writing and Speeches.
6. Dr. Dibya Doley, Assistant Prof. Department of Sociology, Silapathar Town College, Silapathar, Dhemaji, Assam.
7. Saikia, U (2013) Borgohain, H (Samajatattic Siddhantar Porichoi) Dibrugarh-1.
8. D, Souza Lawrance (2012) (Political Views and Thoughts of Dr. Ambedkar).
9. Dr. Grishma Manikrao Khobragade, Kalyan, Dist.Thane. Maharashtra.
10. Rajshekar, V.T. Caste – a Nation within the Nation. Bangalore :Books for Change: 2007.
11. Ambedkar, B.R. Annihilation of Caste. Nagpur: Samata Prakashan, 1944.
12. Thangaraj, P. (Ed) Selected Thoughts of Dr. Ambedkar. Madras: Puratchikkanal Publications, 1980.
13. Thaper, Romila, Syndicated Hinduism, New Delhi: Critical Quest, 2010.
14. Bahujan Sanghatak, New Delhi, Dt. 16 November, 1998.

Index

D

E

F

G

M

N

S

T

U